The Employment Relationship

The issue of who is or is not in an employment relationship has become problematic in recent decades as a result of major changes in work organization as well as in the adequacy of legal regulation in adapting to such changes. In different parts of the world there is increasing difficulty in establishing whether or not an employment relationship exists in situations where the respective rights and obligations of the parties concerned are not clear, where there has been an attempt to disguise the employment relationship, or where inadequacies or gaps exist in the legal framework or in its interpretation or application. Vulnerable workers appear to suffer most in these situations. At the same time, social partners and labour administrators have emphasized that globalization has increased the need for protection against circumvention of national labour legislation by contractual and/or other legal arrangements.

The employment relationship is under ever-closer scrutiny, not only by labour lawyers, but also by workers, employers and the judiciary. Changes in the world of work have modified traditional notions of the employment relationship. These changes in the 'standard employment relationship' shape the scope of protection and application of labour legislation and automatically affect the way labour law is implemented.

This book presents the ways the scope of labour legislation applies to the realm of the employment relationship. Terms, notions, definitions, laws and practice in the various regions of the world are herein reported.

The Employment Relationship

A Comparative Overview

Edited by

GIUSEPPE CASALE

HART PUBLISHING ● OXFORD AND PORTLAND, OREGON
INTERNATIONAL LABOUR OFFICE ● GENEVA
2011

Published in the United Kingdom by Hart Publishing Ltd
16C Worcester Place, Oxford, OX1 2JW
Telephone: +44 (0)1865 517530
Fax: +44 (0)1865 510710
E-mail: mail@hartpub.co.uk
Website: http://www.hartpub.co.uk

Published in North America (US and Canada) by
Hart Publishing
c/o International Specialized Book Services
920 NE 58th Avenue, Suite 300
Portland, OR 97213–3786
USA
Tel: +1 503 287 3093 or toll-free: (1) 800 944 6190
Fax: +1 503 280 8832
E-mail: orders@isbs.com
Website: http://www.isbs.com

Published in Switzerland by the
International Labour Office
Route de Morillons 4
CH-1211 Geneva 22
Telephone: +41 22 799 7828
Fax: +41 22 799 6938
E-mail: pubvente@ilo.org
Website: http://www.ilo.org/publns

British Library Cataloguing in Publication Data

Data Available

ISBN: 978–1–84113–420–8 (Hart)

978–92–2–123302–2 (ILO)

Typeset by Columns Design XML Ltd, Reading
Printed and bound in Great Britain by
CPI Antony Rowe Ltd, Chippenham, Wiltshire

Preface

This book offers a comparative analysis of the changing legal notions of the employment relationship in different regions of the world. It starts with an overview of the work of the International Labour Organization concerning the employment relationship and then goes on to analyse the different ways in which, during the past few decades, industrialized and transition economies have witnessed a progressive crisis of the regulatory frameworks sustaining criteria for determining the employment relationship. The latter is mainly based on 'traditional' notions of subordinate employment and autonomous self-employment.

More and more atypical and/or non-standard working arrangements have emerged and this has had repercussions on the national notions of the employment relationship, including the division between subordination and autonomy. This development has brought changes to labour law systems across different countries worldwide, especially those which had based their systems on the notions of dependent and subordinate employment to build the respective personal scope of application of the law. Thus it has had the effect of triggering a deregulatory trend that some legal scholars have defined as 'the way out of labour law'.

This book was written at a time when no single solution to the problems under analysis had been found. In this regard, it should be seen more as a product of time: a way of analysing the various attempts made in different countries to address the problematic new scenario. It presents the various regulatory approaches that are being developed, tries to highlight the main common trends and issues at stake, and in some depth seeks to find the areas of expansion of the legal notion of the employment relationship. It also provides, here and there, ad hoc regulations for a number of atypical and/or non-standard forms of employment.

Needless to say, one of the big challenges in preparing this volume has been to keep abreast of the constantly evolving legal framework at the various levels. For a number of reasons, it was decided to leave out many examples which were too old, and sometimes, in my modest judgment, not strictly essential to the structure of the book. All in all, the work here seeks to state the situation at the beginning of 2008.

Of course, the area of study has evolved and will continue to do so, and thus the work will require further amendment. Nonetheless, this volume stands on its own, for it gives a global overview of current legal and practice relating to the notion of the employment relationship.

Finally, I would like to thank most warmly all the contributors to the book. All of them participated enthusiastically in the preparation of the different chapters. I hope that this volume will be valuable reading for government officials, workers, employers, researchers, academics as well as legal practitioners.

Giuseppe Casale
Director
Labour Administration and Inspection Programme
November 2010

Acknowledgements

I would like to take this opportunity to thank the colleagues and friends who contributed in one way or another to the preparation of this volume, for their continuous support and cooperation.

I am particularly grateful to ILO former colleagues Enrique Marin and Slava Egorov, with whom I had many discussions around the issue of the employment relationship. Special thanks to Professor Gianni Arrigo, who contributed with critical comments on the first draft.

In addition, I would like to thank Johanna Ruefli of the Labour Administration and Inspection Programme, who worked hard in typing and re-typing all the corrections.

A word of thanks is also due to ILO colleagues Humberto Villasmil, Colin Fenwick and Mario Fasani, who contributed with substantial updates on the law and practice of different regions of the world.

Finally, special appreciation goes to Charlotte Beauchamp, Elvira Lesaffre and Chris Edgar of ILO Publications for their support and commitment in making sure that this volume was in final shape before entering the publishing process.

Many thanks to all of them,

g.c.

Contents

Table of Cases

Australia

Canada

Table of Cases

Europe

India

Lesotho

Malaysia

Namibia

Singapore

Swaziland

Table of Cases

South Africa

United Kingdom

United States of America

Venezuela, Bolivarian Republic of

Zimbabwe

Table of Legislation

Table of Legislation

Benin

Botswana

Brazil

Canada

China

Colombia

Dominican Republic

Europe

Table of Legislation

France

Gabon

Germany

Table of Legislation

Table of Legislation

Swaziland

Tanzania, United Republic of

United Kingdom

United States of America

Uruguay

Venezuela, Bolivarian Republic of

Viet Nam

Zimbabwe

Table of ILO Instruments

ILO Conventions and Recommendations

The Employment Relationship: A General Introduction

1

G**IUSEPPE** C**ASALE***

The subject of the employment relationship has been on the agenda of the International Labour Conference (hereafter 'the ILC') for several years. The issue of who is or is not in an employment relationship, and what rights and protections flow from that status, has become problematic in recent decades as a result of major changes in work organization and the adequacy of legal regulation in adapting to those changes. Such changes have accelerated as a result of globalization, characterized by a rapid economic integration among countries driven by the liberalization of trade, investment and capital flows, as well as rapid technological change.[1] As a response to this phenomenon, in November 2001, the Governing Body of the International Labour Organization (hereafter 'the ILO') established the World Commission on the Social Dimension of Globalization (hereafter 'the World Commission') as an independent international body to respond to the needs of people as they cope with the unprecedented changes brought about by globalization.[2] The World Commission looked at the various facets of globalization,

* Director, Labour Administration and Inspection Programme (LAB/ADMIN), ILO, Geneva. I wish to express my sincere thanks to two ILO former colleagues who inspired this chapter: Prof Enrique Marin and Dr Slava Egorov.

[1] See ILO, Country studies on the social impact of globalization: Final report, Working Party on the Social Dimensions of the Liberalization of International Trade, doc GB.276/WP/SDL/1 (276th Session Geneva November 1999) para 2. This document contains the results of a survey carried out in seven countries to collect information on the effects of globalization and trade liberalization on the attainment of the ILO social objectives.

[2] The Commission consisted of two Co-Chairs (HE Ms Tarja Halonen, President of the Republic of Finland, and HE Mr Benjamin William Mkapa, President of the United Republic of Tanzania), 29 members and 5 ex officio members. The World Commission officially ended its work once the World Commission's Report was released, but a number of the Commissioners, including the two Co-Chairs, are actively involved in a range of initiatives related to the follow-up of the Report's recommendations. (For details, see: www.ilo.org/public/english/fairglobalization/follow/index.htm.)

the diversity of public perceptions of the process, and its implications for economic and social progress. It searched for innovative ways of combining economic, social and environmental objectives, based on worldwide expertise. It has made its recommendations seeking to build upon a broad understanding among all key actors. The World Commission's final report 'A fair globalization: Creating opportunities for all', released on 24 February 2004,[3] focused, inter alia, on the impact of globalization on employment and proposed that in order to achieve a fair globalization that creates opportunities for all, decent work[4] should become a global goal to be pursued by every country and the international community.

Further to the establishment of the World Commission, the Governing Body of the ILO set up a Working Party on the Social Dimension of Globalization (hereafter 'the Working Party') as the 'institutional anchor' in terms of the role and mandate of the ILO in the follow-up of the World Commission's final report. At its 92nd Session in June 2004, the ILC discussed the Report of its Director-General, Mr Juan Somavia, entitled 'A fair globalization: The role of the ILO'.[5] This Report in fact placed the work of the World Commission on the agenda of the ILC for discussion.

The 2004 ILC debate on globalization provided the 'political direction' for the future role of the ILO in promoting a fair globalization. Further debates in the Working Party resulted in the priorities outlined by ILO tripartite constituents for follow-up action by the International Labour Office (hereafter 'the Office') to the World Commission's recommendations.[6] It was emphasized that there was widespread support for making decent work a global goal and that every effort should be made to advance all four of its components:

— employment generation;
— promotion of labour standards;
— protection and support for workers displaced by industrial restructuring;

---

[3] See ILO, World Commission report 40–45 at www.ilo.org/public/english/wcsdg/docs/report.pdf.

[4] For more detail about decent work as a primary goal for the ILO, see ILO, Report of the Director-General to the 87th Session of the International Labour Conference, June 1999, on Decent Work, at www.ilo.org/public/english/standards/relm/ilc/ilc87/rep-i.htm; Report of the Director-General on 'Reducing the decent work deficit: A global challenge' to the 89th Session of the International Labour Conference, June 2001, at www.ilo.org/public/english/standards/relm/ilc/ilc89/rep-i-a.htm; the ILO Strategic Policy Framework 2002–05 on Consolidating the decent work agenda at www.ilo.org/public/english/standards/relm/gb/docs/gb279/pdf/pfa-6.pdf; and the ILO Decent work pilot programme at www.ilo.org/public/english/bureau/dwpp/.

[5] The text of the Report is available at www.ilo.org/public/english/standards/relm/ilc/ilc92/pdf/adhoc.pdf.

[6] See ILO, www.ilo.org/public/english/fairglobalization/follow/index.htm.

— reinforcement of social dialogue as an important tool to bring about more equitable outcomes in the workplace.[7]

The impact of globalization is quite uneven in terms of the degree to which it benefits countries, enterprises and their workers. Globalization has frequently been preceded or accompanied by legislative and institutional reforms. The nature and pace of changes occurring in the world of work, and particularly in the labour markets, have given rise to new forms of employment relationship which do not always fit within the traditional parameters. Patterns of employment are becoming more and more complex as the range and variety of work arrangements expand, leading to opportunities as well as risks. As a result, traditional concepts and certainties are being challenged. While these changes have increased labour market flexibility, they have also led to a growing number of workers whose employment status is unclear and who are consequently outside the scope of the protection normally associated with the employment relationship. Job security and the protection which has been built around the employment relationship are being affected. This can also have an adverse impact on the competitiveness and viability of enterprises. These developments are on the increase worldwide and challenge the relevance of labour laws which for many countries have been an instrument for the orderly organization of the relationships between major labour market players, ie employers and workers.

A major feature of the employment relationship, one that can be found in different countries and legal traditions, is the hierarchical power of employers over employees. The hierarchical power consists mainly of three related elements: (i) the power to assign tasks and to give orders and directives to employees (directional power); (ii) the power to monitor both the performance of such tasks and the compliance with same orders and directives (control power); (iii) the power to sanction both the improper or negligent performance of the assigned tasks and disobedience to given orders and directives (disciplinary power).

The presence of hierarchical power in a working relationship has been traditionally established—either statutorily or by case law—as the distinctive element of employment in contrast to self-employment, and accordingly as an access key to the wide range of regulations set out to protect employees in the different jurisdictions. The abovementioned reduction of hierarchy and parcelization of work has materially changed the way in which working activity is performed. Together with the spread of new activities in the service sector and the growing

---

[7] See ILO, Report of the Working Party on the Social Dimension of Globalization. Overall reactions by the Working Party to the work of the World Commission, doc GB 289/16, (289th Session Geneva March 2004) para 8.

use of information technology in business, these developments have challenged traditional legal categories of working relationships based on such models as the blue-collar employee working in an assembly line of a big, bureaucratic and vertically integrated firm. New working practices came to lawyers' attention that did not easily fit into either employment or self-employment. In particular, they embodied new forms of integration of work in business organizations whereby the coordination exerted by firms upon the relevant workers did not match all the elements of hierarchical power as construed by legal experts and case law.

Significant problems of classification therefore emerged with reference to growing number of working activities in which directional power and hierarchical organization were loosened, or in which at least they displayed new features. The risk was either an exclusion of working relationships deserving the legal protection afforded to employees by the legislator from the scope of the employment, or an inclusion in the same scope of workers that did not deserve such protection. Neither exclusion nor inclusion could be determined taking into account the mere written or oral declaration of the parties, since courts—in the majority of jurisdictions—must rely principally on the factual circumstances and characteristics of the relevant relationship. As we will see in the following chapters, in order to avoid a borderless expansion of the scope of employment, labour courts initially adopted a rigorous and narrow approach whereby directional—and accordingly, hierarchical—power was deemed present only where the worker was subject to directional, organizational and disciplinary control of the relevant employer, this being shown by the issue of specific orders and by the exertion of an assiduous monitoring and control of the working activity. Yet this approach carried the risk of excluding from the scope of the employment relationship and from the relevant legal protection a wide range of working activities that—due to the abovementioned changes in the production system—did not display such stringent characteristics yet nonetheless deserved such a legal protection on the basis of a systematic construction of labour regulations. Over the years and in order to address such problems, the judicial approach in a good number of countries became more flexible when dealing with working activities displaying forms of hierarchical power differing from traditional ones. According to the ensuing rulings, hierarchical power, and therefore employment, is also present when a person performs her working activities—on a continuous, loyal and diligent basis—following the general directives issued by such a subject according to programmes and purposes of the relevant firm. Nonetheless, new working activities are still challenging legal categories: in most of the European jurisdictions a growing number of workers are in a grey area between employment and self-employment, their working relationships only partially fulfilling the requirements of employment under the relevant laws.

The problem is becoming a serious one not only in Europe, but also in Latin America, Asia and Africa, as is testified by the following contributions to this volume. In a good number of countries there is no protection—or at least no significant protection—for self-employees, who operate in an empirical grey area that is not covered by any legal structure, with no 'median' legal category covering the area between employment and self-employment.

At the same time, it should be noted that under the post-Fordist system, a material amount of production stages are now contracted out which are more and more significant in the production cycle. Activities as important as accounting, marketing and client care are entrusted to third parties. This has been defined as 'horizontal' outsourcing. The reasons for this business practice are multifaceted. On the one hand, firms may have recourse to third parties in search of specialized suppliers of delicate and high-skilled activities. In this respect they may turn to a supplier which performs a business activity better than they could do, both with regard to the quality of the relevant output and on the relevant cost, related for instance to the experience curve effect: this may also be in order to acquire a competitive advantage vis-à-vis their competitors.

In this context, contracting out is also driven by business strategies aimed at reducing workforce costs. By way of example, firms might use suppliers whose overall labour cost is lower than their own, because the relevant workers are non-unionized or in any event receive lower wages. Workers' protection has traditionally been centred on the universal notion of the employment relationship, based on a distinction between dependent and independent work. The employment relationship has historically proven to be a key point through which labour law rights and benefits are rendered to both employers and workers. The employment relationship is a legal notion widely used in countries around the world to refer to the relationship between an employee (frequently referred to as a 'worker') and an employer for whom the employee performs work under certain conditions, in return for remuneration. It is through the employment relationship, however defined, that reciprocal rights and obligations are created between the employer and the worker.[8]

Despite the changes currently taking place in the global labour market, there is strong evidence that the employment relationship continues to be the predominant pattern of work arrangement in many countries around the world. The legal framework governing the employment relationship is an important component for managing these changes. The failure to adapt labour laws, however, can result in the

---

[8] International Labour Conference (95th Session) The employment relationship Report V(1) (Geneva 2006) 3.

perpetuation of regulations that are ill-suited to the new realities of the contemporary global labour market.[9] The debates over the future of the employment relationship and its legal framework are gaining momentum at both national and international levels, and the ILO remains at the forefront of this debate.

1.1 A Debated Issue at the International Level

As mentioned above, the issue of who is or is not in an employment relationship has become more and more problematic in recent decades. From a comparative point of view, there is increasing difficulty in establishing whether or not an employment relationship exists in situations where: a) the respective rights and obligations of the parties concerned are not clear; or b) where there has been an attempt to disguise the employment relationship; or c) where inadequacies or gaps exist in the legal framework, or in its interpretation or application. Contractual arrangements can have the effect of depriving employees of the protections they are due. Moreover, vulnerable workers appear to suffer more from such arrangements. More and more, ILO member States and their social partners have emphasized that the globalized economy has increased workers' need for protection, at least against circumvention of national laws by contractual and/or other legal arrangements.

In the framework of the transitional provision of services, it is also important to establish who is considered a worker in an employment relationship, what rights the worker has, and who is the employer. This is the background against which the ILO and its constituents worked, reaching an outcome which was the adoption of the Employment Relationship Recommendation, 2006 (No 198).

To be sure, the question of the employment relationship has, in one form or another, been on the agenda of the ILC for over a decade as the reference point for examining various types of work relationships. In recent years, the ILC has held discussions on self-employed workers, migrant workers, home workers, private employment agency workers, child workers, workers in cooperatives, and workers in the informal economy and in the fishing sector. It has also addressed the issue in the course of discussions on social security and maternity protection.

---

[9] 'In my view labour law has to show a greater capacity of adaptation if it wants to continue to play a significant role in the new social and economic environment. The changed environment is challenging the very essence of the classic model: namely the idea that national law—and similarly collective bargaining—can regulate with "imperative" effects and through unitary rules all the major contents of labour relations. Flexibility is the key word, which goes against imperative and rigid labour law': T Treu, 'Labour law and social change', public lecture, (Geneva, International Labour Office, November 2002).

The 1997–98 Discussions on Contract Labour

In 1997 and 1998, the ILC discussed an item on contract labour[10], with a view to adopting a Convention and a Recommendation.

Concerns about this kind of work arrangement had been repeatedly expressed on several occasions in ILO industrial committees' meetings since the 1950s. A number of conclusions and resolutions had been adopted. They called for appropriate measures to be taken in order to provide the workers concerned with adequate protection.[11] The original intention of the 1997–98 ILC discussions on contract labour was therefore to establish rules to govern the situations wherein workers involved in various contracting and subcontracting arrangements either do not enjoy or only partially enjoy labour law protections, rights and benefits because of the uncertainty of their employment status.

The 1997–98 ILC discussions on contract labour faced significant conceptual ambiguity in what might be understood by contract labour and contract workers. On the one hand, the delegates had a certain idea in common about the subject under discussion, particularly, of the workers whose situation they were trying to regulate, including for example workers recruited through intermediaries, or those who work for a contracting/subcontracting enterprise, or certain economically dependent self-employed workers. Reference was also made to concealed employment and ambiguous relationships. On the other hand, the wide variety of such situations raised the question of the advisability of dealing with them separately.

The discussion concerning so-called 'triangular' work arrangements (through intermediaries) proved to be especially difficult. In this regard, account should be taken of the fact that the 1997 ILC discussed and adopted the Private Employment Agencies Convention, 1997 (No 181) and its accompanying Recommendation (No 188),[12] which regulate work though private employment agencies. As a result, the

---

[10] The term 'contract labour' was, at that time, used to refer to different ways of employing workers through different types of arrangements between enterprises and workers (often through intermediaries) whereby one or both parties (or more parties, including intermediaries) interpret the arrangement as different from a genuine employment relationship. In the proposed text of the Convention, contract labour was defined as 'work performed for a natural or legal person (referred to as a "user enterprise") by a person (referred to as a "contract worker") where the work is performed by the worker personally under actual conditions of dependency on or subordination to the user enterprise and these conditions are similar to those that characterize an employment relationship under national law and practice'. That definition included both direct (bilateral) and 'triangular' (through intermediaries) arrangements (International Labour Conference (86th Session), 'Contract labour', Reports V(1), (2A) and (2B) (Geneva, 1998) 8).

[11] See International Labour Conference (85th Session) (Geneva, 1997) 72.

[12] The texts of Convention No 181 and Recommendation No 188 are available at www.ilo.org/ilolex/english/convdisp1.htm and www.ilo.org/ilolex/english/recdisp1.htm, respectively.

distinction between the scopes of application of Convention No 181 and possible instruments on contract labour became a high priority item during the contract labour discussions.

The divergences of opinion on the subject were exacerbated by terminological and conceptual difficulties. The term 'contract labour' immediately sparked off lengthy debates. Although it is widely used in a significant number of countries, this expression does not provide a clear description of its content. Furthermore, it is understood differently from one country to another and does not have a precise generic meaning, much less the legal breadth to encompass the diverse work situations in which it arises.

It is noteworthy, however, that during the 1997–98 debates, delegates from all regions repeatedly alluded to the employment relationship, in its various forms and with different meanings, as a concept familiar to all. After lengthy debate, it was decided at the end of the second discussion in 1998 through an ILC resolution that the Committee on Contract Labour had begun to identify situations where workers require protection and had made progress on these issues. The resolution invited the Governing Body of the ILO:

— to place these issues on the agenda of a future session of the ILC with a view to the possible adoption of a Convention supplemented by a Recommendation, if considered necessary by the ILC; and

— to hold meetings of experts to examine at least the following issues arising out of the 1997–98 ILC deliberations on contract labour:

– which workers, in the situations that have begun to be identified in the Committee, are in need of protection;

– appropriate ways in which such workers can be protected, and the possibility of dealing separately with the various situations;

– how such workers would be defined, bearing in mind the different legal systems that exist and the language differences.[13]

---

[13] For the reports of the Conference Committee on Contract Labour and the discussion of the reports in plenary, see ILO, Record of Proceedings, International Labour Conference, 85th Session, Geneva, 1997, 20th Sitting, 18 June, and Provisional Record No 18; and Record of Proceedings, International Labour Conference, 86th Session, Geneva, 1998, Provisional Record Nos 16 and 21. The following documents were prepared by the Office to serve as a basis for these discussions: ILO, 'Contract labour', Reports VI(1) and (2), International Labour Conference (85th Session) (Geneva, 1997); and International Labour Conference (86th Session), 'Contract labour', Reports V(1), (2A) and (2B) (Geneva, 1998).

National Studies

Further to the resolution adopted by the ILC in 1998, the Office undertook a series of national studies.[14] The objective of these studies was to help identify and describe the principal situations in which workers lacked adequate protection, as well as the problems caused by the absence or inadequacy of protection, and to suggest measures to remedy such situations.

To prevent ambiguities arising from the proliferation of terms[15] used to refer to the different situations that occur, the authors of the national studies tried to avoid the use of such terms, and concentrated on describing each situation in law and in practice which reflected the trends.[16] Difficulties arose in determining the scale and patterns of these situations because of the limited statistical information available.[17] However, most of the authors had access to a variety of authoritative sources in support of their analyses and conclusions.

The research undertaken confirmed the universal importance of the employment relationship, on which labour protection systems are largely based, while highlighting the deficiencies affecting the scope (in terms of persons covered) of the regulations governing this relationship.

---

[14] Further to 20 national studies undertaken by the Office in preparation to the ILC 1997–98 discussion on contract labour (see: International Labour Conference (85th Session) 'Contract labour', Report VI(1) (Geneva, 1997) 1, another set of 38 national studies was carried out during 1999–2002 (See: International Labour Conference (95th Session), 'The employment relationship', Report V(1) (Geneva, 2006) 5. Most of these studies may be consulted at www.ilo.org/public/english/dialogue/ifpdial/ll/wp.htm.

[15] The specialist literature frequently uses expressions and terms such as 'atypical', 'precarious' or 'flexible employment'; 'new forms of employment'; 'non-conventional forms of employment'; 'contracting out', 'externalization', 'outsourcing', or 'temporary workers', but not in the traditional sense meaning persons who work for a limited time, but specifically those recruited through a temporary employment agency.

[16] The studies drew a distinction between the following four types of situation, which were also referred to in the discussions on contract labour: subordinate work, triangular relationships, self-employment, and self-employment under conditions of dependency (economic or other). Particular reference was made to specific cases in which workers frequently lack protection, such as those of truck drivers in transport enterprises, certain workers in department stores, and construction workers.

[17] In 1993, the 15th International Conference of Labour Statisticians (ICLS) adopted a Resolution concerning the International Classification of Status in Employment (ICSE), which provides improved guidelines for the production of statistics on the different contractual situations of workers, to reflect the different types of economic risk and authority they have in their jobs in more detail than is reflected in a rough distinction between paid employment and self-employment. In 1998, the 16th ICLS discussed a report on national practices in the production of such statistics, which showed that very little work had been done to provide better statistics on these issues. The 16th ICLS concluded that more work was needed both in national statistical offices and by the ILO to improve the situation (see International Labour Conference (16th Session) (Geneva 1998), Report of the Conference, doc ICLS/16/1998/V, appended to Governing Body document GB.273/STM/7, 273rd Session, Geneva, November 1998. However, only limited work has been possible in the ILO, and the situation seems to have been similar in national statistical offices. There is no discussion of this issue scheduled for the 17th ICLS, which met from 24 November to 3 December 2003.

Giuseppe Casale

Meeting of Experts on Workers in Situations Needing Protection

A tripartite Meeting of Experts on Workers in Situations Needing Protection was held in Geneva in May 2000.[18] The experts participating in the meeting adopted a common statement[19] that noted that the global phenomenon of transformation in the nature of work had resulted in situations in which the legal scope of the employment relationship (which determines whether or not workers are entitled to be protected by labour legislation) did not accord with the realities of working relationships.

According to the experts, this has resulted in situations whereby workers who should be protected by labour law were not receiving that protection in fact or in law. It was also evident that while some countries had responded by adjusting the scope of the legal regulation of the employment relationship, this had not occurred in all countries.

The 2003 Discussion on the Scope of the Employment Relationship

The scope of the employment relationship was included in the agenda of the 91st Session of the 2003 ILC for a general discussion with a view to focusing on the labour protection of dependent workers, ie the rights, entitlements and obligations of dependent workers under laws, regulations or collective agreements which derive from and depend on the existence of an employment relationship.

During the discussions, many delegates emphasized that the concept of the employment relationship is common to all legal systems and traditions. There are rights and entitlements which exist under labour laws, regulations and collective agreements and which are specific or linked to workers who work within the framework of an employment relationship. One of the consequences associated with changes in the structure of the labour markets, the organization of work and the deficient application of the law is the growing phenomenon of workers who are

---

[18] The Office prepared the following document as the basis for discussions at the meeting: ILO, Meeting of Experts on Workers in Situations Needing Protection (The employment relationship: Scope), basic technical document (Geneva 2000), doc MEWNP/2000, at www.ilo.org/public/english/dialogue/ifpdial/publ/mewnp/index.htm. The report of the Meeting is contained in ILO, Report of the Meeting of Experts on Workers in Situations Needing Protection, doc MEWNP/2000/4(Rev), appended to Governing Body document GB.279/2, 279th Session, Geneva, November 2000, at www.ilo.org/public/english/standards/relm/gb/docs/gb279/pdf/gb-2.pdf.

[19] See ILO, Annex 2 to the Report of the Meeting of Experts on Workers in Situations Needing Protection.

in fact employees but find themselves without the protection of an employment relationship. The view was shared among the tripartite constituents that labour laws should be applied to those who are in employment relationships and that the wide variety of arrangements under which work is performed by a worker could be put within an appropriate legal framework.[20]

The conclusions adopted at the end of the 2003 ILC discussion noted that the ILO should envisage the adoption of an international instrument on this topic. A Recommendation was considered as an appropriate response, and it should focus on disguised employment relationships and on the need for mechanisms to ensure that persons with an employment relationship have access to the protection they are due at the national level. Such a Recommendation should:

— be flexible enough to take account of different economic, social, legal and industrial relations traditions and address the gender dimension;
— take into account recent developments in employment relationships;
— provide guidance to member States without universally defining the substance of the employment relationship;
— not interfere with genuine commercial and independent contracting arrangements; and
— promote social dialogue and collective bargaining as a means of finding solutions to the problem.

The 2006 Discussion on the Employment Relationship

The 2003 ILC general discussion showed that the problem under consideration is a complex and growing phenomenon, the possible solutions are diverse and constantly evolving and, at the same time, many common elements and trends can be found in the responses across different countries and regions. The importance of action at the national level was emphasized throughout the discussion. The conclusions stated that action at the national level should include the development of a national policy framework in consultation with the social partners, collection of statistical data, clear policies on gender equality, and better compliance and enforcement. This was similar to the approach proposed by the Meeting of Experts

---

[20] See ILO: 'Conclusions concerning the employment relationship', in International Labour Conference (95th Session), 'The employment relationship', Report V(1) (Geneva, 2006) 72–77, at www.ilo.org/public/english/standards/relm/ilc/ilc95/pdf/rep-v-1.pdf.

in 2000. The parameters of a possible international standard on this topic were outlined in the 2003 ILC conclusions which guided the Office in its further preparatory work.

In March 2004, the employment relationship was put on the agenda of the 95th Session of the ILC (2006) for a single standard-setting discussion. To this end, the Office prepared a report on the law and practice[21] of member States representing different regions, legal systems and traditions. The report included a questionnaire designed with a view to preparing a Recommendation based in essence on the conclusions adopted during the 2003 ILC general discussion on the scope of the employment relationship. The questionnaire consisted of 18 questions. From the substantive point of view, these focused on such issues as the content of the national policy of protection for workers in an employment relationship and the role of national tripartite constituents in its development and implementation, the determination of the existence of an employment relationship, the settlement of disputes concerning the employment status, compliance and enforcement, and non-interference in civil or commercial contracting.

Seventy-eight Governments submitted their replies to the questionnaire, 63 of which indicated that their replies were prepared after consultations with the most representative employers' and workers' organizations; 34 governments sent the replies of employers' and workers' organizations separately. All the replies and the Office's commentaries on these replies and on the proposed text of the Recommendation were published in early 2006 in Report V(2A).[22] The draft text of the Recommendation prepared by the Office was published in Report V(2B).[23] The proposed Recommendation consisted of 18 draft paragraphs and four parts. The latter covered national policy for the protection of workers in an employment relationship, the determination of the existence of an employment relationship, the monitoring of labour markets and organization of work as well as the implementation of measures within the framework of national policy, and international exchange of information.

To a great extent, the 2006 ILC deliberations,[24] built upon the previous debates during the contract labour discussions in 1997–98 and the scope of

---

[21] International Labour Conference (95th Session) 'The employment relationship', Report V(1) (Geneva, 2006).

[22] See International Labour Conference (95th Session), 'The employment relationship', Report V(1) (Geneva, 2006), at www.ilo.org/public/english/standards/relm/ilc/ilc95/pdf/rep-v-2a.pdf.

[23] International Labour Conference (95th Session), 'The employment relationship', Report V(1) (Geneva, 2006), at www.ilo.org/public/english/standards/relm/ilc/ilc95/pdf/rep-v-2b.pdf.

[24] See International Labour Conference (95th Session), Provisional Record No 21, Fifth item on the agenda: The employment relationship (single discussion), Report of the Committee on the Employment Relationship (Geneva, 2006), at www.ilo.org/public/english/standards/relm/ilc/ilc95/pdf/pr-21.pdf.

employment relationship discussions in 2003, showed the topicality of the issue. Although the deliberations proved to be sometimes very difficult (especially regarding the presumption and indicators of the existence of an employment relationship, as well as 'triangular' relationships), they resulted in the adoption by the 2006 ILC of the Employment Relationship Recommendation, 2006 (No 198).[25]

The analysis below will therefore focus on major elements of the discussions and studies leading to the adoption of Recommendation No 198, which consists of three major components:

— National policy of protection for workers in an employment relationship.
— Determination of the existence of an employment relationship.
— Monitoring and implementation.

1.2 National Policy Protecting Workers in an Employment Relationship

The employment relationship is a universal concept with common elements which can be found in countries with different legal systems and cultures as well as different economic and social environments. Nevertheless, its evolution and the laws and practices governing it vary from country to country, as do the problems associated with it. The national authorities, in cooperation with the social partners, should lead the search for appropriate and viable solutions.

Already in the technical document submitted by the Office for discussion at the Meeting of Experts 2000, attention was drawn to the importance of establishing a principle which would commit member States to tackling the problem of legal uncertainty affecting the scope of the employment relationship by means of a systematic policy based on common but flexible premises. That principle would lead to the formulation and application of a national policy aimed at the continuing clarification and adjustment of the scope of labour legislation, based on observation of the evolution of employment relationships. This process would require a dynamic policy on the part of the competent authorities to monitor the form in

---

[25] The text of the adopted Recommendation is available at www.ilo.org/ilolex/english/recdisp1.htm.

which employment relationships are evolving and the timely introduction of necessary changes in standards.[26] The Meeting agreed that the elements of a national policy might include but not be limited to:

— providing workers and employers with clear guidance concerning employment relationships, in particular the distinction between dependent workers and self-employed persons;
— combating disguised employment which has the effect of depriving dependent workers of proper legal protection;
— not interfering with genuine commercial or genuine independent contracting;
— providing access to appropriate resolution mechanisms to determine the status of workers.[27]

As stated in the conclusions concerning the employment relationship adopted during the 2003 ILC general discussion,[28] the collection of statistical data and the undertaking of research and periodic reviews of changes in the structure and patterns of work at national and sectoral levels should be part of this national policy framework. The methodology for the collection of data and for undertaking the research and review should be determined after a process of social dialogue. All data collected should be disaggregated according to sex, and the national and sectoral level research and reviews should explicitly incorporate the gender dimension of this question and should take into account other aspects of diversity. National labour administrations and their associated services should regularly monitor their enforcement programmes and processes. This should include identifying those sectors and occupational groups with high levels of disguised employment and adopting a strategic approach to enforcement. Special attention should be paid to those occupations and sectors with a high proportion of women workers. Innovative programmes of information and education and outreach strategies and services should be developed. The social partners should be involved in developing and implementing these initiatives.

The parameters of a possible future Recommendation outlined in the conclusions adopted by the 2003 ILC guided the Office in the preparation of the abovementioned questionnaire contained in the Report V(1) prepared for the 2006

---

[26] See ILO, Meeting of Experts on Workers in Situations Needing Protection (The employment relationship: Scope). Basic technical document. MEWNP/2000 (Geneva, 2000), paras 205, 206, 212.

[27] See ILO, Report of the Meeting of Experts on Workers in Situations Needing Protection, doc MEWNP/2000/4(Rev), appended to Governing Body document GB.279/2, 279th Session, Geneva, 2000, 38–39.

[28] See ILO, Provisional Record No 21, International Labour Conference, 95th Session, Geneva, 2006, Fifth item on the agenda: The employment relationship (single discussion), Report of the Committee on the Employment Relationship, 21–52.

ILC. This questionnaire was drawn up to ascertain the views of member States on the possibility of adopting a Recommendation on the subject and on the elements that might be included in such a Recommendation. The Recommendation, as proposed by the 2003 ILC, was conceived of as a promotional instrument having the advantage of encouraging member States to formulate and progressively implement national policies that had a common objective but were designed to take into account national circumstances. The questionnaire suggested the following elements as part of this policy:

— Development and implementation, or continuation, of a national policy which would aim to review at appropriate intervals and, if necessary, clarify and adapt the scope of legislation in order to guarantee adequate protection to workers within the framework of an employment relationship.

— Guidance of the determination of the existence of an employment relationship by the facts, irrespective of the arrangement, contractual or otherwise, agreed between the parties.

— Determination of the protection of workers within the framework of an employment relationship in accordance with national law and practice, but in any event conducting of the relevant policy in a transparent manner with the participation of the most representative organizations of employers and workers.

— Elements of a national policy:
  − Provisions for those concerned, in particular employers and workers, and guidance on how to determine the existence of an employment relationship.
  − Combating disguised employment relationships.
  − Establishing clear rules addressing, inter alia, situations where employee(s) of a person ('the provider') work for another person ('the user')[29] and where it is unclear:
    • who the employer is;
    • what are the conditions of work, including remuneration, taking into account the principles of equal opportunity and treatment;
    • how to establish joint and several liability of the provider and the user in such a manner that the employees are effectively protected;
    • how to avoid interfering with civil or commercial contractual relationships;

---

[29] The so-called 'triangular' relationship.

- how to ensure access to appropriate dispute resolution processes and mechanisms to determine the employment status of workers; and
- how to provide for effective and efficient enforcement.

The replies sent to the Office by the governments as well as employers' and workers' organizations revealed that the idea of a national policy to allow an examination of the employment relationship situation with a view to adopting specific measures was considered central to the discussed recommendation, and that it was supported by most of the governments, as well as by employers' and workers' organizations. On the one hand, there was a concern expressed in the replies that the legislative framework should be stable and coherent. On the other, there was a desire to ensure that the review in question did not infringe certain principles of workers' acquired rights. Certain employers' organizations took the view that there could be no question, once a revision of legislation has been undertaken, of broadening its scope. Some workers' organizations, by contrast, stated that the scope of labour legislation, as well as its application, should be examined. One government considered that it was for each country to decide whether or not it needed to review its legislation. Another government considered that it was not appropriate to add new obligations concerning the revision of legislation. A number of employers' organizations expressed their special concerns with regard to the question of the so-called 'triangular' relationship, saying that care must be taken to ensure that there was no interference in commercial arrangements between a provider and a user, and that there was no allocation of responsibilities arising from the employment relationship to the user as such that they become liable for the obligations of the employer provider. One employers' organization added that subcontracting or other legitimate ways of structuring work should not be demonized, in order to not discourage innovation.

Further to these replies, the relevant provisions in the text of a proposed Recommendation were drafted accordingly and submitted to the 2006 ILC for discussion in Report V(2B). In comparison with the questionnaire, some modifications were made. During the 2006 ILC discussion, this part of the proposed instrument underwent a number of drafting changes, and two new paragraphs (6 and 7) were introduced in the adopted text.

1.3 Determination of the Existence of an Employment Relationship

An employment relationship depends on the existence of objective conditions, ie on the form in which the worker and the employer have established their respective positions, rights and obligations. This is to say that for the purposes of the national policy of protection for workers in an employment relationship, the determination of the existence of such a relationship should be guided primarily by the facts relating to the performance of work and the remuneration of the worker, notwithstanding how the relationship is characterized in an contrary arrangement that may have been agreed between the parties.

The issue of the determination of an employment relationship was central throughout the employment relationship debate at the ILO, including the 1997–98 ILC discussions on contract labour,[30] and as can be seen from the contributions to this volume, the general rules applicable to the determination of an employment relationship derives from case law and statutory provisions. If we look at such a circumstance from an employment relationship viewpoint, in order to speak of employment, there must be some hierarchical power relationship—even if it is only negligible. As mentioned above, hierarchical power allows the working activities of employees to be moulded and directed according to firms' aims and requirements, without any need to obtain the relevant consent, whereas the counterpart's consent is normally required in order to amend the activities to be performed in other types of contract. This juridical feature of the contract of employment corresponds to its socio-economic function of providing employers with flexible working capacity. This applies also to working relationships whereby the employee is endowed with a material degree of executive autonomy and broadened discretion. As we will see in the following pages, these were the problems that Italian courts have had to face in dealing with working activities in which hierarchical power has taken forms different from the traditional ones. Even in such cases, we have seen, the courts have maintained that hierarchical power is in any case essential to the employment relationship. That is to say that no employment relationship can exist in the absence of hierarchical power, the latter also being—taking into account the relevant factual circumstances—the power to issue general directives, according to the programmes and purposes of the firm, to a person who is bound to perform her working activities on a continuous, loyal and diligent basis.

---

[30] See International Labour Conference (85th Session), 'Contract labour', Report VI(1) (Geneva, 1997) 26–33.

With regard to the duty of loyalty, it is worth noting that some students have construed it under a broad meaning, namely as a duty to be available to perform any activity the employer may require on the basis of its different business need, if no demotion occurs. Therefore, it could be said that the aforementioned basic juridical feature of the contract of employment, together with the relevant socio-economic function, recurs also when the employment relationship is carried out in loose hierarchy conditions and/or environments.

Until now, whilst speaking generally of hierarchical power and highlighting its flexibility content, we have principally seen just one of its three main elements: the power to assign tasks and to give orders and directives to employees, namely directional power. But the other two elements thereof are also of use in achieving flexibility and ultimately in reducing what are defined to be 'transaction costs'. The control power affords employers with the possibility of monitoring how working activities are discharged, thus eventually allowing them also to adjust such activities if needed, also by making recourse to directional power. At the same time, there are types of contracts where the power to check how the counterparts' duties are discharged is usually exerted at the end and not during the period of the performance. This results in a quicker and, at the end of the day, more flexible way to coordinate the activities of different subjects in the firm: this also because of the third hierarchical element, namely the disciplinary power. On closer inspection, then, disciplinary power is a mighty instrument of flexibility and transaction costs reduction. As to the former, disciplinary power allows employers to sanction activities deviating from their orders and directives. In this sense, it provides a powerful means for enforcing same orders and directives. Moreover, since it is exerted on a private basis—as it is not necessary to take legal proceedings in order to make use of it—it is a swift means of enforcement. Accordingly, disciplinary power is a means of both deterrence and sanction against non-compliance when firms must rapidly adjust their activities to contingent and unpredictable needs through new orders and directives.

With regard to transaction costs reduction, as complying with employer's orders and directions is an employee's contractual duty, sanctioning any non-compliance will result in enforcing the contract of employment without need to resort to courts: this materially cuts the contract's enforcement costs and therefore reduces transaction costs as a whole. Furthermore, disciplinary power also fosters the flexibility of firms because it allows them to graduate sanctions to the relevant breaches. Most notably, and almost uniquely in the field of contracts, it makes it possible to lawfully sanction a breach of contract without terminating it. This allows enforcing internal rules without the need of entering into a new relationship and bearing the relevant transaction costs.

Thus far, we have shown some of the features of the employment relationship that render it an important device for business organization, as it provides employers with a great deal of flexibility. Accordingly, it should follow that the internalization of activities—of which the employment contract is a central tool—allows businesses to be run in a more flexible way and ultimately also enables them to take advantage of hierarchy as a way to reduce transaction costs. Nonetheless, we should notice that under the post-Fordism system, firms look principally for flexibility, and also that the number of outsourced activities has increased, in comparison with Fordism. From the above, it seems that this reasoning is inconsistent. It is therefore convenient to examine the second facet of the costs trade-off mentioned above, namely 'organization costs'. The latter are the costs any organization faces in carrying out an activity on its own, such as dispersion of resources, arrangement of methods and devices of coordination and hierarchy, as well as some costs related to limitation of hierarchy within the organization. In this regard, the determination of an employment relationship has traditionally gone together with a growing set of regulations afforded by the law and by industrial relation devices in order to protect one of the parties of the relationship, namely the employee. As we have seen above, the definition of employment has traditionally had a legal-technical basis rather than a socio-economic one, the key element of employment being hierarchical power and not economic dependence on the employer, or at least at the very beginning. From a legal viewpoint, the hierarchical/coordination power is at the centre of the employment relationship; that is, the regulatory protection of employees has traditionally focused on hierarchical power in order to reduce it. In this sense, such protection has provided for measures such as reduction of working hours, regulation of overtime, limitations on employers' control power, impediments to demotion and most notably the possibility for employees to organize and bargain collectively.

Collective organization not only allows for reducing competition among workers in order to bargain for better working condition. It also entails a reduction of hierarchical power of employers. Hierarchical power allows employers to organize their business. However, such an organization activity is rarely carried out on an individual basis. Since organization implies the coordination of different parts and outputs, it is commonly exerted on a plural and collective basis. As for work organization, orders and directives are normally issued with regard not to a single worker but rather towards teams, line stages or establishments.

This gives rise to a shift between the level at which hierarchical power is exerted—which is plural—and the individual worker who is subject to hierarchical power. It has been underlined that collective organization allows employees to participate on a plural and collective basis, and therefore to place themselves on the same level of their employers. This results in a limitation of hierarchical power, which is confronted with another plural power, that of the collective organization. When, for instance, employees collectively bargain to regulate working time or output audits or working environment conditions at a shop or plant level, they control and limit the firm's hierarchical power.

This is true also for regulation governing the mere individual employment relationship, such as statutory rules establishing disciplinary procedures, forbidding demotion, regulating transfers of workers or providing redress against unfair dismissal. As to the latter, it is usually perceived as a gross impediment of flexibility, as it—depending on the remedies afforded to the relevant employee—could hinder the possibility of the firm to adjust the size of its workforce to the contingent business situation.

In light of the above, employers see the set of employment protections as limiting their hierarchical power and therefore ultimately causing a reduction of flexibility for the whole business. Such a reduction is perceived as a cost for the firm, notably as an organization cost. Said costs are the other side of the coin with respect to internalizing working activities as a means of reducing transaction costs. Accordingly, in deciding whether to carry out a production phase on an internal basis or to outsource it, firms will also take into account the trade-off between organization costs and transaction costs.

Moreover, some other circumstances must be taken into account in trying to draw an analysis about the reasons that cause firms to have recourse to either internal or contracted-out production.

First, the employment contract is not the sole device through which firms can afford themselves flexibility by means of a hierarchical relationship, whereby they can adjust terms and conditions of the counterpart's performance to their business needs, avoiding or limiting transaction costs. Second, the employment contract is not a monolithic type of contract, as there are very different forms of employment. With regard to the first consideration, it is worth mentioning a species of contractual relationship which in recent decades has increasingly come to the attention of lawyers and economists, namely 'relational contracts'. The main features of relational contracts are their incompleteness and their extension in time. Actually, the latter feature could be deemed to be the cause of the former. Given the impossibility for parties to take into account every circumstance that will occur throughout the relevant relationship—this being due to unpredictability, bounded rationality of the parties or prohibitive transaction costs—the same parties decide to leave unspecified many parts of the contract's terms and conditions, so as to be able to determine them during the same relationship. As a consequence, they draft what could be said to be a framework agreement setting out just the basic rules governing their business relationship, such as criteria of determining the relevant compensations, the minimum or maximum entity of the supply, and reasons for or notice of termination. Other terms of the contract (eg the actual entity of the supply, the number or frequency of orders) are therefore left to the parties' future determination. This allows for adapting the performance of the parties to the contingent business conditions and therefore affords a good deal of flexibility to the relevant contractual relationship. However, it is worth noting that not only is the entity of the supply usually not specified in advance in relational contracts, but also the means through which disputes between the parties are settled. As the settlement of disputes necessarily occurs after the conclusion of the contract, it might be attained also through extra-juridical mechanisms. Such mechanisms are most notably the reputation and economic dependence of the parties. As to the latter, it is necessary to highlight the role of what has been defined 'idiosyncratic investments'. These are investments that are very difficult to reallocate to other business relations because of their specificity with regard to a particular relation. Idiosyncratic investments can be both tangible (such as special machinery, special premises near to the counterpart's location, etc) or intangible (such as specific training, skills, know-how, etc). Furthermore, idiosyncratic investments can either be symmetric or asymmetric among the parties, as there can be relations in which just one of the parties bears idiosyncratic investments or in which one party bears a far higher amount in comparison to the other party. As idiosyncratic investments are difficult to reallocate, they act as an incentive to the party who has borne the investments to prolong the relevant business relation to the greatest extent. In a situation of asymmetric idiosyncratic investments, just one of the parties has this kind of incentive; the other parties are neutral or would find it less onerous to make recourse to their counterpart, who will therefore be in a much weaker business position. Moreover, such a position could be further weakened in a situation whereby the counterpart is the party's sole customer.

In this case, the counterpart could abuse its stronger business position, as the weaker party lacks business alternatives both for its idiosyncratic investments and its mono-customer situation. Termination of the relationship, while being neutral or almost neutral for one party, could potentially lead to the bankruptcy of the other party. Accordingly, the stronger party could unilaterally determine features and conditions of the relevant business relationship, particularly by specifying new details of the counterpart's performance, as they were left unspecified pursuant to the incompleteness of the contract. Moreover, the same party could also interfere with the counterpart's business organization by imposing standards of production and supply that were ever more convenient and specific to its business (this, incidentally, fostering the idiosyncrasy of the counterpart's investments). In this way, the stronger party could position itself in a hierarchical relationship to the counterpart: most notably it could establish hierarchy by making recourse to market instead of internal organization. As curbing transaction costs is a common effect of hierarchy, this kind of hierarchical relation would result also in lower organizational costs in comparison to internalization of business activities.

If we look for instance at labour costs, the stronger party could impose a low-wages policy in order to reduce the cost of the relationship. If a crisis in demand occurs, it would not have to deal with redundancies, as it would not have a legal relationship with the other party's employees. Moreover, it could also interfere with the business organization by unilaterally specifying quantity and quality of outputs and ultimately dictating 'performance rules' to the other party. This kind of action would be made easier in the post-Fordist system whereby even internal production phases have greater executive autonomy, vertical integration no longer being an essential feature of business organization. By abusing its business position in relational contracts, a firm could afford itself a level of hierarchy similar to the one exerted towards an internalized production stage, without the need to arrange an internal organization and the attendant costs. This kind of business relationship embodies what has been called 'hierarchical market relationships'. If the stronger party is a big firm, it could have a large number of hierarchical market relationships with different suppliers, independent contractors and franchisees, this giving rise to what has been called 'asymmetrical cluster firms'.

The term 'asymmetrical' is meant to distinguish this type of business organization from symmetrical cluster firms, namely a network of firms having genuine market and non-hierarchical market relationships between them, thus cooperating on a parity and not on a hierarchy basis.

Asymmetrical cluster firms have recently experienced increasing attention from economists, sociologists and, obviously, lawyers and legislators.

In this context, certain acts of legislation aim at avoiding excesses in terms of incompleteness of contract, as a way to counter abusive business practices. Accordingly, they render null and void clauses whereby one party can unilaterally amend terms and conditions of a contract or terminate a contract without reasonable notice. It follows that parties must determine or set criteria for determining their activities under the contract. Most notably, such an approach forbids the abuse of the other parties' economic dependence and sets out that economic dependence must be ascertained taking into account parties' opportunities to find business alternatives. The rationale of such rules is therefore aimed at reducing the possibilities of misusing a business position by means of relational contracts. Such contracts are relevant in the employment relationship, since the latter assumes a variety of forms, including the so-called 'non-standard forms of employment' that are perceived by firms as more flexible than the standard. One of the main causes of such flexibility is found in their temporality. Although not all non-standard forms of employment are on a fixed-term basis (eg part-time employment could be permanent), nevertheless this is usually a common feature. Temporality affords flexibility to the same extent that it allows firms to plan the duration of working relationships in order to adjust the size of their workforce to the contingent business needs. On the other hand, temporary forms of work are also more rigid than the standard employment relationship in some aspects. We will now look at developments in the case law.

Case law

The mutual rights and obligations of the parties became the focus for the definition of the nature of work relationships. The fundamental term of a contract of employment was the performance of work under the employer's supervision and control in exchange for wages. Non-compliance with the employer's reasonable demands was a fundamental breach of the contract entitling the employer to terminate the contract. Therefore, the case law indicator of 'subordination and control' became all-important in the characterization of an employment relationship. Initially, this indicator was simply understood as direct control exercised by an employer over the work performed by the worker. However, with technological and organizational changes, many employers could no longer directly supervise and control their more highly trained or specialized workers. As a result, the indicator of actual exercise of subordination and control was supplemented by a number of other indicators, including the 'business' indicator (whether the worker is in business on his or her own account) and the 'integration' indicator (whether the worker performs the duties as an integral part of the business of the user enterprise). Further developments in work organization, increased specialization of production and the growing diversity of contractual arrangements brought to the existence a number of other indicators including, inter alia, the following:

— the extent to which the user enterprise determines when and how work should be performed, including instructions on where and how to do the work, working time and other conditions of work;

— the extent of supervisory authority and control of the user enterprise with respect to the work performed, including disciplinary authority;

— whether the work is performed on a regular and continuous basis;

— whether the worker does the same work as that normally performed by the regular employees of the user enterprise;

— whether the work performed is contractually stipulated as an activity or as a result ('final product');

— the extent to which the work performed is integrated into the normal activities of the user enterprise;

— whether the user enterprise pays the amounts due to the worker periodically and according to pre-established criteria;

— whether the worker performs work exclusively for a particular user enterprise;

— the extent to which the user enterprise makes investments and provides tools, materials and machinery, among other things, to perform the work concerned;

— whether the worker undertakes any risk in the business sense or, alternatively, has any expectations of profits associated with the delivery of his or her services as distinct from a fixed commission;

— who pays fiscal and social security contributions—the user enterprise or the worker; and

— whether the user enterprise trains the worker.

In practice, no single indicator is decisive per se, but it is a combination, usually, of two or more of these indicators that determines whether or not there is a genuine employment relationship. From the contributions to this volume, it is possible to discern that the 'subordination and control' indicator is frequently given a high priority, which in most legal regimes is considered to be the hallmark of an employment relationship. However, some experts are sceptical of the efficiency of this kind of multi-indicator review. They assert that under such a test the relationship itself remains largely undefined as a legal concept, since the relevance of different criteria may vary according to the circumstances. Therefore, it is believed that various formulations of indicators are no more than a determination of the degree of dependency (or independence), for which there is no exclusive measure. It has been emphasized that various factors are not exclusive or inclusive but are merely extensions along the same continuum of dependency, which certainly includes subordination and control, and therefore the distinction between an independent contracting and an employment relationship lies in facts, not in law.

In the so-called 'triangular' relationship,[31] the identification of an employer is of crucial importance. In order to resolve the issue, the judiciary determines

---

[31] Normally, an employment relationship involves two parties: the employer and the employee. There are, however, more complex situations whereby one or more third parties are involved, in what is sometimes termed a 'triangular' employment relationship. Such a relationship occurs when the employee of an enterprise is made available by his or her employer to another enterprise to perform certain work or provide certain services. Such

whether it is the user enterprise that exercises the requisite control and economic domination over the workers concerned or whether it is the enterprise that provides these workers. Decisions are normally grounded in employment legislation. In jurisdictions that provide for recognition of two or more employers as a common employer, the courts recognize both enterprises as employers.

Statutory Regulation

Where legislative policy seeks to determine an employment relationship, various statutory techniques are used for this purpose, including the following:

— providing for definitions of 'contract of employment' or 'employment rela-tionship' and spelling out certain indicators, many originally developed by the judiciary, according to which a contract or a relationship is defined as a contract of employment or an employment relationship;

— determination of specific types of contractual arrangements in which the workers concerned are regarded either as employees or as self-employed;

— easing the burden of proof for the workers concerned; and

— removing incentives to disguise an employment relationship.

Many national labour laws contain provisions on the employment relationship, particularly with regard to its scope. Some provisions deal with the regulation of the employment contract as a specific contract (whereby a worker agrees to perform certain work for and under the authority of an employer, who in turn undertakes to provide the necessary conditions for this work and to pay remuneration), its definition, the parties and their respective obligations. Other provisions are intended to facilitate recognition of the existence of an employment relationship and to prescribe administrative and judicial mechanisms for monitoring compliance and enforcing these laws.[32]

---

situations can be beneficial to all concerned. A wide variety of civil (commercial) law contracts can be used to formalize an agreement for the provision of work or services. Such contracts can have beneficial effects for the provider's employees in terms of employment opportunities, experience and professional challenges. From a legal standpoint, however, such contracts may present a technical difficulty as the workers concerned may find themselves interacting with two (or more) interlocutors, each of whom assumes certain functions of a traditional employer. Whereas a 'triangular' employment relationship normally presupposes a civil or commercial contract between a provider and user enterprises, it is possible that no such contract exists and that the provider is not a proper enterprise, but an intermediary who does not undertake any employer responsibility vis-à-vis the workers concerned.

[32] See International Labour Conference (95th Session), 'The employment relationship', Report V(1) (Geneva, 2006) 19–38.

Giuseppe Casale

Definitions

In many countries, the legislation contains a substantive definition of a contract of employment, worded in such a way as to establish what conditions constitute such a contract and hence what distinguishes it from other contracts; in other countries, however, the legislation is less detailed and the task of determining the existence of an employment contract is largely left to case law. The description of the conditions for determining whether work is being performed under an employment contract varies in wording and level of detail from one country to another. Thus, the most commonly used terms are 'dependency', 'subordination', 'supervision', 'direction', 'control', 'authority' of the employer, or the latter's 'orders' or 'instructions' or for the 'employer's account'. Some legal systems use the terms 'subordination' and 'dependency' as alternatives or together, either with different meanings or as synonyms. Sometimes, the law assigns a different meaning to each word, and each is accompanied by a different qualifier: 'legal subordination' and 'economic dependency'. 'Legal subordination' is understood to mean that the employer or his or her representatives direct or are likely to direct the performance of the work. There is deemed to be 'economic dependency' where the sums received by the worker constitute his or her only or main source of income, where such sums are paid by a person or enterprise as a result of the worker's activity, and where the worker does not enjoy economic autonomy and is economically linked to the sphere of activity in which the person or enterprise that may be considered as the employer operates. It is interesting to note that in case of doubt, 'economic dependency' may be used as a factor for determining whether there is an employment relationship.

From the various contributions to this volume, it is possible to see that some labour laws define not only the employment contract but also the employment relationship, understood to mean the fact of performing a service, irrespective of the nature of the agreement under which it is performed, placing the employment contract in the broader context of the employment relationship.

In some other jurisdictions, the employment contract is simply described as a contract between an employer and an employee, without referring to the abovementioned conditions characterizing it as an employment contract. However, the legislation of these countries may have provisions giving a clear idea of the conditions in which the parties are bound by such an employment relationship. For example, provisions governing a worker's duties often include the obligation to respect the employer's orders and instructions—which is an important indicator for determining the existence of an employment contract.

Determination by Law

In some legal systems, labour laws describe certain potentially ambiguous or controversial situations as employment relationships, either in general or under certain conditions, or at least presume they are employment relationships (for example, professional athletes and artists, models, professional journalists, sales representatives, travelling salespersons, insurance salespersons, sales promoters and various public transport workers (drivers, operators, conductors, etc). In other cases, labour legislation specifies whether a given type of work is excluded from its scope or whether or not it gives rise to a contract of employment, depending on the conditions under which it is performed, for example, when home work is deemed to be employment if it is neither discontinuous nor sporadic. On the other hand, work done by persons performing work or services directly for the public, or home work that is performed discontinuously or sporadically, is not deemed to give rise to an employment contract, and neither is work done by a student or graduate of higher education or secondary vocational and technical education for a specified period to fulfil a practical work requirement, even if the enterprise where this work is done provides food, transportation or an allowance in lieu of such benefits.

Conversely, legislation may specify that certain work relationships are not employment relationships, or exclude certain categories of workers from their scope, while other laws authorize the government to make such exclusions. The most common is the total or partial exclusion of public servants and similar workers and, less frequently, public sector workers. In some other countries, labour legislation authorizes the government to adapt the scope of employment legislation to include in it certain categories of workers as parties to contracts of employment.

Burden of Proof

In cases of determination of an employment relationship, the application of the general rule of contract law, whereby the burden of proof rests on the complainant, could make it very difficult or sometimes impossible for the worker to show that he or she is in an employment relationship with the plaintiff. In an employment relationship, it is the employer who has the upper hand, particularly because he or she controls the sources of information. That is why labour laws in many countries have provided certain measures to ease for the workers concerned the burden of proof of the existence of an employment relationship.

It is common for labour legislation to expressly provide that the employment relationship may be proved by any of the usual means, or by any means permitted by law. In some instances, the law may provide that contracts of employment are consensual, ie concluded merely by the consent of the parties without further formalities. In other instances, however, the law may require that the contract be in writing for various reasons relating to compliance or to evidence; or it may proceed from the assumption that the employment relationship exists based on the fact that services are provided. An important element of certainty, which also makes it easier to prove the existence of an employment contract, is the obligation on the part of the employer to inform employees of the conditions applicable to the contract by providing a written contract, a letter of engagement or other documents indicating the essential aspects of the employment contract or relationship. Non-compliance with this obligation may cause the worker to question his or her employee status. Conversely, having the written information in question makes it easier for the worker to prove that status.

With the same aim of easing the burden of proof, some laws provide for a presumption of the existence of an employment relationship. This presumption might be considered either as 'substantive' or as 'procedural'. The 'substantive' presumption implies that under certain conditions spelled out in legislation, the relationship is deemed to be an employment relationship. The 'procedural' presumption means that if certain indicators are present, the relationship is deemed to be an employment relationship, unless the alleged employer proves otherwise or unless it is evident that the parties entered into a different kind of contract.

During the international debate at the ILO, together with the role of case law and statutory regulation in the determination of the existence of an employment relationship, other important issues were highlighted. These included:

— effective access to justice in accordance with national law and practice;
— the role of collective bargaining and social dialogue as a means of finding solutions to questions related to the scope of the employment relationship;
— respect for and implementation of laws and regulations concerning the employment relationship through labour administration services, including labour inspection and their collaboration with the social security administration and the tax authorities; and
— removing incentives to disguise an employment relationship.

As a matter of curiosity, in the replies to the questionnaire contained in Report V(1), the question concerning indicators of the existence of an employment relationship proved to be of considerable interest to governments. For example, 41 governments mentioned indicators that could be included in the proposed Recommendation; several endorsed those mentioned in the questionnaire. One government preferred the 'common law' approach. Another considered that indicators were not relevant to determining the existence of an employment relationship. One indicated that such indicators should be derived from law and jurisprudence. Another stated that they should be defined by national law and practice, that their inclusion in the instrument could be interpreted as implying an exhaustive list, and that some indicators might not be universally recognized. Finally, one government considered that, given the diversity of employment relationships, it was virtually impossible to cite all valid indicators.

Whereas the trade union replies were supportive with regard to the question concerning indicators of the existence of an employment relationship, the employers' organizations stated that these factors should be defined not in the instrument but by the national authorities, as they were based on different concepts in different countries. According to the employers' organizations, an instrument containing a list of such factors would not be useful and, according to one organization, would be at variance with the agreement that the Recommendation should not universally define the content of the employment relationship. On the other hand, one employers' organization recalled that national legislation and practice may not provide for measures of protection in the case of disguised employment relationships, and consequently the instrument should set out clear provisions in this area. At the same time, employers' organizations opposed the very idea of an international definition of the employment relationship. They argued that the definition and scope of that relationship depended on a wide range of national characteristics and that any attempt to introduce the concept of common indicators would only lead to disagreements and dissatisfaction among the social partners.

Further to the replies received, the relevant provisions in the text of a proposed Recommendation were drafted accordingly and submitted to the 2006 ILC for discussion in Report V(2B). With reference to the questionnaire, a number of modifications were made. During the 2006 ILC discussions, this part of the proposed instrument underwent a number of drafting changes, and one new paragraph (17) was introduced in the adopted text.

1.4 Monitoring and Implementation

Reviewing changes in the labour market and in the organization of work as well as advising governments on the implementation of national policy concerning the employment relationship, are among the major issues addressed in the debates in the ILO concerning the employment relationship.

In the technical document prepared by the Office for the Meeting of Experts held in 2000, attention was drawn to the fact that the monitoring of employment relationships was a major political and technical challenge for governments. To address this, it was suggested that a consensus-building tripartite mechanism be devised as a focal point for common observation and analysis of the developments in the labour markets and organization of work, with the specific task of identifying the functional and dysfunctional trends emerging in employment relationships. The body responsible for monitoring employment relationships could suggest corrective measures to fine-tune relevant legal provisions or their application, as well as economic and social initiatives to correct the dysfunctional trends, including initiatives to ensure that necessary statistics are collected on a regular and systematic basis. Respectively, the following points were proposed to the experts for discussion:

— Periodic review of law and practice.
— Creation of a tripartite mechanism to facilitate the formulation and application of the national policy concerning the employment relationship.
— Practical guidelines for governments on specific ways of developing and implementing the national policy.

The experts agreed that countries should adopt or continue a national policy under which they would review at appropriate intervals and, if necessary, clarify or adapt the scope of the regulation of the employment relationship in the country's legislation in line with current employment realities. The review should be conducted in a transparent manner with participation by the social partners.[33]

The general discussion in 2003 revealed that changes in the structure of the labour market and in the organization of work were leading to changing patterns of work both within and outside the framework of the employment relationship. In some situations, it may be unclear whether the worker is an employee or is genuinely self-employed. Collection of statistical data and the undertaking of research and periodic reviews of changes in the structure and patterns of work should be part of

---

[33] See ILO, Report of the Meeting of Experts on Workers in Situations Needing Protection, doc MEWNP/2000/4(Rev), appended to doc GB.279/2, 279th Session, Geneva, November 2000, 38–39.

the national policy framework relating to the employment relationship. The methodology for the collection of data and for undertaking the research and reviews should be determined through a process of social dialogue. All data collected should be disaggregated according to sex, and reviews should explicitly incorporate the gender dimension to take into account other aspects of diversity.

The question on whether the instrument should provide for the establishment of a review and advisory mechanism was included in the questionnaire contained in Report V(1) prepared by the Office for the 2006 ILC discussion. Most of the replies were positive and acknowledged the potential benefits and importance of such a mechanism, although a number expressed reservations as to its nature and scope. For example, one reply indicated that the mechanism should not be too restrictive, and should depend on the capacities of the country concerned. Other replies asked whether the mechanism should be new or whether an existing mechanism could also meet the requirements of the international instrument under discussion; one government considered that States should have total freedom to determine the appropriate mechanism. The replies given to the subsidiary questions concerning consultation (frequent intervals, representation of organizations on an equal footing and experts' reports or technical studies) were generally similar and positive.

Further to the replies received, the relevant provisions in the text of the proposed Recommendation were drafted accordingly and submitted to the 2006 ILC for discussion in the Report V(2B). In comparison with the questionnaire, a number of modifications were made. During the 2006 ILC discussion, this part of the proposed instrument underwent a number of drafting changes and one new paragraph (22) was introduced in the adopted text.

1.5 Final Paragraph

Throughout the debates in the ILO, the Employer delegates were concerned that the new Recommendation might have adverse effects on Convention No 181 concerning private employment agencies. In this regard, they proposed the following new paragraph for introduction in the newly developed recommendation: 'Nothing in this Recommendation should be construed as affecting the meaning or the application of the Private Employment Agencies Convention, 1997 (No 181), or the Private Employment Agencies Recommendation, 1997 (No 188)'. After the discussion, the following text was introduced in the Recommendation as Paragraph 18: 'This Recommendation does not revise the Private Employment Agencies

Recommendation, 1997 (No. 188), nor can it revise the Private Employment Agencies Convention, 1997 (No. 181).'

Follow-up Resolution

At the end of the 2006 ILC discussion, a number of Government delegates proposed a resolution to instruct the Director-General of the Office to help all ILO constituents to better understand and address the difficulties encountered by workers in certain employment relationships. Noting that Paragraphs 19–22 of the newly adopted instrument recommend that the ILO member States establish and maintain monitoring and implementing national policy mechanisms, the resolution's objective was to ensure and reinforce assistance for such mechanisms, the collection of up-to-date information and comparative studies, and the promotion of good practice.

The adopted resolution invites the Office to:

— assist constituents in monitoring and implementing mechanisms for the national policy as set out in Recommendation No 198;

— maintain up-to-date information and undertake comparative studies on changes in the patterns and structure of work in the world, in order to:

- improve the quality of information on and understanding of employment relationships and related issues;
- help better understand and assess these phenomena and adopt appropriate measures for the protection of workers;
- promote good practices at the national and international levels concerning the determination and use of employment relationships; and
- undertake surveys of legal systems to ascertain what criteria are used nationally to determine the existence of an employment relationship and make the results available to the ILO member States to guide them, where this need exists, in developing their own national approach to the issue.[34]

---

[34] For the text of the adopted resolution, see International Labour Conference (95th Session), Provisional Record No 21 (Geneva, 2006) 21/80, available at www.ilo.org/public/english/standards/relm/ilc/ilc95/pdf/pr-21.pdf. See also *The Employment Relationship: An Annotated Guide to ILO Recommendation No 198*, Paper No 18, (Geneva, ILO, 2008).

1.6 Conclusions

Comparative research and debate, including those within the ILO, have recognised that the employment relationship remains one of the most challenging issues in the labour market. The question of whether an employment relationship exists between two parties is of crucial importance for many reasons, not least of which is that most jurisdictions link workers' protection and access to social security to the existence of such a relationship. From a comparative viewpoint, the trend towards more flexible working arrangements generated to a great extent by globalization has affected the employment relationship debate. It is no longer a matter of purely academic interest, but it touches the day-to-day life of workers and employers in the world of work. Whereas many countries have already adopted measures to deal with this issue, many others are interested in finding a balanced approach to the development of national policies to address it. The ILO is expected to give initial guidance on this matter and the adoption of Recommendation No 198 is an important step in this direction.

The comparative research carried out by the ILO and the following discussions have shown that major labour market players recognized the need to address the issue of the employment relationship internationally. In this regard, the adoption of Recommendation No 198 and its accompanying resolution is a result of serious efforts at the international level. At the same time, the complexity of the problem continues to be there, and this is proved by the contributions of the various authors who have accepted to share their own experiences taking into account the law and practice in several regions of the world. This issue will continue to be under the scrutiny of labour lawyers, judiciaries, and law and policy-makers. This proves that the text of the Recommendation No 198 could be of support to those who would like to clarify such an issue in their respective national legal regimes.

The Employment Relationship: a Comparative Analysis of National Judicial Approaches

2

Nicola Countouris[*]

2.1 Introduction

Adapting the employment relationship to the realities of twenty-first century labour markets has become an important policy goal for many national governments and, unsurprisingly, supranational organizations. As put by Deakin and Wilkinson, 'It is no exaggeration to think of the classification of work relationships as the central, defining operation of any labour law system. … Without classification, the law cannot be mobilised.'[1] Whilst the protection offered by labour legislation is universally linked to the existence of an employment relationship between a worker and an employer, a number of technological, legal and, ultimately, political changes are contributing to rendering more tenuous and opaque the legal manifestations of such relationships, thus complicating the legal classification of work and the very application of employment protection legislation.[2] Clearly these trends provide an opportunity for 'disguising' the dependent work relationship as self-employment to avoid the regulatory, social and fiscal costs associated with subordinate work relationships. No less worrying, however, is that they often cast genuine uncertainties over the nature of some more complex work arrangements located in a conceptual 'grey zone' between employment and self-employment.

---

[*] Lecturer at the Faculty of Laws of University College London. This chapter is up to date as of June 2007, the date it was completed. I am grateful to Professor Mark Freedland for comments on earlier versions. The usual disclaimer applies.

[1] S Deakin and F Wilkinson, *The Law of the Labour Market—Industrialization, Employment and Legal Evolution* (Oxford, Oxford University Press, 2005) 4.

[2] For an early comprehensive comparative analysis on the subject, see the 'Supiot Report' of 1998, A Supiot et al, 'Transformation of labour and future of labour law in Europe—Final report' (June 1998), available at http://ec.europa.eu/employment_social/labour_law/docs/supiotreport_en.pdf. See also the more recent and extremely comprehensive report produced by the ILO: International Labour Conference (95th session), 'The employment relationship—Fifth item on the agenda', Report V(I), available at www.ilo.org/public/english/standards/relm/ilc/ilc95/pdf/rep-v-1.pdf.

The debate that took place during the June 2006 International Labour Conference (ILC), and the adoption of the Employment Relationship Recommendation, 2006 (No 198),[3] forcefully highlighted a quasi-unanimous agreement on the perceived need to embark on a regulatory process leading to a clearer conceptualization of the legal notion and definition of the employment relationship. This emerging national and supranational consensus is perhaps the best testimony to the so-called 'universality' of the employment relationship, that is to say the fact that in Scandinavian, as in Latin American countries, the 'protection offered by national laws and regulations and collective agreements [is] linked to the existence of an employment relationship between an employer and an employee'.[4] Unsurprisingly, given the crucial importance of the notion of the employment relationship in any labour law system, the ILO is not the only international body currently exploring novel ways of clarifying the 'classification' and definition of the employment relationship. Recently, the European Union has also suggested that it may seek to develop a supranational regional agenda engaging with the national reform discourses on the notion of the employment relationship.[5]

This chapter was written at the request of the International Labour Office as part of the follow-up to the Resolution Concerning the Employment Relationship.[6] Since one of its main purposes is to collect and disseminate information, the paper makes extensive use of easily accessible internet sources. Its sections seek to provide a contextual and comparative analysis of a number of national notions of the employment relationship as emerging from judicial practice, and effectively seeks to provide the legal background against which Paragraph 4(a) of Recommendation No 198 should be read and understood. The paper is divided into four main sections, followed by a concluding section. Section 2.2 provides a synoptic analysis of the types and notions of employment relationship currently informing labour law systems, by reference to a selection of national jurisdictions. It should be emphasized that the common denominator of all systems is the traditional binary model of

---

[3] ILO, International Labour Conference (95th session), 'Recommendation concerning the employment relationship' (Geneva, 2006), available at www.ilo.org/ilolex/cgi-lex/convde.pl?R198.

[4] ILO Recommendation No 198, Preamble.

[5] Commission (EC), 'Modernising labour law to meet the challenges of the 21st century' (Green Paper) COM (2006) 708 final, particularly at 10–13. Available at http://ec.europa.eu/employment_social/labour_law/docs/2006/green_paper_en.pdf.

[6] International Labour Conference (95th session), Report of the Committee on the Employment Relationship—Provisional Record (Geneva, 2006) 21/80. ILO Governing Body, Follow-up to resolutions adopted by the 95th session (2006) of the International Labour Conference and other matters arising (297th session of the Governing Body, Geneva, November 2006). Available at www.ilo.org/public/english/standards/relm/gb/docs/gb297/pdf/gb-3.pdf.

the employment relationship[7] whereby working persons are either categorized as dependent employees or, alternatively, as autonomous self-employed workers.[8] However, it will be pointed out that several labour law systems are premised on more complex and multilayered notions of the employment relationship that uphold the existence of intermediate statuses of quasi-dependent or parasubordinated workers, enjoying some of the—substantive or procedural—employment protection rights typically associated with dependent employment. It will be stressed, however, that the *nomen iuris* of each type of labour relationship is of little or no value if seen outside the context of jurisprudential reasoning and of its practical application. Thus, the following section 2.3 highlights the ways in which courts tend to apply these labels to actual types of work relationships. In particular this section analyses the various legal tests adopted by national judiciaries, and the indicia of employment status that are typically used to clarify the legal categorization of complex work arrangements. Finally, section 2.4 will further narrow down the analysis in section 2.3 and assess the extent to which some, broadly speaking, economic criteria of dependence/autonomy (eg bearing the risk of loss/chance of profit within a work relationship or being economically dependent upon a sole 'client') are used to attach specific legal statuses to particular groups of working people.[9]

The chapter, as may already be obvious, is essentially case-law focused, and addresses statutory intervention in this area of labour law only cursorily and tangentially. This is not to downplay the importance of hard law, or for that matter, of other softer forms of regulation.[10] On the contrary, it is thought that for the latter to be analysed in a full and coherent way, a separate and distinct type of analysis would be necessary. For similar reasons this chapter does not discuss the complex issue of work relationships involving multiple parties, and it will focus exclusively on the ways in which courts construct essentially bilateral work relations.

---

[7] On the use of this term, see S Deakin, 'The Comparative Evolution of the Employment Relationship' (CBR Working Paper No 317, December 2005) 7, available at www.cbr.cam.ac.uk/pdf/WP317.pdf.

[8] See para 4(a) of Recommendation No 198.

[9] See in particular Paragraph 13 of Recommendation No 198.

[10] Just to mention some of the most recent interventions in this area, *cf* the Australian Independent Contractors Act 2006, available at www.comlaw.gov.au/ComLaw/Legislation/Act1.nsf/0/14A30999 C898119ACA25729600026A39/$file/1622006.pdf and, on the 'softer' side of the regulatory spectrum, see the South African December 2006 Code of Good Practice: Who is an Employee, available at www.labour.gov.za/download/11880/Notice%201774%20-%20OHS%20-%20Who%20is%20an%20employee.pdf and the 2004 Irish Code of Practice determining Employment or Self-employment Status of Individuals, available at www.welfare.ie/publications/codeofpract.pdf.

2.2 The Changing Notion of the Employment Relationship: The Binary Divide and Beyond

This section of the chapter provides a spectrum of the existing legal notions of the employment relationship emerging from a selection of legal systems. It will be highlighted that, at a first level, all legal systems recognise a fundamental divide between what, using the wording of Recommendation No 198, could be defined as the 'distinction between employed and self-employed workers',[11] but that some systems have progressively recognized new and intermediate 'quasi-subordinate' types of work relationships that do not fall squarely under the paradigm of either employment or self-employment. The analysis will highlight both the similarities and the considerable differences existing in terms of taxonomy, scope and protection afforded to the various employment relationships in the different legal systems.

The dichotomy between employment and self-employment is at the heart of the classification of work relationships. The binary notion of the employment relationship grew out of a series of profound economic, political, social and legal changes that took place in the European continent between the eighteenth and the early twentieth centuries.[12] Whilst undeniably the Industrial Revolution[13] and the growth of the capitalist 'firm'[14] played a crucial role in the emergence of the binary divide[15] between employees and the self-employed, there is little doubt that the consolidation of an all-embracing unitary notion of the contract of employment, exercising a centripetal force in respect of a vast variety of work relationships, was just as much a product of deeper political pressures of the nineteenth and twentieth centuries, as it was of economic ones. For instance, if it is true that the new industrial production arrangements caused a decline in 'intermediate forms of labour sub-contracting',[16] legislation and to some extent judge-made legal principles also had an important role in further curbing the use of some of these pre-industrial employment practices, often by explicitly outlawing some of them. In the case of Britain, a country whose doctrinal analysis has been so influential for other common law systems, legal history suggests that a more complete 'contractualization' of the

---

[11] Paragraph 4(a) of Recommendation No 198.

[12] B Veneziani, 'The Evolution of the Contract of Employment' in B Hepple (ed), *The Making of Labour Law in Europe: A Comparative Study of Nine Countries up to 1945* (Mansell, London, 1986).

[13] M Weber, 'The Origins of Industrial Capitalism in Europe' in WG Runciman (ed), *Weber Selections in Translations* (Cambridge, CUP, 1978) 335–36.

[14] RH Coase, 'The Nature of the Firm' (1937) 4 *Economica* 386.

[15] This term was first used by M Freedland, 'The role of the contract of employment in modern labour law' in L Betten (ed), The *Employment Contract in Transforming Labour Relations* (The Hague, Kluwer, 1995) 17–27.

[16] S Deakin, *The Many Futures of the Contract of Employment* (CBR Working Paper No 191, December 2001), at 2, available at www.cbr.cam.ac.uk/pdf/wp191.pdf.

employment relationship was very largely the result of the socialising influence of welfare state legislation,[17] and of a wider set of political and legal pressures geared towards the 'decasualization'[18] of work and discouraging heterogeneity in employment relationships. As Lyon-Caen put it : 'Whatever one may say, there has never been a single legal model. But diversity did not receive any public encouragement and it encountered some limits, notably in what judges would draw from the general rules' (author's translation).[19]

But whatever the reasons behind the emergence of the contractual notion of subordinate employment and of the establishment of the employee/self-employed dichotomy, it is a fact that this distinction has acted as the blueprint for casting the scope of application of modern, twentieth-century century labour law systems. Typically the distinction is grounded in statutes and labour or civil codes, although in most cases legislation alone provides an insufficiently precise description of either or both notions, effectively assigning to the national judiciaries the role of spelling out the exact definition and content of the terms.

In Brazil[20] the distinction between *empregado*[21] and *trabalhador autônomo*[22] is as crucial for determining the scope of application of labour legislation as the concepts of *lavoratore subordinato*[23] and *lavoratore autonomo*[24] in Italian law, those of *Arbeitnehmer* and *freier Dienstvertrag* in German law[25] or the concepts of employee working under a contract of employment/contract of service and of self-employed contractor working under a contract for services adopted in most common law based legal systems,[26] such as those of the United Kingdom,[27] Australia,[28] and to a

---

[17] S Deakin and F Wilkinson, *The Law of the Labour Market* (Oxford, OUP, 2005).

[18] O Kahn-Freund, 'Status and Contract in Labour Law' (1967) *Modern Law Review* 642.

[19] A Lyon-Caen, 'Actualité du contrat de travail' (1988) *Droit Social* 541.

[20] See JF Siqueira Neto, *Informe Sobre as Situações de Trabalho e de Proteção dos Trabalhadores no Brasil* (OIT, Geneva, 1998), available at www.ilo.org/public/english/dialogue/ifpdial/downloads/wpnr/brazil.pdf.

[21] See art 3 of the *Consolidação das Leis do Trabalho*, available at www.trt02.gov.br/geral/tribunal2/legis/CLT/TITULOI.html.

[22] For a recent analysis on the distinction between the *empregado* and *trabajador autonomo*, see N° 00032–2007–106–22–00–6 of the *Tribunal Regional do Trabalho da 22a Região* available at www.trt22.gov.br/institucional/varas/floriano/sentencas/2007/2007_02/ST_00032–2007–106–22–00–6.pdf.

[23] *Articolo 2094 Codice Civile* available at www.jus.unitn.it/CARDOZO/Obiter_Dictum/codciv/Lib5.htm.

[24] On the definition of the *contratto d'opera*, the main type of *contratto di lavoro autonomo*, see *Articolo 2222 Codice Civile* at www.jus.unitn.it/CARDOZO/Obiter_Dictum/codciv/Lib5.htm.

[25] See R Wank, 'Diversifying Employment Patterns—the Scope of Labor Law and the Notion of Employees', Paper presented at the 7th Comparative Labor Law Seminar of JILPT in March 2004, available at www.jil.go.jp/english/events_and_information/documents/clls04_wank2.pdf. See also A Supiot, *Beyond Employment—Changes in Work and the Future of Labour Law in Europe* (Oxford, OUP, 2001) 7, available at http://fds.oup.com/www.oup.co.uk/pdf/0–19–924305–0.pdf, www.jil.go.jp/english/events_and_information/0309_report.htm.

[26] For a comparative analysis of some systems heavily influenced by the common law notion of contract of employment, see S Vettori, *The Employment Contract and the Changed World of Work* (Aldershot, Ashgate, 2007).

certain extent the United States.[29] South Africa[30] and Canada,[31] albeit not fully fitting the pure common law system paradigm, have also shaped their labour protection systems on the basis of the employee/self-employed divide, partly due to the historical influence of other European legal systems. The universality of the employment relationship is such that even countries like Japan,[32] far removed from most of the eighteenth- and nineteenth-century European historical vicissitudes, have eventually espoused a binary model of employment relationship and the concept of subordinate employment. 'According to prevailing academic opinion, the main characteristic of a worker covered under [art 9 of the Japanese Labour Standards Law] is the existence of a subordinate relationship with an employer'.[33] Although the analysis and comparison between industrialized and newly industrializing countries is always bound to raise complications,[34] it is worth noticing that countries such as India and China have also cast their labour law systems around the notion of the dependent contract of employment. Section 16 of the Chinese Labour Act 1994 provides that 'A labour contract is the agreement reached between a labourer and an employing unit for the establishment of the labour relationship and the definition of the rights, interests and obligations of each party. A labour

---

[27] s 230(1)-(2) ERA 1996, available at www.opsi.gov.uk/ACTS/acts1996/96018-ah.htm. See also M Freedland, *The Personal Employment Contract* (Oxford, Oxford University Press, 2003) and by the same author, 'United Kingdom—National Study for the ILO Workers' Protection' (Geneva, ILO, 1999), available at www.ilo.org/public/english/dialogue/ifpdial/downloads/wpnr/uk.pdf.

[28] B Creighton and R Mitchell, 'The Contract of Employment in Australian Labour Law' in L Betten (ed), *The Employment Contract in Transforming Labour Relations* (The Hague, Kluwer, 1995) 129. See also J-C Tham, 'The Scope of Australian Labour Law and the Regulatory Challenges Posed by Self and Casual Employment', Paper presented at the 7th Comparative Labor Law Seminar of JILPT in March 2004, available at www.jil.go.jp/english/events_and_information/documents/clls04_tham2.pdf.

[29] On the very circular definition of 'employee' in US legislation, see s 3(e) of the Fair Labor Standards Act 1938, as amended, available at www.dol.gov/esa/regs/statutes/whd/FairLaborStandAct.pdf. See also KG Dau-Schmidt and MD Ray, 'The Definition of "Employee" in American Labor and Employment Law', Paper presented at the 7th Comparative Labor Law Seminar of JILPT in March 2004, available at www.jil.go.jp/english/events_and_information/documents/clls04_dauschmidt2.pdf.

[30] See S Vettori, *The Employment Contract and the Changed World of Work* (Aldershot, Ashgate, 2007). See also H Cheadle and M Clarke, 'South Africa' (Geneva, ILO, 1999), available at www.ilo.org/public/english/dialogue/ifpdial/downloads/wpnr/sa.pdf.

[31] See s 167 of the Canada Labour Code, available at http://laws.justice.gc.ca/en/showdoc/cs/L-2/bo-ga:l_III//en#anchorbo-ga:l_III and see the considerations on the Canadian notion of 'employee' in HW Arthurs, *Fairness at Work—Federal Labour Standards for the 21ˢᵗ Century (2006)* 57 available at www.fls-ntf.gc.ca/doc/fin-rpt-e.pdf and the very detailed analysis inch 4 of MJ Bernier et al, *Les Besoins de Protection Sociale des Personnes en Situation de Travail non Traditionnelle* (2003), available at www.travail.gouv.qc.ca/actualite/travail_non_traditionnel/Bernier2003/BernierReportChap4.pdf.

[32] See M Asakura, 'Workers' Protection in Japan' (Geneva, ILO, 1999) available at www.ilo.org/public/english/dialogue/ifpdial/downloads/wpnr/japan.pdf.

[33] S Ouchi, 'Labor Law Coverage and the Concept of "Worker"', Paper presented at the 7th Comparative Labor Law Seminar of JILPT in March 2004, available at www.jil.go.jp/english/events_and_information/documents/clls04_ouchi.pdf.

[34] O Kahn-Freund, 'On Uses and Misuses of Comparative Law (1974) *Modern Law Review*, 1.

contract shall be concluded where a labour relationship is to be established'.[35] Article 3 of the Draft Labour Contract Law, presented in March 2006 and currently being discussed before the National People's Congress, provides that:

(1) The term 'Labour Relation' as referred to herein shall mean the relationship causing any rights and obligations subject to which an Employer employs any labourers as its employees who shall provide paid labour service under the administration of such Employer.

(2) A 'labour contract' as referred to herein shall mean the agreement by which an employment relationship between an Employer and its employees is established, with their rights and obligations clarified thereunder.

The relevance of the notion of the 'contract of service' is also quite apparent in Indian law, albeit in the context of a more varied spectrum of employment practices.[36] Here the core of labour protection legislation is enjoyed by those subjects falling within the definition of 'workman' of s 2(s) of the Industrial Disputes Act 1947.[37] The term refers to 'any person (including an apprentice) employed in any industry to do any manual, unskilled, skilled, technical, operational, clerical or supervisory work for hire or reward, whether the terms of employment be express or implied'. As we are recently reminded by SB Sinha J, of the Supreme Court of India, the definition of the term effectively requires the '[d]etermination of the vexed questions as to whether a contract is a contract of service or contract for services'.[38]

While there is little doubt that the binary notion of the employment relationship has exercised a formidable and 'universal' influence on the scope of application of most employment protection systems around the world, it should also be clear that, in this area of law more than in others, the devil is in the detail. In fact, the 'universality' claim needs to be approached with at least three caveats in mind. Firstly, whilst the binary notion of the employment relationship is still the dominant cast used to mould the personal scope of application of labour laws, a growing number of national jurisdictions are moving towards more articulated and multifaceted systems of classification including one—or more—'hybrid' notions of work relationship that do not display all the characteristics of dependent work but neither all those of self-employment. Some typical examples of this trend are the Italian

---

[35] Text available at http://english.ibd.com.cn/news/readcredit.asp?newsid=98.

[36] www.ilo.org/public/english/dialogue/ifpdial/downloads/wpnr/india.pdf.

[37] Text of the Act available at http://pblabour.gov.in/pdf/acts_rules/inustrial_disputes_act_1947.pdf.

[38] *Workmen of Nilgiri Coop Mkt Society Ltd v State of Tamil Nadu & Ors* [2004] (101) FLR 137 [32], available at www.judis.nic.in/supremecourt/qrydisp.asp?tfnm=25859.

notion of *lavoratore parasubordinato*,[39] the German concept of *arbeitnehmerähnliche Personen*,[40] and, with some degree of approximation, the British concept of 'worker'.[41] Secondly, even a superficial analysis of the national definitions of 'employee' included in statute law and—perhaps most importantly—in court decisions, inevitably suggests that the numbers and types of personal work relationships incorporated within each national concept of 'dependent employment' vary from system to system and that the ability of each national definition of 'contract of employment' to cope with the ever-growing diversity in the provision of personal work varies from country to country. The British notion of 'contract of employment', as the next section will highlight, is possibly narrower than, for instance, the French notion of *contrat de travail*. Thirdly, it is arguable that while the classificatory exercise discussed in the present section is of vital importance for any labour law system, there is no doubt that the consequences of this exercise very much depend on the amount of substantive rights attached to each employment status. Put simply, there is little value in having a broad definition of 'employee' if the latter category of workers enjoys little or no substantive protection. Inevitably, a closer analysis of the labour systems discussed in the previous paragraphs would quickly reveal that the quantity and quality of the substantive rights and protections afforded to employees in, say, the United Kingdom, France and China differs and, one may say, differs considerably. Also, the ability of each national system to effectively enforce its existing standards varies from country to country.

The third caveat discussed above will be only cursorily discussed in this chapter, as it arguably falls partly or wholly outside its declared scope. The second one will be analysed in more detail below, in sections 2.3 and 2.4. The following paragraphs of this section focus instead on the progressive emergence, in a number of national legal systems, of some more articulated and multifaceted systems of classification, often including some intermediate quasi-subordinate types of statuses.

---

[39] See, in general, A Perulli, *Economically dependent/quasi-subordinate (parasubordinate) employment: legal, social and economic aspects* (Brussels, EC, 2003), http://ec.europa.eu/employment_social/news/2003/sep/parasubordination_report_en.pdf.

[40] See s 12a of the 1974 law on collective agreements (*Tarifvertragsgesetz*), available at http://bundesrecht.juris.de/tvg/__12a.html.

[41] See for instance s 54(3) of the National Minimum Wage Act 1998, available at www.opsi.gov.uk/acts/acts1998/80039–g.htm#54.

Beyond the Binary Divide: The Notion of Quasi-Subordinate Work

According to some authors, the binary divide, important as it may have been in the past, no longer provides a satisfactory tool for shaping the scope of application of employment law since, over the last few decades, a number of hard-to-define work relationships have effectively contributed to the growth of a grey area located between the traditional concepts of employee, on the one hand, and of self-employed, on the other. As such, workers engaged under these types of 'intermediate' relationships retain, at least formally, a considerable discretion over the manner and timing of performance of their work, but they may also be economically dependent on the payment of 'fees', or wages, for their subsistence just as any dependent employee and may be subject to some form of entrepreneurial control or coordination of their activities for a certain amount of time. '[H]ere, the question is not to verify that the law is being correctly applied in a specific case. On the contrary, [the 'grey zone' notion] casts doubt as to the accuracy of the legal categories (employed and self-employed) and of the legal and case law criteria on which the classifications are based'.[42]

The proliferation of these 'hard to categorize' work relationships has led some legal systems to effectively coin some new types of employment status, usually but not exclusively by carving them out of the notion of self-employment. A good example of this trend would be the German notion of *arbeitnehmerähnliche Person*. This category was first 'typified' by section 12a of the 1974 law on collective agreements (*Tarifsvertragsgesetz*) and defined as 'Personen, die wirtschafltlicht abhängig und vergleichbar einem Arbeitnehmer sozial schutzbedürftig sind', that is to say, 'persons who [in spite of their formal independence] are economically dependent and, like an employee, in need of social protection'. To be in this category the worker has to work alone, and the major part of his work (for example, one-third of his total income, for journalists and artists) must come from a single employer. At the outset, 'quasi-employees' were afforded the same procedural labour rights recognized for 'dependent workers', with section 5 of the *Arbeitsgerichtsgesetz* covering employees as well as 'other persons who, because of a lack of economic autonomy, are treated as dependent workers'. In 1994, protection against sexual harassment in the workplace was extended to the *arbeitnehmeränliche Personen* under section 1 of the *Beschaftigtenschutzgesetz*. Traditionally, German economically dependent workers have also enjoyed a statutory entitlement to holidays and leave, under

---

[42] A Perulli (n 39) 15.

section 2 of the *Bundesurlaubsgesetz* 1963, and to social security contributions and protection and health and safety regulations.[43]

A similar set of rights was bestowed to the Italian *parasubordinati* by a series of statutory interventions. Law 533/1973, modifying for this purpose Article 409 of the Italian Civil Procedure Code, prescribed that the labour dispute regime should also apply to the 'relationship of agency, of commercial representation and other relations of collaboration materialising in a continuous and coordinated provision, predominantly personal even if not of entirely personal character'. To put it simply, the labour process rules will apply when the provision of the service presents itself as characterized, in practice, by a predominantly personal activity of continuous and coordinated collaboration in an enterprise (the so-called *co.co.co.—collaborazioni coordinate e continuative*—which in practice is a loose category of *parasubordinati*). The focus in Italy is not, as in Germany, on the economic need for social protection, but instead on the expectation, and power, of the employer to *coordinate* the activities of the worker (in the limited sense that he can expect to see his interest in having a sequence of 'result performances' satisfied), despite the lack of subordination.[44] The characterizing elements of *parasubordinazione*, as inferred from Article 409(3), are collaboration, coordination, continuity and the predominantly personal provision of labour. Italian courts have more or less consistently held that *parasubordinazione* is effectively a circumscribed sub-species of self-employment. The Italian Constitutional Court is adamant about the fact that 'the category of parasubordination [is only relevant] from a procedural and not also from a substantive point of view [and it does] not provide a hermeneutic criterion for extending to these types of relationships, that remain on the area of self-employment, the substantive areas typical of subordinate employment'.[45] But this minimalist understanding of *parasubordinazione* has to be seen in the context of a growing level of statutory and collective intervention. Statute, after progressively seeking to extend to *co.co.co* workers a series of rights and entitlements in the areas of social security and health and safety,[46] sought to provide with legislative decree 276/2003 a more comprehensive regulation of these forms of work. The result was the creation of a new

---

[43] *Sozialgesetzbuch-SGB*, §7, s IV, Book IV. See A Hoeland, 'A Comparative Study of the Impact of Electronic Technology on Workplace Disputes: National Report on Germany' (2005) *Comparative Labor Law & Policy Journal* 152–53.

[44] V Pinto, 'La Categoria Giuridica delle Collaborazioni Coordinate e Continuative e il Lavoro a Progetto' (Massimo D'Antona Working Paper 34/2005) 7, available at www.lex.unict.it/eurolabor/ricerca/wp/it/pinto_n34–2005it.pdf.

[45] Corte Costituzionale, *Sentenza N 365 del 24 Luglio 1995*, available at www.cortecostituzionale.it/ita/attivitacorte/pronunceemassime/pronunce/schedaDec.asp?Comando=RIC&bVar=true&TrmD=&TrmDF=&TrmDD=&TrmM=&iPagEl=1&iPag=1.

[46] See art 2(b) of the legislative decree 124/1993, art 2(26) of Law 335/1995, and art 59(16) of Law 449/1997 as amended by art 51(1)of Law 488/1999.

sub-category of quasi-subordinate contracts known as '*lavoro a progetto*'[47] introducing a series of, perhaps modest, formal and substantive requirements—ranging from a duty to conclude the contracts in writing by specifying the nature and duration of the 'project'[48] to that of the statutory suspension of the relationship during pregnancy—further accentuating the hybrid and self-standing nature of this type of work relationship. Collective bargaining has also sought to ameliorate the level of protection granted to *lavoratori parasubordinati*.[49] Earlier data made available by Nidil, the largest trade union of atypical workers, suggested that some 102 collective agreements had been signed by 2004, and that the number of *parasubordinati* directly covered amounted to circa 100,000.[50] From a substantial point of view all the agreements typically cover health and safety legislation, while the second most common provision was the requirement that the contract be in written form and that a copy be given to the worker. As for the minimum duration of the contract, the latter is usually placed at two months. Working time is typically excluded from the scope of these agreements, while the issue of pay is tackled in a variety of ways ranging from forfeit-payments to explicit references to analogous collective agreements signed by typical workers' unions, and most of the agreements provided for remuneration to be matched with that of typical workers on a monthly basis.[51] However, in spite of these improvements, recent surveys still suggest that these atypical workers clearly perceive themselves as a relatively under-protected and precarious category of economically-dependent workers.[52]

In recent years, the idea of introducing some new notions of employment relationships that fall in the conceptual, and regulatory, grey zone between employment and self-employment has spread slowly but progressively both within and outside Europe. Since 1997, UK statutes and statutory instruments have progressively extended to the category of 'workers' a series of important rights, ranging

---

[47] Article 61 of legislative decree 276/2003, available at www.parlamento.it/leggi/deleghe/03276dl.htm.

[48] Interestingly, the first judicial decisions in cases where the project was not specified in the contract provided that the relationship be transformed into a standard open-ended subordinate employment relationship. *Cf* T Torino 5 aprile 2005, in (2005) *Rivista Italiana di Diritto del Lavoro* 849. On the same point see also *Circolare del Ministero del Lavoro e delle Politich Sociali n 1/2004*.

[49] For a comprehensive list of collective agreements signed by Nidil-CGIL, one of the most representative trade unions in the sector, see www.nidil.cgil.it/pagina.php?Id_Tipologia=9&Id_Pag=42&Colore_Pagina=1&Id_Voce=9&Tipo_Voce=1.

[50] Nidil, 'Nessun Lavoro Senza Diritti e Tutele. La Contrattazione di NIdiL-Cgil nel Lavoro Atipico' (2004) 86, available at www.atipici.net/atipici/osservatorio/files/contrattazione_NIdiL-Cgil.pdf.

[51] For a detailed analysis, see S Leonardi, 'Parasubordinazione e Contrattazione Collettiva. Una Lettura Trasversale' (IRES, Milan, 2001), available at www.atipici.net/osservatorio/files/Parasubordinazione_e_contrattazione_collettiva_IRES.pdf.

[52] IRES, *Il Lavoro Para-Subordinato A Rischio Di Precarietà: tra Scarsa Autonomia, Dipendenza Economica e Mancanza di Prospettive* (Milan, IRES, 2006), available at www.ires.it/files/rapporto_compl_nidil_26ott2006.pdf.

from a minimum wage to working time.[53] The notion of 'worker' is defined by statute as being broader than the notion of 'employee' and as including the latter as well as 'any other contract, whether express or implied and (if it is express) whether oral or in writing, whereby the individual undertakes to do or perform personally any work or services for another party to the contract whose status is not by virtue of the contract that of a client or customer of any profession or business undertaking carried on by the individual'.[54] In the recent Employment Appeal Tribunal decision of *James v Redcats*, a case dealing with a courier engaged under a 'self-employed courier agreement' who was eventually re-classified as being a 'worker', Elias J stated that:

> There are three elements to the definition. First, there must be a contract to perform work or services. Second, there must be an obligation to perform that work personally. Third, the individual will not be a worker (or indeed a home worker) if the provision of services is performed in the course of running a profession or business undertaking and the other party is a client or customer. In practice the last two are interrelated concepts....[55]

In recent years, and even months, courts and tribunals have shown some degree of generosity in affording the status of 'worker' to a number of 'atypicals'.[56] However, it should be pointed out that 'workers' do not enjoy all rights afforded to standard employees, and that they are excluded from important statutory protections such as unfair dismissal legislation and eligibility for redundancy compensation.

The examples of 'grey area' work relationships should not lead one to assume that this type of debate is exclusive to the European continent. For instance, a notion of 'quasi-subordinate' work very similar to the Italian concept of *parasubordinazione* has recently started to emerge in some quarters of Brazilian legal reasoning and jurisprudence, and the Canadian concept of 'intermediate worker' has a long history dating back to the early decades of the twentieth century.[57]

---

[53] See ERA 1996 s 230(3), NMWA 1998 s 54, WTR 1998 reg 2. Some basic rights pertaining to collective labour law, also refer to the term 'worker'. See TULRCA 1992 s 296(1), ERA 1999 s 13.

[54] See s 54(3) of the National Minimum Wage Act 1998, at www.opsi.gov.uk/acts/acts1998/80039–g.htm#54.

[55] *James v Redcats* [2007] IRLR 296, also available at www.employmentappeals.gov.uk/Public/Upload/06_0475fhRCDM.doc.

[56] See in particular cases such as *Byrne Brothers v Baird* [2002] IRLR 96 and also *James v Redcats* [2007] IRLR 296.

[57] See *Carter v Bell & Sons* [1936] OR 290 (CA) (QL).

In 1998, the report compiled by JF Siqueira Neto for the ILO highlighted the progressive emergence in Brazilian law of some forms of *trabalho 'independente-dependente'*.[58] In the absence of ad hoc legislation for these forms of work, some employment tribunals have sought to develop an autonomous understanding of what is increasingly defined as *trabalho parasubordinado*. In 2000 Judge Monteiro de Barros, of the Tribunal Regional do Trabalho da 3ª Região, pointed out that 'the contraposition between subordinate employment and autonomous employment has exhausted its historical function ... The most attentive *doctrina* has suggested a new typology (coordinated work, or parasuborinated work), with an adequate level of protection, less than that foreseen for subordinate work and greater than that applied to autonomous work'.[59] These ideas have been further considered by subsequent case law, most recently in *Processo N 00628.2006.006.14.00–0* of December 2006.[60] In this case the tribunal highlighted the jurisprudential debate over the notion of quasi-subordinate work. However, the judge pointed out that as a typology of coordinated work is non-existant, there is no better legal way to characterise this particular work contract than as an employment relationship, although he then went on to say that in the case of instance the 'moto-boy' failed to meet the tests of dependent employment.

The Canadian concept of 'intermediate worker' has a long-rooted history dating back to the mid-1930s and the Ontario Court of Appeal decisions of *Carter v Bell & Sons*.[61] In discussing the terms and the nature of the relationship, JA Middleton opined:

> There are many cases of an intermediate nature where the relationship of master and servant does not exist but where an agreement to terminate the arrangement upon reasonable notice may be implied. This is I think such a case. The mode of remuneration points to a mercantile agency pure and simple, but the duties to be performed indicate a relationship of a more permanent character.[62]

This concept eventually managed to permeate some Canadian labour law statutes, and effectively carved out of the ambit of commercial law a number of formally

---

[58]   See JF Siqueira Neto, *Informe Sobre as Situações de Trabalho e de Proteção dos Trabalhadores no Brasil* (Geneva, OIT, 1998) s 7.

[59]   RO no 17.231/2000 of 26/04/2000 available at http://as1.mg.trt.gov.br/jurisprudencia/acordaoNumero.do?evento=Detalhe&idAcordao=180440&codProcesso=176535&datPublicacao=26/04/2000&index=3.

[60]   Available at www.trt14.gov.br/acordao/2007/Mar_07/Data05_03_07/00628.2006.006.14.00–0_RO.pdf.

[61]   [1936] OR 290 (CA) (QL).

[62]   ibid 5.

independent workers and repositioned them within the protective scope of employment law for the purposes of collective bargaining and, mainly through judicial intervention, for the purposes of reasonable notice of the termination of the relationship. The rationale for this approach is fairly evident from the definition of 'dependent contractor' provided by section 1 of the Labour Relations Act, and will be quite familiar to those English labour lawyers who considered the reasoning behind decisions such as *Ready Mixed Concrete*[63] to be ill-conceived:

> 'Dependent contractor' means a person, whether or not employed under a contract of employment, and whether or not furnishing tools, vehicles, equipment, machinery, material, or any other thing owned by the dependent contractor, who performs work or services for another person for compensation or reward on such terms and conditions that the dependent contractor is in a position of economic dependence upon, and under an obligation to perform duties for, that person more closely resembling the relationship of an employee than that of an independent contractor.[64]

Clearly the perceived inadequacies of the binary notion of employment relationship are progressively triggering a series of national responses aimed at regulating the 'grey area' between employment and self-employment. Not all systems are approaching this trend by creating an intermediate notion of work relationships. France, for instance has traditionally sought to enforce its binary system by relying on statutory presumptions of status. The French Labour Code has introduced a number of professional categories, often referred to as *situations mixtes*, in its livre VII, and Article L 751–1 for instance, introduces a statutory presumption of employment status for *voyageurs représentants placiers* (door-to-door salespersons), regardless of whether they work for one or more employers. And not all authors would agree that the creation of an intermediate category of workers is necessary or beneficial even if, as we saw above,[65] the consequence of its absence can often be that Brazilian 'moto-boys' ultimately receive a lower level of protection than British 'self-employed couriers'.

In Australia the notion of 'dependent contractor' has struggled to develop amid a considerable degree of controversy. In 2000, the Independent Report of the Victorian Industrial Relations Taskforce considered that

---

[63] *Ready Mixed Concrete v Ministry of Pensions* [1968] 2 QB 497.

[64] www.e-laws.gov.on.ca/DBLaws/Statutes/English/95l01_e.htm.

[65] A strong and lucid defence of the contract of employment can be found in G Davidov, 'The Reports of My Death are Greatly Exaggerated: "Employee" as a Viable (Though Overly-Used) Legal Concept', in G Davidov and B Langille (eds) *Boundaries and Frontiers of Labour Law: Goals and Means in the Regulation of Work* (Oxford, Hart, 2006), available as an article at http://papers.ssrn.com/sol3/papers.cfm?abstract_id=783484.

There is also a view that somewhere between genuine employees and genuine independent contractors, that a third category of contractors is starting to emerge. This category is defined as those workers who are self-employed, but at the same time are dependent on the hiring organization to whom they provide their services. They are basically dependent on a regular employer for work, much like an employee is dependent on an employer for a wage. While workers in this third category may not yet account for a substantial share of the workforce, their numbers look set to grow.

With self-employed people now rising to around eleven per cent of the Australian labour force, it is estimated that at least thirty-eight per cent of the self-employed are treated by employers as dependent contractors who are difficult to distinguish from ordinary wage and salary earners.[66]

Those authors and legal systems that suggest that the binary notion has not and should not exhaust its classificatory and protective functions believe that more could be done in order to clarify and, perhaps, expand the definition and concept of contract of employment, either through statutory or judicial intervention. The following section of this paper examines the ways in which the notion of 'contract of employment' is defined and conceptualized in a number of national jurisdictions and the relationship of these national definitions with Recommendation No 198.

2.3 The Contract of Employment in Legal Practice: The Role of Judiciaries

As seen in the previous section, the contract of employment plays a fundamental 'gatekeeping' function in all employment protection legislation ('EPL') systems. Typically, if workers are employed under a contract of employment, their employment relationships will be deemed to fall within the scope of application of labour law. If they are not, their work relationships will be regulated, partly or totally, by commercial law or by contract law. Given the crucial role of the contract of employment as the gatekeeper of EPL systems, one would have expected legislation to set out clearly, if not incontrovertibly, its exact defining elements. However, this is hardly the case and, as argued by Benjamin:

---

[66] At 146–47. Available at www.business.vic.gov.au/busvicwr/_assets/main/lib60093/irtaskforcereport-fulldocument.pdf.

> Conventional definitions of an employee have allowed wide scope for the courts to determine who is covered by labour law ... the remarkable fact is that the key question in labour market regulation ... is left for the courts to determine, with legislation often giving very little guidance.[67]

While case law has undoubtedly been the main legal influence shaping the definition of contract of employment during the twentieth century, the following sections of this chapter will reveal that in some jurisdictions other types of regulatory instrument also concur to the classification of work relationships. For instance, in a number of systems, statute sets 'hard law' legal presumptions of employment status, or provides, often with the backing of social partners, 'soft law' codes of practice aimed at guiding judicial or, increasingly, administrative bodies in their determinations on the nature of work relationships.

But the following paragraphs of this section will focus exclusively on the reasoning and judicial tests used by courts in identifying the notion of contract of employment. It will be pointed out that judiciaries have had, and continue to have, a tremendous influence over the actual meaning of dependent employment. A comparative analysis of the approach adopted by courts in performing this delicate classificatory function will inevitably reveal a series of differences and, in fact, the existence of slightly broader or narrower legal concepts of subordinate employment. However, there are also a number of similarities. For instance, in all systems the classification of the contact of employment is a question of both law and, perhaps primarily, of fact. This should hardly be surprising since, after all, the concept of employment relationship is by its very nature a relational and factual one, and presupposes the actual performance of a series of acts that may cast a completely different light on the formal terms of the contract itself. As such, the legal classification of a work relationship will typically require an ex post facto investigation into the legal consequences of the conduct of the parties involved. Another common feature is that, ultimately, no system of classification solely relies on a single defining test or 'index' of subordination. While it is correct to discuss and analyse tests such as the 'control test', the 'integration test' or the 'mutuality of obligations test' in isolation, and while at times some tests can be more influential than others in determining the employment status of a worker, in practice courts will use a multiplicity of tests and consider a vast range of 'subordination indicia' in order to finalize their determinations. Another common trend is the growing tendency of most national, and supranational, judiciaries to come to terms with the

---

[67] P Benjamin, 'Beyond the Boundaries: Prospects for Expanding Labour Market Regulation in South Africa', in G Davidov and B Langille (eds) *Boundaries and Frontiers of Labour Law: Goals and Means in the Regulation of Work* (Oxford, Hart, 2006) 192.

changing world of work by trying to expand, as far as possible, the legal notion of dependent employment to include some new forms of personal work. The Italian notion of '*subordinazione attenuata*',[68] the ever-growing use of the concept of 'employment relationship' by the European Court of Justice in the context of discrimination and health and safety legislation, are but two of several examples of expanded notions of subordination. The following paragraphs will look at these trends while discussing the main features of the notion of contract of subordinate employment emerging from judicial practice, in a comparative perspective.

The employment relationship is perhaps irrevocably linked to the notion of subordination of one person to another. Be it through the 'control test' devised by English courts in *Yewens v Noakes,*[69] or though the concept of '*lien de subordination juridique*',[70] typical of French law and of other civil law systems, all national notions of contract of employment are premised on a paradigm of work that is based on an inherently vertical power relationship between employer and employee. Clearly socio-economic changes have strained the narrow readings of most of the early definitions of employee or salaried worker. In this respect, most common law based systems have taken the lead from the jurisprudential decisions of English courts and have progressively adopted and adapted most of the 'new tests' devised by UK judges to their national circumstances. A trace of this 'spillover' effect can be found in the illuminating words of Benjamin:

> The seminal article written by Sir Otto-Kahn Freund, persuaded [the South African Courts] to reject the 'control' test and adopt the approach that an employee is someone who is part of the employer's business … usually referred to as the 'organization' or 'integration' test.[71]

The control test, as developed in *Yewens v Noakes,*[72] was eventually rephrased in somewhat broader terms in *Ready Mixed Concrete,*[73] which considered whether the employing entity has the right to give orders and directions regarding the workers' *activities* rather than the workers themselves, and thus emphasising the legal elements of dependence over the more personal ones. The more generous *integration* test, developed by Lord Denning in *Stevensons,*[74] sought to take into account the extent to

---

[68]   See, for instance, Cass Civ 6 luglio 2001, n 9167.

[69]   *Yewens v Noakes* (1880) 6 QBD 530.

[70]   *Arrêt Bardou*, Civ., 6 julliet 1931, DP 1931.1.121.

[71]   P Benjamin, 'An Accident of History: Who Is (and Who Should Be) an Employee under South African Labour Law' (2004) *Industrial Law Journal* 791.

[72]   *Yewens v Noakes* (1880) 6 QBD 530.

[73]   'Control includes the power of deciding the thing to be done, the way in which it shall be done, the means to be employed in doing it, the time when, and the place where it shall be done', [1968] 2 QB 497.

[74]   *Stevenson v McDonald & Evans* [1952] 1 TLR 101.

which a person's activity is structurally part of the business. Another generous test, which will be further discussed in one of the following sections of this chapter, is the *economic reality* test, essentially assessing whether the worker takes the ultimate risk of loss or chance of profit (see *Hall v Lorimer*[75]). The *mutuality of obligations* test, perhaps the most important and equally most problematic test, assesses whether the relationship implies some sort of mutual promise by the employer to provide future work and a corresponding one by the employee to accept that work, typically described as a 'mutual promise of future performances', which British courts are so reluctant to find in the context of casual, intermittent and agency workers (see cases such as *O'Kelly*, and *Carmichael*).[76] In their investigations English courts will typically take a pragmatic approach and use a variety of tests and consider a wide range of factors in assessing the nature of the relationship. The so-called *multi-factor* test provides that:

> The tribunal should consider all aspects of the relationship, no single feature being in itself decisive and each of which may vary in weight and direction, and having given such balance to the factors as seems appropriate to determine whether the person was carrying on business on his own account.[77]

Most of these tests have reverberated across other jurisdictions influenced, directly or indirectly, by English legal reasoning. In *Workmen of Nilgiri*, the Indian Supreme Court pointed out that:

> The control test and the organization test … are not the only factors which can be said to [be] decisive. With a view of elicit the answer, the court is required to consider several factors which would have a bearing on the result: (a) who is [the] appointing authority; (b) who is the pay master; (c) who can dismiss; (d) how long alternative service lasts; (e) the extent of control and supervision; (f) the nature of the job, e.g. whether, it is professional or skilled work; (g) nature of establishment; (h) the right to reject.
>
> With a view to find out reasonable solution in a problematic case of this nature, what is needed is an integrated approach meaning thereby integration of the relevant tests …[78]

Also there is no doubt that Indian judges are fully aware of the fact that judicial tests are context- and time-contingent.

---

[75] *Hall v Lorimer* [1992] 1 WLR 939.

[76] *O'Kelly v Trusthouse Forte Plc* [1983] IRLR 369 and *Carmichael v National Power Plc* [2000] IRLR 43.

[77] *O'Kelly v Trusthouse Forte Plc* [1983] ICR 736.

[78] *Workmen of Nilgiri Coop Mkt Society Ltd v State of Tamil Nadu & Ors* [2004] (101) FLR 137 [32] available at www.judis.nic.in/supremecourt/qrydisp.asp?tfnm=25859.

The decisions of this Court lead to one conclusion that law in this behalf is not static. In *Punjab National Bank* vs. *Ghulam Dastagir* [(1978) 1 ILJ 312 (1978) 2 SCC 358], Krishna Iyer, J. observed 'to crystalise criteria conclusively is baffling but broad indications may be available from decisions'.[79]

Ever since *Smit v Workmen's Compensation Commissioner*, South African jurisprudence in this area of labour law has been effectively dominated by the so-called 'dominant impression' test.[80] The test, which seems, prima facie, to draw inspiration from the multi-factor test seen above, as well as from the Roman law distinction between *locatio operarum* and *locatio operaris*, invites the adjudicator to consider all aspects of the contract, without limiting herself to ascertaining the existence of a right of supervision or control, that is not seen as the conclusive element of the employee relationship. It should be noted, however, that this test has been criticized by a number of academic authors. Brassey forcefully argued that the test leads to a 'maze of casuistry without much principle',[81] while Benjamin has pointed out that 'is is not a fully fledged "multi-factoral" test [and] fails to give appropriate weight to the significance of control [and the] organization's tests'.[82] Recent decisions suggest that adjudicators do not, however, base their determinations solely on the 'dominant impression' test to the exclusion of others. In the recent *Taljaard v Basil Real Estate*, Commissioner Juries pointed out that:

> here are different tests to consider … The first test I would look at is the control test … The second test is the organization test … Finally, I will apply the dominant impression test, which considers a multiplicity of factors.[83]

Australian case law has also drawn heavily from the English common law understanding of the contract of employment. In the leading case of *Stevens v Brodribb Sawmilling Co*[84] the High Court rejected the 'organization test' (para 16) and

---

[79] ibid.

[80] *Smit v Workmen's Compensation Commissioner* 1979 (1) SA 51 (A), more recently considered in *SA Broadcasting Corporation v McKenzie* (1999) 20 ILJ 585 (LAC) and *Somerset West Society for the Aged v Democratic Nursing Organisation of SA &others* (2001) 22 ILJ 919 (LC). A description of some of the tests used can be found in C Bosh, 'Who is an Employee' (2003) 3:18 *Labour Law Updates* 1, available at www.law.wits.ac.za/cals/2003.vol. 3%20no.18.pdf.

[81] M Brassey, 'The Nature of Employment' (1990) *Industrial Law Journal* 919.

[82] P Benjamin, 'An Accident of History: Who Is (and Who Should Be) an Employee under South African Labour Law' (2004) *Industrial Law Journal* 791.

[83] *Taljaard v Basil Real Estate* (2006) ILJ 861 (CCMA).

[84] *Stevens v Brodribb Sawmilling Co* (1986) 160 CLR 16 available at www.austlii.edu.au//cgi-bin/disp.pl/au/cases/cth/high_ct/160clr16.html?query=Stevens%20v%20Brodribb.

highlighted the relevance of the 'degree of control' exercised by the employer (para 9). However, it pointed out that:

> the existence of control, whilst significant, is not the sole criterion by which to gauge whether a relationship is one of employment. The approach of this Court has been to regard it merely as one of a number of indicia which must be considered in the determination of that question ... Other relevant matters include, but are not limited to, the mode of remuneration, the provision and maintenance of equipment, the obligation to work, the hours of work and provision for holidays, the deduction of income tax and the delegation of work by the putative employee.[85]

A long but declaredly non-exhaustive 'Summary of the law on distinguishing employees from independent contractors' can be found in the Australian Industrial Relations Commission decision of 2003, *Abdalla v Viewdaze Pty Ltd*.[86] More recent cases suggest that the use of a multi-factor test is almost an inescapable fate, in spite of the fact that, ultimately, it leaves a considerable degree of discretion to the interpreter performing the delicate balancing act between the relative weight of the different indicia. In *ACT Visiting Medical Officers Association v AIRC*, a case dealing with the complexities of the employment status of members of the medical profession, the Federal Court of Australia pointed out that:

> The problem ... is that while the above factors may be indicative of a relationship of employment they are not determinative. Moreover the Full Bench was cognizant of each of these factors but was also conscious of factors pointing to the opposite conclusion ...[87]

Ultimately, the decision of whether a person is an employee or self-employed does not seem to rest on a clear-cut line, and the use of multiple tests and indicia is not a panacea. The conclusion of the Australian Industrial Relations Commission in *Abdalla* is clearly illuminating when they point out that it will often be the case that 'the various indicia point in both directions such that the case falls close to the ill-defined dividing line between employment and independent contract'.[88] Although in other cases common law reasoning will allow the interpreter to say that '[a]lthough there are some unusual features to this matter it is not so close to the

---

[85] para 9.
[86] [2003] AIRC 504 [34]. Available at www.austlii.edu.au//cgi-bin/disp.pl/au/cases/cth/AIRC/2003/504.html.
[87] [2006] FCAFC 109 www.austlii.edu.au//cgi-bin/disp.pl/au/cases/cth/FCAFC/2006/109.html.
[88] [2003] AIRC 504 [38].

dividing line that I have any doubt that the relationship should be properly characterized as that of an employee and an employer'.[89]

It must be pointed out that the use of several tests, or at least of numerous indicia, for assessing the nature of a given employment relationship is not the exclusive privilege of common law based systems. Most civil law systems will also try to base their assessment on more than one indicator of subordination, typically by first trying to ascertain whether the personal services are provided under some sort of legal dependence, and—when this assessment is not obvious—by recourse to other secondary indicators.

Supiot argues that French judicial authorities are increasingly adopting the so-called *'faisceau d'indices'*[90] technique. The traditional approach to defining the notion of *travail dépendant* focuses on the quest for indications of a legally subordinate relationship between a worker and his employer. In the famous *arrêt Bardou* the Court de Cassation explicitly linked the existence of the employee status to the existence of a 'lien de subordination du travailleur à la personne qui l'emploie' and not to the 'faiblesse ou la dépendance économique dudit travailleur'.[91] But over the past few decades, 'ce critère de la subordination s'est considérablement enrichi et complexifié'.[92] This new complexity has pushed French judges towards 'enlarging the notion of contract of employment' by exploring whether the worker is exercising his freedom to work or his freedom to undertake. Effectively this has led to the adoption of two new tests. The first one is that of 'integration into an organized service', in which the courts ask themselves whether the beneficiary of the service is actually directing and controlling the terms and conditions for the execution of the work, as opposed to the mere execution of the work.[93] The second test, called *'participation dans l'entreprise autrui'*, is a negative one, in which the courts verify that the worker is neither employing other workers for the performance of the required service, nor that he has his own clientele, or that the he is the bearer of the enterprise risk.[94]

In a recent judgment, the Areios Pagos (the Greek Supreme Court) confirmed that in deciding whether a relationship is one of εξαρτημένης εργασίας (dependent labour), to which employment law should apply, or a σύμβαση έργου (contract of service) regulated by contract and commercial law, '[t]he court will decide ... by evaluating the totality of the real elements through which the relationship

---

[89] *Advance Resource Services Pty Ltd t/as Progress Couriers and Taxi Trucks v Charlton* [2006] SAIRC 79, available at www.austlii.edu.au//cgi-bin/disp.pl/au/cases/sa/SAIRC/2006/79.html?query=Abdalla%20v%20View daze%20Pty%20Ltd.

[90] A Supiot, 'Les nouveaux visages de la subordination' (2000) *Droit Social* 139.

[91] Civ 6 julliet 1931, DP 1931.1.121.

[92] Supiot (n 90) 140.

[93] Jurisprudence Hebdo-prese: Cass. Ass. Plén. 18 juin 1976 D 1977, J, 1973.

[94] Soc. 7 déc. 1983, *Bull civ* V, n 592 p 423.

operated'.[95] While the primary distinctive criterion between the two notions of employment is 'the provision of labour as such and not its result',[96] the Court went on to consider indicia of 'legal dependence' (νομική εξάρτηση) such as the 'control over the time and manner of the provision of labour', working time obligations, the nature of the instructions given to the worker, the payment of wages and other elements of remuneration.

Italian courts have similarly developed a great number of tactics for the detection of the kind of employment relationship, often referred to as 'subsidiary' indicia (*'indici empirici c.d. sussidiari'*[97]) for the detection of *'subordinazione'*, whenever the latter is not obvious or easily discernible as such. With the judgment Cassazione, Sezioni Unite, 30 giugno 1999 n 379, it became clear that the *'faisceau d'indices'* strategy is not alien to the Italian judicial system. The Corte di Cassazione pointed out that:

> [W]here the element of the subjection of the worker to someone else's directives cannot be easily appreciated, one must refer to complementary and subsidiary criteria—such as collaboration, continuity of performance, observance of predetermined working time, payment at regular intervals of a predetermined remuneration, coordination of working activity to the organisational structure provided by the employer, absence of even the slightest entrepreneurial structure—that, though without any decisive power on their own, can be evaluated globally as indications providing evidence of subordination.[98]

This plurality of tests and indicia builds on the firm basis provided by the other traditional tests of *'collaborazione'*, *'continuità'*, 'risk' and 'object of performance', the latter being identified with the provision of labour resources to the employer rather than with a specific 'result'. There is no doubt that Italian courts are still predominantly concerned with identifying 'technical-functional subordination [as] the principal criterion for distinguishing [employment] from autonomous work ..., while it utilizes in a subsidiary way a plurality of so called symptomatic criteria emerging from practice'.[99] The terms of the hierarchical relationship between the concept of subordination and the various indicia is, however, out of question as, 'the absence of *eterodirezione* cannot be surrogated by any of the subsidiary indicia'.[100]

The same type of analysis seems to be inspiring Brazilian judges conducting this type of enquiry. The starting point is that 'A distinção principal, ... encontra-se

---

[95] Αρείου Πάγου 376/2006, Τμ. Β/II, in (2006), Επιθεώρησις Εργατικού Δικαίου 1245.

[96] Ibid 1244.

[97] E Ghera, 'Subordinazione, Statuto Protettivo e Qualificazione del Rapporto di Lavoro' (2006) *Giornale di Diritto del Lavoro e Relazioni Industriali* 10.

[98] E Ghera, *Diritto del Lavoro* (Bari, Cacucci, 2000) 70.

[99] Ghera, 'Subordinazione" (n 97) 11.

[100] Ibid.

na chamada subordinação jurídica' ('The main distinction ... is found in what is termed legal subordination').[101] This is not, however, the end of the story, and Brazilian courts appear to have developed an extremely sophisticated set of indicators of subordinate employee status:

> [T]he employee relationship is, thus, one of the modalities of the employment relationship .... For it to emerge the following requirements must be present: work provided by a physical person; work provided personally; non-eventuality/continuity; onerousity and subordination.
>
> ...
>
> The employee, then, is directed by the employer since he is inserted in an enterprise that ... is organized and directed by the employer. Finally [the] absence of the responsibility of an employee in respect of the fate of the enterprise [means that] he will never suffer the risk of the business. He may participate to the profits of the enterprise, but never to the losses.[102]

Judges and Change: Recent Developments and More Generous Approaches

The previous section highlighted the crucial role that judicial reasoning has in 'breathing life' into the normally unrevealing and at times vague statutory definitions of 'employee', 'contract of employment' and 'dependent work'. Courts and tribunals have developed a vast array of legal tools and concepts to approach the classification of employment relationship. While most systems tend to take a rather pragmatic approach to this type of enquiry, and will typically use the whole panoply of legal devices at their disposal, there is no doubt that each and every system has a preferred 'instrument of choice'. As such, the test of 'mutuality of obligations' has emerged as the most widely and consistently used device in English tribunals and courts. South African courts will typically rely on the – according to some – rather vague 'dominant impression' test. 'Legal subordination' will be the first line of enquiry for most judges in civil law systems, whether European or not. Indian courts seem quite keen on using tests such as the control and integration tests. However no system will disdain other approaches and most will engage in a 'multi-factor test' type of enquiry, when necessary.

In some respects this fragmented panorama suggests a certain degree of elusiveness and perhaps a lack of predictability, if not coherence, in judicial

---

[101] *Processo no 00032–2007–106–22–00–6,* available at www.trt22.gov.br/institucional/varas/floriano/sentencas/2007/2007_02/ST_00032–2007–106–22–00–6.pdf.

[102] *Processo no 00090–2007–105–22–00–3,* available at www.trt22.gov.br/institucional/varas/piripiri/sentencas/2007/03/RT-90–07.pdf.

practices. There is hardly any doubt that even the most sophisticated and structured system concedes a considerable degree of discretion to the interpreter. On the other hand, there is also no doubt that 'judge-made law' is perhaps a necessary evil in a context of rapid changes. If one accepts the—perhaps simplistic—view that changes in the system of production are the main factor in the growing fragmentation of the types and forms of work relationships, then there is hardly any doubt that case law should have a comparative advantage over statute in adapting the legal framework to the changing world of work, with legislation eventually following suit. And indeed there are some indications that in recent years, and even months, judicial reasoning has risen to the task of adapting the notion of the employment relationship and has partly modified some of its earlier, perhaps more restrictive, classificatory approaches.

As far as the United Kingdom is concerned, it is fair to say that part of the impetus towards the expansion of the scope of application of employment law to wider categories of personal work providers has derived from the European Court of Justice. Famous decisions, such as *ex parte EOC*,[103] addressed some of the legislative exclusions provided by statute for part-time workers. In cases such as *Preston*[104] and *Allonby*,[105] the ECJ partly reformulated the reasoning behind the 'mutuality test' and the continuity requirement, and showed a willingness to adopt a more relational and less — strictly speakingm – contractual notion of the employment *relationship*, at least in the context of equal treatment legislation. But British courts have also taken some important steps in this direction, for instance with decisions such as *Cornwall County Council v Prater*[106] and *ABC News Intercontinental Inc v Gizbert*,[107] where the 'mutuality of obligation' test was reinterpreted, respectively for the purposes of establishing continuity of workers in casual or discontinuous work relationships, and for the purposes of taking into account the 'good faith' of the parties providing and accepting personal work services.

Italian courts have also sought to grapple with the changing notion of the employment relationship by introducing an attenuated notion of subordination. In *Decision 9167 of 2001*, the Corte di Cassazione pointed out that with:

> the evolution of the systems of organisation of labour, increasingly characterized by the tendency to outsource or tertiarize whole sectors of the cycle of production or series of

---

[103] *R v Secretary of State for Employment ex p Equal Opportunities Commission* [1994] IRLR 176, HL.
[104] *Preston v Wolverhampton NHS* [2001] 3 All ER 947.
[105] Case C-256/01 *Allonby* [2004] IRLR.
[106] *Cornwall CC v Prater* [2006] IRLR 362.
[107] *ABC News Intercontinental Inc v Gizbert* [2006] WL 2469644.

specific professional skills, subordination becomes less and less significant, because of the impossibility of exercising full and direct control over the different phases of the activity performed.[108]

In a subsequent decision, the Court stressed that:

> Subordination is an essential element of dependent labour; nevertheless it can also be present in attenuated forms by reason of the specific organization of labour and of the type of provision (particularly in the case of simple provisions, of the same type or repetitive) and can be perceived, in these specific circumstances, as making available to the employer the labour resources of the worker with continuity, loyalty and diligence, according to the directions given by the other party.[109]

Italian academic authors suggest that in these cases, the elements of 'collaboration' that are present in the employment relationship are such as to justify a degree of subordination, albeit an 'attenuated' one, even just understood as 'simple availability of the worker to the directives of the enterprise'.[110]

Another example of this judicial trend could be found in the French *arrêt Labanne*[111] of 2000 stating that a person who drove a taxi under an automatically renewable monthly contract labelled as 'contract for the lease of a vehicle equipped as a taxi' and who paid a sum described in the contract as 'rent', had to be treated as an employee. Again, putting aside the details of the decision of the Cour de Cassation, what is striking is the willingness of the French judges to go beyond the contractual and formal absence of dependence and to characterise the taxi driver as an employee 'because the economy of the contractual relationship was leaving him no real freedom in his activity'.[112] As Supiot et al maintain, the *Labanne* decision:

> distances itself from the path traced [by earlier case law]. It distances itself from the *arrêt Société Générale* as it allows the existence of a contract of employment although the supposed employer (the taxi renting business) did not have the power to give orders to the taxi renters,

---

[108] Cass 06.07.2001 n 9167, in (2002) II RIDL 272.

[109] Cass 27.11.2002 n 16805, in (2003)3 MGL 127. See also Cass 10.03.2004 n 5508; Cass 9.4.2004 n 4797; Cass 9.4.2004 n 6983.

[110] E Ghera, 'Subordinazione, statuto protettivo e qualificazione del rapporto di lavoro', in D Garofalo and M Ricci (eds) *Percorsi di Diritto del Lavoro* (Bari, Cacucci, 2006) p 332.

[111] Ruling No 5371 of 19 December 2000. *MM Labanne c/Soc Bastille taxi et autre*. See A Jeammaud 'L'avenir sauvegardé de la qualification de contrat de travail. À propos de l' *arrêt Labanne*', DS, (2001), 227. The decision is available at www.legifrance.gouv.fr/WAspad/Visu?cid=100032&indice=1&table=CASS&ligne Deb=1.

[112] F Adine Flammand and M-L Morin, 'L'activité professionnelle indépendante: quelle protection juridique?' (2001) *Le Notes du Lirhe*, 6. Also available on www.univ-tlse1.fr/lirhe/publications/notes/346–01. pdf.

that could work the hours they wanted and in the areas of their choice. It distances itself from the *arrêt Bardou* in that the subordination of the taxi driver is, in this case, an economic subordination and not a legal one.[113]

As new developments in human resource management strategies increasingly water down the elements of formal dependence and formal continuity, with a labour force increasingly being obtainable on an as-required basis, judiciaries seem to be evolving their understanding of the changes affecting the employment relationship and are broadening their notions of dependence, control, continuity and subordination. One such evolutionary trajectory would seem to suggest an increasing attention to the element of 'economic dependence' (as opposed to mere legal or formal dependence) as a new distinctive criterion for the assimilation of providers of personal services into the category of subordinate employees.

2.4 Economic Dependence as a (New) Distinctive Criterion?

The quest for the Holy Grail in the classification of employment relationships has pushed several authors and a number of legal systems to suggest that the regulatory framework should pay more attention to the substantive and economic aspects of dependence, rather than to the more formalistic and legal ones, particularly since the latter have become increasingly evanescent in recent years. The basic idea behind this type of suggestion is that if a worker provides his or her services under a formally autonomous contractual arrangement to a single (or *mainly* to a single) 'client-principal', the latter should be held to be his or her 'employer' for the purposes of labour protection (and presumably also social security and tax) legislation. And conversely, if a person provides his services to several 'employers' or clients, he or she will then be appropriately defined as an independent provider of services. As put by the English Court of Appeal in *Hall v Lorimer*, a case dealing with the employment and tax status of a freelance vision mixer, doing work for a number of production companies:

> The extent to which the individual is dependent upon or independent of a particular paymaster for the financial exploitation of his talents may well be significant ... [I]n the present case ... the most outstanding feature to my mind is that the taxpayer customarily

---

[113] A Supiot, J Pellissier and A Jeammaud, *Droit du Travail* (Paris, Dalloz, 2006) 324–25.

worked for 20 or more production companies and that the vast majority of his assignments, as appears from the annexures to the stated case lasted only for a single day.[114]

German law embraced a regulatory approach based on the notion of economic dependence, albeit in the limited field of social security law, between 1998 and 2002.[115] With the adoption of Law No 3843 of 28 December 1998 the German legislator introduced a catalogue of four criteria qualifying the employment relationship as one of dependent labour for the purposes of social security. The newly introduced section 4 of paragraph 7 of the *Sozialgezetsbuch* (SGB) stated:

> In case of persons, who are in paid work and who in connection with their activity do not employ any employee liable to insurance deductions with the exception of family members, who work *regularly and principally only for one employer*, who perform services which are typical of employed people, who are in particular subject to instructions given by the employer and are integrated in the work organisation of the employer, or who do not engage in any business activity, it is assumed that they are employed for remuneration, when at least two of the above mentioned criteria are met. The first sentence does not apply to commercial agents, who organise their work substantially in freedom and who can decide upon their working hours.[116]

In 1999, this wording was partly modified, and a fifth criterion was added, so that the section in question read as follows:

> In case of a person, who is in paid work, ... it is presumed that she/he is an employee when at least three of the following five criteria can be found:
>
> 1. when in connection with his/her activity the person does not regularly employ an employee liable to social insurance contributions, whose remuneration from this employment exceeds regularly 325 Euros per month;
>
> 2. the person works on a *continuous basis and principally only for one employer*;
>
> 3. his/her employer or any other comparable employer allow similar activities to be performed regularly by his/her employees;
>
> 4. her/his activity does not show features which are typical of an entrepreneurial activity;
>
> 5. her/his activity appears to correspond to the activity which she or he has performed before for the employer on the basis of a subordinate employment relationship.

---

[114] *Hall v Lorimer* [1994] ICR 218.

[115] *Gesetz zu Korrekturen in der Sozialversicherung und zur Sicherung der Arbeitnehmerrechte* (BGBI I s 3843 v art 3, modifying § 7 of Book IV of the Social Security Code). *cf.* W Däubler 'Working people in Germany' (1999) *Comparative Labor Law & Policy Journal* 78. On the changes of this definition, see the critical commentary in R Wank, 'Germany', in 'Labour Law in Motion' (2005) *Bulletin of Comparative Labour Relation* 19.

[116] Emphasis added.

The first sentence does not apply to commercial agents, who organise their work substantially in freedom and who can decide upon their working hours. The presumption can be rebutted.[117]

These laws unequivocally focused their attention on a number of criteria that revolved around the notion of financial and economic dependency[118] and on the absence of any genuine entrepreneurial economic activity. Unsurprisingly, some commentators considered this an implicit weakness of the Act[119] and opposed any temptation to extend the same reasoning beyond the social security domain. In fact the definition preferred by the Federal Labour Court (*Bundesarbeitsgerichte*—BAG) and the majority of scholars in the labour law domain is the very simple one that an 'employee is one who is, on the basis of a contract in civil law, obliged to work in the service of somebody else'.[120] And in any case the 'three out of five' criterion was repealed with the adoption of the Law of 23 December 2002[121] and do not feature in the current wording of paragraph 7, section 4 of the SGB.

A recent decision of the South Australian Workers Compensation Tribunal[122] can help us to reconstruct the relevance of this element, or rather the lack of it, in Australian case law:

> In *Re Porter* (at 185) Gray J said there was no particular reason why a court should ignore the practical circumstances and cling to the theoretical niceties. The level of economic dependence and the manner that dependence might be exploited, 'will always be relevant factors in the determination whether a particular contract is one of employment'.
>
> …
>
> However there is a countervailing view. The issue is examined in Creighton and Stewart (2005) (see par [11.39]). The text concludes that nothing in *Hollis v Vabu Pty Ltd* (above cited) suggests a 'reality' test or that economic dependence was an indicia. This would appear to accord with South Australian authority by which I am bound[:] *Mason & Cox Pty Ltd v McCann* (1999) 74 SASR 438 at pars [27], [29][123]

---

[117] Law of 20 December 1999 (BGBl 2000 s 2). Emphasis added.

[118] *cf.* A Supiot, *Beyond Employment* (Oxford, OUP, 2001) 15.

[119] *cf.* H Buchner in U Müchenberger, R Wank and H Buchner, 'Ridefinire la nozione di subordinazione? Il dibattito in Germania'(2000) *Gironal di Diritto del Lavoro e Relazioni Industriali* 344.

[120] *Preis*, ErfK, sec 611 BGB, note 45. See R Wank, 'Germany', in 'Labour Law in Motion' (2005) *Bulletin of Comparative Labour Relations* 19.

[121] BGBl 2002 I s 4621.

[122] *Harnas v Sita Australia Pty Ltd and WorkCover Corporation of SA by its Agent Employers Mutual Ltd* [2007] SAWCT 25 available at www.austlii.edu.au/au/cases/sa/SAWCT/2007/25.html.

[123] ibid paras 47–49.

It is worth highlighting that some European academics and, often, judges, have rather consistently rejected the adoption of a widened notion of economic dependence. '*La notion de subordination économique est, en effet, trop imprécise*'[124] as a great number of persons may depend economically on others, albeit keeping their professional, independent, status; such are the supplier integrated in a network of distribution or a 'franchised' tradesman, the '*agriculteur sous contrat*', the artisan working for an industrial enterprise.[125] On the same line of reasoning, Ghera seems convinced that a situation of *dipendenza economica* may occur even outside subordinate employment. 'Even if one can admit that the position of economic inferiority of the worker conditions his contractual autonomy and characterizes his social position … it cannot be confused with the subordination of the provider of work to the direction and organization of the enterprise'.[126] Undoubtedly, as discussed above in respect of the *arrêt Labanne*, there have been decisions that have suggested a growing relevance of the notion of economic dependence. However, the majority of continental European conceptualizations of the idea of subordination still appear irrevocably linked to its more legal, and contractual, aspects. In another recent decision involving taxi drivers, the Cour de Cassation pointed out that:

> le lien de subordination est caractérisé par l'exécution d'un travail sous l'autorité d'un employeur qui a le pouvoir de donner des ordres et des directives, d'en contrôler l'exécution et de sanctionner les manquements de son subordonné; que le travail au sein d'un service organisé peut constituer un indice du lien de subordination lorsque l'employeur détermine unilatéralement les conditions d'exécution du travail; que l'existence d'une relation de travail ne dépend ni de la volonté exprimée par les parties ni de la dénomination qu'elles ont donnée à leur convention, mais des conditions de fait, dans lesquelles est exercée l'activité des travailleurs.[127]

The notion of economic dependence appears to be of determining relevance in the Canadian and German[128] definitions of intermediate employment relationship. For instance, Canadian labour law appears to pay due regard to the importance of 'economic dependence' in defining the notion of 'dependent contractor'. Already in the 1960s Arthurs claimed that 'a new term is needed: "dependent contractor", they are dependent economically although legally contractors'.[129] As discussed above in

---

124   J Pélissier, A Supiot and A Jeammaud, *Droit du travail* (Paris, Dalloz, 2000) 151.
125   Pélissier et al (n 124) 151–52.
126   Ghera, *Diritto del Lavoro* (n 98) 64.
127   *Soc. 1 décembre 2005 Sté Copagau, RJS* 2/06 n 147.
128   See above under para 2.2.
129   HW Arthurs, 'The Dependent Contractor: A Study of the Legal Problems of Countervailing Power' (1965) *The University of Toronto Law Journal*, 89. For an in-depth analysis, see MJ Bernier et al, *Les Besoins de Protection*

section 2.1, the statutory definition of 'dependent contractor' is premised on the idea that the worker 'performs work or services for another person [and] is in relation to that person in a position of economic dependence'. The regulation of the 'dependent contractor' relationship mirrors some, but not all, the regulatory aspects of the 'employee' relationship, and this mainly for the purposes of collective bargaining rights.[130] However, this minimalist understanding has to be seen in the light of a rather more generous framework provided by some judicial decisions. First and foremost, courts have consistently held that 'dependent contractor' relationships are usually terminable only by providing reasonable notice, a circumstance that approximates the relationship to the common law protection provided to employees in several common law systems.[131] In fact, in some recent decisions Canadian courts have held that when an intermediate category dependent contractor relationship is close to a typical employee relationship, the notice period is likely to be the same in both situations.[132] Secondly, some recent decisions have given a rather broad interpretation to the collective bargaining context of the 'dependent worker' statutory notion. In *Old Dutch Foods Ltd v Teamsters Local Union*[133], the Supreme Court of British Columbia upheld the purposive definition of 'collective bargaining' given by the British Columbia Labour Relations Board.[134]

This, however, does not seem to be so in the case of the British notion of intermediate 'worker'. In spite of some strong academic arguments in favour of a concept of 'worker' based on an economic dependence notion,[135] Elias J in the recent Employment Appeal Tribunal decision of *James v Redcats*, opined that:

> I accept that in a general sense the degree of dependence is in large part what one is seeking to identify—if employees are integrated into the business, workers may be described as semi-detached and those conducting a business undertaking as detached—but that must be assessed by a careful analysis of the contract itself. The fact that the individual may be in a subordinate position, both economically and substantively, is of itself of little assistance in defining the relevant boundary because a small business operation may be as economically

---

Sociale des Personnes en Situation de Travail non Traditionnelle (2003), available at www.travail.gouv.qc.ca/actualite/travail_non_traditionnel/Bernier2003/BernierReportChap4.pdf.

[130] For the definition of the term under Part I of the Canada Labour Code see its s 3 available at www.hrsdc.gc.ca/en/lp/lo/fll/part1/legislation/clc1a.shtml.

[131] *Carter v Bell & Sons (Canada) Ltd* [1936] OR 290 (CA); *Paper Sales Corporation Ltd v Miller Bros Co (1962) Ltd* (1975) 7 OR (2d) 460.

[132] *JKC Enterprises Ltd v Woolworth Canada Inc* (2001) 12 CCEL (3d) 51 (Alta QB).

[133] 2006 BCSC 313 available at www.courts.gov.bc.ca/jdb-txt/sc/06/03/2006bcsc0313.htm.

[134] ibid para 40 of the decision.

[135] G Davidov, 'Who is a Worker?' (2005) *Industrial Law Journal* 57–71.

dependent on the other contracting party, as is the self employed worker, particularly if it is a key or the only customer.[136]

But while economic dependence does not yet appear to enjoy the necessary degree of authority to shape the binary divide of the employment relationship, or even the intermediate notions of work relationship, some authors have argued that it should play a more important role *de jure condendo*. According to Deakin and Morris, a more 'inclusionary' strategy could be derived,[137] from the use of a renewed 'dependency' test, more linked to the economic aspects of the dependence between worker and employer, rather than to the formal and legal ones. Such renewed use of the test could well be inferred, for instance, from important cases such as *Lorimer*,[138] in which the considerable number of clients of Mr Lorimer, was seen as a clear indication of the fact that he was *not* economically dependent upon any of them. The reasonable conclusion from this line of reasoning should be that when a worker is de facto and consistently economically dependent upon a single client or business, he should be considered an employee. 'An emphasis on economic dependence, so defined, would arguably produce greater predictability than the open-ended multiple test, in which any one of a number of factors could turn out to be essential in tipping the balance on one side or the other.'[139]

2.5 Conclusions

As argued throughout this chapter, the notion, scope and definition of the employment relationship have clearly emerged as one of the most complex, but also topical areas of the twenty-first century labour law debate. Recommendation No 198 clearly has the merit of interfacing with this debate in a timely fashion. Paragraph 4 of the Recommendation explicitly addresses a number of fundamental difficulties that increasingly emerge in respect of the legal conceptualization and definition of the employment relationship. Perhaps the most pressing of all these difficulties is the one described in Paragraph 4(a), implicitly addressing the thorny issue of 'ambiguous' employment relationships. In fact most, in not all, of the remaining

---

[136] *James v Redcats* [2007] IRLR 296 [48], available at www.employmentappeals.gov.uk/Public/Upload/06_0475fhRCDM.doc.

[137] S Deakin and G Morris, *Labour Law* (London, Routledge, 2001) 168.

[138] *Hall v Lorimer* [1994] ICR 218.

[139] Deakin and Morris (n 137) 168.

problems mentioned in this paragraph—such as 'disguised employment relation-ships', 'multiple parties' relationships, identifying the 'employing entity', efficient dispute resolution mechanisms and legal certainty, training of decision makers and other parties involved—are in some respect the consequence of the fundamental lack of precision in the difficult conceptualization of the *binary* notion of the employment relationship.

As noted by Freedland,[140] it might be imagined that such a quest for legal certainty would be pursued by the laying down of clear definitional and mandatory norms concerning the personal scope of employment law.

> Instead, however, Recommendation No. 198 takes a gentler processual approach. … All that said, it should not be thought that the processual and 'soft law' character of this measure bespeaks a weakness of motivation on the part of the ILO. Instead, I suggest that the proponents of this measure took the view that this was the furthest point to which they could hope to advance in the face of no small degree of policy disagreement at supra-national level and considerable conceptual diversity or at least lack of conceptual reconciliation as between member States in the ways that they approach the formulation of the personal scope of employment laws. Given the constraints imposed by that conceptual and practical context, Recommendation No. 198 represented a significant normative achievement.[141]

The analysis carried through this chapter would prima facie suggest that the ILO's caution is in many respects well founded and justified. There is no doubt that the employment relationship is characterized by some elements of 'universality'. The divide between employment and self-employment is clearly emerging as the most universal feature of the employment relationship debate. The fundamental gate-keepers deciding who falls within these definitions and who does not are national judicial authorities. Another common feature is that courts will normally take a pragmatic approach in classifying the work relationship, and use all the tools at their disposal in carrying out their assessment. The 'indicators' listed in Paragraph 13 of the Recommendation are all, by and large, used by national judiciaries in what is clearly emerging as a consistent and universal 'multi-factor' test. Another universal feature is that most national judiciaries are progressively realizing that their under-standing and appreciation of the legal notion of the employment relationship has to keep abreast of the constant changes affecting the factual notion of the employ-ment relationship, that is to say the changes in work practices and in the contractual construction of work arrangements. As seen above, the first few years of this

---

[140] M Freedland, 'Application of Labour and Employment Law Beyond the Contract of Employment' (2007) *International Labour Review* (forthcoming).

[141] ibid.

millennium have seen a number of inherently 'expansive' interpretative approaches emerging within several national, and supranational in the case of the European Court of Justice, judiciaries. These are important common trends that fully justify the ILO attempt to coordinate national practices.

However, it is also evident that national differences exist and are grounded in far reaching legal and political traditions. The most obvious distinction is between those systems which, like that of France, seek to enforce a strictly binary notion of the employment relationship and those which—like those of Italy, Germany and Canada—have developed, or—as in the case of Brazil and perhaps Australia—are tempted by the idea of developing new intermediate categories of 'quasi-dependent' work. A fundamental problem for this latter group of countries is what sort of protection should be afforded to these workers. While this type of discourse inevitably brings into the debate the role of national parliaments and the social partners—an aspect of the debate that is beyond the declared scope of this chapter—it is clear that national judiciaries have an important role in clarifying the notion, function and raison d'être of these new intermediate types of employment relationship. As pointed out in section 2.4 of this chapter, some systems seem to be inclined to emphasise the relevance of 'economic dependence' as a distinctive element of this type of relationship, although clearly a number of national judiciaries are clearly not attracted by this prospect. There are strong indications that in some systems (for instance, that of Canada, and perhaps in the not too distant future a number of EU Member States) the time might be right for a progressive extension of an increasing number of employment protection rights typically afforded to standard employees. Again this is an extremely important aspect of the overall debate, but one that falls outside the scope of this chapter. However, it should be noted that the International Labour Organization is also clearly well placed to address this aspect of the discourse. As noted a few years ago by the Office *'it is untrue that ILO standards are only for those in the formal economy where there is a clear employer-employee relationship. Most ILO standards refer to "workers" rather than the narrower legal category of "employees".*'[142]

The existence of these non-negligible national differences makes Recommendation No 198 all the more important. In an increasingly 'globalized' world, the national definitions of employment relationship have a global impact. This is increasingly evident within the European Union, but the development of other

---

[142] International Labour Office, *Report VI Decent Work in the informal economy—Sixth item on the agenda* (Geneva, June 2002) 45. Emphasis original.

transnational modes of provision of services, such as the GATS Mode 4,[143] further suggest that the debate needs to be coordinated at a supranational level.[144]

There is still no 'philosopher's stone' in the employment relationship debate. A growing number of academic authors are increasingly suggesting an abandonment of the ever-so-elusive binary distinction in favour of more universalistic approaches to defining the scope of application of employment and social rights.[145] Other authors have suggested the creation of a *'système unique de protection de l'emploi'*[146] and of a *'contrat du travail unique'*[147] effectively with the intention of reducing the degree of fragmentation affecting the concepts of the contract of employment and dependent work at large.[148] But for the time being, it is perhaps appropriate to conclude this chapter with Bob Hepple's perceptive intuition that 'we are in what Gramsci might have described as an "interregnum" in which "the old is dying, and the new cannot be born"'.[149] Recommendation 198 is arguably here to facilitate the transition.

---

[143] See the World Trade Organization website at www.wto.org/english/thewto_e/whatis_e/tif_e/agrm6_e.htm.

[144] The Preamble of Recommendation No 198 highlights that 'in the framework of transnational provision of services, it is important to establish who is considered a worker in an employment relationship, what rights the worker has, and who the employer is'.

[145] Alain Supiot has come to epitomize these more avant-garde types of analysis. See A Supiot, 'The transformation of work and the future of labour law in Europe: A multidisciplinary perspective'(1999) 138(1) *International Labour Review*, 31–46. M Freedland, is another author currently suggesting a progressive abandonment of the contract of employment as the fulcrum of employment protection legislation. See M Freedland, 'From the contract of Employment to the Personal Work Nexus' (2006) *Industrial Law Journal* 1 and by the same author, 'Application of Labour and Employment Law Beyond the Contract of Employment' (2006) *Oxford University Comparative Law Forum* 4, available at http://ouclf.iuscomp.org/articles/freedland.shtml.

[146] O Blanchard and J Tirole, *Protection de l.emploi et procédures de licenciement* (Paris, La Documentation française, 2003), available at http://lesrapports.ladocumentationfrancaise.fr/BRP/034000592/0000.pdf.

[147] P Cahuc and F Kramarz, *De la précarité à la mobilité: vers une Sécurité sociale professionnelle* (Paris, La Documentation française, 2004), available at http://lesrapports.ladocumentationfrancaise.fr/BRP/054000092/0000.pdf.

[148] And arguably also with some of the protections attached to the traditional employment status. See P Morvan, 'La Chimère du Contrat de Travail Unique, la fluidité et la créativité' (2006) *Droit Social* 959.

[149] B Hepple, 'The Future of Labour Law' (1995) *Industrial Law Journal* 305.

Subordination, Parasubordination and Self-Employment: A Comparative Overview in Selected Countries in Latin America and the Caribbean **3**

Eduardo J Ameglio and Humberto Villasmil*

3.1 Introduction: The Principal Legal Characteristics of the Employment Systems

The issue of the determination of an employment relationship has been on the legal agenda for several years in the countries examined in this comparative study, notably Argentina, Brazil, Colombia, Costa Rica, Dominican Republic, Uruguay and the Bolivarian Republic of Venezuela.

Argentina, Brazil and Uruguay (together with Paraguay) form MERCOSUR, a regional integration treaty that has worked to harmonize the economic and social policies of its members since 1991. A brief description of the context in which this regional integration process is taking place might be useful in order to better understand how the legal systems of these three countries have introduced criteria for the determination of an employment relationship.

These three countries incorporated fundamental labour rights into their respective constitutions a long time ago. For example, article 14 bis of the Argentine Constitution establishes that:

> Labour in its various forms shall be protected in laws, laws to ensure that workers have: dignified and equitable conditions of work; a limited work-day; paid rest and leave; fair

* The original chapter was prepared by Prof E Ameglio of the Universidad de la República Oriental del Uruguay. In this revised version, Dr H Villasmil has introduced legislative examples from other Latin American and Caribbean countries.

retribution; a minimum and mobile living wage; equal remuneration for equal work; participation in the profits of enterprises, with control of production and involvement with management; protection from arbitrary dismissal; stability for public employees; free and democratic trade unions, recognized simply by inclusion on a special register. . . .

The same spirit can be found in the Federal Constitution of Brazil, which addresses social rights in chapter II and in article 6 declares employment, among other things, as a social right. Article 7 lists the rights that the Constitution gives to workers, the most prominent including: the protection of employment against arbitrary dismissal or dismissal without just cause; unemployment benefits; minimum wage; participation in profits; length of work not exceeding eight hours per day and 44 hours per week; paid weekly rest; annual leave and insurance against workplace accidents. The same can be said of the Uruguayan Constitution, which devotes section II to Rights, Duties and Guarantees and establishes in article 7 that 'the inhabitants of the Republic have the right to be protected in the enjoyment of their life, honour, liberty, security, employment and property'. Article 54 outlines the scope of this protection and notes that 'The law must recognize, for a person in an employment or service relationship, as a worker or employee, the independence of their moral and civic conscience, fair remuneration, the limitation of the working day, weekly rest, and physical and moral hygiene'.

In this regard, employment enjoys special protection as a constitutional right in these countries as well as in other countries in the region such as Colombia and Venezuela. In addition, employment is protected without any additional qualification, so it covers the subordinate employment typical of an employment relationship as well as free or autonomous work. It should be noted that the notion of employment relationship is considered by the enacted legislation. For example, in Argentina, the field of individual employment law is regulated by the Employment Contract Act 1974 (hereafter 'ECA'). Since it was approved, this law regulating the employment relationship has undergone various reforms. In the 1990s the reform tended towards increasing flexibility, but more recently it has tended towards greater security/protection.

Individual employment relationships in Brazil are regulated through the Consolidated Labour Act 1943 (hereafter 'CLA'). This extensive law deals with the individual employment contract in section IV. Since it was enacted, this law has had a variety of reforms and has been supplemented with the adoption of various additional laws, but throughout this time it has maintained its nature to guarantee and protect employment.

In Uruguay, the situation is somewhat different because the individual employment relationships are regulated through a collection of laws that have been adopted in a non-systematic manner since 1915. The level of legislative intervention is high, and the protective nature of the standards is well defined.

As we can see, we have before us legal systems where the law is the formal source that defines the duties and obligations under an employment relationship. Labour law, then, operates under constitutional principles which recognize that labour/employment, in its widest sense, deserves special protection.

Moving on from this brief introduction, let us examine the underlying issues around the notion of an employment relationship.

3.2 The Notion of the Employment Relationship

The employment relationship is defined by Argentina's ECA in several articles. Article 4 defines the concept of employment and provides that '… any legal activity that is done for the benefit of somebody with the facility to manage it, through remuneration, constitutes employment for the purposes of this act'. This article determines that what is being regulated is onerous human labour carried out under the direction of another (the employer).

Article 21 of the ECA provides that:

> … there shall be an employment contract, whatever its form or name, whenever a physical person is obliged to do something, carry out labour or provide services for the other person and dependent on them, for a determined or undetermined period of time, by the payment of remuneration. Its clauses with regard to the form and conditions of provision shall submit to the provisions of public order, statutes, collective agreements or rulings with like power, and habits and customs.

The same can also be found in the Venezuelan labour legislation, where at article 8° of the Regulation on the Organic Labour Act, the 'primacy of fact over the form or appearance of legal documents, which stem from an employment relationship' is a general principle.

In Colombia, article 53 of the Constitution (1991) asserts 'the principle of the primacy of fact over formal arrangements between parties to an employment relationship'. In this regard, the Constitutional Court of Colombia has recently completed the process of ratifying legislation, which is now completed and consolidated, regarding the scope of the principle of the primacy of fact over form in the field of employment relations. In its ruling No T-992/05 of 29 September 2005, the Court stipulated the following:

Regarding the principle of the primacy of fact over form in the field of employment relations, this Court has indicated:[1]

> The primacy of fact over formal arrangements between parties to an employment relationship is a constitutional principle (Constitution, art. 53). The voluntary provision of physical or intellectual labour by one person to another, in conditions of subordination, constitutes an employment relationship, irrespective of the nature of the agreement under which it is performed, and labour standards thus apply, in addition to other legal provisions and agreements in the field. The effective provision of labour, in itself, is sufficient to entitle the worker to certain rights which are necessary to ensure his well-being, health and living. National and international labour legislation, taking into account the transcendental nature of labour and the key interests they protect, must be strictly applied whenever the essential elements of an employment relationship are present, without taking into account the will of the parties involved or how they may wish to define or qualify the contract.

In line with the above, a judge must focus on the material conditions of the relationship, its characteristics and the facts, which in reality determine the type of relationship that exists between the contracting parties, rather than how they define their relationship. In ruling C-166 of 1997, the Constitutional Court of Colombia also underlined the relationship between the principle of the primacy of fact over formal agreements in an employment relationship and the primacy of substantive law, suggested deference to the material content of the employment relationship, indicated the effects of the implementation of labour standards and once again stressed that the principle aimed to prevent the employer from taking advantage of the worker's subordinate position. In this regard, it stipulated the following:

> This principle relates to the principle of the primacy of substantive law[2] over outward form, as laid down in article 228 of the Constitution, with respect to the administration of justice.
>
> In the eyes of the Judge, and according to the explicit provisions of the Constitution, the material content of the said relationship, its characteristics and the facts which determine it in reality matter more than the words used by the contracting parties to define their relationship, or the form they wish to give it.
>
> It is this relationship, confirmed in practice, namely the certain and indisputable personal provision of a service in conditions of dependency on the employer, which must be examined to ensure that the relevant legislation is fully applied.
>
> This is in case the employer takes advantage of the subordinate position and need of the worker in order to benefit from their services without entering into the corresponding legal relationship which, in terms of their own obligations, is governed by the labour legislation in

---

[1] For example, see rulings C-555 of 1994, T-166 of 1997, T-426 and T-501 of 2004 (Colombian Constitutional Court).

[2] Article 228 of the Constitution.

force, and by using contractual terms which serve to disguise the reality of the relationship, in order to place it within the remit of different legislation . . ..

To conclude, the principle of the primacy of facts in the field of labour relations allows us to determine the real relationship between the employer and the worker, the material truth pertaining to the facts and actual situations that arise. As a result, it is possible to confirm the existence of an employment contract and challenge the legal documents used to disguise it either as a civil contract, a commercial contract, or even a service contract.

The determination of the employment relationship through 'the primacy of fact' notion is also stated in the 1999 Constitution of Venezuela which, in article 89, stipulates that:

> No law may lay down provisions which change the inalienability and progressive nature of labour rights and benefits. In the field of labour relations, reality holds sway over form or appearance . . ..

In other countries in the region, the same notion is recurrent in legal texts. For example the 1992 Labour Code of the Dominican Republic includes this notion in its Fundamental Principles:

> Principle IX. The employment contract does not reside in documents but in facts. Any contract is void if it was concluded on the basis of fraud, whether by simulating contractual terms that do not pertain to an employment contract, through the use of intermediaries or by any other means. In such cases, this Code shall continue to regulate the employment relationship.

Articles 83 and 93 of Panama's Labour Code enshrine the principle of the primacy of fact.[3] Article 63 rejects the validity of any simulation, either in documents and contracts, or in the presentation/substitution of supposed employers. This article complements the provisions of article 62, which define the employment contract and the employment relationship, and which stipulate that if the legal presumption applies, they will pertain to an employment relationship, however that may be defined.[4]

---

[3]   RM Torrazza and VT De León, *La Relación de Trabajo (Campo de aplicación)* (Panama, Estudios nacionales, 2001), available at www.ilo.org/public/english/dialogue/ifpdial/downloads/wpnr/panama.pdf.

[4]   'Article 63. In order to determine an employment relationship or the parties to this relationship, the court shall not take account of simulated documents and contracts, the participation of intermediaries as alleged employers, or the establishment or fictitious operation of a legal entity as employers'. (Labour Code of Panama).

Panamanian case law has explicitly upheld this legislative concept. The ruling of the Third Chamber of the Supreme Court of Justice, of 17 July 1981, may serve as an example:

> In the same way that article 63 refers to the simulation of contractual terms or simulated participation of an alleged employer in the signing of the contract, article 93 rejects the validity of any fraudulent contracts where a legal entity (company) is falsely presented as providing a service, when in fact this entity is a natural person, namely a worker. Falsely presenting a worker as a company is current practice in certain types of outsourcing. The provisions of the Labour Code are very specific and reject this practice.[5]

Meanwhile, the rulings of Peru's Constitutional Court have been consistent,[6] and have even allowed, at least implicitly (if not in the letter of the law), that the principle has a constitutional basis which stems from the principle of the protection of constitutional rights:

> 4. The difficulty lies in determining whether civil contracts and annexes undersigned by the prosecuting party and the defendant . . . are invalid. As a result, if the principle of the primacy of fact applies, they could be considered permanent employment contracts and, consequently, it must be established whether the plaintiff may only be dismissed for just reasons relating to her ability or behaviour.
>
> 5. With respect to the principle of the primacy of fact which is an element implicit in our legal system and, specifically, upheld by the inherently protective nature of our Constitution, this College has stipulated that, in view of this principle . . . in the event of any discrepancy between what occurs in practice and what is stated in documents and agreements, the former must be favoured, namely, that which occurs within the realm of facts.[7]

In Costa Rica, the Second Chamber of the Supreme Court of Justice has ruled regularly and consistently on this matter, particularly in its ruling in Case 03–000121–0505-Res: 2006–00401 at 15.18 on 31 May 2006:

---

[5] 'Article 93. The simulated participation of a legal entity in the provision of services or labour shall not prevent the corresponding natural person being considered a worker. The relevant case shall be dealt with by a Labour Court, and the hearing shall involve both the legal person and the employer.' (Labour Code of Panama)

[6] Ruling of the Constitutional Court 991–2000 (Justification 3) provides that 'according to the principle of the primacy of facts, it is clear that, beyond the text of the respective contracts, the labour involved subordination, dependency and permanence, and thus it is incorrect to view the above-mentioned employment relationship as casual. The principle of the primacy of fact is implicit in our legal system and, more specifically, imposed by the inherently protective nature of our Labour Code, which considers it a duty and a right, the basis for social welfare, a means of self-realization (art 22°) and, furthermore, the primary focus for the State's attention (art 23°). In other words, the Constitution requires the employment relationship to be viewed in precisely these terms.'

[7] EXP. No 1411–2007-PA/TC.

Regarding the matter at hand, in vote No. 236 at 10.00 on 02/10/1992, this Chamber indicated that: 'in relation to the subject in question, the principle of the primacy of fact must apply and it is sufficient to prove the existence of an economic community, a group of legal or moral persons who operate together, in order to hold all of them responsible vis-à-vis the labour provided by the worker. In these situations, one must look beyond the formal appearance of a company, in order to reveal the truth and avoid preventing the worker from effectively exercising their rights . . .'. It is a well-known fact that developments in economic relations at a global level, as well as the recent trend towards integration, have resulted in the emergence of new and extremely diverse forms of company structures created in the process of developing their commercial activities. In the field of Labour Law, as in other branches of the law, this situation has often required the redefinition of certain legal concepts and the creation of new procedures, in order to regulate new situations; and, in other cases, also adapting existing legal concepts to foster and promote primarily social and economic relations. In a number of cases, this Chamber has expressed the opinion that, in terms of criteria, the worker is not obliged to know, for certain, who his real and actual employer is (see, for example, Vote 319 at 9.40 a.m. on 23/12/1998 and Vote 981 at 10 a.m. on 7/12/2000). We must remember that labour law, being a social law, aims to compensate for the normally latent inequality between the worker and the employer, especially if one takes into account the range of tools which the latter has at their disposal in order to evade their responsibilities (in this regard, see our ruling 1 at 9.30 am on 18/01/2004). Particularly in cases involving groups of economic interest, we have stressed that it goes against the concept of contractual good faith to insist the worker must know exactly who his employer is (Vote 995 at 11.10 a.m. on 12/11/2004).

In addition, the notion of the 'primacy of fact', in the field of Latin American labour legislation, including the jurisprudence and the legal doctrine, there is also the recognition of the notion of 'presumption'. For example, article 15 of the Labour Code of the Dominican Republic stipulates that: 'It is presumed, until proven otherwise, that an employment contract exists in all personal employment relationships. . . .'

Meanwhile, Panama's Labour Code stipulates in article 66 that: 'It is presumed that an employment contract and an employment relationship exist between the person who personally provides a service or labour and the person who receives this service or labour'.

In exactly the same vein, article 65 of Venezuela's Organic Labour Law stipulates that: 'An employment relationship is presumed to exist between the person providing a personal service and the person receiving it ...'.

The Constitutional Court of Colombia has regularly and consistently upheld the following legal doctrine:[8]

---

[8] Ruling T-992/05.

In order to determine whether an employment relationship exists, one must take into account the provisions of article 23 of the Substantive Labour Code, amended by Law 50 of 1990, which stipulates the fundamental elements of an employment relationship, these being: (i) the activity is personally performed by the worker, (ii) continuous subordination or dependence of the worker on the employer, which permits the latter to require compliance with orders given at any point, regarding the means, time or quantity of the work, and to impose regulations with which the worker must respect for the duration of the contract. All this must be done without affecting the honour, dignity and basic rights of the worker, and in accordance with agreements or international conventions on human rights in force in the country, and (iii) the payment of a salary as remuneration for the service.

If these prerequisites are met, it is understood that an employment contract exists. Therefore, however the parties may qualify or define the situation, the employment contract is real and fact has primacy over formal arrangements.

As a guarantee which favours the worker, article 24 of the Substantive Labour Code provides that '*It is presumed that all personal labour relations are governed by an employment contract*', which suggests that it may be contested if the employer can prove otherwise, that is to say, if they can demonstrate that the worker's personal services were not provided with a view to receiving remuneration, or in the spirit of fulfilling an obligation which required dependence or subordination.[9].

In addition to this, the Constitutional Court of Colombia stated the following, concerning the presumption of an employment relationship and the inversion of the burden of proof:

In ruling C-665 of 1998, this Court indicated that the employer, in order to challenge the presumption, must prove before the constitutional court judge that the relationship which exists stems from a civil or commercial contract and that the provision of services is not governed by labour legislation. Under these circumstances, it is not sufficient to merely produce the labour contract as proof. The Judge, basing his ruling on the constitutional principle of the primacy of fact over form, shall examine the evidence presented, in order to determine whether this presumption may be contested.

The same ruling, regarding the transfer or inversion of the burden of proof in order to challenge the legal presumption of the existence of an employment relationship, stipulated the following:

This presumption states that all personal labour relations are governed by a contract which, by its nature, implies the transfer of the burden of proof to the company owner. The employer, in order to challenge the presumption, has to prove before the judge that, in reality, the contract is actually a civil or commercial contract, and the provision of services is not

---

9 Ruling C-1110 of 2001.

governed by labour legislation, without relying solely on the presentation of the corresponding contract. It is the judge, on the basis of the constitutional principle of the primacy of fact over formal arrangements between parties to an employment relationship, who shall examine the facts of the case, using various investigative methods, in order to verify that this is indeed the case and that, as a result, the presumption may be challenged.[10]

The notion of 'presumption' of the existence of an employment relationship is to be found in other countries, such as Venezuela. The legal doctrine of the Supreme Court of Justice of Venezuela has specified, in a schematic and well-illustrated manner, the presumed distribution of the burden of proof involved in any challenge to the claim:

(1)   The defendant must prove the nature of their relationship to the worker if, in challenging the worker's claims, they have admitted that a service has been personally provided which they do not class as constituting an employment relationship, but rather as a commercial relationship, for example (presumption of a prima facie claim, as set out in art 65 of the Organic Labour Law).

(2)   The plaintiff must prove the nature of their relationship to the employer if, in their challenge to the plaintiff's case, the defendant has denied that a service has been personally provided.

(3)   If the defendant does not deny the existence of an employment relationship, the burden of proof is inverted for all remaining claims presented before the court which concern the employment relationship. That is to say, it is the defendant who must prove the inadmissibility of the worker's claims. At the same time, the defendant must also provide proof to support any new arguments for rejecting the claims of the plaintiff.

(4)   Arguments put forward by the plaintiff are admissible if the defendant does not deny or explicitly refute them in their case, and if they have not placed on the court's records any evidence that could challenge the arguments of the plaintiff.

(5)   Arguments presented by the plaintiff as part of their case are admissible if the defendant has not given grounds for their dismissal, or provided the court with any evidence that could challenge the plaintiff's claims.

In the case of Argentina, it should be noted that for the legal presumption to hold, the effective performance of the work must be proven. In order to determine whether work is performed in a dependent or autonomous manner, the principle of the primacy of facts should be applied. Article 25 of ECA considers a '... worker,

---

[10]   Ruling C-665/98.

for the purposes of this act, [to be] the physical person who undertakes or provides services under the conditions set out in articles 21 and 22 of this act, whatever the method of provision'.

The question 'who is an employer?' is considered by article 26, which states that an '… employer [is] the physical or legal person or persons, whether or not they are a corporate entity, requiring the services of a worker'.

When defining partner employees, article 27 lists the concepts describing what is understood as dependence by noting that somebody is an employee when they provide the company '… all or most of their activity in a personal and regular manner, while subject to the instructions or orders that are or could be given to them for the completion of an activity, they shall be considered to be a dependent worker …'.

In Argentina's legal system, these six articles are the source for the definition of work, for the employment contract and the employment relationship, for the legal presumption of the existence of an employment relationship and for a definition of workers and employers. Thus, not all types of employment are protected by the ECA, just work that is carried out for somebody with the facility to manage it.

This characteristic of work is present in the definition of the employment contract when it is specified that it is provided for another, and dependent on them. This notion of dependence becomes the key to the protection provided in the ECA. However, it should be noted that the ECA has no legal definition of dependence per se, but it is the joint analysis of these provisions that show the element of dependence.

More and more, the work done by the jurisprudence in Argentina confirms the importance of the legal aspects of dependence, but at the same time as it is happening in other countries, there is a trend suggesting that economic dependence is a relevant element.

Different from Argentina, Brazil's CLA does not contain exhaustive regulation of the employment relationship. It simply establishes in article 442 that 'an individual employment contract is the tacit or expressed agreement corresponding to the employment relationship'.

Unlike the ECA, the CLA does not define the employment contract and the employment relationship separately, but instead it compares both concepts.

In Brazilian labour law, the employment contract, also called a contract of activity, is the genus, while the employment relationship is the species. This means that the main elements of the employment relationship generated by the employment contract shown in the jurisprudence are: the employee should provide services personally; they should be services related to the normal activity of the employer;

the work should be remunerated by the employer; and lastly, these services should be provided in a manner legally subordinate to the employer.[11]

The protection derived from the standards contained in the CLA does not apply to any employment relationship, but only those employment relationships where the work is done in a subordinate manner. Therefore, types of work not protected by these standards include self-employed and casual, '*avulso*',[12] temporary, that which occurs in rural areas, transport, administration, brokerage and commercial representation, provided that they are performed by a physical person.

In addition, in the Brazilian legal system, subordination is the fundamental concept that opens the way to the protective standards contained in the CLA. There is no legal definition of subordination and it is the jurisprudence that has been given the task of formulating a definition.

As far as Brazil is concerned, Amauri Mascaro Nascimento defines subordination as the situation in which workers find themselves, resulting from a contractual limitation of free will in order to give their employers managerial power over their activities.[13] This author adds that subordination and managerial power are two sides of the same coin, and it is the situation in which employees find themselves during the employment relationship with regard to their employers. The employer has the legal authority to exercise managerial power over the activity being carried out by the worker, not over his or her person.

Turning now to the Uruguayan legal system, we note that none of the many laws regulating the individual employment relationship contain a definition of the employment contract or of the employment relationship as such.

Doctrine and jurisprudence has shown the three typical elements characterizing the employment contract to be personal provision of service, remuneration, and subordination or dependence.[14] According to this interpretation trend, personal provision of service and remuneration are the two main obligations taken on by the worker and the employer as a result of the employment contract. The very personal nature of the link with the worker is the essence of the contract. The employer's obligation to pay for the work excludes unpaid work from the employment relationship. Therefore, in the Uruguayan labour law system, the central concept defining the area of application for the labour standards is subordination or dependence. Note that subordination and dependence are terms used indistinctly, and that they have not been defined by law.

---

[11]   AM de Barros, *Curso de Direito do Trabalho*, 2nd edn, (Sao Paolo, LTR, 2006) 204.

[12]   In Portuguese, *avulso* means separated, isolated or loose.

[13]   AM Nascimento, *Iniciação ao Direito do Trabalho*, 32nd edn (Sao Paulo, LTR, 2006) 105.

[14]   HH Barbagelata, *Derecho del Trabajo,*2nd edn (Montevideo, FCU, 1999) Book I Vol 2 181.

As Barbagelata notes:

> in general the concept of legal subordination predominates, understood from the idea of separateness of the work and from the circumstance that the employer is the one who gives orders, monitors and directs the activity. In the same way, it has been claimed that it is a situation with a certain permanence or continuity, or that occasional provision of services has been excluded from its scope.[15]

In line with the definition of subordination developed by doctrine, jurisprudence has noted that:

> '... the subordination accepted by labour law—a fundamental characteristic of the employment contract that distinguishes it from the *locatio operis*—is not the capricious subjugation of one person to another, but rather what legal doctrine calls legal subordination and is shown in three aspects: economic subordination (seeking a salary), hierarchical subordination (the managerial role of the employer, disciplinary power), technical or strictly work-related subordination (the duty of the worker to adhere strictly to the instructions of the provider of work).[16]

From the above analysis of the three labour law systems, one could say that subordination or dependence is the key concept determining the scope of the employment relationship. In this regard, the Argentinean ECA, which mentions this concept expressly, prefers to use the word 'dependence' rather than 'subordination' (arts 21, 22, 27). However, we know that both jurisprudence and doctrine in countries such as Argentina, Brazil and Uruguay use the two terms interchangeably.

The notion of subordination and dependency is also a characteristic of the majority of legal systems in Central America. For example, the Costa Rican legal system defines the characteristics and elements of the employment relationship, and the way in which subordination or dependency is determined, in the following manner:

> ... three elements legally determine the character or nature of an employment relationship: a) the personal provision of a service; b) remuneration; and c) legal subordination. Jurisprudence and legal doctrine have established that, in general, subordination or dependence is an essential factor in determining whether or not an employment relationship exists. This is due to the fact that other legal relationships exist which also involve the provision of services, performance of work and remuneration, and which make up so-called 'grey zones' or 'borderline cases' ... As a result, subordination has been defined as 'a state involving the

---

[15] Barbagelata (n 14) 184.
[16] N Nicoliello, *Revista Derecho del Trabajo* (Montevideo, FCU, 2004) Book XIV p 252.

restriction of a worker's autonomy in the provision of services or labour, by means of a contract; and which stems the power of the employer or company owner to direct the other party. . . . it is a state of real dependence, which stems from the employer's right to direct and give orders, and the employee's corresponding obligation to obey these orders . . . which means that it is sufficient . . .for the right to direct to exist, rather than the opportunity to do so, and to substitute one's will for that of the person providing the service, whenever the person giving the orders deems it necessary. . . .[17]

Although labour law systems in Latin America analyse the concept of subordination from different angles, addressing the economic, hierarchical, technical and legal aspects, one could argue that in each country, the legal aspect of subordination is considered to be the core.

On a closer look, subordination and legal presumption are key elements in Argentina's ECA. The law provides that the presumption is still valid for non-labour models. Faced with evidence of the effective provision of a service, the law presumes there to be an employment contract behind it. Of course, to apply these legal notions, the principle of the primacy of fact becomes particularly important. This principle, that has been extensively developed by Américo Plá Rodríguez '. . . means that when there is conflict between what is happening in practice and what is shown in documents or agreements, preference should be given to the former, that is, what is happening on the ground'.[18]

In all labour law systems in the region, there is acknowledgement that there are other forms of work which have multiplied in recent times, and which are not covered by the protective statute resulting from labour law and hence from the determination of an employment relationship. In addition to the above, let us see now what are other criteria developed in the legal systems for determining an employment relationship.

3.3 Criteria for Determining the Employment Relationship

The leading example in Venezuelan jurisprudence in this matter involves ruling No 489 of the Chamber for Labour and Social Matters of the Supreme Court of Justice, dated 13 August 2002, in *Mireya Beatriz Orta de Silva v the National Federation of Academic Teaching Staff of Venezuela (FENAPRODO-CPV)*:

---

[17] Ruling of the Second Chamber of the Supreme Court of Justice, 14 September 2007.
[18] A Plá Rodríguez, *Los Principios del Derecho del Trabajo*, 3rd edn (Buenos Aires, Depalma, 1978) 313.

Without being exhaustive, a list of criteria, or indicators, which can determine the existence of an employment relationship between the person providing their work or services and the person receiving them was:

a)   the manner in which the work is carried out . . .

b)   working time and other working conditions . . .

c)   means of remuneration . . .

d)   personal labour, supervision and disciplinary control . . .

e)   investment, provision of tools, materials and machinery . . .;

f)   other: . . . estimate of profit or loss for the person performing the work or providing the service, regular nature of the work . . ., the worker performs their work exclusively for the contracting company . . .[19]

Now, in addition to the criteria mentioned above, the Chamber has added the following indicators:

a)   the legal status of the alleged employer.

b)   if the person concerned is a legal person, their corporate statutes and corporate purpose must be examined to determine whether the company is a functioning business, whether it fulfils its fiscal obligations, whether it claims any legal deductions, whether it has a book-keeping system, etc.

c)   the ownership of the goods and consumables used to verify the provision of a service.

d)   the nature and quantum of the remuneration received for the service, especially if the amount received is significantly more than that paid to workers doing a similar or identical job.

e)   specific criteria relating to the provision of a service on behalf of another party ....

When looking at the labour law systems in Argentina, Brazil and Uruguay, it has always been the concept of subordination or dependence that determines whether or not we are dealing with an employment relationship. However, in recent years, there has been a lively debate on this criterion among Latin American scholars. For example, as Adrián Goldin notes: '... it would appear to be useful to characterize the process of constructing the concept of labour dependence as the result of the inductive recognition of the points that historically set apart the manner in which

---

[19]   AS Bronstein, Ambito de Aplicación del Derecho del Trabajo, Ponencia del Congreso Internacional de Derecho del Trabajo y de la Seguridad Social, Caracas, Venezuela, 6–8 May 2002.

the typical industrial worker and the owner of the production organization join themselves together within a capitalist society'[20].

In this regard, several indicators have emerged both in doctrine and jurisprudence for the determination of an employment relationship. Some of them can be defined as core elements. In the three countries examined here, the core element is that of working for another, that is, providing a service to benefit the employer. The worker makes his capacity for work available to a third-party, in return for receiving remuneration. In this relationship, the worker does not take on the financial risks of work, his obligation being limited to making his capacity for work available to an employer. The worker is in a position of duality with regard to the financial risks of work and with regard to the means of production.

This aspect is also noted by Alonso Olea when he states that the initial and direct attribution of the fruits of the labour to the employer is an integral part of the reason for the contract, which in turn is a necessary and structural consequence of his separation from the means of production and the organization of the work.[21]

In contrast, the employer has the ability to manage, control and supervise this capacity for work. There is therefore an employment relationship when work is done for another person (whether physical or legal), and that person has the ability to manage and control that work.

In Argentinean doctrine, as a result of an analysis of the current legal provisions, there is a lot of emphasis on the fact that the subordinate worker is now joining a separate business structure. In that regard it is noted that '… if the dependent relationship is defined by the personal incorporation of the subject working in an organization that is separate from him, with the effect that the outcome of his work will result in the production of a good or service, it seems that what defines the possibility of a dependency as regulated by labour law is the presence of an enterprise, defined in law as 'the organization of personal, material and immaterial means organized under management in order to achieve economic ends or profits'[22].

Brazilian doctrine states that subordination has various levels of intensity according to the type of work. However, it appears to be well defined in the case of employees of low rank, but becomes more vague and complex with regard to managerial employees and intellectual workers.[23]

---

[20] A Goldín, 'El concepto de dependencia laboral y las transformaciones productivas', (1996) II(14) *Relaciones Laborales y Seguridad Social* 132.

[21] O Alonso, *Introducción al Derecho del Trabajo*, 5th edn (Madrid, Civitas, 1994) 34 ff.

[22] A Perugini, *La Relación de Dependencia* (Buenos Aires, Hammurabi, 2004) 64.

[23] Nascimento (n 13) 107.

As Daniel Rivas states, in Uruguayan doctrine, 'the idea that the characteristic subordination of the employment contract implies that the worker is obliged to work under the management of the employer predominates'.[24] In other words, it is the employer who, in exercising managerial power, defines the place and time of the provision of labour.

From the above, it could be said that in the large majority of countries in Latin America, there still exists difficulty in establishing whether or not an employment relationship exists. Although the criteria of subordination or dependence continue to be the core elements for determining an employment relationship, it is also true that other indicators have emerged and they need to be systematized in the respective labour law systems. This would reduce what are considered to be the grey areas between employment and self-employment.

3.4 The Grey Areas between Employment and Self-Employment: A Contribution of the Legal Doctrine

Labour law today is evolving constantly as it adapts to the many changes occurring in the economic and social sphere.

From the experience of these labour law systems, the concept of subordination appears to be insufficient to cover all forms of employment activity that exist in the world of work. In this regard, reference could be made to Supiot's opinions on this very notion. Supiot notes that 'the notion of subordination no longer enables us to address the many diverse forms of employment, and so a new legal regime for workers should be established, that goes beyond the current limits of salaried work'[25].

Córdova stresses that subordination generated a splendid series of legal findings and eradicated many abuses, but barely three-quarters of a century after its consecration it also began to show signs that it was too narrow a circle. He concludes by affirming that subordination, which still appears in texts today as an

---

[24] D Rivas, *La subordinación—criterios distintivos del contrato de trabajo* (Montevideo, FCU, 1995) p 35.

[25] A Supiot, 'Introducción a las reflexiones sobre el trabajo' (1996) 115 *Revista Internacional del trabajo* N§ 6, 663.

essential element of the employment relationship, is becoming a limiting and somewhat obsolete factor in the modern conception of work.[26]

Along the same lines, Gino Giugni levels criticism at subordination as a formal criterion with priority over real criteria such as the existence of an imbalance of contractual strength, which has contributed to distortions of the system, because it has overprotected relationships that were already occurring in relatively balanced conditions and has left out social relationships where there is intense exploitation.[27]

With a view to overcoming such limitations in the use of the criterion of subordination as the only/core element to determine an employment relationship, there has been a lively debate in Latin America with a view to advancing new proposals. One prominent trend when examining the new proposals is the application of labour law to all types of work, whether subordinate or not.

Analysing the future of labour law in 1989, Barbagelata noted that '…from the perspective of the future of workers we must admit definitively that every one of us that is in or outside an employment relationship is a worker Labour Law should include everyone'.[28]

Umberto Romagnoli is also of the same opinion, when he writes about the notion of working citizenship, precisely because it guarantees citizens a level of social protection based on criteria of need, independently of the normative qualification of the function that they perform in and for society.[29]

As Oscar Ermida Uriarte and Hernández Álvarez recall, this trend can be seen as a return to the past, because half a century ago Paul Durand and Mario Deveali noted that labour law was heading towards becoming the legal code regulating all human work.[30]

There is then in the Latin American debate a consistent trend to recognize that labour law, without major reformulation, should be the legal instrument to regulate all types of human work, and not only to apply it to dependent work.

Thus appears a second line of thought towards the formulation of a new labour law to cover a type of work that is in between dependent and independent

---

[26] E Córdova, *Evolución del Pensamiento Juslaboralista—Estudios en Homenaje al Prof. Héctor-Hugo Barbagelata, 'El papel de la industrialización y el principio de subordinación en la evolución de la legislación laboral'* (Montevideo, FCU, 1997) 135–36.

[27] G Giugni, 'Diritto del Lavoro (voce per una enciclopedia)' (1979) 1 *Giornale di Diritto del Lavoro e di Relazioni Industriali* 21–22.

[28] H-H Barbagelata, 'El futuro del Derecho del Trabajo', X Congreso Iberoamericano de Derecho del Trabajo y de la Seguridad Social, Montevideo, 1989, 27.

[29] GL Caen, *Evolución del Pensamiento Juslaboralista—Estudios en Homenaje al Prof. Héctor-Hugo Barbagelata, 'El derecho del trabajo ¿Qué futuro?'* (Montevideo, FCU, 1997) 441

[30] O Ermida Uriarte and O Hernández Alvarez, 'Crítica de la subordinación' (2003) XLV 206 *Revista Derecho Laboral* 247.

work. This type of work that goes beyond the limits of subordinate work would need a new regulation in the three labour law systems considered here, and later.

To be sure, 'work is not only a model of production but also a model of life in which interdependence is the prevailing factor, rather than dependence or subordination'.[31] The new labour law should develop and draw up a normative framework around the concept of interdependence that, as we can see, is halfway between subordination and autonomous work.

Goldin and Feldmen in Argentina are thinking along the same lines of a legal technique that proposes the development of a labour law for a third category of workers. They believe that in the country there is a need to create '... a category or concept that is sufficiently broad, so as to cover the various types of work that require protection (whether or not they have an actual employment contract) and it should be given a minimum and indispensable stock of protection'.[32]

Supiot also supports this trend, when discussing the grey areas between subordinate and independent work, he establishes that it would be appropriate to create hybrid forms of protection therein. This grey area would justify the partial application of labour law to workers who, because they are legally independent, depend on the person paying for the work.[33]

The common element in all these positions is the need to redevelop a new protective law for work that is legally independent while being economically dependent, or to adapt classic labour law to these new methods of work. In this way, a notion has developed in Italian doctrine of a 'parasubordinate worker', in German doctrine of 'quasi-subordinate workers', and in France of 'goodwill managers', where there is a partial application of labour law.

With regard to parasubordinate workers, in Uruguayan doctrine Márquez Garmendia and Beñarán Burastero share the view of those highlighting the need for a specific set of standards for this form of work,[34] and implying that the application of the economic dependence would be the main criterion for defining 'para-subordination'.

In Brazil, economic and social transformations have thrown the traditional dichotomy between self-employment and subordinate work into crisis. To deal with this new situation, a third genre has slowly been developed along the lines of

---

[31] Córdova (n 26) 136.

[32] AGS Feldman, 'Protección de los trabajadores. Informe argentino', consultation carried out by ILO within the framework of the studies for the discussion of an International Convention on subcontracting, October 1999, 85.

[33] A Supiot, 'Wage employment and self-employment', Report to the 6th European Congress for Labour Law, Warsaw, September 1999, 160.

[34] PB Burastero 'Trabajadores parasubordinados', in *Cuarenta y dos Estudios sobre la descentralización empresarial y el derecho del trabajo* (Montevideo, FCU, 2000) 266.

parasubordinate work. According to the opinion of Alice Monteiro de Barros, institutionalizing parasubordinate work would involve reframing labour law in Brazil and it would imply a re-definition of the legal situations that could then be covered by the law. The usefulness of defining this third genre would lie in the possibility of including so-called borderline situations or grey areas in the scope of protection, comprised of, among others, intellectual workers, whose work is difficult to qualify legally.[35]

From a comparative viewpoint, we can see that Argentina, Brazil and Uruguay do not seek to replace the concept of subordination, but rather to introduce compensatory rules to balance out the negotiating inequality of the contracting parties. This inequality appears to be the element that should be corrected and addressed by labour law.

In the countries examined here, the concept of economic dependence is, without doubt, a difficult notion to frame in law. Defining it in abstract legal categories is not easy, because there are many levels, and because the contracting parties are almost always economically unequal. The difficult task is to find objective parameters to demonstrate the economic dependence of a worker. In this regard, it is mainly the role of the labour judge to examine and apply criteria to specific cases with a view to developing jurisprudence consonant to the protection of the worker.

An additional argument on the determination of an employment relationship concerns the existence of a legal presumption of the existence of a dependent relationship between an employer and an employee.

The notion of a legal presumption of the existence of dependent work would help the judge to apply labour standards, and at the same time would clarify that independent or autonomous work would be regulated by civil and/or commercial law, as it has been until now, in three legal systems.

Autonomous work has been defined in three legal systems as 'the physical person who carries out labour or provides a service freelance, autonomously, in exchange for a reward.'[36]

This has been developed through labour jurisprudence that considers the autonomous worker as someone 'who works for their own gain, that is to say independently, outside the realm of the organization and the management of the person paying the salary, in a regular, personal and direct manner and assumes the economic risk of applying their capacity for work.'[37]

---

[35] de Barros (n 11) 278 and 279.

[36] D Rivas, 'El trabajo autónomo', in *Cuarenta y dos Estudios sobre la descentralización empresarial y el derecho del trabajo* (Montevideo, FCU, 2000) 266.

[37] Rivas (n 36) 246.

More recently, in Uruguay, both labour doctrine and jurisprudence have examined the multitude of new forms of employment that, in one way or another, disguise a genuine employment relationship. As Mangarelli notes, in Uruguayan law, 'in recent years service provision has regained ground to the detriment of the employment contract, being one of the instruments used to carry out enterprise decentralization'. The author goes on to add that 'this change does not herald its predominance in the future, or the spread of employment contracting into the field of Civil Law. It is a sign of growth in the service provision sector of employment.'[38]

In light of the evidence that labour has developed into an autonomous form, provided by independent workers, there are doctrinal trends highlighting the need to create a set of standards to protect this method of work. The regulation contained in the civil or commercial code is not sufficient or adequate and therefore a set of standards must be created that should take into account the nature of the autonomous worker today.

In that regard, Rivas has advanced the idea that in the Latin American context there should be a law protecting independent work, adapted to the range of activities and professions, as well as to the social and economic diversity of people who personally provide autonomous work.[39] This would be in line with the opinion that no matter the form of employment, the law should be in the position to provide protection to every worker.

3.5 Contracting Methods in the Labour Market

The labour markets in Latin America and the Caribbean are highly fragmented. Technological changes, the need to reduce cost in order to maintain or increase competitiveness, and the globalization of markets have resulted in significant and permanent restructuring of production units. To confront these new challenges, enterprises have adopted the strategy of concentrating their activities on the areas of greatest specialization, and externalized incidental or complementary services or processes. Therefore, the large production units, where advances in technology and research are focused, have links with many external providers with a wide variety of legal forms.

---

[38] C Mangarelli, 'Arrendamiento de servicios', in *Cuarenta y dos Estudios sobre la descentralización empresarial y el derecho del trabajo* (Montevideo, FCU, 2000) 281

[39] Rivas (n 36) 249.

In this context, we experience a dual labour market: on one side a typical subordinate work being done in what we could call central production units, and on the other side autonomous work, which can be economically dependent, and in some cases even disguised, and that is to be found mainly in the world of the suppliers. More and more, the reality in countries like Argentina, Brazil, Colombia, Costa Rica, Dominican Republic, Uruguay and Venezuela is characterized by workers who are directly linked to the central production units covered by the labour standards developed in each legal code with a clear aim to protect them, while on the borders of these core production units there is a more precarious labour market, one that creates employment links between suppliers and their workers, and commercial links between suppliers (in many cases small or medium-sized enterprises) and the core production units.

This reality has not been ignored by the labour law of each country. For example, the Argentinean ECA provides that workers who have been contracted by third parties with a view to supplying them to the enterprises, will be considered as direct employees of those using their services, and establishes joint responsibility between the employers for all costs arising from the employment relationship and the social security scheme (article 29). Meanwhile in Brazil, the CLA establishes in article 455 that in cases of subcontracting, the subcontractor is responsible for the costs resulting from the employment contract, but the worker has the right to claim any labour costs that the subcontractor has not complied with, from the principal employer. According to the practice, it is illegal to outsource or subcontract activities which constitute the central aim or focus of the enterprise (end activities) and that only mid-level activities can be subcontracted or outsourced. As a result, it is permitted to subcontract temporary, security service, maintenance, cleaning and specialized service staff related to incidental activities rather than to the principal activities of the core production unit. The same can be said for Uruguay, where the law provides joint responsibility between the principal and subcontracting enterprises for all labour and social security costs due to the worker contracted by the subcontractor (Act 18.098 article 1).

Closely linked to this form of employment is the hiring of temporary workers through temporary work agencies. Although as yet, only Uruguay has ratified ILO Convention No 181 on Private Employment Agencies, there are laws in Argentina and Brazil that regulate the operation of these agencies as well. In Argentina, an employer who hires workers though a temporary agency is jointly responsible for covering labour and social security costs. Temporary workers are covered by the collective agreement and can be represented by the trade union of the agency enterprise (Act 24.013 articles 75 and 76). As well, in Brazil, the aim of the temporary work agency is to provide specialized staff, for determined periods, to another enterprise that needs them. The temporary worker has the right to a salary equivalent to that earned by a permanent worker of the same category. In turn, if the temporary work agency is insolvent, the client enterprise is jointly responsible for labour and social security costs due to the temporary worker (Act 6.019 of 3 January 1974 and regulatory decree No 73.841 of 13 March 1974).

Uruguay has recently regulated the supply of staff. The first difference with the other two systems is that the supply is of both temporary and permanent staff. According to Uruguayan law, there is joint responsibility between the supplying enterprise and the client enterprise for all the labour and social security costs of the temporary worker. In addition, the temporary worker cannot receive labour benefits lower than those received by the permanent workers of the user enterprise (Act 18.099 articles 1 and 5).

The other method of hiring regulated by the three legal systems is the provision of goods or services by cooperatives of workers. The levels of legal independence between the core production units and the supplier cooperatives vary, and in many cases can include a genuine employment relationship.

In Argentina, the predominant trend is usually to exclude the work of members of a cooperative from the rules for dependent workers, except in cases of fraud, a hypothesis provided for in Act 25.877 article 40, which authorizes the labour inspectorate services to check that cooperatives comply with labour and social security standards and whether its members are working in accordance with labour law, which supposes that there is a distinction between the non-member dependents and the members of the cooperatives. Moreover, the last section of article 40 expressly provides that cooperatives cannot behave as enterprises supplying temporary or seasonal services, or in any other way offer the services of job placement agencies.

In Brazilian law the employment relationships of members of cooperatives are not covered by the labour standards, unless fraudulent situations are established. In accordance with the Civil Code of 2002, a cooperative is a simple society that, according to Act 5.764 of 1971, has the freedom to choose its target, which could be any kind of service, operation or activity. Doctrine has classified cooperatives into three categories: production, consumption and credit.[40]

More recently, according to José Dari Krein, since the mid-1990s, becoming a labour cooperative has been the best way of reducing cost, avoiding the application of the labour standards, within the framework of a policy of outsourcing services. It should be noted that hiring through cooperatives still presents fiscal and budgetary

---

[40] See de Barros (n 11), 212.

advantages that are notably greater than other forms of hiring, since it guarantees greater freedom for the employer to adjust the labour force to the production needs, without having to give notice or pay indemnities.[41]

In Uruguay, Act 17.794 regulates the operation of cooperatives of production or incidental labour. It is in this legal form that former workers from enterprises that have gone bankrupt have kept their posts, managing the assets in liquidation. In order to promote the rescue of these enterprises by the workers, the law allows the bankruptcy judge to appoint a cooperative made up of the former workers to be the receiver of the assets of the enterprise. The law has a novel solution, in that it enables the social security body to pay the workers' unemployment benefits in cash in advance, as long as they are invested in their entirety in shares in the cooperative in order to provide it with capital.

Experience suggests that in some cases the former workers, supported by the facilities given to them by this act, have, by transforming themselves into cooperatives, managed to revive enterprises and thereby save their jobs. All in all, it can be said that the role of the cooperative in the Uruguayan labour market does not appear to be a fraudulent means of hiring labour.

This fragmentation of the labour market has stimulated the hiring of autonomous workers by principal enterprises. Undoubtedly, the new business strategies with regard to the specialization of activities have enabled processes or services to be delegated to truly independent workers, who in many cases are economically dependent, since they focus their activity on only one contracting party. It is also true that in the field of autonomous work the three codes give a hypothesis of fraud. In certain situations, fraud is provoked by the standard, principally because of the lower cost of taxation for autonomous work compared to dependent work. For example, this very last issue is expressly mentioned in ILO Recommendation No 198, which refers to these situations in Paragraph 17 and notes that '… Members should develop, as part of the national policy referred to in this Recommendation, effective measures aimed at removing incentives to disguise an employment relationship.'

On closer inspection, in Brazil, the labour law has facilitated the hiring of workers who formally appear to be independent, through what is known as the hiring of the 'legal person'. The process of '*pejorización*', as it is currently known, has resulted in a change in the labour market in Brazil. Workers who formally appear to be independent register with the tax directorate as a legal person, and provide their services through a commercial relationship. A worker hired in this manner does not

---

[41] JD Krein, *Tendencias recientes en las relaciones de empleo en el Brasil 1990–2005* (Campinhas, 2007) 168 and 169.

enjoy the labour benefits or social security benefits that a dependent worker has, and this method of hiring involves lower cost for the employer.

In order to expand the jurisdictional scope of the employment relationship, the recent constitutional amendment No 45 was broadened and the jurisdiction of the Labour Courts can now hear cases arising from any kind of employment relationship. Labour law is then applied to all cases related to work, including autonomous workers, liberal professionals, commercial representatives and agents.[42]

In Argentinean law, the self-employed worker also has particular regulation, particularly with regard to taxes. According to Ramírez Gronda:

> ... it is important to distinguish dependent workers from those that, although they are doing tasks that may be identical, are not in that situation. The main problem is that human labour can be subject to various contracts—such as hiring, enterprise, free provision,—in many of which there is some element of subordination, and it is indispensable to identify which are regulated by the discipline specifically designed to regulate salaried work and which are not, a task not without obstacles. On the one hand there is a vague reasoning for the employment contract when compared to that of other civil or commercial contracts, on the other hand, because there is often a malicious will among the contracting parties, particularly on the side of the enterprise, seeking to simulate a commercial contract with a view to avoiding the application of labour law, which is always more expensive.[43]

In Uruguay, the figure of the individual enterprise is the instrument that the law uses to register autonomous workers with social security. The social security contribution for an autonomous employee is much lower than for a dependent worker. This has led to abusive use of individual enterprises that in many cases are a cover for dependent work, which is registered with social security as autonomous.

In these three countries the law establishes a tax and labour system (self-employed in Argentina; legal person in Brazil; individual enterprise in Uruguay) that is less costly for the independent worker than for the dependent worker. This process of deprofessionalizing the employment relationship is increasing, since a disguised employment relationship entails savings for both parties, particularly for the person benefiting from the service.

The above examples are the most common methods of hiring in the countries covered in this study. In the formal economy we can identify the labour market generated by the central enterprises or organizations and the peripheral market comprising the world of suppliers or subcontractors. In the first circle, workers are

---

[42] N Maunzich, 'Enmienda Constitucional N° 45 y las nuevas competencias: de la extensión al fortalecimiento de la justicia del trabajo' (2006) 1 *Revista del Departamento de Derecho del Trabajo y de la Seguridad Social, Facultad de Derecho de la Universidad de San Pablo* 139.

[43] D Ramírez Gronda, *Tratado de Derecho del Trabajo* (Buenos Aires, La Ley, 1964) 558.

linked directly to enterprises, under the protection of the traditional labour law standards. In the second circle, new methods of hiring appear, which in some circumstances have lesser levels of protection.

3.6 Conclusions

In conclusion, we should bear in mind that the labour laws in a good number of countries in Latin America and the Caribbean have responded positively to the growth of new forms of hiring. The sharing of labour responsibilities (shared or subsidiary) among the employers, has led to a great advance in the level of protection. In this sense, it can be said that national legal systems have responded to the changes in the labour market by making sure that workers' protection be centred on the notion of the employment relationship. In the legal tradition of Latin America, the employment relationship has proven to be a core issue through which labour rights and benefits are rendered to both workers and employers. In these systems, the employment relationship continues to refer to the protection of those workers who find themselves in a disguised employment relationship. Although one big issue still remains to be solved, that of the so-called 'triangular relationship', it is also true that these legal systems introduce a joint responsibility for the intermediary agency and the employer to cover benefits and costs to workers. Nonetheless, we will still have to wait some time before a consolidated jurisprudence re-affirms the appropriate ways—legal and not—in which workers in need of protection can be effectively protected, as well as the possibility of dealing separately with the various situations. The judicial bodies of countries in Latin America and the Caribbean will speak through their sentences.

Subordination, Parasubordination and Self-Employment: A Comparative Study of Selected African Countries $\quad$ **4**

Paul Benjamin* (assisted by Urmilla Bhoola**)

4.1 Introduction

In an insightful contribution to the immense body of literature on the changing nature of employment, Clive Thompson has commented that: 'the standard model of employment is now one of inherent variability. Work has changed and is changing for both better and for worse.'[1] Edward Webster, in an overview of research on the changing nature of work and employment in Southern Africa, suggests that economic liberalization has increased competitive pressures resulting in three different 'worlds of work': those who have benefited from global integration, those who continue to survive in employment but under worse conditions and those who 'make a living' in informal and unpaid work.[2]

The transformation of work has polarized employment relations. The inhabitants of the world of work range from the knowledge workers of the 'new economy' to the precarious and vulnerable workers who make their living through informal work and sub-contracted labour. These latter workers are poorly paid and employed in unstable jobs which more often than not fall outside the scope of collective bargaining and legal protection. The burgeoning informalization of the last three decades has been a change for the worse as a growing proportion of

---

    * Practising Attorney, Cape Town (South Africa); Professor of Law, University of Cape Town. The author wishes to acknowledge the assistance in locating material from their countries of Herbert Jauch (Namibia), Peter Dunseith (Swaziland) and Mabathoana Khotle (Lesotho), as well as Grahame Matthewson who put me in touch with them.

    ** Judge of the Labour Court, South Africa.

    [1] C Thompson, 'The Changing Nature of Employment' (2003) 24 *Industrial Law Journal (SA)* 1793.

    [2] E Webster, 'Making a Living, Earning a Living: Work and Employment in Southern Africa' (2005) 26(1) *International Political Science Review* 55–71.

workers survive without regular benefits or employment protection.[3] In qualifying types of relationships terms such as 'atypical' or 'non-standard' no longer carry the descriptive power that they did some 20 to 30 years ago when they were first used to identify an emerging labour market trend in the developed economies. Precariousness has become a norm and in much of the developed world it is the dominant form of employment. Everywhere, labour law touches fewer lives than it once did.

In this context, the ILO Employment Relationship Recommendation, 2006 (No. 198), seeks to ensure that the scope of application of labour legislation is appropriate and thereby provide for the protection of employees, particularly vulnerable employees in non-standard employment relationships. The Recommendation proposes that countries should adopt a policy to clarify and, if necessary, to adapt the scope of labour legislation in order to ensure the effective protection of workers 'who perform work in the context of an employment relationship.'

This paper identifies the emerging new relationships and describes them within the framework of the current labour markets in South Africa and other African countries. This provides the context in which it is possible to examine legislative provisions, policy proposals and judicial interpretations dealing with the scope of the employment relationship and responses to the increasingly complex task of identifying employment relationships and ensuring effective protection.

In a recent paper on the challenges of labour law in Southern Africa, Fenwick, Kalula and Landau have suggested that in the developing world, the challenges to orthodox labour law concepts are greater than in the industrialized world. These challenges, they argue, arise from the extent to which work is performed by 'own-account' workers in the informal economy, as well as the widespread unemployment and under-employment experienced in so many developing countries.[4] The high degree of informalization of work also poses major challenges for the foundational labour law activity: identifying and defining employment relationships. The extent of this challenge is illustrated by the fact that among Southern Africa's total population of about 200 million, only 1 out of 10 people have a job in the formal sector.[5] The informal sector itself is diverse, containing a myriad of different forms of work: what these forms have in common is that—to a lesser or greater degree—they are performed outside of the realm of labour law. This challenge is

---

[3] For general accounts of informalization, see G Standing, *Global Labour Flexibility: Seeking Distributive Justice* (Basingstoke, Macmillan, 1999) and J Fudge, 'The Legal Boundaries of the Employer, Precarious Workers, and Labour Protection' in G Davidov and B Langille, *Boundaries and Frontiers of Labour Law* (Oxford, Hart Publishing, 2006).

[4] C Fenwick, E Kalula and I Landau, 'Labour law: a southern African perspective' in T Tekle (ed) *Labour law and worker protection in developing countries* (Oxford, Hart Publishing and Geneva, ILO, 2010).

[5] H Jauch, *Labour Markets in Southern Africa* (Windhoek, Labour Resource and Research Institute, 2004).

not unique to Southern Africa, or even Africa, and is shared by many Latin American and Asian countries.

Informal work ranges from archetypal 'informal sector' activities such as street-hawking (or vending), to jobs that were formerly performed as part of public sector or large private sector entities that have been 'outsourced' into informal arrangements, leaving workers with reduced (and in some cases, no) labour protection. A significant example is the 'dumping' by South African municipalities of waste disposal services into a range of different outsourcing arrangements, all of which have resulted in a loss of benefits and protection for employees.[6]

Work in the formal and informal spheres is highly inter-connected. Street vendors form part of the marketing strategies of world's largest multinationals: Unilever sells its soaps through street-traders and Coca-Cola rents out kiosks to them to sell its beverages. Issues of 'disguised employment', a central concern of the Employment Relationship Recommendation, permeate all levels of work in the informal economy. Recent studies in South Africa show extensive movement by workers between employment in the formal and informal economies.[7]

Despite increasing informalization, conventional employment remains the fundamental legal relationship regulating work. Employees have not chosen to opt out of traditional employment into entrepreneurship and other forms of self-employment to the extent that this may have occurred in developed economies. The South African workplace is less characterized by relationships involving 'parasubordination', in which the worker personally performs the labour in the presence of continuity and coordination by a principal, but in the absence of subordination. In Europe, this concept is used to describe a middle ground between self-employment on the one hand and employment (or subordination) on the other.

Parasubordination incorporates a notion of economic dependence to identify those relationships that contain elements of both atypical and typical employment.[8] This is essentially self-employment accompanied by a number of characteristics of employment which entitle the 'employee' to protection under labour legislation.[9]

---

[6] Samson, M "Organising in the informal economy: A Case Study of the Municipal Waste Management Industry in South Africa" (Geneva, ILO, 2003)

[7] Between 2000 and 2004, 53.7%—moved between formal employment, informal work and unemployment. 18.3% of workers initially employed in informal work moved into formal employment see I Valodia, L Lebani, C Skinner and R Devey 'Low-Waged and Informal Employment in South Africa', (2006) 60 *Transformation: Critical Perspectives in Southern Africa* .

[8] See S Liebman, 'Employment situations and workers' protection: Italy' (Paper prepared for Meeting of Experts on Workers in need of Protection, Geneva, 2000).

[9] Liebman (n 8) cites as examples of 'parasubordinate' new professions such as merchandisers and telemarketers. However, traditional professions such as corporate directors and auditors also claim this status. The professional categories that contain the greatest number of registrations are research/consultancy and teaching/training.

However, the influence of this development is reflected in the fact that 'economic dependence' has become one of the criteria utilized to identify a statutory employment relationship.

This paper proceeds to examine the changing forms of employment in South Africa. This is followed by an examination of the criteria utilized to identify the employment relationship in South Africa and an account of how South African legislators, policy-makers and tribunals have responded to changes in the form of work. The discussion is then broadened to track these developments in a number of other countries in the Southern African Development Community (SADC). The final section examines responses in more detail, in two particular areas in which legal uncertainty has been utilized to deprive employees of labour law protection: triangular employment relationships and temporary contracts.

4.2 Changing Forms of Employment in South Africa

Recommendation 198's challenge to governments is to review the scope of application of its labour laws to ensure that workers receive effective protection. This raises very substantial issues. It requires that the diversity of employment relationships within the labour market is identified and analysed. This requires that statistics reflect the range of non-standard and informalized work. This is no easy task, and its complexity is exacerbated by the sectoral varieties in non-standard and informalized work and employment.

In South Africa, the need for a response to informalization has begun to dominate the labour law agenda. Early post-apartheid policy documents such as the Department of Labour's 1996 Green Paper on Employment Standards noted the rise of non-standard employment relationships, but were not able to document its extent and diversity. In 2002, 6.6 million people were engaged in full-time employment, 3.1 million were engaged in atypical employment[10] and 2.2 million were engaged in informal work.[11] The following year, in June 2003, the national Growth and Development Summit noted the need for 'measures to be taken to promote decent work and to address the problem of casualization'. This led to a research project co-ordinated by the Department of Labour on the changing nature of work

---

[10] Atypical employment includes temporary, part-time and outsourced work as well as approximately 1.1 million domestic workers.

[11] E Webster, and K von Holdt, 'Work Restructuring ad the Crisis of Social Reproduction: A Southern Perspective' in Webster and von Holdt (eds), *Beyond the Apartheid Workplace: Studies in Transition* (Durban, University of Kwazulu-Natal Press, 2005).

and atypical forms of employment. Its report, which was tabled in the NEDLAC in October 2004, showed the extent to which the growth of non-standard employment had eroded the quality of labour protection and called for a reappraisal of policies and legislative provisions.

This report conceptualizes the changes in work in South Africa in terms of two interrelated processes: casualization and externalization. Both represent shifts from the norm of the standard employment relationship which is understood as being indefinite (permanent) and full-time employment, usually at a workplace controlled by the employer. Casualization refers to the displacement of standard employment by temporary or part-time employment (or both). Externalization refers to a process of economic restructuring whereby employment is regulated by a commercial contract rather than a contract of employment. In the case of externalized work, this includes situations where the nominal employer does not in fact control the employment relationship.

Informalization, as indicated above, refers to the process by which employment is increasingly unregulated and workers are not protected by labour law. 'Informalization' covers both employees who are nominally protected by labour law but are not able to enforce their rights and those who are not employees because they have the legal status of independent contractors.

The research attempts to quantify the extent of casualization and externalization and how this has eroded labour protection in South Africa. The report notes that these questions cannot be answered by reference to official sources of statistics and contains recommendations to address the inadequate collection and analysis of data. The report proposes an extensive package of possible legislative and institutional responses and acknowledges that any changes must take account of relevant costs and benefits to employers, workers and society. However, a NEDLAC negotiation process on this issue is still ongoing and no proposals for draft legislation have yet emerged.[12]

The predominant form of restructuring in South Africa's post-apartheid labour market has been externalization through triangular employment relationships involving employees supplied by temporary employment services ('TES') such as 'labour brokers'. Externalization has also taken the form of outsourcing, subcontracting and the transfer of assets to employees or former employees. There has

---

[12] Department of Labour, 'Synthesis Report: Changing Nature of Work and "Atypical" forms of Employment in South Africa', (unpublished paper, Pretoria, 2004) and J Theron, 'Labour's casualisation cancer spreads' (2005) 29(2) *SA Labour Bulletin* 27–31.

also been an increase in independent contracting as a mechanism to disguise employment, casual employment, the use of short-term or fixed-term contracts and temporary and seasonal work. Firms have reduced standard employment to reduce labour costs and minimise the risks associated with employment. This has produced two forms of labour market segmentation—the first is between full-time employees and those who have been casualized (part-time or temporary workers), and the second is between 'core' enterprise employees and those working through externalized arrangements.

In sectors such as construction and mining, industry subcontracting has expanded to a wider range of operations, including those previously seen as 'core' functions. Massive retrenchment in the clothing industry have led to a marked growth in the informal production of garments, with many manufacturers and retailers sourcing directly from home workers. Similar trends have been noted in the shoe manufacturing sector, which was all but devastated by imports. Retailers have replaced full-time permanent workers with casual and part-time employees, and outsourced activities to smaller companies, or to businesses in the informal sector or home workers. Employer policies to shift the burden of risk such as ill-health (especially HIV-AIDS) onto employees and their families have also contributed to growing informalization. Local government authorities have outsourced functions such as waste disposal to a range of formal and informal contractors.[13]

Recent empirical studies have utilized concepts of social security in relation to work and employment in order to ascertain the extent to which the growth in the informal economy and in atypical forms of formal work has led to work being a source of risk and vulnerability for some categories of workers. An important study of residents of Kwamsane, KwaZulu-Natal divides security into eight separate components: income, health, education, employment and skill reproduction, place of work, demand, capital, and the ability to manage risk.[14] The authors use 18 indicators for the wage employed and six for the self-employed to estimate the extent of formality of employment in order to assess the components of work-related security for those in different employment statuses.

The study tested for the presence or absence of the following 18 attributes for those in wage work:

(i) permanent work;

---

[13] This overview is drawn from the following sources: H Cheadle and M Clarke, 'National Studies on Worker's Protection: South Africa' (Paper prepared for Meeting of Experts on Workers in need of Protection, Geneva, 2000); Webster (n 2); Samson (n 6).

[14] F Lund and C Ardington, 'Employment Status, Security and the Management of Risk: A Study of Workers in Kwamsane, KwaZulu-Natal' (2006) UKZN Centre for Development Studies: Working Paper No 45.

   (ii) job acquired through formal job search;

  (iii) more than five workers;

  (iv) written contract;

   (v) paid by cheque or electronic transfer (not cash);

  (vi) work at fixed location;

 (vii) regular pay;

(viii) paid leave;

  (ix) paid sick leave;

   (x) 13th cheque;

  (xi) bonus;

 (xii) employer contribution to pension fund;

(xiii) employer contribution to medical aid;

(xiv) employer contribution to life insurance;

 (xv) unemployment insurance fund;

(xvi) member of a trade union;

(xvii) protection from arbitrary dismissal;

(xviii) housing allowance (from employer/through place of work).

Using these attributes, those in wage work were classified into three distinct clusters reflecting different levels of formality/ informality.

Self-employed people were separated into two groups: own account workers and employers. The following attributes were used as indicators of the degree of formality of employment:

   (i) regularity of employment (whether the business is considered permanent);

  (ii) regularity of income (how regular income flows are);

 (iii) requires a licence;

 (iv) fixed premises;

  (v) keeps a set of accounts.

These indicators of formality and informality were used to investigate security and risk in different types of employment.

The study concluded that the self-employed were generally more vulnerable than those in wage employment, and that women were more likely to be self-employed than men, often earning less than men. However, those in the least formal wage employment were more vulnerable in a number of respects than the self-employed. Employment status determined access to risk management mechanisms such as savings and insurance; most of those with low incomes (both wage workers and the self-employed) tended not to have work-related risk coverage and could not access services from formal or informal financial service providers. In general, the income security of self-employed people is exceptionally vulnerable to illness, and this will become an increasingly severe constraint in the context of AIDS-related illnesses.

As the authors point out, increasing numbers of people work at the borderline between self-employment and waged employment with the result that the simple distinction between 'formal' and 'informal' conceals a great deal of variation. They therefore argue that it is necessary to find a way of exploring similarities and differences in working conditions across self-employment and waged employment, to see whether there may be a place at the more precarious end of wage employment which has similar characteristics to those found in self-employment. The identification of specific patterns and forms of insecurity may provide a basis for labour law to make a more targeted response to identifying what protections vulnerable workers may require.

4.3 The Notion of the Employment Relationship

In South Africa, as in most other Southern African countries, the employment relationship is defined primarily by distinguishing between employees and independent contractors. This is sourced in the common law distinction between contracts of employment (service) and contracts for services (independent contractor) inherited from South Africa's Roman-Dutch law (common law) orientation.

In South Africa (as well as Namibia), the terminology of contract is introduced through the exclusion from statutory protection of 'independent contractors', a term which is not defined in any of the country's statutes.

An employee is:

(a)   any person, excluding an independent contractor, who works for another person (or the State) and receives, or is entitled to receive, remuneration; and

(b)   any other person who in any manner assists in carrying on or conducting the business of an employer.

The definition of 'employee' was not at issue in the extensive negotiations that led to the adoption of South Africa's post-apartheid 1995 Labour Relations Act. The existing definition was incorporated unaltered into that Act as well the Basic Conditions of Employment Act 75 of 1997('BCEA'), the Employment Equity Act 55 of 1998 ('EEA') and the Skills Development Act 9 of 1999 ('SDA'). The Namibian Labour Act 1992 used the same definition and this has been retained in that country's 2007 Labour Act. While this definition is open to an expansive interpretation, South African courts have tended to interpret it conservatively.

More commonly in the South African Development Community region, countries that limit the scope of the employment relationship to employees engaged under a contract of employment do so by confining their application expressly to those who have a contract of employment. This includes Swaziland's 1980 Employment Act, Botswana's 1982 Employment Act, the Lesotho Labour Code of 1992 and Zimbabwe's 2005 Labour Act. This approach is typically found in older legislation with colonial-era origins in countries such as Nigeria and Kenya. Other statutes in the region that apply a purely contractual definition include South Africa's Compensation for Occupational Injuries and Diseases Act 1993. These definitions typically cover employees working under a contract of employment, whether express or implied and whether oral or in writing.

Two countries that currently have statutory definitions of employment that seek to broaden the categories of protected workers are Swaziland and Tanzania. The Swaziland Industrial Relations Act No 1 of 2000 has a definition which expressly disavows the contractual model and the Tanzanian Employment and Labour Relations Act 2004 also seeks to expand protection to dependent workers who are not employees. Zimbabwe's Labour Act 17 of 2002 introduced a definition of employee which considerably expanded its scope and made 'economic dependence' the key definitional element. However, this was short-lived and was subsequently repealed by the Labour Act 7 of 2005, which restored the previous contractual definition. The implications of these different approaches are examined in greater detail later in this chapter.

Despite the preceding Green Paper, a policy document identifying regulatory problems associated with the non-standard employment, South Africa's 1997 BCEA retained the standard employment relationship as the normative model for employment.[15] While the BCEA's cautiousness has been criticized, it can be attributed to a concern that inadequate information was available at the time on patterns of non-standard employment. The Act did extend greater protection to part-time workers and seasonal and other intermittent workers. An administrative capacity to regulate unprotected work was established within this statutory dispensation by giving the Minister the power to apply provisions in the BCEA or sectoral determination made in terms of it to persons other than employees, however the need for the substantive regulation of non-standard work was not addressed. In 2002, this power of extension was extended to all labour legislation. To date, little use has been

---

[15] S Godfrey and M Clarke, 'The Basic Conditions of Employment Act amendments: More questions than answers' (2002) 6 *Law Democracy and Development* 1.

made of the Ministerial power to extend the scope of laws. However, the Department of Labour has proposed that the Minister should use this power to broaden the restriction on work by under-age children, to achieve full compliance with international instruments regulating child labour. The power to extend the scope of application of labour law by Ministerial notice is also contained in the Namibian and Tanzanian labour statutes.

4.4 The Criteria Defining the Employment Relationship

Traditional Tests

Since 1979, the South African courts[16] have used a multi-factoral 'dominant impression' test to identify who is an employee. This approach, which requires an adjudicator to take a conspectus of all aspects of the employment contract and relationship in the circumstances of each case, is now used by courts in most SADC jurisdictions.

Before this decision, the South African courts, like the courts in many other countries, sought a single definitive touchstone to identify the employment relationship. Since the 1930s, South African courts have been influenced by the English courts. In 1952 the English courts, following the publication of a seminal article by Sir Otto Kahn-Freund, rejected the 'control' test to adopt an 'organization' or 'integration' test.[17]

However, in the decisive *Smit* decision,[18] South Africa's highest court at the time, the Appellate Division of the Supreme Court, rejected both approaches. It held that an employer's right of supervision and control was not the sole defining feature of an employment relationship while also rejecting the 'organization test' as 'vague and nebulous'. Under the 'dominant impression' approach, the existence of a right of supervision or control, while an important consideration, is not conclusive proof of the existence of a contract of employment.

---

[16] *Smit v Workmen's Compensation Commissioner* 1979(1) SA 51 (AD).

[17] Kahn Freund argued that the control test is well suited to identify employment relations where there is a 'combination of managerial and technical functions in the person of the employer'. This assists to identify a relationship such as those between a farmer and a farm worker or a factory owner and an unskilled worker. However, he argued that it was not adequate to deal with the technical and economic developments of 1950s industry (O Kahn-Freund, 'Servants and Independent Contractors' (1951) 14 *Modern Law Review* 504).

[18] *Smit v Workmen's Compensation Commissioner* (n 16).

This decision identified the following factors as being the most important legal characteristics of the contract of service or subordination (employee) and the contract of work (independent contractor):

Contract of service	Contract of work
1. Object of a contract is to render personal services.	Object of contract is to perform a specified work or produce a specified result.
2. Employee must perform services personally.	Contractor may usually perform through others.
3. Employer may choose when to make use of services of employee.	Contractor must perform work (or produce result) within period fixed by contract.
4. Employee obliged to perform lawful commands and instructions of employer.	Contractor is subservient to the contract, not under supervision or control of employer.
5. Contract terminates on death of employee.	Contract does not necessarily terminate on death of employee.
6. Contract also terminates on expiry of period of service in contract.	Contract terminates on completion of work or production of specified result.

The Labour Appeal Court established under the 1995 LRA continued to apply interpreting the definition of an employee in the 1995 Act.

The 'dominant impression' test has been criticized by legal scholars from the outset because it says nothing about the legal nature of the contract of employment and gives no assistance in difficult cases on the border between employment and self-employment.[19] In a 1997 Labour Court decision, Judge R Zondo, who subsequently became the Judge-President of the Labour Appeal Court, echoed these concerns, saying that the 'dominant impression' test was unsatisfactory because of the uncertainty it created.[20] Yet the courts continued to apply it, leaving a very significant and increasing number of workers vulnerable to abuse by employers who deliberately sought to disguise employment relationships as independent contracts.

The 'dominant impression' test also continues to be used to determine the employer's vicarious liability to third parties for wrongful conduct by an employee.

---

[19] E Mureinik, 'The Contract of Service: An Easy Test for Hard Cases' (1980) 97 *South African Law Journal* 246; M Brassey, 'The Nature of Employment' (1990) 18 *Industrial Law Journal* 920.

[20] *Medical Association of SA & others v Minister of Health & another* (1997) 18 ILJ 528 (LC) 536 [D]–[E].

In general terms, an employer will not be liable for the wrongdoing of an independent contractor unless the employer is in some way personally at fault. The courts have described their approach as a 'topological' one in which, in addition to the employer's right to exercise control, factors to be taken into account in determining whether the individual is an employee include:

(a) the existence or non-existence of a right of supervision on the part of the employer;
(b) the manner of payment (whether the employee is paid a fixed rate or by commission);
(c) the relative dependence or freedom of action of the employee in the performance of his or her duties;
(d) the employer's power of dismissal;
(e) whether the employee is preclude from working for another;
(f) whether the employee is required to devote a particular amount of time to his or her work;
(g) whether the employee is obliged to perform his or her duties personally;
(h) the ownership of the working facilities and whether the employee provides his or her own tools and equipment;
(i) the place of work;
(j) the length of time of employment; and
(k) the intention of the parties.[21]

Disguised Employment

The ILO describes 'disguised employment' as an employment relationship that 'is lent an appearance that is other than the underlying reality'.[22] Recommendation 198 proposes that states should introduce a National Policy which includes measures to combat disguised employment. In the immediate aftermath of the enactment of the post-apartheid labour law dispensation, the practice of seeking to exclude workers from labour legislation by 'converting' them into 'independent contractors' became a high-profile issue. A number of labour consultancies, notably COFESA,[23] were proponents of this approach. Employees were advised that the expedient of changing the language of contracts would allow them to avoid the clutches of

---

[21] *Stein v Rising Tide Productions CC* (2002) 23 ILJ 2017 (C) 2024
[22] ILO, *The Scope of the Employment Relationship* (Geneva, 2003) 24.
[23] The Confederation of Employers South Africa (COFESA) was established in 1990 as both a labour consultancy and an employers' organization.

labour laws and policies without in any way adjusting shop-floor practices. After some hesitation, the South African courts have shown an increasing awareness of the extent of this issue and have managed to fashion an effective legal response to the cruder forms of disguised employment. This has required the courts to move away from an approach focused on the wording of the contract.

The conventional approach to identifying a contract of employment proceeded from the premise that the legal relationship must be gathered from a construction of the contract between worker and employer. However, in subsequent cases, the courts have had to confront the discrepancies between contractual wording and the realities of working life. In a 1998 decision, *Niselow v Liberty Life*, the Supreme Court of Appeal indicated that when categorising an employment relationship, the terms of the contract could be departed from if a party contended that the contract was a simulated transaction, had been amended or was vague and ambiguous.[24] However, the onus of establishing this lay on the party making that allegation: in these circumstances, the employee.

The Court's responded to the rise of disguised employment by adopting an approach whereby the contractual relationship is not definitive as to the nature of the legal relationship, and a court must examine the true nature of the relationship between the parties, particularly where a party is induced into a relationship that deprives him or her of the protection granted by the status of employment.[25] The courts have characterized contracts in which employees are 'converted' into independent contractors without any change in how they perform their work as a 'bizarre subterfuge'[26] and a 'cruel hoax and sham'[27] to deprive employees of the protection of labour law.[28] By the time of these decisions, the Department of Labour published proposals in 2000 to introduce a presumption of employment into legislation as a response to this form of disguised employment. A number of

---

[24]   At 166A.

[25]   *Rumbles v Kwa-Bat Marketing* (2003) 24 ILJ 1587 (LC). This approach is similar to that adopted by the British courts. In *Young and Woods Ltd v West* [1980] IRLR 20 (CA) the Court of Appeal upheld the approach of the Employment Appeal Tribunal to look beyond the contractual expression of the relationship to decide whether the individual was an employee as a matter of fact. The Court notes that the failure to do this would make employees vulnerable to being pressed into self-employment by employers wishing to avoid statutory responsibilities.

[26]   *Motor Industry Bargaining Council v Mac-Rites Panel Beaters and Spray Painters (Pty) Ltd* (2001) 22 ILJ 1077 (N) 1091 [I]–[J].

[27]   *Building Bargaining Council (Southern & Eastern Cape) v Melmon's Cabinets CC & another* (2001) 22 ILJ 120 (LC) [21].

[28]   Treating genuine employees as independent contractors can have disastrous consequences for the employers concerned, particularly where there is effective enforcement. Bargaining councils have succeeded in having employers who do not register with the council jailed for contempt of a court order requiring them to register with the council (*Business Day* 8 June 2000).

arbitrators also made awards in which they expressed a preference for an 'economic realities' approach to analysing working relationships.[29]

These cases dealt with low-skilled workers who were pressurized into accepting a fraudulent independent contractor status. In another line of decisions, the Labour Courts have dealt with cases of disguised employment in which skilled personnel have voluntarily assumed the status of independent contractors in order to obtain tax benefits. When this relationship sours and the contractor seeks to reclaim the status of employee in order to obtain compensation or reinstatement on the basis of an unfair dismissal, the courts initially have been unwilling to assist the employee because (in the language of one of the judgments) they are seeking to 'have their cake and eat it'.

In *CMS Support Services v Briggs*,[30] the Labour Appeal Court dealt with a case in which a consultant had provided services through a closed corporation, to obtain tax advantages. The Court found that as there was no personal contract between the respondent and the employee—the consultant was not an employee. This conclusion was reached on the basis of an examination of the contract alone, and the court emphasized that the contractual relationship was the primary mechanism for determining the relationship. Likewise, the Labour Court case of *Bezer v Cruiser International CC*[31] concerned an employee who established a closed corporation at the suggestion of her employer, even though the day-to-day relationship did not change: the employer continued to set her hours of employment and the employee was not entitled to work for other clients. The court found that while the relationship remained in substance one of employment,[32] the claimant was not an employee, because of her election to contract through the closed corporation.[33] These two decisions gave precedence to form over substance by holding employees to a legal characterization of their employment relationship which differs from the underlying reality because they voluntarily agreed to that characterization in order to obtain benefits under different legislation. This approach, it is suggested, misconstrues the nature of disguised employment, focusing only on the benefit gained by the employee and not on the advantages for the employer or the cost to the State. In neither case did the Court ask, as they are required to do by the second leg of the definition of an employee, whether the individual assisted the employer to conduct its business.[34]

---

[29] Thompson and Benjamin, *South African Labour Law* BB1–4.

[30] *CMS Support Services v Briggs* (1998) 19 ILJ 271(LAC).

[31] *Bezer v Cruiser International CC* (2003) 24 ILJ 1372 (LAC).

[32] ibid [55].

[33] ibid [57].

[34] *Niselow v Liberty Life Association of SA Ltd* 1998(4) SA 163 (SCA) 168F.

The introduction in 2002 of presumptions of employment in s 200A of the LRA and s 83A of the BCEA has resulted in the Court being less inclined to assist employers who persuade high-level employees to utilise alternative corporate forms to disguise employment in a manner that the parties assume to be mutually beneficial.

One such case is *Denel (Pty) Ltd v Gerber*,[35] which concerned an individual who claimed to be an employee even though she was 'employed' by a private company which in turn had been contracted to provide services to a client. The Labour Appeal Court found that in reality, Gerber was employed by Denel (Pty) Ltd and that the Labour Court had jurisdiction to consider her unfair dismissal claim. The LAC then added an important caveat. Since the employee had represented to the tax authorities that she had been employed by a number of entities other than Denel (Pty) Ltd, she was required to correct any misrepresentation she had made to them. In other words, the Court was indicating that an employee could only expect the assistance of the Labour Courts if she accepted that all public authorities should treat her as an employee, even where this was to her disadvantage.

The prominent labour lawyer Andre Van Niekerk[36] criticized this decision on the basis that where parties agree, quite lawfully and in anticipation of whatever advantage they perceive, services should be supplied on an independent contractor–client basis. This should not be disregarded only because on the facts the relationship bears some resemblance to a contract of employment. He argues that public policy should frown on the employee who wants the benefit of not being an employee yet, when the relationship breaks down, the benefit of being an employee. It is suggested that this argument repeats the error that distinguished the reasoning in earlier cases such as *Briggs* because it fails to take into account the fact that 'disguised employment' between an employer and a well-paid worker for their assumed mutual benefit amounts to a misrepresentation to the state by both parties as it excludes the employee from social security schemes such as skills development, unemployment and worker's compensation. While it may not be appropriate on policy grounds to give such an employee effective unfair dismissal protection, this should be done without accepting their characterization of the employee as a self-employed person operating its own business, when this evidently is not the case. It is suggested that the approach of the South African Labour Appeal Court in *Denel v Gerber* is an appropriate method of resolving this dilemma.

---

[35]   *Denel (Pty) Ltd v Gerber* [2005] 9 BLLR 849 (LAC).
[36]   A van Niekerk, 'The Definition of an employee revisited' (2005) 15(2) *Contemporary Labour Law* 11.

Paul Benjamin

Tests Introduced by Statutory Presumption and the Code of Good Practice

The Presumption

In 2002 the South African Government introduced a rebuttable presumption of employment into the principal labour statutes.[37] This was accompanied by a direction to the National Economic Development and Labour Council to prepare a Code of Good Practice to provide guidance in identifying whether an employment relationship exists. The presumption was a response to the widespread practice of disguised employment through 'independent' contracting described above.

The presumption applies only to employees earning below a prescribed earnings threshold[38] but applies irrespective of the contractual arrangement in terms of which a worker is hired. It is triggered if the worker can show that one of a number of factors listed in the Act is present in the working relationship. The employer must then show that the worker is not an employee. These factors are:

(a) the manner in which the person works is subject to the control or direction of another person;

(b) the person's hours of work are subject to the control or direction of another person;

(c) in the case of a person who works for an organization, the person forms part of that organization;

(d) the person has worked for that other person for an average of at least 40 hours per month over the previous three months;

(e) the person is economically dependent on the person for whom he or she works or renders services;

(f) the person is provided with tools of trade or work equipment by the other person; or

(g) the person only works for or renders services to one person.

Five of the seven factors reflect considerations that formed part of the conventional approach to identifying employment relationships. However, two of the factors are worthy of particular comment because they signify an intention to break with the past. The inclusion of a version of the 'organization' test appears to indicate an intention to reintroduce elements of this approach rejected more than

---

[37] The presumption is found in s 200A of the Labour Relations Act 66 of 1995 and s 83A of the Basic Conditions of Employment Act 75 of 1997.

[38] R115 572 with effect from 14 March 2003. See GNR 356 GG 25012.

two decades earlier. However, it is introduced as one of the factors that trigger the presumption, not as a single decisive test of employment. The presumption introduces the notion of 'economic dependence' into South African law and the courts are now required to give meaning to this term. The Code of Good Practice provides extensive guidance on this issue which we examine in the following section.

A concrete example that highlights the significance of economic dependence as a factor is the position of 'home workers' who undertake work for manufacturers in the clothing industry. An application of conventional approaches might lead one to hold that they are not employees either because they are not supervised in their work or because they are engaged to perform specified tasks (for instance, sowing a garment or part of a garment). Neither of these factors relate to the relative bargaining position of the workers who may be in a position of real economic dependence on those employers who supply them with work. In evaluating whether these home-workers are employees or not, the court must consider whether they conduct their own business.

It has been suggested that the presumption offers an opportunity to initiate a process of challenging the assumptions that underlie the traditional distinction between employees and independent contractors.[39] While the courts have had limited opportunity to apply the presumption to the position of marginal workers, the introduction of the presumption has given the Labour Appeal Court the confidence to apply an increasingly purposive interpretation to the issue of who is an employee.

In the first of these judgments, the court held that the definition of an 'employee' includes a person who has concluded a contract of employment to commence work at a future date but who has not yet started work. The court acknowledged that while this construction did not accord with a literal construction of the definition of an employee, an expansive interpretation was justified to avoid hardship and absurdity and was consistent with the progressive legislative development of labour protection.[40] This approach is consistent with that of the Constitutional Court, which adopted a purposive approach when interpreting the definition of the term 'worker' in s 23(2) of the Constitution to include military personnel who are expressly excluded from the ambit of the LRA and other labour legislation.[41] In *Denel v Gerber*, discussed earlier, the LAC held that even where the

---

[39] J Theron, 'The erosion of workers rights and the presumption as to who is an employee' (2002) 6 *Law, Democracy and Development* 1.

[40] *Wyeth SA (Pty) Ltd & others v Manqele* (2005) 26 ILJ 749 (LAC).

[41] *SANDU v Minister of Defence and Another* 1999 (4) SA 469 (CC).

presumption does not apply because the employee is above the threshold of earnings, the factors listed may nevertheless be used as a guide for the purposes of determining whether the true nature of the relationship between the parties is one of employment.

In a very significant decision in 2009, the Labour Appeal Court has held that there are three 'primary criteria' for determining whether a person is an employee. These are:

(a) an employer's right to supervision and control;
(b) whether the employee forms an integral part of the organization with the employer;
(c) the extent to which the employee is economically dependent upon the employer.[42]

The presence of any one of these three factors is sufficient to establish in ordinary circumstances that the person is an employee. The fact that these primary criteria have been identified does not preclude an employee relying on other factors associated with the 'dominant impression' test although this is only likely to occur in the most exceptional of cases.

The extent to which South African courts have moved away from reliance on a contractual model of employment is also captured by the Labour Court in *White v Pan Palladium SA (Pty) Ltd*,[43]:

> The existence of an employment relationship is therefore not dependent solely upon the conclusion of a contract recognized at common law as valid and enforceable. Someone who works for another, assists that other in his business and receives remuneration may, under the statutory definition qualify as an employee even if the parties inter se have not yet agreed on all the relevant terms of the agreement by which the wish to regulate their contractual relationship.

Code of Good Practice

The Department of Labour's Code of Good Practice: Who is an Employee (Notice 1774 of 2006, GG 29445, 1 December 2006) was developed to provide guidance on identifying the employment relationship. The Code was developed by the tripartite forum NEDLAC over a three-year period. Its final text was revised to ensure

---

[42] *State Information Technology Agency (Pty) Ltd v Commission for Conciliation Mediation & Arbitration & others* (2008) 29 ILJ 2234 (LAC); *Pam Golding Properties v Erasmus & others* (2010) 31 ILJ 1460 (LC).
[43] *White v Pan Palladium SA (Pty) Ltd* (2006) 27 ILJ 2721 (LC) 2727[J]–2728[A].

consistency with the ILO Recommendation 198, a copy of which is attached to it. The Code provides guidelines for interpreting diverse forms of employment relationships, including ambiguous employment relationships, disguised employment, atypical or non-standard employment and triangular employment relationships. The Code seeks to locate the issue of identifying employment relationship within the context of purposive legislative interpretation. The Code emphasizes that no single factor is decisive of an employment relationship and encourages adjudicators to examine the realities of each relationship rather than confining themselves to the legal structuring.

The Code is a 'soft law' policy document which serves as an aide to the interpretation of the law. It does not create new obligations or alter the statutory definition. The Code endorses the approach taken by the LAC in *Denel v Gerber* that where the presumption does not apply because the employee falls above the threshold of earnings, the factors listed may nevertheless be used as a guide for the purposes of determining whether the true nature of the relationship between the parties is one of employment. The Code analyses the factors listed in the presumption, as well as the distinction drawn in the common law between independent contractors and employees. It also lists other factors that are significant in determining the existence of an employment relationship. These include:

— *Remuneration and benefits.* The Code emphasizes that the fact that an employee receives fixed payments at regular intervals regardless of output is not necessarily definitive of an employment relationship in the same way that variable payments do not necessarily indicate the existence of an independent contracting relationship. The Code emphasizes that the manner and method of payment is one factor that may, along with others, lead to the conclusion that a person is or is not an employee. In this regard, the Code can be seen as be somewhat more equivocal than the Recommendation[44] which identifies the 'periodic payment of remuneration' to the worker as a potential as an indicator of an employment relationship.

— *Provision of training.* The Code stipulates that in general the provision of training indicates an employment relationship but that training as part of a contractual relationship is not necessarily inconsistent with an independent contractor relationship.

— *Place of work.* The Code states that regular work at the employer's premises generally point to employment, but that this is not necessarily the case. Where work involves repairs or other services that have to be performed at the

---

[44] See para 13(b).

employer's premises, or where the independent contractor leases premises from the employer, the place of work is not definitive. In fact, in certain instances employees such as home workers may be required to work outside the employer's premises, but are still subject to the employer's control and may even use the employer's tools

The Code suggests that 'economic dependence' as a factor listed in the presumption, will not be present if the applicant is genuinely self-employed or retains the capacity to contract in the market. On the other hand, a part-time employee may be economically dependent on a number of part-time employment contracts, or a full-time employee may also be allowed to take on other work in his/her spare time, but this will not mean the employment relationship no longer exists. Economic dependence therefore relates to the entrepreneurial position of the person in the marketplace. An important indicator that a person is not dependent economically is that he or she is entitled to offer skills or services to persons other than his or her employer. The fact that a person is required by contract only to provide services for a single 'client' is a very strong indication of economic dependence. Likewise, depending upon an employer for the supply of work is a significant indicator of economic dependence.

The CCMA and Labour Court have now adopted an approach according to which they look beyond the legal structuring of the relationship and ascertain the true nature of the relationship. This has enabled them to reject fabricated independent contractual arrangements and focus on the 'underlying economic realities'. 'Difficult' cases in which there has been a finding that an individual is an employee include the following:

(a) An estate agent engaged as an independent contractor and paid only commission was an employee because of the degree of control that the company and its managers had over the agent.[45]

(b) An individual retrenched after 30 years' service and immediately re-engaged to do the same work as an independent contractor was an employee even though she signed a number of contracts with the respondent and another entity to supply her services. As the individual was ignorant of the nature or purpose of the agreement with the second entity, the agreement was not binding on her.[46]

(c) An individual described in his contract as a 'subcontractor' and paid on presentation of invoices for work performed was an employee. Factors

---

[45] *Linda Erasmus Properties Enterprise (Pty) Ltd v Mhlongo & others* [2007] 6 BLLR 530 (LC)).

[46] *De Greeve v Old Mutual Employee Benefits/Life Assurance Co (SA) Ltd* [2004] 2 BALR 184 (CCMA).

influencing this decision were that the applicant's pay was calculated on an hourly basis, he had been required to utilize the company's clock card system, his assistants were also remunerated by the employer and the employer had a practice of appoint subcontractors as employees after a period if they performed their work satisfactorily.[47]

(d)   Workers covered by a framework casual employment agreement regulating a pool of about 2,000 workers whom the employer, a parastatal operator of harbours, could drawn upon to meet its day-to-day demands for labour were classified as a 'special class of employees', even though they did not have an individual contract and had no right to be engaged to perform casual work.[48]

(e)   A medical intern, who was instructed to vacate her post at the end of her internship, was deemed an employee, as she had received a salary and had been occupied full-time in the service of the respondent.[49]

(f)   A sex worker employed by a massage parlour is an employee despite the fact that prostitution is a criminal offence for both the sex worker and the client. The Labour Appeal Court concluded that despite sex work being unlawful, sex workers should be entitled to the benefit of the constitutional right to fair labour practices unless it would be contrary to public policy to grant a legal remedy. The Court held that while it would be inappropriate for a sex work to be reinstated or compensated for a dismissal without a valid reason they should nevertheless be accorded a hearing before dismissal. The court also held that it would be inappropriate to allow a trade union of sex workers to register for the purposes of collective bargaining.[50]

On the other hand, cases in which there has been a finding that the claimant was not an employee include:

(a)   An individual who was paid a monthly cash retainer to assist a company with its labour relations and who performed certain tasks for it on one or two days a month at the company's premises was not an employee. He had no office, the company respondent had no control over his working hours and he referred to the company in all correspondence as a client.[51]

(b)   An individual who operated a franchise in terms of a franchise agreement was

[47]   *Durand & another v C A Engineering* [2005] 10 BALR 1033 (MEIBC).
[48]   *NUCCAWU v Transnet t/a Portnet* (2000) 21 ILJ 2288 (LC).
[49]   *Andreanis v Department of Health* [2006] 5 BALR 461 (PHWSBC).
[50]   *'Kylie' v CCMA & others* (Case No. CA 10/08).. The prominent labour lawyer Halton Cheadle, hearing the matter as an Acting Judge of the Labour Court had earlier concluded that while sex workers were employees, it would be contrary to public policy for the courts to grant them any relief in respect of a claim for unfair dismissal. See *'Kylie v CCMA & others* (2008) 29 ILJ 1918(LC).
[51]   *Quinn v Hendrik Sand van Heerden (Pty) Ltd* [2007] JOL 1975 (CCMA)

an independent contractor and not an employee. While the franchiser company assisted him by allocating clients, he was not economically dependent as he also sourced his own clients and was responsible for his own profitability. The fact that he operated under the franchiser's brand did not make him an employee.[52]

(c)   An applicant who was a member of an organization which placed individuals as 'independent contractors' at various sites to act as security guards was not an employee.[53]

(d)   A newspaper art critic was not an employee, as the newspaper was not bound to accept his contributions; he was free to work for other publications and was not treated in the same way as other employees..[54]

(e)   An applicant who was employed to file reports and was paid per report was an independent contractor. Nothing prevented the applicant from working for persons other than the respondent, and the respondent did not regulate his hours of work.[55]

(f)   A trainee on a bursary loan from the respondent to help him attend college was not an employee, in spite of the fact that he worked occasionally for the respondent during his training.[56]

(g)   A freelance radio talk show host was an independent contractor because the parties had a contract providing that a radio announcer would provide the talk show through a close corporation.[57]

(h)   An individual, who had concluded a partnership agreement that was a bona fide statement of the terms of the relationship of the parties, was not an employee.[58]

These cases show the extent to which adjudicators have taken an increasingly wide range of factors into account in endeavouring to identify the true nature of employment relationships. Nevertheless, a tendency to resolve matters by reference to contractual language has not been totally eradicated.

---

[52] *Rodgers v Assist-U-Drive* (2006) 27 ILJ 855 (CCMA).
[53] *Hanyane v Urban Protection Services* [2005] 10 BALR 1086 (CCMA).
[54] *Lewis v Independent Newspapers Cape Times* [2002] 11 BALR 1162 (CCMA).
[55] *Kaingane v Trio Data Business Risk Consultant* [2004] 12 BALR 1538 (CCMA).
[56] *Mokone v Highveld Steel and Vanadium* [2005] 12 BALR 1245 (MEIBC).
[57] *Jordison v Primedia Broadcasting (Pty) Ltd* [2000] 2 BALR 140 (CCMA).
[58] *Greyling v Appies Inc* [2007] JOL 18869 (CCMA).

Sectoral Responses

A significant proportion of South African workers have their minimum conditions of employment, including minimum wages determined by sectorally specific standards. There are two sources of these standards:

Collective agreements negotiated by bargaining councils, which are voluntary statutory collective bargaining institutions that allow trade unions and employer's organizations to bargain wages and minimum conditions of employment for their sectors. Subject to representivity criteria, these agreements may be extended by the Minister of Labour to all employees in the sector. Presently, 41 bargaining councils covering a total of approximately 900,000 employees operate in the private sector.[59] In 2002, the statutory functions of bargaining councils were extended to include 'extending the services and functions of the council to workers in the informal sector and home workers'.

Sectoral determinations made by the Minister of Labour on the advice of the Employment Conditions Commission which set minimum conditions of employment including minimum wages for unorganized sectors. This has led to the setting of minimum wages for the first time for domestic workers, farm workers, forestry workers and in the highly informal taxi and hospitality sectors. In addition, minimum wages continue to be set for contract cleaning, wholesale and retail, and private security.

These sectoral instruments contain a range of responses seeking to ensure the adequate protection of vulnerable employees. These include:

(a) The Building Industry Bargaining Council in the Western Cape has used a range of strategies to regulate outsourcing to labour-only subcontractors get compliance with their agreements. The Council obtained the agreement of the institutions that provide and finance large-scale housing to only contract builders registered with the Council. The Council also introduced a clause into its agreement that prohibits subcontracting to unregistered firms. The Council has also offered services, including a payroll service and an employment bureau, to attract smaller employers to the Council. The result has been a steady increase in the number of employers, particularly small employers and subcontractors, registered with the Council and complying with its agreements.[60]

---

[59] S Godfrey, J Maree, D du Toit and J Theron, *Collective Bargaining in South Africa: Past, Present and Future* (Cape Town, Juta, 2010).

[60] Goldman, T (2003) 'Organising in the informal economy: A Case Study of the Building Industry in South Africa' (Geneva, ILO); S Godfrey, J Theron and M Visser (2007) 'The State of Collective Bargaining in SA', Working Paper, Development and Policy Research Unit, University of Cape Town, 2007.

(b)   Trade liberalization and the huge influx of cheap shoes brought the local footwear industry to the verge of collapse. The retrenchment of footwear workers saw an upsurge in informal shoe-making operations and home working, undermining the labour standards set by the Leather Industry Bargaining Council. Employers and unions responded by revising the footwear collective agreement to classify firms into one of three categories: formal, semi-formal and informal. Firms categorized as formal pay 100 per cent of the set wage rate and comply with the rest of the agreement (although negotiations at the company level can reduce the wage rate to 80 per cent). Semi-formal firms comply with the agreement but are required to pay only 75 per cent of the set wage rates (although negotiations at the company level can reduce the wage rate to 60 per cent). Informal firms are excluded from the agreement entirely (but must still register with the Council).[61]

(c)   The National Bargaining Council for the Road Freight Industry requires 'owner-driver' individuals who are employers while at the same time drivers, to comply with the limits on working hours applicable to employees.

(d)   A number of bargaining councils regulate the operation of temporary employment services in their sector.

(e)   The sectoral determination for domestic workers applies to domestic workers who are independent contractors.

(f)   The sectoral determination for the retail sector deals allows part-time employees (those working less than 27 hours per week) to receive the same benefits on a proportional basis as full-time employees or to be paid a cash premium instead of benefits.[62]

4.5   The Scope of the Employment Relationship in Other African Countries

In this section, we examine the approach taken by both legislators and adjudicators to identify employment relationships in several different Southern African jurisdictions. A range of different influences contribute to a complex pattern of

---

[61]   S Godfrey, J Theron & M Visser (2007) (n 61).

[62]   The determination provides two models for employing workers who work less than 27 hours a week. The employee and employer may agree that the employee receive a wage that is 25% higher than the prescribed minimum wage. Employees who conclude such an agreement do not qualify for a night shift allowance, paid sick leave, family responsibility leave and only receive two weeks of annual leave, while other employees receive three. Part-time employees who do not conclude these agreements receive all benefits on a proportional basis.

similarity and difference within the region. In this regard, mention should be made of the differences in legal traditions between, for example, the French-speaking and the English-speaking African countries. Herewith, some examples on how the determination of the criteria of the employment relationship is dealt with in law and practice.

Namibia

The Namibian Labour Act 2007 defines an employee as:

> an individual, other than an independent contractor, who—
>
> (a)   works for another person and who receives, or is entitled to receive, remuneration for that work; or
>
> (b)   in any manner assists in carrying on or conducting the business of an employer.

The definition is the same as that in South African labour legislation except that the exclusion of 'independent contractors' is contained in the stem (the opening words) rather than in sub-paragraph (a) as in the South African version. This definition was included in Namibia's first post-independence labour statute, the Labour Act of 1992, an omnibus labour code developed with considerable ILO assistance and retained in the 2004 Labour Act, which was passed by Parliament but never came into force.

However, as the South African courts have held that persons who are independent contractors are excluded from both elements of the definition of an employee, the effect is the same. Accordingly, the Namibian definition amounts to a less ambiguous version of the South African approach.[63]

One consequence of locating the Namibian definition within the omnibus labour 'code', which deals with all aspects of employment law including occupational health and safety, is to restrict the coverage of occupational health and safety law to employees who are covered by other labour laws. This is unlike South Africa, where the Occupational Health and Safety Act 1993 has a significantly wider definition of an 'employee'. A further consequence is that it restricts the application of the prohibition on child labour to the employment of children as employees, rather than a wider range of work performed by children.

---

[63]   The only reported judgment in Namibia on the scope of the employment definition is one in which a judge unsuccessfully claimed to be an employee.

Paul Benjamin

Swaziland

The definition of an employee in the Swaziland Industrial Relations Act No 1 of 2000 is an example of a definition that seeks to extend the scope of the legislation to workers other than contractual employees. The Act defines an 'employee' as:

> a person, whether or not the person is an employee at common law, who works for pay or other remuneration under a contract of service or under any other arrangement involving control by, or sustained dependence for the provision of work upon, another person.

This definition explicitly extends the scope of the Industrial Relations Act to two categories of workers who may not be able to establish that they have contracts of employment. These are:

(a) any person who works under an arrangement in terms of which that person is under the control of another person;

(b) any person who works under an arrangement in terms of which there is a sustained dependence for the provision of work upon another person.

The Swaziland Labour Court has described the implications of this definition in the following manner:

> This extended definition means that the Industrial Court may even have jurisdiction over independent contractors and their principals, provided that the necessary degree of control or sustained dependence for work is shown to be present in the relationship … The Act extends its protection to 'quasi-employees' who, while not being employees, are nevertheless to be distinguished from autonomous self-employed persons because they are subject to a degree of control or dependence which makes them vulnerable to exploitation or unfair treatment … It is not necessary to lay down a demarcation line for Swaziland, but it is safe to say that where a natural person earns his livelihood solely from services rendered to one other person or institution, then he is regarded as an employee whether the services are rendered under a contract of service or some other arrangement.[64]

In this case, an individual employed by Swazi TV in 1993 as a 'commissioned salesperson' and later as a 'Freelance Sales Advertising Executive' was found not to be an employee under the extended definition in the 2000 Act. He was paid a commission on all sales he generated, as well as a petrol allowance, but was responsible for his own business expenses and transport. The contract made no provision for supervision or control of the manner in which he worked. This led the

---

[64] *Percy Lokotfwako v Swaziland Broadcasting Corporation t/a Swazi TV* (151/2007).

court to conclude that he was not a conventional employee and it then inquired whether he may have been a 'quasi-employee' in terms of the extended definition of employee because of control by, or sustained dependence for work upon, Swazi TV.

The Court found an absence of control as he had no fixed hours of work, was not subject to discipline for failing to meet his target, did not work from the company's premises and was given free rein in the manner in which he secured advertising contracts. A requirement that he conduct and dress himself properly did not in the Court's view indicate any significant degree of control. As the contract did not preclude him from working for others and did not require him to personally render the contracted services, the Court held that he could not be said to be dependent upon Swazi TV for work. The Court pointed out no further evidence was before the Court of his dependence for the supply of work.[65]

A number of aspects of this definition are worthy of comment. Firstly, the definition expressly states that there are persons who may be covered who are not employees under the common law. This makes it abundantly clear that the purpose of the definition includes covering persons who have not concluded a contract of employment. Secondly, in creating an extended category of employees beyond the confines of the common law, the statute does not make use of the terminology of contract. The use of the term 'arrangement' may well lower the burden of what a worker must establish to show that they fall into one of these two categories by making the question of whether a contract came into existence irrelevant. Thirdly, in creating the extended category of employees, the definition identifies two elements, either of which is sufficient to trigger coverage by the Act. These are the presence of control or a sustained dependence for the provision of work. The emphasis on control is important as in the case of vulnerable employees, the presence of control remains the most important indicator that a relationship is one of employment. The notion of 'sustained dependence for the provision of work' is a narrower formulation than the notion of 'economic dependence' included in the presumption of employment in the South African and Tanzanian statutes. However, the linking of dependence to the provision of work targets the source of dependence with greater clarity making issues of interpretation and application more certain.

Swaziland's Employment Act No 5 of 1980 continues to define an employee in purely contractual terms. An 'employee' is 'any person to whom wages are paid or are payable under a contract of employment'. The term 'contract of employment' is

---

[65] ibid.

in turn defined as a 'a contract of service, apprenticeship or traineeship whether it is express or implied and, if it is express, whether it is oral or in writing'.

The inconsistent usage of the definition of an employee in Swaziland's labour legislation creates very significant anomalies with non-contractual 'quasi-employees' having collective labour rights under the Industrial Relations Act, but no protection against unfair dismissal or minimum standards on issues such as hours of work and leave, for instance, which are dealt with in the Employment Act. They are also excluded from the wage-fixing machinery. This inconsistency may have the consequence that Swaziland's Parliament is in default of its obligations under the country's constitution. Section 32(4) of the Constitution of Swaziland requires Parliament to enact laws to:

(c) ensure that every *worker* is accorded rest and reasonable working hours and periods of holidays with pay as well as remuneration for public holidays; and

(d) protect *employees* from victimization and unfair dismissal or treatment.

The Employment Act is currently subject to review and hopefully this opportunity will be used to end this anomaly.

United Republic of Tanzania

The Tanzanian Employment and Labour Relations Act 2004 defines an employee as:

an individual who has –

(a) has entered into a contract of employment;

(b) has entered into any other contract under which:

(i) the individual undertakes to work individually for the other party to the contract; and

(ii) the other party is not a client or customer of any profession, business or undertaking carried on by the individual.' (section 4)

This expanded definition of an 'employee' is supplemented by the relevant minister having the power to deem individuals falling outside the definition as employees as well as a presumption of employment modelled on the South African provision. While there are significant influences from the South African LRA in the Tanzanian legislation, the definition of an 'employee' is drawn from the definition of a 'worker' contained in s 230(3) of the UK Employment Rights Act 1996. The concept of worker has been described as creating a 'middle category' between employee and self-employed.[66] The UK Employment Appeals tribunal has said that this provision must be understood in the light of its purpose of extending labour law to some of the people who do not fall under the definition of an employee and have used an 'economic dependence' test to determine whether individuals fall within this broadened definition.[67] However, unlike the Swaziland definition discussed above, the extending provision does use the language of contract.

Lesotho

As indicated in the preceding section, the Lesotho Labour Code, 1992 has a contractual definition of an employee. The scope of the Lesotho Labour Code emerges from a series of interlocking definitions:

(a) An employee is a person who works under a contract of employment with an employer.

(b) A contract of employment is a contract in terms of which an employee enters into the service of an employer.

(c) An employer is any person who employs any person under a contract of employment.

Like Namibia, these definitions are located in an omnibus statute. A draft Bill currently being debated by Lesotho's National Advisory Committee on Labour (NACOLA) has recommended that the definition of an 'employee' be broadened for the purpose of the regulation of 'child labour' and occupational health and safety.

The Lesotho Code contains a separate definition of a 'domestic servant' as 'any person *employed* in or about a private residence' in a range of different capacities which are specified in the definition. A significant difference of opinion has emerged over the significance of this separate definition. Arbitrators in Lesotho's Directorate of Dispute Resolution and Prevention (DDPR) have interpreted the fact of this definition as signifying an intention to exclude domestic workers from the ambit of the legislation and have therefore rejected claims for unfair dismissal brought by domestic workers on the basis that they fall outside of the scope of the Act. On the other hand, the Lesotho Government treats domestic workers as falling within the scope of the law and utilises the wage-setting machinery in the Act to set

---

[66] ACL Davies, *Perspectives on Labour Law* (Cambridge, CUP, 2004) 87.

[67] Davies (n 66) 88.

minimum wages for 'domestic servants'.[68] There is no doubt that the latter view is the preferred one. The fact of a separate definition of a specific category of employees such as 'domestic servants' does not in itself indication an intention to exclude them form the relevant legislation in the absence of any express exclusion. This conclusion is strengthened by the fact that the definition of domestic servants uses the term 'employed' which supports the conclusion that they are a sub-category of employees.

Arbitrators of Lesotho's DDPR have had to deal with a number of cases involving triangular employment relationships. In one such case, an arbitrator ruled that workers who were employed by a cell-phone provider without written contracts but in accordance with its HR Procedures were employees of the company and not of services company to whom the cell-phone provider had outsourced the running of a call centre. The approach of the arbitrator was that, in the absence of a written contract, the nature of the relationship had to be inferred from the conduct of the parties. Factors that influenced the arbitrator to conclude that they were employees of the cell-phone provider were that it had given them an induction programme and that their entitlement to leave and staff benefits such as medical aid, death cover and cell phone had been determined in accordance with the company's HR Manual.[69]

Outsourcing arrangements also come to the fore in two arbitrations arising out a decision by a car-rental firm to outsource their security services to a security company that was to be formed by the company's chief of security. The service agreement was concluded while the security company was in an incipient stage and had not obtained either a trading licence or a registered office. In the first case heard, the company raised as a defence to a claim for unfair dismissal brought against it by the security guards that they had been employed by their chief security officer in his personal capacity. This argument was rejected, on the basis that the relationship between the car-hire company and its chief security officer was not one of independent contracting. Factors that they took into account were that the company was its only client, the chief of security was guaranteed work by the car-hire company and the security company was the car-hire company's 'own creation'. Applying what it termed an 'economic realities' approach, the arbitrator found that chief security officer's economic dependence on the car-hire firm meant that he was still one of its employees and that he had engaged the security officers on behalf of the car-hire firm. The arbitrator was severely critical of a large international company engaging an unlicensed company to meet its security commitments.[70]

---

[68]   S Msweti, 'Labour Talk' (2003) 6(46) *Public Eye*.
[69]   *Motsieloa Lebete and Itumeleng Makoetlane v Vodacom Lesotho* (DDPR A0142/05).
[70]   *Ntahli Motlane and 18 others v Imperial Fleet Services (Pty) Ltd* (DDPR A 1089/02)

However, in a subsequent case, a different arbitrator reached the conclusion that because the service agreement with security officer had been concluded prior to the security guards commencing employment and because the car-hire firm had no contracts of employment with the security guards they were not its employees.[71] The arbitrator in this case accepted the car-hire firm's explanation that the reason it had paid the security guards was because it was assisting their former employee to set up a security business. The arbitrator in the previous case had accepted that this was an indication supporting the employee's view that they were employees of the security company.

In another case, an arbitrator used the factors listed in the presumption of employment in South African labour legislation as a basis for concluding in a default hearing that in the absence of evidence from the employer that a sales consultant (referred to as an 'independent field agent') who recruited clients for a business and was paid on a commission basis was an independent contractor and not an employee. The arbitrator was influenced by the fact that the company exercised no control over the individual's days and hours of work.[72]

Zimbabwe

Zimbabwe has traditionally had a contractual test to determine what a statutory employee is. For instance, the Labour Relations Act 1985 defined an employee as:

> any person employed by or working for an employer and receiving or entitled to receive any remuneration in respect of such employment or work.

It also defined a contractor as:

> a person who renders to an employer services which are related to or connected with the employer's undertaking.

These definitions have been interpreted as reflecting the common law distinction between contracts of employment and contracts of service.

The Zimbabwean courts have been influenced by the approach of the South African courts. Initially a 'supervision and control' test was adopted, but this was

---

[71] *Nteboheleng Mphutlane v Imperial Fleet Services* (DDPRA1568/03)
[72] *Gladys Mamoroesi Mokhali v Star Lion Gold Coin Investment* (DDPR A494/02).

replaced by a 'dominant impression' or 'composite' test, in terms of which supervision and control remains an important factor, but is not the sole determinant of who is an employee. A prominent Zimbabwean scholar has argued that the test was developed to give flexibility to employers and courts and has criticized it because of its failure to indicate the weighting that should be attached to different factors.[73] This results in a situation in which different courts can come to different conclusions on the same facts.

Examples of decisions by the Zimbabwean courts are:

(a) Insurance personnel were held to be independent contractors despite the fact that they were given a list of customers by the employer, supplied with office space, were not allowed to work for any other insurance company, were on the company's medical aid scheme and work under a hierarchy of managers. The factors that lead the court to this conclusion were that they were described in their contacts as contractors; they had flexible working hours were paid on commission.[74]

(b) A taxi driver who had flexible hours, was paid on commission and was described in his contract as an independent contractor was held to be an employee because this was consistent with the purpose of the Labour Act to advance worker's interests.[75]

The Labour Act 17 of 2002 introduced a definition of employee which considerably expanded its scope and which made 'economic dependence' the key definitional element. The definition of an employee for this period was:

> any person who performs work or services for another person for remuneration or reward on such terms and conditions that the first mentioned person is in a position of economic dependence upon or under an obligation to perform duties for the second-mentioned person, and includes a person performing work or services for another person:
>
> (a) in circumstances where, even if the person performing the work or services supplies his own tools or works under flexible conditions of service, the hirer provides the substantial investments in or assumes the substantial risk of the undertaking; or
>
> (b) in any other circumstances that more closely resemble the relationship between an employee and employer that that between an independent contractor and hirer of services.

---

[73] M Gwisai, *Labour and Employment Law in Zimbabwe* (Harare, 2006).

[74] *Southampton Insurance Co Ltd of Zimbabwe v Mutuma & Anor* 1990 (1) ZLR 12.

[75] *Chiworese v Rixi Taxi Services Co-op* HH-13–93.

However, this was subsequently repealed by the Labour Act 7 of 2005 which restored the previous definition.[76] The report of the Parliamentary Committee that preceded the 2002 Act had also proposed the retrospective transformation of all contract and casual workers who had been employed for more than 12 months into permanent workers. However, this proposal was not introduced. The 2002 Labour Act was influenced by South Africa's post-apartheid 1995 Labour Relations Act, and was prepared by a Parliamentary Committee that included a number of trade unionist who had been elected as opposition MPs.[77]

Morocco

The Labour Code 2004 of Morocco specifically includes groups of workers that are often unprotected, such as salespersons and home workers.

> Section 2. The provisions of the Labour Code apply also:
>
> (i)   to workers whose enterprise manager puts them at the disposal of his or her clients in order to deliver any services requested;
>
> (ii) to persons engaged to carry out sales-related activities in premises provided by the enterprise in a different location and under conditions set by the enterprise;
>
> (iii) to home workers.
>
> Section 6. 'Wage earners/salaried workers' include every person who is engaged to carry out a professional activity under the direction of one or more employers in return for remuneration, whatever the nature and method of payment.

In addition, s 8 of the Labour Code extends its scope of application to home workers and provides guidance as to what constitute essential elements of such employment:

> Section 8. 'Home workers' under the present Code are considered to be wage earners/salaried workers, without there being a need to assess whether there is any legal subordination, any direct and habitual control by the employer, whether the place where they work and the tools they use belong to them or not, whether they supply with the work all or part of the basic materials used when these materials are sold to them by the person giving the work who subsequently purchases back the finished object, or are given to them by a supplier who is determined by the person giving the work and from whom the wage earners must get supplies, or whether they procure any additional materials themselves:

---

[76] Gwisai (n 73) 55.
[77] For a full discussion, see Gwisai (n 73) 26–31.

if they satisfy the following two conditions:

(i) they are responsible, either directly or through an intermediary, for accomplishing work for one or more enterprises in return for remuneration;

and

(ii) they work alone or with an assistant or with their spouse and non-salaried children.

In other countries also, one can find that the *tâcheron* system is practised. The principal entrepreneur is required to keep a list of all the *tâcherons* with whom he has signed a contract. The labour codes further regulate the joint liability of the principal entrepreneur with regard to the *tâcheron*'s obligations vis-à-vis his/her workers.

Benin

In Benin, the Labour Code No 98–004 of 1998 at s 75 says:

> The *tâcheron* is a secondary entrepreneur [*sous-entrepreneur*] who him/herself recruits the labour force required for a job, and who signs a written contract with an entrepreneur for the execution of a given job or for the provision of certain services in return for a negotiated price. The contract must be submitted, in duplicate, to the Labour Inspector within 48 hours of being countersigned by the entrepreneur.

The following s 76 provides that when the work is performed within the premises or building site of the principal entrepreneur, the latter is entirely liable for workers' claims arising out of their employment in the event of the *tâcheron*'s insolvency. However, when the work is performed within premises or building sites that do not belong to the main entrepreneur, then the latter is liable only of the payment of the workers' wages.

Finally, s 78 states that the entrepreneur must maintain a list of the *tâcherons* with whom he/she has signed contracts.

Gabon

In Gabon, the Labour Code—Act No 3/94 of 21 November 1994 at s 113 states that the *tâcheron* is a certified and independent master worker (*maître ouvrier*) or secondary entrepreneur, who signs a contract with an entrepreneur or with the head of a work site/job manager for the execution of a given job or for the provision of certain services, in return for a fee negotiated between the parties. The '*tâcheronnat*' contract must be in writing.

The following s 114, provides that the *tâcheron* is forbidden to sub-contract, in whole or in part, the contracts that he/she has entered into. This is in line with s 116, which states that in case of insolvency of the *tâcheron*, and in accordance with the contract signed with the principal entrepreneur or head of a work site/job manager, the co-signatory is jointly (*solidairement*) responsible for the obligations of the *tâcheron* as regards the workers and this applies up to the level of the amount due from the principal entrepreneur to the *tâcheron*. Workers who have a claim are entitled to lodge such claims directly against the principal entrepreneur or head of a work site/job manager without prejudice to any restitution claim that the latter themselves may make against the *tâcheron*.

Triangular Employment Relationships: Contrasting Approaches in South Africa and Namibia

Article 4.1 of the Recommendation 198 requires that a country's national policy should ensure that protection is available to all forms of employment relationships, including those involving multiple parties. As one of the publications prepared in preparation for the adoption of the Recommendation noted, the challenge in respect of triangular employment relations lies 'in ensuring that employees in such a relationship enjoy the same level of protection traditionally provided by the law for employers that have bilateral employment relationships, without impeding legitimate private and public business initiatives'.[78]

As indicated earlier in this chapter, the primary vehicle for informalization in South Africa has been the process of externalization through triangular employment relationship. The inadequate regulatory framework for temporary employment services ('TESs'), still more commonly referred to by their previous appellation of labour brokers, has provide the opportunity for this process. There has been an exponential growth in the number of TESs, with an increase from 1,076 in 2000 to 3,140 in 2006.[79] Significantly, the largest rise came in 2000, at a stage when the courts begun to cast a more critical eye over the use of 'independent' contracting as a mechanism for disguised employment. An estimated 800,000 workers (equivalent to 9 per cent of the workforce) are placed daily by TESs.[80] The rise of labour hire has

---

[78] ILO, *Report V(1): The Employment Relationship*. (Geneva, International Labour Office, 2005).

[79] These figures reflect registrations with the Services SETA in terms of the Skills Development Act.

[80] This information is extracted from the web-site from the website of the Confederation of Associations in the Private Employment Sector (CAPES): www.capes.org.za.

also been at the centre of Namibian response to informalization. In this section, we examine the contrasting policy responses to this trend in these two neighbouring countries.

South Africa

South Africa's LRA and BCEA both define a "'temporary employment service' ("'TES'") as:

> any person who, for reward, procures for or provides to a client other persons
>
> (a) who render services to or perform work for, the client; and
>
> (b) who are remunerated by the temporary employment service.[81]

TESs fall within the broader category of private employment services agencies as defined in the Skills Development Act. Although this Act empowers the Minister to issue regulations requiring private employment service agencies to register with the Department of Labour, no such regulations have yet been published. TESs are required to register as employers with Sectoral Education and Training Authorities under the Skills Development Act as well as with bargaining council in the sectors in which they operate. However, neither of these institutions have regulatory control over TESs. The Employment Equity Act renders a client and TES jointly and severally liable for unfair discrimination,[82] and under s 57(1), for purposes of affirmative action, a person whose services have been procured by a TES will be deemed to be an employee of the client if that person is placed with the client for an indefinite period or for a period of three months or longer. No similar deeming provision is contained in any other labour legislation. A TES is not the employer for the purposes of compliance with health and safety legislation.

In terms of both the LRA and the BCEA, a TES is the employer of the person placed. However, the client-enterprise is jointly and severally liable for breaches of the statutory labour standards, contracts of employment, collective agreements and arbitration awards. However, the concept of joint and several liability does not extend to unfair dismissal protections. A proposal to this effect in the initial draft

---

[81] A temporary employment service falls within the definition of a private employment agency as contemplated by the Private Employment Agencies Convention 181, 1997. However, the Convention does not deal specifically with the security of employment of workers engaged through private employment services.

[82] s 57(2).

Bill that was submitted to NEDLAC for negotiation was removed during the Parliamentary hearings as a result of representations by the organization representing TESs.

Whether an individual who is on the books of a TES and is supplied to one of its clients is an employee or an independent contractor, is determined by the nature of working relationship between that individual and the client and the person placed with it.[83] The *Code of Good Practice: Who is an Employee* points out that an adjudicator must be satisfied that the relationship between the client and the TES is genuine and not a subterfuge to avoid labour legislation. However, as Van Niekerk points out, applying the 'dominant impression' test to the relationship between agency worker and the client is extremely complex.

Although it is likely that the default liability of TES has encouraged more responsible contracting patterns, the lack of limitation in respect of the period for which an employee is provided by a TES has allowed employers to permanently outsource recruitment and employment functions. These employees are without security of employment because the client's decision to terminate employment or work is conveyed from client to the TES and therefore falls outside of the employment relationship and beyond the reach of labour law. A statutory provision intended to facilitate the supply of temporary staff has therefore become a vehicle enabling permanent triangular employment of workers who are without any security of employment.

Namibia

The issue of labour hire has also been a dominant controversy arising out of processes of flexibilization n Namibia. According to Jauch, labour hire emerged in Namibia in the late 1990s for the supply of employees for short periods as well as those who work on a full-time and ongoing basis for the client company.

Namibia's labour hire industry is dominated by one large company, which originated in South Africa and now operates across Namibia. Jauch estimates that there are at least 10 labour hire companies in Namibia. They supply mostly unskilled and semi-skilled workers to client companies in various industries, including mining, fishing, and retail. Their clients include private companies and also state-owned enterprises. Almost all labour hire companies retain a substantial part (15–55 per cent) of workers' hourly wage rates as their fee. Labour hire workers are paid significantly less than permanent workers and they usually do not enjoy any benefits.

---

[83] *LAD Brokers v Mandla* (2001) 22 ILJ 1813 (LAC).

While most employees hired in this way are registered with social security, many do not receive any paid leave or severance pay in the event of retrenchment. As in South Africa, they have no job security and their employment contract with the labour hire company is terminated as soon as the commercial contract between the labour broker and its client ends.

Namibia's first post-independence Labour Act of 1992 did not specifically regulate the issue of labour hire. Namibia's 2004 Labour Act[84] and the initial Labour Bill presented to Parliament in 2007 proposed regulating the use of labour hire. However, during the debates in the National Assembly, the Bill was amended to prohibit any form of labour hire. In the 2007 Act, the Namibian legislature provided that 'No person may, for reward, employ any person with a view to making that person available to a third party to perform work for the third party' (cl 128[1]).[85] As a result of a legal challenge brought by the country's largest labour hire firm, the clause never came into effect and in late 2009, Namibia's highest court held that a total prohibition on labour hire violated the country's constitution.[86] Despite this development, the approach proposed in the 2004 Act and 2007 Bill deserves careful scrutiny. These proposed regulating 'employment hire services' (EHS), a term covering any person who runs a business of procuring or providing individuals to render services or work for a client. Individuals whose services are supplied to the client are employees of the employment hire service for all purposes under the Labour Act. However, the client of the employment hire service is jointly and severally liable for breaches of the Act, a collective agreement, contract of employment or binding arbitration award.

This approach is based on the framework of the South African approach, but there are a number of very significant differences which indicate a keen awareness of the problems of regulation and enforcement encountered in South Africa. The first of these differences is that the definition of an EHS is wider than a TES, in that it is not a requirement that the service remunerate the employee. The provisions of the section apply to any organization that supplies employees for reward, irrespective of how the remuneration takes places. Most importantly, the joint and several liabilities between hire service and employer applies to the employee's protection against unfair dismissal. This would provide a basis for placed employees to challenge the decision of the client to terminate his or her services. A significant

---

[84]   This Act was passed but never came into effect.
[85]   This account is based on Herbert Jauch 'Namibia's Ban on Labour Hire in Perspective' *The Namibian* (3 August 2007). See also G. Klerck, 'Rise of the temporary employment industry in Namibia: A regulatory "fix"' (2009) 27(1) *Journal of Contemporary African Studies*, 1, 85–103 and H. Jauch, 'Namibia's Labour Hire Debate in Perspective' (Windhoek, Friedrich Ebert Stiftung (FES), 2010).
[86]   *Africa Personnel Services (Pty) Ltd v Government of Republic of Namibia and Others* [2009] NASC 17.

procedural innovation is that an employee seeking to enforce his or her rights may do so against either the employment hire service or the client or both in accordance with this Act. In South Africa, the employee is required to proceed against the TES as employer and can only draw the client into litigation where the TES defaults on its liability. It was also proposed that an employee of an EHS would remain an employee during periods in which they do not work but remain on the EHS's books. The Bill proposed severe penalties for employment hire services and client companies who breach the law: a fine of up to N$80,000 or imprisonment for up to five years or both. In contrast, the South African statute creates no criminal liability. A final difference arises out of the fact that the EHS and client are jointly and severally liable for compliance with all the employer's obligations under the Labour Act including occupational health and safety standards. This differs from the position in South Africa, where it is the client who has sole responsibility. While it will generally be the client who will have the day-to-day obligation to provide a healthy and safe workplace, the joint and several liabilities would require the hiring service to monitor health and safety conditions in the workplaces to which they supply employees.

This extensive package of regulation did not persuade Namibia's law-makers that the abuses of labour hire could be controlled, and instead they opted to prohibit employment hire. The exploitative practices used by 'labour hire' firms were seen as being reminiscent of the contract labour system utilized prior to independence and were rejected as permitting a 'new form of slavery'. However, the fact that the Namibian policy-makers adapted the South African model to remove its shortcomings means that the clause in the Bill, while not part of Namibian law, may serve as a welcome contribution to debates on the reform of this area in the law in South Africa as well as other African countries in which triangular employment is mushrooming.

Temporary Employment Contracts

As indicated above, the employment of workers through short-term fixed contracts has been one of the dominant mechanisms for informalizing work. In this section, we examine the extent to which labour legislation has been able to meet the Recommendation's proposal of 'ensuring that employed workers have the protection they are due'.

Under apartheid, virtually all African workers in South Africa were employed on fixed term (most commonly annual) contracts. Employees who were not resident in urban areas were required to return to a homeland (or in the case of foreign workers, their home country) to renew their contract. This prevented these workers gaining rights of permanent residence in urban areas in terms of the influx control legislation that controlled the South African labour market. Several of the key Labour Court cases in the early 1980s concerned whether these 'contract' workers were protected against unfair dismissal. The Court rejected the arguments of employers and held that employees engaged through this system on successive contracts should be regarded as having been in ongoing employment and that a failure to renew the contracts could amount to an unfair dismissal on either substantive or procedural grounds. The obvious artificiality of the contractual arrangements enabled the Court to give precedence to substance over form, a task that took considerably longer when identifying the employment relationship.

This historical context informs the provisions in the 1995 LRA that an employer's failure to renew a fixed-term (or maximum term)[87] contract amounts to a dismissal if the employee can show that he or she had a reasonable expectation that the employer would renew the contract on the same or similar terms (s 186(1)(b) of the Labour Relations Act). To succeed with such a claim, the employee must show that he or she in fact expected that the contract would be renewed and that, after taking into account all relevant factors, the expectation was reasonable.[88] In the absence of these circumstances, the failure to renew a fixed-term contract irrespective of its duration is not an unfair dismissal. Factors that the courts have taken into account in determining whether an employee's expectation of a renewal was reasonable include:

(a) the wording of the contract;
(b) undertakings made by the employer or a representative of the employer to the employee;
(c) custom and practice in regard to renewing contracts;
(d) the availability of the post;
(e) the purpose or reason for having concluded the fixed-term contract;
(f) the extent to which the employer gave reasonable notice to the employee;
(g) the nature of the employer's business.[89]

Widespread use is made of fixed-term contracts by temporary employment services, contract cleaning firms and security services, among other sectors, even where the employees concerned are in effect employed indefinitely. An indication of the

---

[87] The Labour Court has pointed out these contracts should be described as 'maximum term contracts', as opposed to fixed-term contracts which do not permit for early termination: *Mafihla v Govan Mbeki Municipality* [2005]4 BLLR 334 (LC). However, this issue does not affect the application of s 186(1)(b).

[88] *Mediterranean Woollen Mills (Pty) Ltd v SA Clothing & Textile Workers Union* (1998) 19 ILJ 731(SCA) 734[C].

[89] *Dierks vs University of South Africa* (1999) 20 ILJ 1227 (LC).

extent of the use of temporary employment contracts can be obtained from the Annual Report of the Commission for Employment Equity which analyses reports, which include information concerning terminations made by large employers, under the Employment Equity Act. These reports (which cover roughly 25 per cent of workers in the formal sector) show that around one-quarter of terminations (covering both dismissals and resignations) could be attributed to the non-renewal of contracts.[90] In contrast, only 6 per cent of the approximately 80,000 dismissal cases referred to the CCMA annually are identified as being about 'contract renewal'. This indicates that employers in South Africa enjoy a considerable level of de jure and de facto flexibility to employ workers under fixed-term contracts.

In most other SADC countries, protection of employees against unfair dismissal is significantly undermined by the limited protection provided to employees engaged on short-term contracts. Section 35(d) of Swaziland's Employment Act excludes 'an employee engaged for a fixed term and whose term of engagement has expired' from protection against unfair dismissal. Swaziland's Industrial Court of Appeal has accepted that employees who were employed from time to time on one month fixed term contracts but had not worked for longer than three months without a break were excluded from challenging the unfairness of their termination.[91] Likewise, in terms of s 66 of the Lesotho Labour Code, the ending of any contract for a fixed period or for performing a specific task or journey can only be a dismissal if the contract expressly provides for it to be renewed. In Namibia, a contract of employment terminates automatically if either the contract or a collective agreement provides for its termination. A termination of a contract of employment in these circumstances does not constitute a dismissal and the employee is unable to bring a challenge based on the unfairness of the failure to renew the contract.

4.6 Conclusions

Growing informalization in the labour market is a feature of several African countries. As a result, growing numbers of workers are not protected by labour law

---

[90] The 2006 Report analysed reports made in October 2005 and the reports of 2,085 employers employing a total of 2,365,259 employees with an average size of 1,134 employees were analysed. The October 2005 reports show that 23% of terminations (72,352 out of a total of 336,399) were occasioned by non-renewal of contracts. According to the 2004 Employment Equity Reports 85,754 (26%) out of a total of 329,077 terminations were due to non-renewal of contracts.

[91] *Swaziland Meat Industries v Nhlabatsi & others* (Appeal Case 142/2005).

and policies. Legislators and policy-makers have introduced a range of policy changes to either expand the scope of legislation or to assist individuals to prove that they are employed in terms of an employment relationship. In the light of the enormity of labour market shifts, it is perhaps surprising that these initiatives have not occupied a more central position in reform agendas. Nevertheless, it is possible to identify significant innovative responses. Adjudicators in the region's courts and arbitration forums have also found themselves torn between adherence to conventional contractual approaches and a recognition of the forms of dependence that occur in the context of non-standard employment relations. This tension indicates the need for all governments in Africa to review, clarify and (if necessary) adapt the scope of their laws to ensure adequate protection for employees in their countries.

Subordinate, Autonomous and Economically Dependent Work: A Comparative Analysis of Selected European Countries

5

ADALBERTO PERULLI[*]

5.1 Introduction

The distinction between 'subordinate employment' and 'autonomous work' is a recurring feature in all European legal systems. Indeed, its historical origin is shared: the Industrial Revolution brought about a reorganization of production that transformed work from a conceptual and normative point of view and resulted in subordinate employment being identified as the dominant type of work. This category covers all those who offer their productive capacity to entrepreneurs, using it for their own economic ends.

Alongside the new legal category of subordinate employment, we find a different, and in some respects more traditional, legal form of exchange between personal commitment and economic remuneration: autonomous work. In this category we have the 'liberal professions' and a growing area of work activities that fall outside the Taylor-Fordist organizational model and are therefore regulated by the principles of civil and commercial law.

The distinction between subordinate and autonomous work, common to all European countries, tends to present itself as a clear-cut dichotomy. Since subordinate work is regulated by principles and rules that are profoundly different from those governing autonomous work, defining a work relationship as subordinate or autonomous has important consequences from both economic and socio-economic points of view. The two definitions thus acquire great importance in and

---

* Professor of Labour Law at the University Ca' Foscari of Venice (Italy).

of themselves, because they determine the respective interests and norms which the legal order establishes for the exchange of work and remuneration.

The two different offsets of interests and norms can be explained if we recall the two major areas of private law applied to the world of work by European legislation: subordinate work is governed by labour law, whereas autonomous work is governed by civil and commercial law.

Labour law, which deals with subordinate work, seeks to find measures to protect the worker, who is considered—legally and socially—to be the weaker party in the contract. Consequently, the legislation has often intervened in the main aspects of the relationship between the subordinate worker and the employer—recruitment, dismissal, remuneration, working hours, etc—and in ways that reduce the usual areas of contractual autonomy. Thus, labour law's treatment of subordinate work can be summarized as extensive legislative protection in favour of the worker.

Autonomous work, on the other hand, is treated as a contract governed by the general rules of civil law and in many cases by commercial law. This corresponds to an essentially different approach at the regulatory level: the autonomous worker is not considered to be the weak party, but rather as substantially and formally equal to the counterparty. With autonomous work, there is no special legislation protecting the worker (except in specific situations, as we will see below); the autonomous worker is in fact considered to be anyone who concludes a contract. For our purposes, the fundamental character of the rules governing autonomous work is the absence of a protective system such as the one protecting the subordinate worker, since the exchange between work and compensation follows market rules.

Clearly, the definition of work as either subordinate or autonomous is linked to a pivotal question: is the work subject to market rules or not? In the case of subordinate work, labour law abstracts the work from market laws and affords the worker specific protections both in relations with the other contracting party and in vulnerable situations (eg accidents, unemployment). In the case of autonomous work, civil and commercial law essentially aims to promote the correct and efficient functioning of market forces.

5.2 The Legal Notion and Its Interpretation by the Jurisprudence

In defining the notions of subordinate and autonomous work, the European states take two approaches:

(a) *Legislative*: the law defines two general unitary notions of subordinate and autonomous work.

(b) *Jurisprudential*: the definitions are provided by cases based on jurisprudence, which identifies a series of indicators or criteria in order to establish if work is subordinate or autonomous.

As we shall see, in some cases a legal system may opt for one of the two approaches, whereas in others—as happens more frequently—the legislative and the jurisprudential approaches are integrated, and the guiding definitions often combine legal and case law techniques.

A further point that should be mentioned concerns the importance legal systems attribute to the abovementioned notions. While all European Union Member States commonly distinguish between subordination and autonomy, linking only subordinate work to protective legislation for the worker, in reality the two notions do not have the same value in all of the legal systems. In some cases, the legislation contains a general, systematic notion of subordination (and autonomy) that tends to identify the whole field of application as falling within labour law. In others, there is no notion of the subordinate worker having general importance, rather the legislation establishes a field of application within more limited and particular disciplines, from which it is not possible to deduce a definition of systematic value.

5.3 Identifying Criteria of Subordinate and Autonomous Work

Since subordination is considered to be a legal notion, a socio-economic meaning of subordination, based on the social and economic dependence of the worker on the employer, should not be considered relevant. Even if a tendency to identify subordination in terms of socio-economic dependence can be found in historical presumptions which led to the formulation of the legal notion through doctrinal and jurisprudential elaboration, such an identification is not present in the content of the technical, legal notion.

As a legal notion, subordination expresses a structural element in the relationship. This is described in Italian as *eterodirezione*, indicating the subjection of the worker to the directional power of the employer. This power consists in the employer's right:

(a) to give instructions to the subordinate worker on how to execute his or her work;

(b)   to sanction possible non-fulfilment;

(c)   to control the worker during work.

Under *eterodirezione*, other subsidiary indicators or criteria exist which define the legal notion of subordination. The following should be emphasized:

(a)   The typology and number of subsidiary indicators can vary from one country to another;

(b)   There are no formalized hierarchies of these indicators;

(c)   The presence of all indicators is not established by the occurrence of one or more of them;

(d)   Their presence or absence does not seem to be decisive for defining the work relationship/contract; rather, they are principally considered as indicators which the judge is free to evaluate.

The indicators that seem the most significant ones for defining subordination are:

—   the presence of an organization on the employer's side;

—   the absence of an economic risk related to production;

—   the payment of a salary;

—   the observance of set working hours;

—   work materials and equipment that are not the worker's property.

The combined and variable use of *eterodirezione*, along with other indicators mentioned above, provide us with the elements of a legal notion of subordination.

In contrast, the notion of autonomous work is essentially the opposite of subordinate work once the latter is defined. We define autonomous work as activities carried out without the obligation of subordination; that is, work not subject to the direction of a third party, and where the indicators of subordination are missing or not present in significant measure.

5.4   The 'Grey Area' between Subordination and Autonomy

The literature often refers to an area lying between subordinate and autonomous work, and also to cases where, according to a binary logic, attribution to either the first or the second category is unclear. There are at least two different types of this 'grey area':

(a)   work activities that do not fit a binary logic because they have features of both subordinate and autonomous work;

(b)   work that has the appearance of autonomous work, but where in reality there is a subordinate work relationship.

This first type of grey area brings up a problem of legal classification, one that should be resolved by using the usual instruments the law provides judges and the competent authorities. Here, for example, the grey area involves 'false autonomous workers': workers who are treated as autonomous workers, but from a legal point of view clearly belong under subordinate work because all the typical prerequisites are present (as established by law or jurisprudence). With the second type of grey area, the correct application of the law should be verified on a case-to-case basis, as there is ambiguity regarding both the legal categories (subordinate work and autonomous work) and the legal and jurisprudential criteria used to classify the work relationship. Here the 'false autonomous work' may signify illegal practices, but rather that the workers in question do not clearly meet the criteria established by legislation to distinguish subordinate from autonomous work. False autonomous workers and workers of unclear status are different and therefore require different legislative solutions. With the former, the problem is one of not applying the legislation in force, while with the latter, the problem is one of interpreting (or updating) the criteria for defining subordinate and autonomous work. For both, the solutions should be sought in the case law.

Resolving the first type of grey area depends in part on the judge's use—whether restrictive or inclusive—of the indicators of subordination, and in particular, his or her interpretation of the principal indicator of directional power. German jurisprudence, for example, has adopted a very flexible concept linked with the idea of a right aimed at making possible the 'functional and a useful participation of the worker at the production process'. By using a very broad notion of directional power, German judges have extended the field of application of labour law so that it encompasses many workers falling in this first grey area. In Italy, there have been changes regarding the interpretation of *eterodirezione*: in the past the courts adopted a rigorous definition that excluded from the condition of subordination all work relationships that did not correspond perfectly to the characteristics of subordinate work. The orientation in current jurisprudence is to take into consideration the new forms of work and the organization of production. Even work activities not subject to continuous and detailed orders but only to general, purely functional directives are classified as subordinate work.

Adalberto Perulli

5.5 Definition of Subordination in Selected European Countries

5.5.1 Italy

The Legislation

Historically, Italian labour law is grounded in the general definition of subordinate work contained in the Civil Code of 1942, according to which a subordinate worker is a person who offers his/her own intellectual or manual work in exchange for a salary under the dependence and direction of the entrepreneur (Civil Code art 2094).

The key criterion is the way the work is carried out: in subordinate work, as opposed to autonomous work, it is carried out 'under the dependence and direction of the entrepreneur'. This concept recurs in article 2104 co 2° c.c. on the 'obligation of obedience', by which the worker 'shall observe the dispositions in the execution and discipline of the job as provided by the entrepreneur and the co-workers upon whom he/she is hierarchically dependent'. The hierarchical relationship that allows the employer to organize and plan workers' activities in the pursuit of his or own interest and to exercise disciplinary power in the case of non-observance is emphasized in article 2086 c.c. on the 'Direction and hierarchy in the enterprise'. This article stipulates that the 'entrepreneur is the head of the enterprise and the co-workers depend hierarchically on him/her'.

In legal terms, the notion of subordination thus becomes the right reserved by the employer to translate the direction and control of the work deriving from a contract into a hierarchical mechanism in order to organize the workers for the attainment of his/her goals (see art 2082 c.c.). In the case of subordinate work, the exchange of work services by means of 'structured' contracts—as economists define the contracts in autonomous work—is replaced by an 'incomplete', open and flexible contractual form by which the worker accepts, within certain limits, adaptive specification of the task of carrying out the work.

This fundamental sense, repeatedly affirmed by the jurisprudence, can be considered as *ius receptum*. Accordingly, 'the essential distinguishing feature of subordinate employment is the existence of a subjection of the worker to the directional, organizational and disciplinary power of the employer'.[1] The other specifying elements of article 2094 c.c. are centred around this fundamental

---

[1] Cass 22 November 1999 no 12926, RIDL 2000 II 633.

concept: 'co-working' meaning the continuous availability or technical and functional subordination of the worker, and 'dependence' seeming to express the 'socio-economic' subordination of the worker with respect to the owner or the production equipment. A constant feature of judicial decisions on the work relationship is the normative index of the work direction, which can be conceptually broken down into the conformity and coordination (in area and time) of the required work with the organization it is part of.

In this context, scholars often make reference to article 2099 of the Civil Code, which concerns remuneration. According to article 2099, the remuneration of workers can be established on the basis of time or performance, and shall be paid according to the modalities and within the terms in use at the place where the work is carried out. In the absence of an agreement between the parties, the remuneration shall be determined by the judge, taking into consideration, if applicable, the opinion of professional organizations. The worker may be remunerated in whole or in part, with a share of the results, or in kind.

If we combine the above criterion of remuneration with the directional power, we have what we might call the principal distinguishing criteria of labour law. In particular, the exercise of directional power is directly related to the changeable requirements of work organization both in terms of the profile of the work and control over execution and discipline of the work, the legal subjection of the worker to the command of the employer. In substance, the exercise of the directional power in subordinate work activates the worker's obligation to conform his/her conduct to a specific order; it legitimates the employer's control over the ways his/her orders are fulfilled. It also makes possible the use of disciplinary sanctions, according to the seriousness of the violation, in the event that there is a change in the technical and functional aspects of subordination relating to the work (art 2106 c.c.).

This contrasts with the 'negative' definition the Civil Code provides for the self-employed worker: a self-employed person is an individual who does not work under the subordinate status in relation to his/her client (Art 2222 c.c. *Contratto d'opera*). Work without the obligation of subordination means that the work is not subject to the direction of another party and that the indicators of subordination are missing or not present in significant measure. This legal definition is not very meaningful in practical terms. Rather, it is more important to bear in mind that self-employment is a complex, multi-faceted category and that this complexity should be reflected in the legislation. This is even true if one looks at the different regional realities and regional policies relating to the employment relationship. In Friuli Venezia Giulia, for example, legislative interventions (Regional Law No 18 of 9 August 2005) have aimed at increasing the quality, stability and number of workplaces, as well as at correcting possible trends towards precarious employment.

Another legislative approach is using instruments introduced to promote equal treatment for workers, as these have proven to be particularly significant in addressing employment relationship issues. In particular, s 46 of Legislative Decree No 165/200, states that:

> Private and public companies employing more than 100 employees have to prepare a report at least every 2 years on the situation of male and female personnel in every profession and report on the gender balance in the number of recruitments, training, professional promotions, levels, changes of categories or qualification requirements, and other phenomena such as mobility, interventions by the Wage Guarantee Fund, dismissals, pre-retirement and retirement, and effectively paid compensation. The report is prepared in conformity with indications from the Minister of Labour, and is transmitted to the company trade unions and to the Regional Counsellor for Equality.

Collective Bargaining Agreements

In Italy, it is not only legislation that governs the employment relationship; more and more, collective bargaining is determining the criteria identifying employment relationships. Many collective agreements provide for observers who are responsible for verifying the effectiveness of the provisions negotiated. The Minister of Labour issued a circular (No 17/2006 of 14 June 2006) to labour inspectorates that gave guidelines for a uniform interpretation of work carried out, for example, in call centres under a project-based employment contract. In addition to collective agreements and despite legislative interventions relating to this type of contract, there were often problems of interpretation and 'disguised' situations which deprived workers having this type of contract of their rights. The circular aimed to create clarity and fight abuses, although most often it was negotiations between the parties that brought clarity to the issues.

The Jurisprudence

The subjection of the worker to the direction of the employer (*eterodirezione*), deemed essential by the jurisprudence when identifying subordination, can appear in different forms, with different effects on the determination of the work relationship. According to one branch of the jurisprudence, the new forms of organization of subordinate employment are bringing about a reduction of employer interventions and controls, justifying the reclassification of employment relationships under subordination even in the case of programmatic directives or predetermined instructions.[2] *Eterodirezione* is also becoming less significant with the ever-growing outsourcing of entire phases of production. With these new realities, the distinguishing criterion for subordination becomes the obligation of putting one's productive energies and using them continuously according to the general instructions of the employer with regard to the enterprise's objectives. Such a modus operandi on the one hand guarantees a certain flexibility vis-à-vis the notion of subordination; it is not excluded from the more or less wide parameters of autonomy, initiative and discretion enjoyed by the worker. On the other hand, this implies the risk of an expansion of the notion that an absence of selective devices of protection can lead to indiscriminate application of labour law in favour of those who theoretically do not need protection.

In recent years, however, a more rigorous and restrictive interpretation of subordination has evolved. Indeed, the general orientation has been that article 2094 c.c. should be interpreted so that the employment relationship is characterized by directives given by the entrepreneur on the execution of the work relationship.[3] Directional power should mean specific and precise orders inherent to the execution of the relationship. Generic, programmatic directives or indeterminate instructions, given their compatibility with autonomous work, are not sufficient for establishing subordinate employment.[4] This does not exclude, however, that there can be 'softened' forms of subordination due to the 'particular organization and type of the work'. In such cases, subordination is identified by the 'continuous, loyal and diligent availability of the worker for the employer according to the instructions of the counterparty'[5]. Legal doctrine on this point observes that the existence of directional power should not be judged in absolute terms, but rather 'in relation to the specific nature of the work'.[6]

This orientation on the one hand responds to the need to delimit the expanding trend of labour law, and thus to understandable demands for rigid selectiveness when defining a work relationship. Moreover, it confirms that *eterodirezione* in its strongest sense is still the technical juridical element, affirmed by a

---

[2]   Cass 20 June 1997 no 5520, Riv it dir lav 1997 II 701.

[3]   Cass 13 May 2004 no 9151, Guida al lavoro 2004 no 24, 12.

[4]   Cass 3 April 1990 no 2680, Riv Giur Lav I 196; Cass 29/01/1993 no 1094, Rep Giur Lav no 4, 3.

[5]   Cass 27 November 2002 no 16805; Cass 7 March 2003 no 3471, Lav Giur 2003, 7, 676 on a doctor in a medical centre or Cass 25 October 2004 no 20669, Dir e Giust 2004, 45, 118.

[6]   F Carinci, R De Luca Tamajo, T Tosi, T Treu, *Diritto del lavoro, 2 – Il rapporto di lavoro subordinato*, (Torino, Utet, 2006), 473. *Cf.* E Ghera, 'Subordinazione, Statuto Protettivo e Qualificazione del Rapporto di Lavoro' (2006) 2 *Giornale di Diritto del Lavoro e Relazioni Industriali* 10, according to which 'the jurisprudence elaborated not only an articulated but also plural notion of subordination. The plurality of models or social types of subordinations is indeed an expression of the plurality of the ways of working and hence, of the diffusion of flexible work forms especially today'.

well-founded congruence between the provisions and the effects.[7] On the other hand, however, this orientation does not adequately include the new forms of subordination created by the decline of the Taylor-Fordist organizational model. Thus some attention is focused on the problematic distinction between subordination and subjection to the market forces typically found in autonomous work.[8]

Clearly, the specific delimitation of the notion of subordination is not at all rigidly predetermined by the law, but rather largely depends on orientations in interpretation and evaluation. To identify the contractual nature of subordinate employment, the jurisprudence has also used a series of subsidiary indicators or criteria ancillary to *eterodirezione* to define subordination, in particular, the continuance (or duration) of the relationship, the distribution of the risk and the will of the parties.

Continuance

The jurisprudence affirms that subordinate employment, as characterized by the subjection to *eterodirezione*, can only come about continuously, given that subordination cannot exist without a continuous carrying out of the work.[9] By contrast, in autonomous work the time of carrying out the work loses its legal importance and only the time of the result of the work is significant. The continuance is thus reflected in the goal of the work (if it is continuous, it means works, and not work), resulting in a complementary subsidiary indicator relating to the 'presence' of the worker in the enterprise (the jurisprudence, mixing the two indicators, talks about a 'continuous presence'). In other words, a sort of gap is created by the jurisprudence which, initiating from the subjection to *eterodirezione*, arrives at continuance. As a functional substitute for subordination, this appears to be among the most efficient subsidiary indicators in cases where active subordination is weakly manifested.

The distinguishing criteria are being reconsidered not so much in terms of how the work was materially carried out, but instead in terms of the legal structure of the obligation as expressed in the contract. Thus a rigorous distinction is being made between the duration and the continuance of the work in a technical sense. This can be characterized by the adequacy of each part of the work to partially

---

[7] In this sense, see Carinci et al (n 6), 468, according to whom the powers and rights of the employer constitute 'not only historically but also in the present, the foundation of labour law, it is the key to resolving a series of interpretation and system problems of labour law'.

[8] L Menghini, 'Subordinazione e dintorni: itinerari della giurisprudenza' (1998) 21 *Quaderni di Diritto del Lavoro e delle Relazioni Industriali* 224.

[9] Cass 24 February 2006 no 4171, Giust civ mass 2006, 2; Corte Appello 6 October 2004, Lav giur 2005, 390.

satisfy the specific interests of the employer in terms of time.[10] Such a characterization cannot indicate autonomous work if the contract foresees the repetition of different activities and the distribution in time becomes the causal element of the contract. The continuance feature is the result of the work's divisibility *ratione temporis* in terms of the employer's interest. Even so, this characterization cannot be exclusive to subordinate employment, for if the latter is essentially a contract with continuous service, then autonomous work cannot always and only be a discrete action.

Risk

The allocation of risk is the ultimate key subsidiary indicator, and in Italy and other countries (especially Germany and France), legal doctrine has recently focused on risk as a more relevant criterion for distinguishing subordinate and autonomous work. An important aspect of subordination is the exemption from entrepreneurial and contractual risk of the subordinate worker. This constitutes a rebalancing, given that the worker is not responsible for the productive result of his/her activity, but only for the correctness of his/her behaviour.[11] In the case of autonomous work, however, risk is borne by the worker (arts 1655 c.c. and 2225 c.c.). If performance of the work becomes impossible for a reason not attributable to him/her, he or she has worked in vain and have the right only to a 'payment for the work carried out in relation to the usefulness of the part of the completed activity' (art 2228 c.c.) or, in the case of contracting, within the limits to which the activity is useful for the buyer (art 1672 c.c.). The risk borne by the employer and by the autonomous worker cannot become a determining factor in a strict sense, as such a rule cannot be considered to be absolute. In the case of subordinate employment, beyond the hypothesis that the contract contains a 'goal' clause, the economic risk of the activity is also borne by the worker if it is piecework (art 2101 c.c.). The same is true for all associative and profit-sharing relationships (art 2102 c.c.). More generally, risk could probably be a valid criterion for reorienting the protective intervention of labour law independently from the distinction of subordination or autonomy, in the sense that the worker requires protection not only because he or she is subject to directional power, but also because he or she does not have (even if formally

---

[10]   P Ichino, *Il tempo della prestazione nel rapporto di lavoro*, I (Milano, Giuffrè, 1985) 15.

[11]   See, among others, Cass 24 February 2006 no 4171, Giust civ mass 2006, 2; Cass 24 October 2004 no 20669, D&G 2004, 45.

autonomous) the typical economic freedom of the entrepreneur. The worker cannot guarantee his or her livelihood in the event of accidents at work and other risks.

The Will of the Parties

Another useful subsidiary indicator is the will of the parties (*nomen iuris*) expressed when they concluded the contract. Traditionally, this has been neglected: interpreters have gone beyond references to the written and conventional will to evaluate 'the overall behaviour' of the contracting parties 'after the conclusion of the contract' (art 1362, co. 2, c.c.). This option is made necessary by the unequal allocation of the power of autonomy that, if not controlled, would allow for fraudulent claims aimed at placing the contractual relationship outside the labour law context. More recent trends in doctrine and the jurisprudence tend to still use the will of the parties as a determining factor. Helped by a cultural climate sensitive to 'neocontractualism' aiming at furthering individual interests and increasing individual decision-making, the parameters of autonomy negotiated according to binding rules are being contested. This should be regarded 'as a consequence, and definitely not as an assumption' of the determination, contesting a priori the favour given by the legal system to subordinate over autonomous employment. The role of the will of the parties would thus allow the necessary passage from the the level of *in rerum natura* to the level of the normative 'should be': here the directional power cannot manifest itself except as the right of intervention, effectively excluding the possibility of self-employment.

This need to re-evaluate the normative function of individual autonomy appears to have changed, given that the most recent jurisprudence confirms that it is no longer necessary to refer to *nomen iuris*, but rather to the actual implementation of the relationship, and that subjection to hierarchical power determines the classification of the relationship as subordinate work. The jurisprudence affirms the relevance of declarations of the will of the contracting parties: 'such declaration[s] constitute ... a fundamental and primary element to resolving ambiguous situations'.[12] This means that when the parties declared their intention to exclude the element of subordination when articulating their reciprocal interests, it was not possible to distinguish—especially in the cases where the elements were compatible with the type of relationship—that subordination was in fact realized during the

---

[12] Cass 29 May 1996 no 4948, DPL 1996, 3338.

relationship.[13] Addressing this problematic issue, s 75 of Legislative Decree No 276 of 2003 introduced a measure called 'certification', with the aim of reducing labour disputes. The Decree consists of a voluntary procedure activated on the basis of a common written request by the parties to the contract, presented before the competent organs to certify the contractual nature of their employment relationship. The 'act of certification' must explicitly mention the civil, administrative, social security or fiscal effects of the certification. Section 81(1) on consultation and assistance to the parties ensures the clarity of the employment relationship status:

> The organs of certification provide consultation and assistance to the contracting parties both as regards the conclusion of the employment contract and its content and with its modifications, in particular regarding rights and the exact categorization of employment contracts.

5.5.2 France

The Legislation

In French law, the concept of subordinate employment derives from legal theory and practice, and is based on the definition contained in the Civil Code. However, the labour code does not contain a general definition of subordinate employment.

The Civil Code distinguishes between the rental of things (*louage de choses*) and the rental of work (*louage d'ouvrage*). The second category, concerning the performance of work, has three sub-groups: *louage des gens de travail, louage des voituriers et louage des entrepreneurs 'à prix fait'* (art 1779(a)).

Case law refers to a link of legal subordination (*le lien de subordination juridique*) with the adjective *juridique,* distinguishing subordinate employment from the concept of economic dependence. Legal doctrine, however, has defined the employment contract as 'an agreement whereby natural persons, the employees, place their labour at the service (or disposal) and under the control of another person, the employer, in exchange for payment'.[14]

With certain types of contracts, the law presumes the existence of an employment relationship, for instance with commercial travellers, sales representatives and travelling salesmen (art L 751–1 of the Labour Code); journalists (art 761–2); and entertainment workers (art 762–1). Article L 751–1 states that:

---

[13] Cass 23/07/04 no 13884, Giust civ mass 2004; Cass.28/03/2003 no 4770, Giust civ mass 2003, 652.

[14] G Lyon-Caen, J Pèlisser, A Supiot, *Droit du travail* (Paris, Dalloz, 1998) 118.

> Agreements covering representatives, travelling salespersons or insurance brokers on the one hand, and their employers on the other hand, shall be deemed—notwithstanding any express language in the contract or its silence on this issue—to be work contracts (*contrats de louage de services*) when the representatives, travelling salespersons or insurance brokers: (1) work for one or more employers; (2) work exclusively and continually in the area of representation; (3) do not carry out any commercial activity on their own account; (4) are bound to their employers by commitments concerning the nature of the services rendered or of the merchandise offered for sale or to be purchased, the region where they must exercise their professional activity, the categories of clients whom they must contact or the rate of remuneration.

Article L 781–1 extends labour law to 'particular groups of workers', including:

> those whose occupation consists mainly of selling all types of goods or products, all types of books, publications and tickets supplied to them on an exclusive or quasi-exclusive basis by one industrial or commercial company, or by taking orders for or receiving the goods to be sold, moved or transported for the account of one industrial or commercial company, where such persons carry out their occupation in premises provided or designated by the aforementioned companies and under the conditions and for a price set by the latter.

As for self-employment, which the Civil Code defines as a contract through which a person undertakes to *faire un ouvrage*, it is covered by numerous laws relating to occupational activities which fall under this category. As mentioned above, case law defines self-employment as a situation where the characteristics of subordinate status are absent.

The Jurisprudence

While the Labour Code does not contain a specific provision for it, even in the 1930s French jurisprudence offered a clearly defined technical and functional notion of subordination.[15] According to the French Supreme Court, the legal condition of a worker with respect to the person for whom he or she carries out work cannot be identified on the basis of 'weakness' (*faiblesse*) or 'economic dependence' (*dépendance économique*), but rather according to other factors. In particular, the Court specified that 'the fact of being an employee necessarily implies the existence of a legal relationship of subordination of the worker to his/her

---

[15] The notion of subordination is a result of the jurisprudence and doctrine inspired by the Civil Code, which considers the employment contract a sort of rental (see para 3), defining it as 'the rental of working people who undertake a service for someone else' (*le louage de gens de travail qui s'engagent au service de quelqu'un*, art 1779(a)).

employer', in the sense that the 'contract puts the worker under the direction, supervision and authority' of the employer.

As in Italy and Spain, in France the fundamental determining elements defining the nature of the employment relationship are the directional power and the degree of entrepreneurial organization. In France, however, very early on the direct authority of the employer over the execution of the working activity ceased to be the only or prevailing criterion for defining subordination and thus classifying the contract as an employment contract, resulting in application of the related protection measures.

The organizational indicator evolved rapidly, using features of the notion of organized service (*service organisé*). Clearly, the initial formulation of unilateralism—that is, the authority and direction—slowly gave rise to a plurality of rules. Such plurality allowed for autonomous workers to come under labour law. The limits of subordination extended to the point where one can clearly discern the considerable relativity of the authority indicator. Here the consideration of the 'organization' of the enterprise, understood both in terms of structure and objectives, seems to be pivotal. The substance of subordination is essentially organizational in French labour law.

The French notion of organization has a dual nature, as judges tend to examine two elements when defining an employment contract. The first is the conditions under which the work is carried out. This primacy derives from the fact that the employment contract brings about subordination. However, the conditions differ in function according to the degree of autonomy that the employer leaves to employees. To bring under labour law those workers who enjoy some technical autonomy, the judges invented the notion of *service organisé*. Thus, authority over the working conditions is the first criterion in defining the employment contract. This authority, however, becomes relative if the employee has the technical competence to render the employer's direction non-essential. The technical independence of the employee is no longer an obstacle when qualifying an employment contract. These developments have obliged judges to enlarge their scope and consequently to abandon the issue of authority. The judiciary focuses not only on the work itself but also on the place of work, the working hours and the equipment used for carrying out the work. If the judges find one of these elements sufficiently convincing, they generally conclude that there is an employment contract.[16] Thus authority in a legal

---

[16] On the working place, Soc, 11 May 1967 *Bull Civ* V n° 607; Soc, 12 June 1974 *Bull Civ* V n° 652; Soc, 11 February 1981 *Bull Civ* V n° 202; on working hours, Soc, 31 May 1961 *Bull Civ* V n° 396; on supply of materials, Soc, 29 October 1985 *Bull Civ* V n° 559.

sense is exercised not only over the employment, but also over the general conditions for carrying out the work. If, on the one hand, the employee can be subject to the employer's directives when carrying out his/her duties, in a second scenario subordination can be the result of a series of constraints that make the employer's directives a general rule. The criterion of authority does not disappear entirely, however: it is still the unilateralism of the person who gives the orders that brings about the subordination. This has made it necessary to distinguish between a central subordination (*subordination centrale*) and a peripheral subordination (*subordination périphérique*).

Since the 1960s, the Cour de cassation has elaborated *service organisé*, the most original aspect of the French interpretation of subordination. While *service organisé* is not the primary indicator of subordination, the Cour has attributed it more importance. Indeed, *service organisé* has become a determining and sufficient indicator for the employment contract. While unilateralism is still considered the essential determining factor of subordination, *service organisé* is considered as a metamorphose of subordination. This metamorphosis has allowed for the application of labour law to doctors, teachers, trade agents and public accountants and counsels, and even to artists, musicians and actors. The subordinate relationship, along the lines of the *service organisé*, continues to be affirmed; it has also become in certain ways the defining criterion for autonomous workers.

The second element to which judges have turned their attention, influenced by social security law, is the economic objectives of the *service organisé*. This analysis has vested the qualification of the employment contract. The 'organized service for the profit of another person' (*service organisé au profit d'autrui*) becomes a criterion for judicial consideration of the objectives of the economic activity. The limits of the *service organisé au profit d'autrui* are the same as those of the unilaterally ordered organization. A worker who does not fall under this unilateralism is thus an independent worker.[17] The *Société générale* decision of 13 November 1996[18] did not change or add anything. Indeed, recalling that the employment relationship is a power relationship and that *service organisé* is only an indicator of subordination, the Cour de cassation only took note of this evidence.[19] On the other hand, it put a significant stop to extending subordination to *service organisé au profit d'autrui*.

---

[17]   See, for example, Soc, 26 February 2002 *Bull Civ* V n° 128.

[18]   Soc. 13 November 1996 *Bull Civ* V n° 386, 275; *JCP E* 1997 n° 5, 21, note J Barthelemy, *Droit Social* 1996, 1067.

[19]   'Cet arrêt de 1996 a eu le mérite de rappeler que la subordination résultait de l'exercice, ou manifestait l'exercice, d'un *pouvoir*' : A Jeammaud, 'L'avenir sauvegardé de la qualification de contrat de travail : à propos de l'arrêt Labbane' (2001) 3 *Droit Social* 234.

The Cour de cassation confirmed the probationary value of *service organisé* in the determination of the dependant relationship. But it also imposed a new way of understanding this service. In effect, in the terms of the decision, the following are considered as subordinate workers:

> workers not for their own activity but for the person from the company which employs them in the frame of an organised service and according to the general directives imposed by it, who took the risks and the profit of its enterprise and under whose dependence they are actually placed, the form, the nature or the validity of their contract and clauses added by the company being of little importance.[20]

The focus of judicial analysis is not only the way the power is exercised, as in the case of a *service organisé au profit d'autrui*, but the objective of its implementation. The Cour substituted the analysis of the means with the analysis of the goals. It is most frequently the goal that determines the legal qualification of the means.

In effect, the reasoning of the judges differs profoundly according to the advancement of the determination. In the case of *service organisé par autrui*, judges usually emphasise that, despite the technical independence of the employee, the employer exercises power over the conditions under which the work is carried out—a rationale of affirmation. In the case of *service organisé au profit d'autrui*, they exclude the economic independence of the worker to only look at the *service organisé* for and in the interest of the employer—a rationale of subtraction.

As one example, Cour de cassation Ruling No 5371 of 19 December 2000 examined the case of a person who drove a taxi under a monthly contract which was automatically renewable. The contract had been termed a 'contract for the lease of a vehicle equipped as a taxi', and the taxi driver had paid a sum described in the contract as 'rent'. The Cour held that this contract concealed a contract of employment, since the taxi driver was bound by numerous strict obligations concerning the use and maintenance of the vehicle and was in a situation of subordination. In addition, in Rulings Nos 5034, 35 and 36 of 4 December 2001, the Supreme Court examined the case of workers engaged in the delivery and collection of parcels under a franchise agreement. The 'franchisees' collected the parcels from premises rented by the 'franchiser' and delivered them according to a schedule and route determined by the latter. In addition, the charges were set by the enterprise, which collected payment directly from the customers. The Supreme Court examined the situation of three 'franchisees' in three separate cases and handed down three rulings on the same day. According to the rulings, provisions of the Labour Code

---

[20] Emphasis supplied.

were applicable to persons whose occupation consisted essentially of collecting orders or receiving items for handling, storage or transport, on behalf of a single industrial or commercial enterprise, when those persons performed their work in premises supplied or approved by that enterprise, under conditions and at prices imposed by that enterprise, without the need to establish a subordinate relationship. This is understood to amount to an extension of the scope of the Labour Code to certain 'franchised' workers.

5.5.3 Germany

The Legislation

There is no general legal definition of employee (*Arbeitnehmer*) or self-employed person (*Selbständiger*) in German legislation. Deriving from the Roman pandectist traditions, the German Civil Code (BGB) historically draws a distinction between work contract (*Werkvertrag—location operis*) and the service contract (*Dienstvertrag—location operarum*),[21] yet this distinction does not correspond exactly to that between employment and self-employment.

The absence of a general notion of subordinate employment has created a sort of paradox, as a number of legislative interventions have established a new sphere of application for subordinate workers by taking for granted a definition that does not exist. It should be mentioned that there are different definitions of a subordinate worker in the various sectors: the most common criterion can be inferred from the content of § 84 I 2 HGB (the Code of Commerce of 1954), which describes an autonomous worker as 'someone who is substantially free to manage his/her own activity and working hours'. A second definition of subordinate worker can be found in the tax law. Others can probably be found in other legislative acts regulating specific issues such as holidays (*Bunsdesurlaubsgesetz*) and dismissals (*Abeitsplatzschutzgesetz*), but only in an indirect way, in the sense that the legislation does not provide definitions in these areas even if it refers to subordinate workers in order to define the field of application of the related laws.

The notion of 'employed' is particularly relevant, and has been elaborated by legislators to define the application of the Social Security Code (*Sozialgesetzbuch*) and tax law.

(a)   *Social security.* The Social Security Code contains a definition of employee (§ 7.1, Book IV). According to this definition, subordinate employment is not

---

[21] R Wank, 'Tipi contrattuali con prestazioni di servizio nella Rft' (1997) 2 *LD* 217 ff, 223.

self-employed work, especially when it is done within the parameters of an employment relationship. Indicators of subordinate employment are that the work is done under the control of another person and that the worker is part of the employer's organization. It is assumed that an individual is an employee within the meaning of social security law when at least three of the following factors apply:

(1) the individual concerned does not ordinarily employ anyone who is covered by compulsory social insurance and whose monthly remuneration from the employment relationship exceeds €400;
(2) the individual has been working for a long time and mainly for one principal only;
(3) this or a similar type of principal usually has similar activities carried out for him/her by employees employed by him/her;
(4) the activity of the individual concerned does not display the typical characteristics of an entrepreneurial activity; and
(5) the activity of the individual is the same as that carried out previously for the same employer under an employment relationship.

Thus, German legislation has considerably broadened the scope of application of the Social Security Act, extending it beyond the limits of subordinate employment to include those individuals, formally self-employed, who find themselves in a position of economic dependence.

(b) *Tax law.* Income tax legislation defines employees as those persons engaged or employed at present or in the past in public services or in private work and who have drawn a salary from this or a previous work relationship. An employment relationship exists as long as a worker must use his/her own labour on behalf and under the control of the employer. Despite the absence of a general legal definition, the dominant opinion in Germany holds that the starting point should be a unique and comprehensive concept that leads back to the full application of the provisions of labour law. To come up with a unified definition of subordinate employment, both legal doctrine and the jurisprudence gave lengthy consideration to the requirement of personal dependence (*persönliche Abhängigkeit*). The Federal Labour Court (*Bundesarbeitsgerichte*—BAG) has indicated that it means that the employer determines the content of the work activity and the placement (*Eingliederung*) of the worker in an organization predefined by others. However, due to the increasing number of cases involving relationships that do not fit the standard employment concept (*Normalarbeitsverhältnis*), the jurisprudence drew up a series of defining criteria for indicating whether the worker is under the control of the employer.

All in all, it could be said that in Germany, in both legal theory and practice, quasi-salaried workers (*arbeitnehmerähnliche Personen*) are considered as belonging to the self-employed category and, more precisely, as forming a subcategory in need of greater protection than that provided most self-employed persons. Some of the legal protections (eg holidays, social security pension benefits) afforded employees are extended to quasi-workers. The characteristics of this category of workers are set out in many legislative provisions, but there is no general definition. Nor can the following individual indicators (specific to Germany) be applied across the board: (i) the absence of economic independence; (ii) economic dependence (as opposed to the personal dependence of subordinate employees); (iii) the need for social protection (as an indicator of economic dependence); (iv) work performed personally without the aid of subordinate employees; and (v) work done mainly for one person, or where the worker relies on one single entity for more than half of his/her total income.

The Jurisprudence

The role of the jurisprudence in this area has been crucially important for at least two reasons. On the one hand, protective measures for subordinate work progressively increased, especially after the Second World War. On the other, no general legal definition or concept of an *Arbeitnehmer* (subordinate worker) or an *Arbeitsvertrag* (employment contract) has been given along with these measures. Thus the legislation has at least partially abandoned its role. In the majority of the cases, the legislators limited themselves to saying that the guarantees provided by the different measures apply to subordinate workers, while omitting the definition (or at most saying that they are divided into blue-collar workers and clerks).

In the German Federal Republic, labour jurisprudence was the main actor in elaborating the concept of the subordinate worker (*Arbeitnehmerbegriff*). To concretize the qualification criteria, the jurisprudence departed from the real facts in the absence of an abstract definition such as that provided by article 2094 of the Italian Civil Code. In particular, German lawmakers took a sociological point of view towards the subject, one best represented by the prototype for subordinate employment: the factory worker with a full-time employment for an indeterminate period (the so-called *Normalarbeitsverhältnis*, or normal employment relationship).

Affirmed as far back as during the Weimar Republic, personal dependence (*persönliche Abhängigkeit*), has remained to this day the fundamental element signifying subordination for the *Bundesarbeitsgericht*. In fact, as made evident by legal doctrine, from a technical, legal point of view, it is an empty formula (*Leerformel*) that cannot per se constitute a criterion for distinguishing between subordination and autonomy. Personal dependence should be verified on a case-by-case basis by the identification of a series of indicators of subordination that allow for understanding the degree of dependence. In fact, also according to the jurisprudence of the *Bundesarbeitsgericht*, it is the degree of personal dependence of the worker that is decisive in establishing whether there is subordination or not.

Before describing individual indicators of subordination, let us examine the method adopted by the labour jurisprudence to determine subordination. The use of the degree of personal dependence highlights how German labour judges and in particular the *Bundesarbeitsgericht* have always privileged a case-by-case approach, affirming that 'for practical reasons and of certainty of the law it is unavoidable in defining subordinate work in a typological way'[22]. According to German jurisprudence and scholarship, a subordinate worker is not a real concept (*Begriff*), but rather a type concept (*Typusbegriff*). This means that subordinate employment should be identified using the 'typological' method, according to which there are no abstract criteria applicable to all types of employment. To determine the presence of subordination—or of personal dependence—it is enough that there exist a sufficient number of the indicators elaborated by the case law to identify the type of a 'subordinate worker'.

Such a jurisprudential approach allows for greater flexibility in terms of distinguishing subordinate from autonomous employment than the interpretative method used by the majority of the judges in Italy. While Italian judges do not make their methods of definition explicit, a careful analysis of the decisions of the last 15 years clearly shows their tendency to adopt 'subsuming' or 'analogical' method. Accordingly, the employment relationship is defined as subordinate only if all the elements of the concrete case can be traced back to the abstract model (in Italian law, art 2094 of the Civil Code). Evidently, this approach introduces a greater rigidity in the qualification process.

Given that the fundamental principle for identifying subordinate employment is personal dependence and that the interpretative method adopted by the German jurisprudence is the typological one, the basic features that determine the degree of personal dependence, and thus the subordination, can be identified.

---

[22] BAG (*Bundesarbeitsgericht*) 23 April 1980, in *AP* (*Arbeitsrechtliche Praxis*) No 34 zu Par 611 BGB Abhängigkeit.

Personal dependence has been defined by the jurisprudence through the elaboration of real indicators of subordination. Legal doctrine later tried a scientific approach. The judges first examined the question of what is the essence of subordination, and affirmed that it is expressed in the first place by the fact that the worker 'offers [his/her] own work in the frame of an organization directed by a third person'.[23] Personal dependence is thus present when the worker is subject to the directional power of the employer, that is, he or she performs a working activity directed by someone else (*fremdbestimmte Arbeit*).

From close examination of the jurisprudential decisions, primary among these indicators is the connection with the organization of the employer (*organisatorische Abhängigkeit*), which can be manifest both in the link with the organization created by the employer with reference to the time and place of the work, and in the need for coordination with other employees. More recently, the absence of real entrepreneurial organization (if the worker uses own workspace and equipment) and the workers' need for social protection (*soziale Schutzbedürftigkeit*) have come to be used. A further element—whether the work activity is useful to others (*Fremdnützighkeit*)—is often recognized by the judges when it is not possible to determine the nature and objectives of the work activity.

German jurisprudence has thus continued to attribute great significance to the element of *eterodirezione* in subordination—even adding another series of indicators—but has adopted a very flexible concept of directional power. Instead of limiting the latter to the employer's directives on the performance of the working activity, German jurisprudence uses the idea of power in terms of the facilitation of the worker's functional and useful participation in the production process. By such a broad use of the traditional identifying requisite of subordinate employment, the judges have extended in a significant way the field of application of labour law, including many relationships belonging to the 'grey area'.

Compared to legal systems such as that of Italy, the absence of legal definition of subordination in the German model has clearly increased the role of German jurisprudence in the determining subordination. German jurisprudence favours the creation of a more elastic notion of subordination, not necessarily linked to the hierarchical dimension of the power of the employer in the enterprise. Despite this, in Germany in the last 15 years the phenomenon of the 'escape from labour law', much denounced in Italy, has been felt and greatly contributed to the increasing phenomenon of the so-called 'new autonomy' (*neue Selbständigkeit*).

---

[23] As affirmed by the BAG (*Bundesarbeitsgericht*) 20 July 1994, in *AP* (*Arbeitsrechtliche Praxis*) No 73 zu Par 611 BGB Abhängigkeit; see BAG 19 November 1997, in *AP* No 133 zu Par 611 BGB Lehrer und Dozenten.

5.5.4 United Kingdom

The Legislation

Like that of other European countries, UK labour law seems to be historically based on a distinction between contracts of subordinate work (contract of employment, contract of service) and autonomous work (contract for service, self-employment labour). As in many other areas of law in the United Kingdom, it is the jurisprudence of the courts that has constructed, in the absence of a unitary and consistent legal definition, the legal notions determining—according to the expression of Kahn-Freund—a real 'case law labyrinth'. In general terms, UK protective legislation is recognized as applying to employees—that is, those hired under a contract of employment. Gradually, on the basis of decisions by the courts in specific cases, the employee has become juxtaposed with the self-employed worker, to whom the rights and obligations included in an individual agreement apply.

Together with case law, the existence and importance of certain statutes should also be recognized. Deakin links a Parliamentary Act (the National Insurance Act of 1946) to the so-called 'unitary notion' of subordinate work (employment under contract of service). It is perfectly congruent with the characteristics of the consolidating production paradigm, and has remained substantially unchanged over the following 30 years. Legislation also includes the Contract of Employment Act 1963 and the Employment Protection Act 1975, conceptual elaborations of the jurisprudence creating a floor of statutory rights. These aimed at guaranteeing a minimum standard of rights for the subordinate worker.

Besides the 'employee' (as defined above), UK law identifies others for whom some protective measures are recognized (see table below). The United Kingdom has experienced the important phenomenon of a selective extension of protective measures through the identification of concentric fields of application. In a widening circle containing the traditional 'employee', the 'worker' has been identified as lying between the subordinate worker (the employee) and the autonomous worker (self-employed). More specifically, the legislation uses the term *worker* to indicate a broader category that includes subordinate workers in cases in which 'the subject undertakes by a contract to carry out personally work or a service for another party and whose status on basis of the contract is not that of a user or a client of a professional or commercial activity carried out by the other party'.[24]

---

[24] See Employment Rights Act 1996 s 230(3); National Minimum Wage Act 1998 s 54(3); Working Time Regulations 1998 SI 1998/1833 reg 2(1); Part-time Workers (Prevention of Less Favourable Treatment) Regulations SI 2000/1551 art 2.

Taken as a whole, recent legislation is a concentric system of protective measures, moving away from the traditional division of the notions of subordinate and autonomous work.

Type	Effects
Dependent entrepreneurs	Health and safety
Professionals (all those who carry out personally a work or a service)	Anti-discrimination legislation
Workers	Wages and hours legislation
Employment relationship	Insolvency and acquired rights directives
Contract of employment	Notice, unfair dismissal, redundancy, written particulars

From the above, it can be said that the law itself authorizes the Government to adjust its scope, a novel response to the growing problem of disguised and objectively ambiguous employment relationships. For example, under s 23 of the Employment Relations Act 1999, the Government may confer employment rights on certain individuals vis-à-vis an employer (however defined), may provide that such individuals are to be treated as parties to employment contracts, and may make provisions as to who is to be regarded as their employer. These powers have not, as yet, been used.

The Jurisprudence

A distinction is made by jurisprudence between the two types of employment by a series of criteria (common law tests) for determining the nature of the employment relationship (eg control, integration, economic reality, mutuality of obligation). For all of these, there are a series of subordination indicators that signify whether the worker is in a situation of subordination (or some degree of subordination) and economic dependence (ie continuing economic dependence). The will of the parties has a secondary role in the judge's determination, as he or she will use that criterion when other criteria do not provide a reliable definition of the relationship. The following are some the tests used in the UK system.

— *Control test.* The degree of discretion and autonomy when carrying out the work, determined using certain parameters (eg duty to obey orders, discretion on hours of work; supervision of mode of working). In general, the element of control includes the power to decide the object of the working activity, how to carry it out, the equipment to use, the time and the place.

— *Integration test.* Subordinate employment is determined not so much by the power of command of the employer as by the fact that the worker is subject to the rules and procedures of the organization (eg disciplinary procedures, inclusion in occupational benefit scheme). The worker and his/her activity are an integral part of the organization structure.

— *Economic reality.* The distribution of the economic risk between the employer, worker and the state (indicators include the method of payment, the freedom to hire others, the provision of own equipment, investment in own business, coverage of sick pay and holiday pay). By this method of definition, it is necessary to verify where the financial risks are located and if the worker can make profit from such allocation. The test is not limited to the evaluation of who bears the risk but considers other elements too, such as the ownership of production equipment, payment methods, and whether the worker organizes the work and thus bears the risks or, on the contrary, he or she is integrated into the commercial activity of someone else. The use of such a test has allowed the courts to classify many casual workers as subordinate workers, for example irregular and atypical workers who, according to other methods (in particular, the mutuality of obligation test, based on the continuity and stability of the contract), remained without protection. This test also casts light on the economic weakness of workers not subject to control who would be considered to be autonomous workers under the control test.

— *Mutuality of obligation,* relating to recruitment conditions, provides formal indicators of whether an individual is a subordinate employee (these include duration of employment, regulation of employment, right to refuse work, customs in the trade). The test refers to the 'reciprocal promises of the parties to maintain the employment relationship of a certain period of time': there is a subordinate employment contract if there is an expressed or implicit contract term that obliges the employer to regularly request the execution of an activity and the worker to carry it out when asked to do so.

These tests were combined and gave way to a multiple test, according to which there is a subordinate work contract if the following three conditions are satisfied:

(a) the worker accepts to work for the employer in exchange for remuneration;

(b) the worker accepts, expressly or implicitly, to be subject to the control of the employer;

(c) the other contractual dispositions are compatible with the existence of the subordinate employment contract.

161

Finally, the vagueness of the concept of 'integration into the organizational structure' in UK law should be noted. Although a few court decisions used this criterion in the 1950s, for example *Stevenson Jordon & Harrison Ltd v MacDonald & Evans*[25] and *Bank voor Handel en Scheepvaart NV v Slatford,*[26] it was apparently not employed in the subsequent decades (see for instance *Ready Mixed Concrete (South East) Ltd v Minister of Pensions and National Insurance*[27]). Due to the diversification of employment relations, however, which makes it difficult to determine the existence of employer control in terms of time, place and means, the concept of 'integration into the organizational structure' has received more attention in recent years.

5.5.5 European Community Law

European Community law has also had to address the definition of the two concepts of employment and self-employment, first and foremost to determine the scope of application of the rules governing free movement. The EC Treaty provisions (arts 39–42) use the general term 'workers', but it is not difficult to see that they refer to subordinate employment. Article 1 of Regulation 1612/1968 recognizes the right of every citizen of a Member State to 'take up an activity as an employed person and to pursue such activity within the territory of another Member State'.

Apart from the example cited above, there is no definition of subordinate employment in European Community law. One would have to consult the now consolidated case law of the European Court of Justice which has, over the decades, prescribed some basic criteria for identifying the concept. First of all, the Court states that it cannot be left to the individual States to define the concept of worker, for we would end up giving them the right to alter the area of application deriving from that definition, with the risk of excluding some categories from the guarantees provided under the Treaty.[28] In order to determine the correct category, we would need to 'have recourse to the generally recognized principles of interpretation, beginning with the ordinary meaning to be attributed to those terms ... in the light of the objectives of the Treaty.'[29]

---

[25] *Stevenson Jordon & Harrison Ltd v MacDonald & Evans* [1952] 1 TLR 101(CA) 111.
[26] *Bank voor Handel en Scheepvaart NV v Slatford* [1953] 1 QB 248 (CA) 295.
[27] *Ready Mixed Concrete (South East) Ltd v Minister of Pensions and National Insurance* [1967] 2 QB 497, 524
[28] Case C-75/63 *Unger v Bedrijfsvereninging voor Detailhandel en Ambachten* (ECJ 19 March 1964).
[29] Case C-53/81 *Levin v Secretary of State for Justice* (ECJ 23 March 1983) [9].

Putting the onus on national laws, in the *Lawrie-Blum*[30] ruling, the Court stated that, in the context of article 39 (formerly art 48) of the EC Treaty, the definition of employment must be based on 'objective criteria which distinguish the employment relationship by reference to the rights and duties of the persons concerned'. Thus the essential feature of subordinate employment is that for a certain period of time 'a person performs services for and under the direction of another person in return for which he receives remuneration.' In Community law, too, a major feature of employment is that the worker performs his/her work under the direction of another person.

In other areas, the definitions are less important in that they cannot be used to demarcate the scope of Community rules. In legislation governing social security for migrant workers, a very broad concept of worker is used, one that is not related to national general definitions of employees and self-employed persons (see art 1 of Regulation 1408/1971). Likewise, with regard to equality, Community legislation covers both categories of workers and does not restrict protection measures to employees only:

(a)   The legislation governing equal treatment of men and women covers both employment and self-employment. Indeed, under Directive 86/613/EC the legislation contained in Directive 76/207/EC is made applicable to employees and self-employed persons alike.

(b)   The scope of application of Directive 2000/78/EC on equal treatment for men and women with regard to employment and working conditions and Directive 2000/43/EC governing the principle of equal treatment of persons irrespective of racial or ethnic origin covers both employment and self-employment (art 3.1(a)), Directive 2002/73/EC modifying Directive 76/207.

The principle of equal treatment also applies to social security schemes for employees (Directives 79/7/EC and 86/378) and self-employed persons (Directive 86/613).

With other aspects of employment relationships, Community legislation adopts two solutions. The first is to omit all reference to the two categories (see Directive 93/104/EC on working hours and Directive 98/59/EC on collective redundancies). The second solution is to refer to national legislation. For example:

---

[30]   Case C-66/85 *Lawrie-Blum v Land Baden-Württemberg*(ECJ 3 July 1986),, [17]. Subsequently Case C-344/87 *Bettray v Secretary of State for Justice* (ECJ 31 May 1989); Case C-3/87 *R v Ministry of Agriculture, Fisheries and Food ex p Agegate Ltd* (ECJ 14 December 1989); Case C-357/89 *Raulin v Minister van Onderwijs en Wetenschappen* (ECJ 26 February 1992); Case C-3/90, *Bernini v Minister van Onderwijs en Wetenschappen*, (ECJ 26 February 1992); Case C-85/96, *Martinez Sala v Freistaat Bayern* (ECJ 12 May 1998).

(a) Directive 96/34/EC, which incorporates the framework agreement on parental leave, 'applies to all workers of both sexes having a contract or an employment relationship defined by law, by collective agreement or based on practices in force in each Member State'.

(b) Directive 96/71/EC, relating to the posting of employed persons states that 'for the purpose of the Directive, the definition of worker shall be that used in the Member State to which the worker is posted'.

(c) The provisions of Directive 97/81/EC, which incorporates the framework agreement on part-time work, 'apply to part-time workers having an employment contract or relationship defined by law, by collective agreement, or based on practices in force in each Member State'.

(d) The rules of Directive 99/70/EC, on fixed-term employment, 'apply to fixed-term workers with an employment contract or relationship governed by law, by collective contracts or based on practices in force in each Member State'.

On the whole, instead of prescribing protection measures based on general definitions of employment and self-employment, Community law focuses much more on the nature of the problems, and therefore on providing protection for workers wherever such a requirement arises. The trend in more recent Community legislation in specific areas—for example equal treatment—is to do away with the distinction between employment and self-employment and to simply use the category of the 'person carrying out work'.

5.6 Economically Dependent Work

As a result of the splitting and decentralization of production, autonomous work has increased in recent years. Whereas in the past there was a progressive expansion of subordinate employment towards former areas of *locatio operis*, today this seems to be reversed, and labour-saving information technologies presage not so much a society without work, as described by Rifkin, but scenarios where subordinate work no longer represents an exclusive way to offer work in coordination with and/or in the interest of another person.

If during the 1990s only one sector of the European labour doctrine paid attention to this phenomenon,[31] it has garnered much interest in current scholarship. Recent inquiries reveal a global trend of increasing self-employment in the 1990s, so much so that in 2000 the OECD dedicated a chapter of *Employment Outlook* to the 'partial rebirth of independent work', especially in the business sector and in services to the community. National reports confirm this to be a very visible trend not only in the European Union but also on the global scale.

It should be underlined that the policies of company streamlining, downsizing and 'dematerialization', besides contributing significantly to the expansion of self-employment, also have many ramifications from both social and legal points of view. The more sharp-eyed social scientists have coined the term 'second-generation' self-employment[32] to highlight the innovative specificity of this new type of work and its distance from the traditional forms of *locatio operis*. While, strictly speaking, these types of 'second-generation' employment generally qualify as self-employment, there is a growing trend towards creating (or extending) legal protection for them. In those countries where this trend has not yet brought about legislative amendments, one can observe in the public debate the desire on the part of different parties for greater protection than is possible under the traditional binary model.

The Italian Legislation

The concept of the economically dependent worker—or quasi-subordinate worker, to use a more accurate term—has existed in Italian law for 30 years now. The first reference to it in legislation dates back to the reform of the procedural rules (*processo del lavoro*), which dealt not only with subordinate employment, but also with agency contracts, sales representation and other collaboration relationships involving continuous and coordinated work, performed mainly in a personal capacity (art 409 no 3, Civil Procedure Code). It was here that the term 'quasi-subordinate employment' was introduced to define forms of self-employment displaying special characteristics, making it similar to subordinate employment.

The extension is not limited to the procedural rules but also concerns the non-validity of relinquishments and settlements concerning quasi-subordinate workers' rights, stemming from legal provisions and collective agreements (art 2113,

---

[31] G Lyon Caen, *Le droit du travail non-salarié* (Paris, Ed. Sirey, 1990); U Romagnoli, "Arriva un bastimento carico di "A"", in D'Antona (ed.), *Politiche di flessibilità e mutamenti del diritto del lavoro: Italia e Spagna* (Napoli, ESI, 1990).

[32] S Bologna, A Fumagalli, *Il lavoro autonomo di seconda generazione* (Milano, Feltrinelli 1997).

Civil Code). However, one cannot conclude from this that in legal terms quasi-subordinate employment is synonymous with the concept of a 'weaker contracting party': the rules applicable to quasi-subordinate workers are only those prescribed by law, and contractual weakness cannot become the prerequisite for extending, by way of interpretation, other protection measures applicable to employees.

The question of quasi-subordinate employment has attracted growing interest in recent years, mainly as a result of the pension reform of 1995 (Act No 335 of 1995), which extended the pension rules for subordinate employees to the self-employed. The Act also provided for the establishment of a special public pension fund for quasi-subordinate workers. The rules governing occupational accidents and diseases were later extended to cover quasi-subordinate workers. Finally, for tax purposes, quasi-subordinate workers' incomes are treated in the same way as employees' incomes.

The extension of subordinate employees' protection to quasi-subordinate workers, however, has not meant that the two are recognized as equals when calculating social security contributions. For Italian quasi-subordinate workers, one-third of the contribution must be paid by the worker, with the remaining two-thirds paid by the client.

Despite this progressive extension of protective measures, one cannot say that quasi-subordinate employment is a third category of employment. In practice, it is still included in the self-employment category. In Italian law, economically-dependent employment is based on three main characteristics:

(a)   continuance;
(b)   coordination;
(c)   the mainly personal nature of the work.

Continuance means that the work is intended to meet a long-term requirement of the other party and that it will take time to complete; in other words, the time period covered in the contract is not brief and discrete. Yet given that self-employed work is aimed at achieving a result, one cannot speak of a long-lasting obligation in the legal sense. It is the de facto continuance of the service that is important. In practice, even in cases where the work is completed in a single effort, the worker may have spent considerable time beforehand preparing the work, so continuance may be said to exist. This criterion is of course met in cases where the 'work' is repeated over time.

Coordination of the work by the client must be distinct from employer control (*eterodirezione*), otherwise the work could be considered subordinate employment. In structural terms, coordination, unlike control, does not imply a close link in terms of the way the work is performed in space and time. Coordination is a functional relationship, a necessary connection between the execution of the work and the organization of the work by the beneficiary (whether the entrepreneur or not). In other words, the obligation on the part of the quasi-subordinate worker to comply with requirements is not as strong as it is for an employee.

The *mainly personal nature of the work* must be understood either in quantitative terms, ie provision of capital or other workers, or in qualitative terms, ie the importance of the service for the business involved. Regarding the quantitative aspect, this means that it is possible to exclude activities that are purely entrepreneurial, for instance, services rendered in the form of a company (partnership or joint stock company), or services rendered by a natural person whose job it is to direct the work of others without being personally involved in that work. With the qualitative aspect, the concept of 'mainly personal' can still be met even if a third party is involved, provided that the worker's contribution is essential and irreplaceable in terms of theoretical knowledge and experience.

To the legal framework described above should be added a recent intervention of Italian legislation regulating *lavoro a progetto* (project work), article 61 of Legislative Decree no 276/2003). The Act reforming the labour market, approved by this Decree, tackled, inter alia, the delicate issue of subordinate employment relationships, the subject of discussion by doctrine and also of an unfortunate series of legislative interventions. The reform's starting point was the assumption that the 'continuous and coordinated cooperation' *(collaborazioni coordinate e continuative—'co. co.co')* of article 409 no 3 of the Civil Procedure Code had been used in an inappropriate and elusive way in labour law legislation: 'a way ... with which reality identified in the turns of the law ways to go over the rigidities and insufficiencies of employment rules'. Consequently, the reform's point of departure should have been that a significant part of the *co.co.co* should be considered as subordinate employment. This gave rise to alarm about the 'disappearance' of *co.co.co* and concerns that the reform would lead to a new rigidity, coupled with the risk of millions of autonomous work activities becoming subordinate employment relationships.[33]

The reform was the source of much ado—perhaps about nothing. The (meta-) typological and temporal requirements imposed by the legislation were that to be legitimately established, cooperation should be linked (*riconducibile*) to a specific project or programme or phase of work (art 61(1)) and have a determinate or

---

[33] P Ichino, *Il contratto di lavoro* (Milano, Giuffrè, 2003); R Del Punta, La scomparsa dei co.co.co., 2003 http://www.lavoce.info/articoli/pagina488.html; A Vallebona, 'Lavoro a progetto: incostituzionalità e circolare di pentimento', (2004) *Argomenti di diritto del lavoro* 293.

determinable duration (art 62(a)) under the sanction of converting *ex lege* the *co.co.co* into an subordinate employment for unfixed term (art 69(1)).

The report attached to the Legislative Decree reveals that the legislator wanted to grant legal recognition to the trend of *lavoro a progetto*, especially visible in the growing service sector. In reality, *lavoro a progetto* representing genuine independent cooperation already has legal recognition in the notion of *prestazione d'opera coordinata e continuative*. This raises a series of questions about the provision. Is it a rule aimed at introducing a new type of contract into the legal system, as it would seem the case in article 62(1), which expressly refers to the *contratto di lavoro a progetto* (project work contract)? Or is it maybe a *tertium genus*, situated between subordination and self-employment? Or is it a simple adjustment to the new legal parameters of cooperation relationships, concretising in a continuous and coordinated working activity (*prestazione d'opera continuativa e coordinata*) article 409 no 3 of the Civil Procedure Code?

From this and related legislation, one gains the impression that there is substantial continuity between the old notion, the rules on *co.co.co*, and the new notion of *lavoro a progetto*. The legal definition expressly refers to the 'mostly personal ... coordinated and continuous cooperation ... without subordination as of Article 409, no 3 of the Civil Procedure Code'. As these are relationships that should be linked to one or more specific projects or programmes of work or phases thereof, *lavoro a progetto* designates a part of what is usually defined as quasi-subordinate employment. It is not a new category, but rather a 'zone' with an open series of relations which, even if typologically they are considered self-employment, present characteristics warranting the extension of some protections guaranteed to subordinate employment (or eventually, new and different guarantees more appropriate to this type of work).

The French Legislation

Unlike in Italian and German legislation, in French legislation the notion of the economically dependent worker does not exist. The scope of labour legislation, beyond subordinate employment, however, has been extended in other ways.

One example is the legal assimilation provided by Book VII of the *Code du travail* (as amended by the Law of 26 December 1969) on 'special provisions relating to some professions' (*dispositions particulières à certaines professions*). Many of the provisions contained in Chapter VII 'alter' the definition of the employment contract, in some cases resulting in the creation of 'employees as determined by law' (*salariés par détermination de la loi*). For some specific categories such as professional journalists (art L 761–2), entertainment artists (art L 762–1) and models (art L 763–1)—and similar rules apply to home employment—there is a legal presumption that workers are employed with an employment contract. This presumption is difficult to argue with when the work is carried out in a permanent way for an enterprise that determines in significant way the conditions of the activity. Judges, however, have denied the existence of an employment contract, only occasionally recalling that the category is 'not without limit'.

The mechanism of the *assimilation aux salariés* is different from—but more interesting and original than—the system of presumption. One part of the provisions of Chapter VII extends the application of the *Code du travail* rules without touching upon the nature of the contract(s) of the interested parties. Without declaring one party to be the employees, it provides a variable range of rules applicable to them when certain conditions relating to the nature or the execution of the activity are present in a specific case.

The provisions of article L 781–1, 2° of the Labour Code which apply to a person employed under an employment contract (*salarié*) are applicable to those whose profession is to sell goods provided exclusively or almost exclusively by an enterprise when such persons carry out their activities in a place provided or accepted by the enterprise and under conditions imposed by that enterprise.

French legislation thus opts to guarantee the operation of the whole protective system offered by labour law to agents, managers of trade funds, concessionaires, exclusive distributors, etc. Yet according to article L 782–1, the rule applies to the branch office managers of the food sector as well, and to *assistantes et assistantes maternelles* in certain measure, due to their integration into the entrepreneurial organization of someone else without changing the legal nature of the contract of agency, concession, franchising, etc.

The jurisprudence on the one hand recognizes that the protective measures are applicable simply by virtue of the existence of the conditions expressed by the Code, without the need to verify the existence of subordination. On the other hand, evaluators must consider not only the formal provisions of the contract, but also whether such conditions actually exist. Moreover, the broad formulation of the rule does not preclude its application to persons who employ subordinate workers, since the conditions of article L 781–1, 2° of the Labour Code are also satisfied by the relationship between the enterprise setting the conditions of sales, purchase, management, etc, and the autonomous worker or the entrepreneur.

It is opportune here to underline how such professional situations can only be partially linked to the 'intermediate entities' known in Italian and German legislation. As observed in comparative law doctrine, French law has indeed created entities of mixed, or rather dual, status. Differing from the quasi-subordinate worker, who is no longer such if he or she becomes an entrepreneur (due to the disappearance of the personal activity in the employment), workers falling within article 781–1 are at once workers assimilated as subordinate workers, and employers/autonomous workers subject to the rules of commercial law with their own clients and dependent employees. Obviously, the two legislative techniques should be distinguished, as they extend the application of the protective rules in different ways. In this they reflect the dual tendency, when considering conditions of economic dependence (*dépendance économique*) or quasi-self-employment (*parasubordination*), of on the one hand responding to legitimate claims for protection and guarantees under labour law, while on the other lessening the legal uncertainty that leads to litigation in grey area situations.

The German Legislation

Germany is another country where the question of economically dependent work has been widely debated. Here too it is possible to retrace the steps taken to develop a suitable legal framework for this type of work.

As with Italy, the first German law to address economically dependent workers—in the German system, *arbeitnehmeränliche Personen* ('workers similar to employees')—was a kind of procedural law. It extended to these workers certain protections that apply to employees. The Procedural Act on labour law (*Arbeitsgerichtsgesetz* § 5) includes among employees 'other persons who, because of a lack of economic autonomy, are treated as dependent workers'. The same terms are used in the Holidays Act (*Bundesurlaubsgesetz* 1963 § 2). Yet perhaps the most relevant legislation is the 1974 Collective Agreement Act (*Tarifvertraggesetz*—TVG § 12a). This Act extends its scope of application to economically dependent persons in need of social protection. The protection is similar to that given to employees in cases where these individuals carry out work for the benefit of other persons under a service or work contract, personally and largely without the collaboration of subordinate employees. Economically dependent workers:

(a) work mainly for one individual; or
(b) receive more than half their total occupational income mainly from one individual; in the event that this cannot be known in advance, and provided that there is nothing to the contrary in the collective agreement, their earnings shall be based on the previous six months. Should the duration of the activity be less than six months, earnings shall be calculated for the whole of that period.

Commercial agents are excluded from this provision.

The Holidays Act introduced a broad definition of quasi-subordinate worker to German law. However, the debate is ongoing regarding the introduction of a general definition of *arbeitnehmeränliche Person*. More recently, protection against sexual harassment in the workplace was extended to *arbeitnehmeränliche Personen* under a 1994 Act (*Beschaftigtenschutzgesetz* § 1). In 1998 and 1999, social security legislation was amended (*Sozialgesetzbuch*—SGB §7 book IV). In an attempt to combat false self-employment, a number of presumptions were introduced to broaden the concept of subordinate employee (c 1 § 6). This resulted in full social security coverage for both employees and *arbeitnehmeränliche Personen*.

A report drawn up by a group of commercial associations and the Chambers of Commerce Association[34] suggested that the introduction of these amendments has had negative effects and brought about the sudden termination of many self-employment contracts or jeopardized their extension. The report includes the following examples:

(a) *Commercial agent in the capital goods sector.* A commercial agent had worked for a medium-sized mechanical engineering company for many years. In 1999, in the wake of the legislative reform, the engineering company terminated the representative's contract for fear that it would have to pay his social security contributions. This stemmed from the fact that the agent had been working very closely with the company; he had even rented a small office on company premises from which he managed his principal's whole distribution system. The agent had explicitly requested this close cooperation so that he could deal more effectively with customers' enquiries. With his further qualification as a mechanical engineer, he was even able to take account of customers' requests in planning.

(b) *Direct selling.* The regulations concerning what is termed 'false self-employment' led to considerable uncertainty among the sales representatives of the Federal Direct Selling Association's member companies. For instance, a large family business, employing sales representatives to distribute cleaning equipment and fully fitted kitchens, had to cut back its production as a result of losing many of its sales representatives due to a climate of uncertainty. Although amended several times, the after-effects of these reforms are still being felt.

(c) *Non-distribution sectors.* Self-employed persons in the building, construction and

---

[34] Federal Association of Insurance Intermediaries (BVK), the German Direct Selling Association, the National Federation of German Trade Associations for Commercial Agencies and Distribution (CDH), the German Association of Chambers of Industry and Commerce (DIHK), *Practical experience report on Economically dependent work/Parasubordination: legal, social and economic aspects* (Bonn/Berlin, 2002).

advertising sectors, data processing experts and freelance contributors to the media have complained about the withdrawal or cancellation of orders and the failure to extend contracts. The principals' fears of the contractual relationships being classed as false self-employment and the resulting large social security contributions was so great that they terminated the relationships, despite the fact that there was a good chance these would not have been so classified.

In summary, we can highlight that in the absence of a general definition of economically independent work, German doctrine and jurisprudence has identified a series of indicators for it. These include:

— the absence of economic autonomy[35];
— economic dependence, as opposed to personal dependence (*persönliche Abhängigkeit*), of subordinate employees[36];
— the need for social protection[37];
— work performed personally, without the aid of subordinate employees[38];
— work done mainly for one person, or where the worker relies on one person for more than half of his or her total income[39].

The UK Legislation

Although there is no definition of quasi-subordinate worker in the United Kingdom, more recent legislation has introduced the category of 'worker', which lies somewhere between (subordinate) employee and self-employed person. This legislation introducing the so-called intermediary category was certainly influenced by the phenomenon of economic dependence. The Employment Rights Act 1996 defines a 'worker' as someone who 'undertakes by a contract to carry out personally a job or a service for another party and whose status, based on the contract is not that of a user or a client of a professional or commercial activity of carried out by

---

[35] Law on Labour Procedure (Arbeitsgerichtsgesetz 1953 § 5); Federal Law on Holidays (Bundesurlaubsgesetz) 1963 § 2; Law on Health and Safety at Work (Arbeitsschutzgesetz) § 2 n 3.
[36] Law on Collective Agreements (Tarifvertraggesetz-TVG) § 12a.
[37] Law on collective agreements (Tarifvertraggesetz-TVG) §12a.
[38] Law on collective agreements (Tarifvertraggesetz) §12a; Social security code (Sozialgesetzbuch-SGB), § 7, Book IV.
[39] Law on collective agreements (Tarifvertraggesetz) §12a; Social security code (Sozialgesetzbuch-SGB), § 7 comma IV, Book IV.

the counterparty'.[40] In identifying the category, one or more jurisprudential criteria serve as the basis for distinguishing between subordinate employment and self-employment. The 'criterion for the determination of the status of worker basically cannot be different from the one used in the case of subordinate workers given that if there is a difference between the latter and the first ones, it refers to the degree and not to the type'.[41]

British fiscal legislation suggests a differentiation of applicable fiscal systems according to the autonomous or subordinate nature of the employment relationship. It is subordinate employment if the worker has to carry out only the directives of the employer, personally and at a given place of work; receives a remuneration on an hourly, weekly or monthly basis; and has the right to payment for overtime. It is self-employment when the person is responsible of his/her own activity and takes up the risk, profit and responsibility for management of the activity.

The Spanish Legislation

A trade union proposal for a law in 2002, aimed at a consistent extension of rights in favour of economically dependent work, was acknowledged by Act No 20/2007. It introduced a real statute for economically dependent autonomous workers.

When the law was first proposed by the *Union de Profesionales y Trabajadores Autónomos* (UPTA), the argument was made that new production models had altered traditional autonomous work 'not only in quantitative terms but . . . [had] substantially changed the traditional morphology on which autonomous work developed'. These 'new mixed ways of working' had some characteristics of subordinate employment even if they were formally considered self-employment. They were situations of para-subordinate or economically dependent work (*trabajo parasubordinado* or *trabajo autónomo dependiente*) where the worker offered his or her activity in a coordinated way to one or more entrepreneurs upon whom he or she was economically dependent.[42]

---

[40] See Employment Rights Act 1996 s 230(3); National Minimum Wage Act 1998 s 54(3); The Working Time Regulations 1998, SI 1998/1833, reg. 2(1); The Part-time Workers (Prevention of Less Favourable Treatment) Regulations SI 2000/1551, art 2.

[41] S Deakin, "Autonomia, subordinazione e lavoro economicamente dipendente", (2004) *Diritto delle relazioni industriali* 599.

[42] *Ley por la que se regula el trabajo autónomo dependiente, exposición de motivos* (Madrid, Instituto Complutense de Estudios Internacionales, 2002) 1.

The Act contains 29 articles and is divided into four parts. The first part defines the field of application and gives a definition of autonomous work, the second gives regulations for autonomous work, the third regulates its collective dimension and the fourth is on social protection. The Act's field of application covers 'those physical persons who habitually carry out an economic or professional lucrative activity personally and directly for themselves and outside the direction and organization and another person'. The Act also applies to economically dependent workers as defined by c III of title II, in particular 'economically dependent autonomous workers who habitually carry out a lucrative economic or professional activity personally, directly and mostly for a physical or legal person, called the client, [and for whom] at least 75 per cent of the income of the work or economic or professional activity carried out economically depends on the latter'.

To be considered an economically dependent worker, a person has to satisfy the following requirements:

(a) He or she does not employ workers on someone else's behalf and does not contract or subcontract partially or totally his/her activity with a third person, either as regards the contracted activity with the client from whom he/she depends economically, or activities which he/she could contract with other clients.

(b) He or she does not carry out his/her activity in a different way from workers carrying out services by other employment contracting modalities for the client.

(c) He or she acquires the productive and material infrastructure necessary for carrying out the activity and independent from his/her client when such activities are economically relevant.

(d) He or she carries out his/her activity with his/her organization criteria without prejudice to the technical indications that he/she can receive from his/her client.

(e) He or she receives an economic counter-provision relating to the results of his/her activity in accordance with the agreement made with the client, by taking up the risk and the opportunities arising from the activity.

5.7 Indicators of Economic Dependence: A Comparison

Comparative analysis reveals a set of criteria or indicators of economic dependence (or quasi-subordination) that highlight similarities with subordinate employment and differences from traditional autonomous work. The most common are the following.

(1) *The personal or mostly personal nature of the work.* In quasi-subordinate employment or economically dependent autonomous work, the work is carried out personally or with a predominantly personal element, ie with a rather limited organization of means and/or human resources. The presence of broad, articulated organization—involving the work and/or goods and capital of others—is a significant indicator affirming the activity's entrepreneurial quality. This normally results in its exclusion from the category of subordinate employment, except for in some instances in German and French legislation.

Even if the parameters of the requirement are ambiguous, the concept of economic dependence is present in both Italian and German legislation. This raises the practical problem of verifying the quantitatively and qualitatively the personal contribution vis-à-vis the organization of means and/or persons that the economically dependent worker uses. Italian legislation (art 409 n 3 c.p.c.) excludes from quasi-subordinate employment those relationships where cooperation takes on a real entrepreneurial character if the activity is carried out within a company (eg of persons or capital, regular or irregular). It is likewise entrepreneurial in a *contratto di agenzia* if the agency (physical person) organized his/her activity with entrepreneurial criteria, according to which (personnel, structure, capital) he or she does not cooperate with somebody else, but manages an autonomous enterprise on his/her own. According to the same indicators, a concessionaire is limited to organizing and directing his/her own co-operators, without any direct personal involvement.

German legislation (para 12a of the TVG) affirms that the work or service should be provided personally and essentially without the cooperation of other subordinate workers—that is, by means of a very simple organization. In interpreting this provision, reference is normally made to the provisions on home-workers, who are defined as working in a freely chosen place alone or with his/her family members according to the orders of a storeowners or an intermediate boss granting the results of his/her activity. A craftsman who works at home, on the other hand, is like someone who produces works and packages goods on the orders of an industrialist or an intermediary subject at the place chosen by him, and with no more than two assistants or home-workers. This means that—as requested by article 409 n 3, c.p.c.—work can be considered personal when the contribution of the titular of the relationship prevails (both from a quantitative and qualitative point of view) over the contribution of any co-workers he or she may use.

(2) *Absence of a direct contact with the market.* A significant number of economically dependent autonomous workers work for buyers who later place the products in the market. In a certain part of German legal doctrine, the absence of a real link with the market represents the main indicator of economic dependence and at the same time the presumption and consequence of the absence of real autonomy on the part of the economic-dependent workers.

(3) *Exclusiveness or quasi-exclusiveness of the contractual relationship granting a monthly or annual income to the worker.* According to Oliver Williamson, people choose the form and the complexity of the contract on the basis of the danger of the 'opportunistic' behaviour of the counterparty. 'Market alternatives are mainly what protect each party against opportunism by his opposite'.[43] This indicator of economic dependence can empirically be translated in terms of the range of buyers, or of the difference between the clients and the restricted buyers. This distinction is considered a central one, not only for its effects on the market but also for the analysis of the changes in the inequality systems and social stratification. The ideal type of autonomous worker with differentiated and multiple clients is the free professional, whose activities may or may not be regulated by professional associations. For professionals with more clients, independence, autonomy and safety in the market are usually guaranteed. In contrast to the free professional with a differentiated income, an autonomous worker with a limited number of buyers has no clients and very few buyers: according to article L 781–1 of the Labour Code, the legal assimilation to subordinate employment of some autonomous working activities is conditioned by whether the person, regardless of his/her activity, is linked to only one supplier on an exclusive (or near-exclusive) basis. The same can be said about the home-worker, who is no longer a home-worker if he or she has his/her own clients and does not work exclusively for one industrial establishment,[44] and for the so-called 'non-employee manager' of article L 782–1, who is generally linked to a company by an exclusive supply clause at an imposed price.

It is these single-buyer situations that legislators consider to be paradigmatic examples of economic dependence in (vertical) contractual relations. The rules on the subcontracting dependence of the economically dependent worker are characterized by the impossibility of turning to other clients without disadvantageous repercussions. In Italian legislation, economic dependence should be verified 'by

---

[43] O Williamson, "Transaction-Cost Economics: The Governance of Contractual Relations", (1979) 22 *Journal of Law and Economics* 247.

[44] Soc 14 October 1970, in *Droit Social*, with a note by J Savatier.

taking into consideration also the real possibilities for the party who suffered an abuse to find satisfying alternatives on the market' (art 9 co 1°, 1 no 192/1998). Given the prospect of finding satisfactory alternatives to the buyer, the subcontractor must balance relationships with private persons with a possible disturbance of market functionality.[45] While the impossibility of finding market alternatives is the only legal evaluative criterion for economic dependence, it is not an exclusive one, since the article leaves open the possibility of identifying other, not expressly named, criteria. On this point, German legislation seems more decisive, referring to the absence of the 'sufficient and reasonable possibilities to turn to another company' (§ 26 of the German Law on Limitations on Competition, GWB). French law stipulates that 'the state of economic dependence' (*l'état de dépendance économique*) is verified when the client or supplier company 'does not have an equivalent solution' (*ne dispose pas de solution équivalente*):[46] Such situations typically present in the case of agents, gas station workers, car concessionaires and franchisees.[47]

Relationships involving restricted or single buyers show the peculiarities of economically-dependent work in the German system: apart from being characterized by the enterprise's voluntary assumption of risk, workers similar to subordinate workers are identified neither by personal dependence (*persönlich abhängig*) nor by subjection to an employer's directives (*weisungsgebunden*). They are identified rather by 'economic dependence', whose primary legal verification relates to work 'carried out mainly for one person' (para 12a TVG).

Understood as such, economic dependence can be identified by a time criterion (how many hours, days, weeks or months the worker worked for only one person) or by remuneration (what remuneration did the worker receive from his/her only buyer, and does this qualify the worker as *arbeitnehmerähnlich*). In both cases, the choice falls to either objective unity or subjective measures. In German law, all the above criteria are often used, but for quasi-subordinate workers, legislators (para 12 TVG) have privileged remuneration: someone who earns on average at least half of his/her total income from a single buyer is considered to be a quasi-subordinate worker. The provision's third element, referring to a particular group of workers, takes a similar approach, requiring that artists, writers and journalists receive one-third of their total income from a single source. How this ratio informs legislative decisions in practice seems evident enough: the need for social protection and the typical guarantees of subordinate employment are considered taking into account whether the worker's main source of income is his/her

---

[45] R Quadri, 'Nullità e tutela del contraente debole, (2002) *Commercio Internazionale* 1143 ff.

[46] Art 8 Ordonnance no 86–1243 of the French anti-trust legislation.

[47] C Osti, "Riflessioni sull'abuso di dipendenza economica", (1999) *Mercato concorrenza regole* 9 ff.

own work or the work, carried out mainly for the only buyer, constitutes the 'basis of his/her livelihood' (*Existenzgrundlage*[48]). The Spanish system, based on the notion of economic dependence set out in Law no 20/2007 on *trabajo autónomo dependiente* (see above), also places considerable emphasis on the income indicator.

The French system uses analogous criteria, where income received on the basis of the contract becomes quite significant in measuring the degree of economic dependence. With no legal benchmark, the profit of the business is left to the judge to evaluate: 'if the essential part of the professional income comes from the same contracting party, it should be considered as a situation of economic dependence'.[49] Legislators implicitly consider this situation to be recurring if it meets the conditions of exclusivity or quasi-exclusivity in article L 781–1 of the Labour Code.

In the Italian system, the criterion of exclusivity, if not explicitly provided by article 409 no 3, c.p.c., can be deduced from the typical requirements of the norm[50]: a situation of economic dependence with respect to either an exclusive contractual clause, or a commitment by the worker in a temporary but significant way to the buyer which limits the former's professional freedom. The jurisprudence, which frequently uses continuity and coordination interchangeably and often identifies continuity with exclusivity, considers the use of this indicator *praeter legem* reasonable, especially where the other requirements of quasi-subordination are uncertain. The main consequence is that a single working activity (*prestazione d'opera*) can satisfy the continuity requirement if the worker spent such a considerable amount of time on the activity that it was possible to conclude that the buyer was the exclusive destination of the working activity. There is no explicit reference (normative or jurisprudential) to the criterion of remuneration. For these reasons, such criteria should be considered as implicitly accepted by the legal models, even if absorbed in the schema of the continuity/exclusivity.

(4) *The inherent or functional relationship of the worker and the activity to the company.* The relationship of the activity of the quasi-subordinate worker to the total goods and resources of the buyer and the former's functional placement in production organized by someone else is characteristic of economically dependent self-employment. This should not be understood, however, as equivalent to the worker's placement in the company organization of the buyer, a characteristic of subordinate employment according to English (integration test), German (*Eingliederung in den*

---

[48] *Cf.* R Wank, *Arbeitnehmer und Selbständige* (München, C.H. Beck'sche Verlagsbuchhandlung, 1988).

[49] G J Virassamy, *Les contrats de dépendance* (Paris, LGDJ, 1986) 139 ff.

[50] M Pedrazzoli, 'Opera (prestazioni coordinate e continuative)', in *Novissimo Digesto Italiano – Appendice*, V (Turin, Utet, 1986) 478.

Betrieb) and, in part, Italian (*collaborazione* in an updated form, article 2094 of the Civil Code) case law tradition. It should rather be understood more generally in the sense of the reference or functional link of the activity to a determinate productive context or cycle. To such ends, German jurisprudence has coined the term *betriebsbezogenheit*, Italian judges use the formula *insertimento funzionale*, and French doctrine and jurisprudence talk about *activité intégrée* (giving rise to an imperfect subordination).

(5) *Absence of directives from the buyer, but presence of a coordinative power when executing the work.* If the economically dependent worker is considered to remain typologically anchored in self-employment, the coordination of the work—as required by article 409 no 3 of the Civil Procedure Code—does not interfere in the autonomous organization of the working activity, but instead confirms its functional link with the activity of the buyer. Indeed, if in practice quasi-subordinate cooperation can contribute to bringing about quasi-hierarchical organizational forms (or even hierarchical ones), on the structural level this does not imply the strict time-place coordination typical of subordination, expressed technically in the exercise by the employer of directional-organizational power.

In this regard, German doctrine affirms that 'in contrast to the subordinate worker, the *arbeitnehmerähnliche Person* is dependent only from an economic point of view and not from a personal one … and for this reason, he/she should not be subject to the directives of his/her buyer'.[51] Similarly, in Italian doctrine *eterodirezione* is reduced in economically-dependent work to the simple power of confirming the required behaviour or the execution of what is in the contract: 'the coordination of article 409 no 3 is not the same coordination that qualifies subordination'.[52] In practice, the question becomes theoretical: where, in economically-dependent work relationships, does the employer's directional power in the subordinate employment end and the coordinative power of the buyer begin? This question has never been answered definitively. In both Italian and German doctrine, the qualitative distinction between coordination and directional power is at times dubious, as 'the first is not and cannot be different from the directional power of the employer if not under a merely quantitative profile',[53] and there is a total compatibility between quasi-subordination and subjection (even if softened) in terms of the directional power of the buyer.[54] The complex distinction that emerges in Italian jurisprudence often

---

[51]   W Grunsky, *Arbeitsgerichtsgesetz Kommentar*, third edition (Munich, Verlag F. Vahlen, 1980).

[52]   M Pedrazzoli, 'Opera (prestazioni coordinate e continuative)', in *Novissimo Digesto Italiano – Appendice*, V (Torino, Utet, 1986) 476.

[53]   G Suppiej, 'Il rapporto di lavoro (costituzione e svolgimento)', in Mazzoni (dir), *Enciclopedia Giuridica del Lavoro* IV (Padova, Cedam, 2002) 49.

[54]   W Herschel, 'Die arbeitnehmerähnliche Person', (1977) DB 1185 ff.

confuses the requirements of coordination and continuity, using such formulas as the 'functional connection with the organization of the buyer for the pursuit of his/her objective', or the 'coordination with the entrepreneurial management reserved to the buyer'. The functional link can be more easily identified if the buyer is an entrepreneur, since the activity of the economically dependent autonomous worker can be perceived—in terms of coordination—as a stage in or instrument of the main productive process. If the buyer is a not an entrepreneur, an 'implicit' coordination can be inferred from the degree of congruence between the activity carried out and the buyer's objectives, according to the programme agreed by the parties.

(6) *Duration of the relationship*. In legislative method, the element of duration finds its classical references in the 'stability' of the assignment (relating to the agency: art 1742 c.c.[55]), or in the 'continuity' of the working activity (art 409 c.p.c.), and more recently in the 'unitary nature' of the relationship (art 34 l n 342/2000) or its 'non-occasional nature' (*collaborazione coordinata*, art 1 co 3, l n 142/2001). These constitute rather flexible criteria and are often used by German and Italian labour law judges. As an example, the Federal Court held that an employment relationship could be linked to economically-dependent autonomous work that lasted more than a year (BAG 13 September 1956), but excluded an organizer of festivals (BAG 16 August 1977) and a conjurer (BAG 6 December 1974) from such status due to the absence of temporal stability of the contractual relationship. Italian judges similarly consider duration to be essential, examining whether the activity of the worker satisfies the client's need for stability in the execution of an activity (*opera*), if there is a repetition of activities (ie the results are linked by continuance), or if the execution of a single *opus* requires prolonged working activity.[56] Collective bargaining also often focuses on the duration of the project or the agreed tasks (in Italy, some collective agreements specify that to have *co.co.co*, the relationship last at least two months), while Legislative Decree no 276/03 states that in reference to *lavoro a progetto*, the duration, determined or determinable, should be clear from the contract and should be linked to one or more work projects or programmes or phases thereof (art 4(c)). This distinguishes it from merely occasional autonomous employment relationships on the basis of the time criterion (the entire duration should not be more than 30 days in a year with the same buyer).

These criteria help to give a general definition of economically dependent work. However, economically dependent work can also be identified referring to

---

[55] G Ghezzi, 'Del contratto di agenzia', (1970) *Commentario del Codice Civile* (ed. A. Scialoja and G. Branca) 2 ff (Bologna-Roma, Zanichelli editore- Soc. ed. del Foro Italiano).
[56] Cass 30 December 1999 No 14722, (2000) Not. Giur. Lav. 297.

specific types of workers. In Germany, for example, the so-called qualifying definition of *arbeitnehmeränliche Person* does not preclude the category's extension to others who may have both personal autonomy and economic dependence: homeworkers (art 1 co 1 e 2 HAG), trade agents (art 92a HGB and art 5 co 3 of the ArbGGT), independent workers in the mass media and 'persons who supply artistic, literary and journalistic work as well as persons who participate in the technical organization of such works' (art 12a co 3 TVG). In this case, the economically dependent worker is defined by his or her professional affiliation and the existence of other specific distinctive characteristics (for example, for homeworkers, art 2 co 1 of the Law of 14 March 1951 requires that assistants be members of the worker's family). The same happens—mutatis mutandis—in French legislation for the mixed-category of professionals who come under subordinate employment.

In Italy, the 'extended' definition in article 409 no 3, c.p.c. could be considered as referring specifically to commercial agents and representatives. However, it should be underlined that in practice the relationship between the general concept (*prestazione d'opera coordinata e continuativa* with a mainly personal character) and the 'extensional' one is not equivalent or alternative (as happens in the German system), but rather hierarchical and cumulative: the agent is no longer a *lavoratore parasubordinato* if his or her work—which is coordinated and continuous typologically—is not predominantly personal.

5.8 Regulation of Economically Dependent Work

It is important to note the extensive use of self-employment as a commercial substitute for subordinate employment at all levels. The trend is becoming increasingly apparent, especially in the European Union, where emerging forms of self-employment have much the same visible features as those of economic dependence. This has prompted legislators to use ambiguous definitions such as *lavoro parasubordinato* or *lavoro a progetto* in Italy, *arbeitnehmeränliche Person* in Germany and *contrats de dépendance à sujétion imparfaite* in France. In some cases, contradictory notions become real oxymorons, for example *trabajo autónomo económicamente dependiente*, recently regulated by the Law No 20/2007 in Spain.

In Europe, national legislation normally follows one of two approaches: (a) assimilation, or (b) the 'selective extension' of protective measures.

Assimilation

This is an expansion of labour law,[57] aiming to broaden the area covered by the rules for subordinate employment to include those self-employed workers who are in a state of economic dependence.

A very good example is the near-total assimilation provided by French law, which uses two different techniques for the purpose. The first is the presumption (in some cases absolute, in others relative) of the use of a subordinate employment contract. The presumption concerns a group of professional activities (which can be carried out *in abstracto* in autonomy) mentioned by book VII of the Labour Code, in particular, home-workers, representatives and canvassers, journalists, artists and models. These professions benefit from a special statute, without which the relationship should be qualified as a contract of *louage d'ouvrage* or *contrat d'entreprise*. A second technique of assimilation involves contracts that in practice produce the conditions prescribed by law independent of the criteria of qualification. The conditions show the lack of genuine economic autonomy of the professionals concerned and their integration into the system of the enterprise with which they have a contract. The contract remains one of execution, eg the lease/management of a trade fund or a concession, etc. Based on article L 781–1, 2 of the Labour Code, the typical guarantees of subordinate employment apply to those whose profession is selling any goods or merchandise supplied exclusively (or almost exclusively) by an industrial or commercial company under the conditions imposed by the latter, or those receiving orders for processing, stocking or transporting for only one commercial or industrial enterprise in a place supplied (or accepted) by the company and under imposed contractual conditions.[58]

The legal particularities are evident in the extreme latitude allowed with respect to contracts involving professions based on exclusivity in sales and acquisition and working on the basis of an order. Judges also tend to establish that such provisions apply when 'the conditions thus stated are indeed present independently from the text of the contract without the need to establish the existence of subordination'.[59] While affirming that the provisions of the Labour Code are

---

[57] M V Ballestrero, 'L'ambigua nozione di lavoro parasubordinato', (1987) *Lavoro e diritto* 41 ff.

[58] In looking at the evolution of Italian doctrine on the subject, it should be noted that toward the end of the 1970s Giuseppe Santoro Passarelli tried to provide a theoretical basis for the construction of the new juridical category of *parasubordinazione*. In so doing, he was utilizing the notion of the weaker employee vis-à-vis the employer. This position remained isolated in doctrine, and even more in the jurisprudence. Today, in presenting new legal experience with *lavoro a progetto*, he has based his analysis more on the outcome of the relationship and utilised the notion of project work as *opus* in accordance with art 2222 of the Italian Civil Code. See G Santoro Passarelli, *Il lavoro parasubordinato* (Milan, Giuffré, 1979); G Santoro Passarelli, 'La nuova figura del lavoro a progetto', in *Annuario di Diritto del Lavoro* (Rome, 2005) 103 ff.

[59] Cass 4 December 2001 (2002) DS 162.

applicable without the need to establish subordination, the Cour de cassation made it clear that this is not a condition for application of article L 781–1: the rule can apply to typical situations of self-employment or even entrepreneurial activities such as agencies or franchises.

Under this rubric, French law has created categories with a mixed, or rather two-sided, statute: under article L 781–1, workers are assimilated at the same time as subordinate workers and employers/autonomous workers, subject to the rules of commercial law, with their own clients and subordinate personnel. Examples include petrol station workers, who are qualified as independent traders by the jurisprudence, and 'non-employee managers' of the branch offices of big companies in the food sector. Even if the latter are assimilated as subordinate workers by article L 782–1 (it expressly refers to art L 781–1), they are qualified as 'directors of establishments in relation to the personnel they employ' (*chefs d'établissements à l'égard du personnel qu'ils emploient,* art L 782–2). Another example of partial assimilation is article L 773–2, which prescribes the application only of a certain number of provisions of the Labour Code to *assistantes maternelles*.

Partial assimilation techniques are present in the United Kingdom, where tax and pension legislation considers some persons as subordinate workers, who on the basis of common law tests are also considered as self-employed (eg contract workers).

Confronted by an enormous increase in self-employment, German legislators intervened in social security law at the end of the 1990s, introducing a system of legal presumptions aimed at significantly broadening the field of subordination by changing § 7.4, Part IV of the *Sozialgesetzbuch*—SGB.[60] In general, the *Korrekturgesetz* received more criticism than approval and was judged insufficient by the very doctrine that had promoted it.[61] This was because it only partially addressed the problem (ie from the point of view of false self-employment and 'apparent autonomy'), and risked creating a very weak determination system. The reform, made up entirely of this legislation, was repealed.

The selective extension of protective measures

Even in Germany there has been a tendency towards a selective extension of labour law protective measures beyond the circle of subordinate workers, applying to

---

[60] M Borzaga, 'Subordinazione e diritto della sicurezza sociale: le riforme fallite nella Repubblica Federale Tedesca', (2002) *Diritto delle Relazioni Industriali* 655 ff.

[61] R Wank, 'Germany', in 'Labour Law in Motion' (2005) *Bulletin of Comparative Labour Relations* 19.

arbeitnehmeränliche Personen the procedural (*Arbeitsgerichtsgesetz* § 5), pension (*Korrekturgesetz* 1998 and *Gesetz zur Förderung der Selbständigkeit* 1999), holidays (*Bundesurlaubsgesetz* 1963 § 2), and collective bargaining protection (*Tarifvertragsgesetz*—TVG § 12°) and, more recently, protections against sexual harassment at the workplace (*Beschaftigtenschutzgesetz* § 1).

Importantly, the United Kingdom has also witnessed extension through the identification of concentric fields of application for protective measures and the breadth of the category of 'worker' (described above). A set of guarantees now applies to workers that were originally reserved to standard subordinate workers. These include the National Minimum Wage Act 1998, the Working Time Regulations 1998 and the Part-time Workers Regulations 2000. According to Point 3.18 of the Blair Government's White Book, *Employment Relations—New Rights for Individuals*, these laws were conceived to apply 'to all those who work for another person, not just those employed under a contract of employment', and the same approach is outlined for the implementation of the EU Working Time Directive. Anti-discrimination rules were extended to an ever-broader group (all those who work or offer a service personally), whereas the rules on safety in the workplace are contained in the circle that presents the maximum circumference, applying also in favour of dependent entrepreneurs. Selective extension also targets specific categories of workers characterized by uncertain status, for example agency workers and home-workers. Both are included in the National Minimum Wage Act, the Working Time Regulations and the Employment Rights Act 1996 (even if with limits to public interest disclosures).

Selective extension is also occurring in Spain, where the Statute of Workers, by excluding self-employment from its field of application, established the possibility of extending labour law legislation to *trabajo realizado por cuenta propia* (freelance work) if a legislator expressly so specifies.[62] This new tendency in legislation has concerned mainly the theme of prevention and safety in the workplace, freedom of trade union organization, and rules on the guaranteed minimum wage (the latter in a limited way with regard to agriculture, for the rental contracts of agricultural plots).[63]

In Denmark, there are legal mechanisms for selective extension, and the concept of economically dependent worker corresponds to the idea of a freelance worker involved in activities such as sales, book-keeping, and consulting in the information technology sector. There are a few legislative provisions that protect

---

[62] Disp final 1 ET 1995.
[63] M C Palomenque López, 'El trabajo autonomo y las propuestas de refundacion del Derecho del Trabajo', 2000 RL 429 ff.

freelancers, notably health and safety in the workplace, maternity leave and the relevant daily allowances.

Mechanisms extending labour legislation to forms of autonomous coordinated and continuous work of a mainly personal nature are a concern in Italy. Since the reform of the Civil Procedure Code of 1973 (art 409 n 3 c.p.c.), there has been an extension of procedural protection and of the rules on renunciation and transactions (art 2113 c.c.) to the *lavoratore parasubordinato*. After a series of legal interventions aimed at offering minimum protection in the field of social security (eg pensions, protection against work accidents and employment sicknesses, maternity protection, sickness allowance), *lavoro parasubordinato* underwent reform. Legislative Decree no 276 of 2003 introduced the new institution of *lavoro a progetto* with the dual intention of combatting fraud by demarcating the field of *co.co.co* and of providing minimal, immutable protection for the real autonomous collaborators. The first objective was pursued by inserting new typological requirements with a selective function (linking the 'old' *collaborazioni* to one or more 'work projects, programmes or phases thereof', according to art 61 co 1). As for the second, some meagre protection was introduced relating to compensation (art 63), sickness, maternity and accidents (art 66), and withdrawals from contracts (art 67). While it may be too early for a definitive evaluation, it should be underlined that the solutions adopted received a cool reception from the trade unions, and were greeted with much severity in most labour law doctrine. The legislator was criticized for questionable techniques, the unsuitability of the selection requirements, deficient protective measures and the inappropriateness of the severe yet inefficient sanction system (art 69).

5.9 Conclusions

As this analysis shows, in European countries modern labour law is based on a distinction between two basic forms of work: subordination and self-employment. While the protective statutes of labour law considered subordinate employment to be the main form, the traditional exclusion of self-employment from the field of application of labour law can be explained by the marginal role of independent work in formerly predominant industrial systems of production. Self-employment in its traditional forms remained without any protective measures, and a great gap was created between the protective legislation for subordinate employment and for autonomous work.

Changes in the organization of work activities (coupled with an increase in the economic importance of different forms of self-employment) and in supply and demand are the main factors behind the 'crisis' of traditional legal arrangements based on the binary opposition of subordinate work and self-employment. The're-engineering', 'outsourcing' and 'downsizing' of the post-Fordist restructuring have helped create a labour market in which the distance between the two forms of employment has diminished. The number of subordinate workers in a position of technical and operative autonomy is on the increase, and a 'new generation' of self-employment with economic dependence is emerging.

While it is not an easy task to find a clear-cut solution to the regulatory problems of employment—and to coordinate public policy among the European Union Member States—we can detect a significant common trend of osmosis between the disciplines of subordinate and other types of work, in particular in the following areas: (a) social security, especially retirement; (b) active employment policy tools; and (c) health and safety at work.

With social security, the tendency is to have a common pension scheme (through the merging of labour laws) covering all types of occupations, whether classified under self-employment or subordinate employment. This is not only the trend in various individual European countries, but it is also the approach taken by the European Union. These trends—backed by a number of welfare schemes, some based on the principle of universal application and some on the need to encourage the free movement of labour—can be seen in Community Regulations 1408/1971 and 1390/1981. These lay down common rules for calculating, for pension purposes, the earnings pertaining to various periods of work in different countries regardless of whether the work is done on a self-employed or employed basis. The European Court of Justice made a decisive contribution to this position by stating that the principle of solidarity of the social security system also applied to the self-employed and to craftsmen as well as to employed workers.

The gradual merging of pension schemes and the costs thereof will have a considerable impact on the distinction between employment and self-employment, as well as on the labour market as a whole. On the one hand, this distinction will become less important (because the two categories will be treated roughly the same), and on the other, indirect labour costs will decrease, thereby reducing the need to resort to false self-employment relationships in an effort to avoid employment costs.

The second area, active employment policy tools, concerns inter alia vocational training, employment services and job creation incentives. Here the perceptible trend is not a merging of the legislation, but rather convergence of its aims and instruments. The common element where training is concerned is that it is a constant factor in efforts to meet market requirements and sustain employability. However, the most widely disseminated method for sustaining employment is the reduction of the contribution burden. Governments have adopted similar incentives to promote types of self-employment, micro-enterprises and cottage industries. Within this framework, there is a tendency to use incentives to promote job opportunities, not only in subordinate employment, but also self-employment and entrepreneurship, particularly in weak sectors and for weak groups. This explains the merging of two components of European employment policy: support for employability and support for entrepreneurship. This is precisely the reason for extending incentives to all types of employment—employment, self-employment and entrepreneurship—which in varying degrees all contribute to providing jobs and facilitating access to the labour market.

Lastly, health and safety, in the broadest sense, covers different forms of work and company organization, protection and the security obligations of employers and workers alike. It thus requires a further set of rules and regulations that will apply to the various occupations without distinction. Putting the onus of safety and related costs on the entrepreneur or the head of the organization is justified, not because of their hierarchical position, but because they have an absolute and objective responsibility to all those who in one way or another may be involved in a dangerous activity. Similarly, it is worth drawing attention to the laws of countries such as the United Kingdom, where the entrepreneur is responsible for taking the necessary steps to ensure the health and safety of all those who are in any way involved in the company's activities, and of those countries where the principals, subcontractors and entrepreneurs are subject to rules designed to prevent them from evading their responsibilities in this area. Such latitude of the health and safety legislation is generally found in the laws of developed countries, and the European Union is no exception to this rule. Harmonization has reached its most advanced stage in the area of protection of the work environment. This involves a combination of hard and soft legal instruments, as well as organizational measures focused on protecting working people from the exposure to health risks, regardless of the specific legal forms in which the activity is carried out.

Legal Regulation of the Employment Relationship in the Asia-Pacific Region

6

Giuseppe Casale, Nicola Countouris, Colin Fenwick, Soo Tian Lee and Joanna Mascarenhas[*]

6.1 Introduction

This chapter gives an overview of aspects of the legal regulation of the employment relationship in selected legal systems of the Asia-Pacific region, namely in Australia, China, India, Malaysia, Singapore and Viet Nam. As will appear, in some of these jurisdictions there have been various attempts in recent times to take steps to clarify, and to help identify, different types of employment relationships. In others, however, legislative intervention has deliberately overlooked the matter of offering ways to identify which workers are in an employment relationship, even while making other major modifications. In Australia, for example, federal laws were introduced in 2006 to protect the rights of independent contractors (not employees), but without attempting to modify the common law definitions of employment or of independent contracting. In China and Viet Nam, laws have been introduced with the express purpose of promoting legally regulated individual employment relationships, but again without specifying how such a relationship should be identified.

Obviously, it would not be possible in a chapter of this scale to seek to provide a historical account of the evolution of the notion of the employment relationship in these six countries. Nor could we provide a systematic review of either the case law or the doctrinal analysis that have shaped the various national legal debates surrounding the employment relationship. Accordingly, we do not try here to deal with these countries at such depth. Nor do we attempt any significant comparative analysis among or between the countries we have selected—not least for the very

---

[*] C Fenwick, Labour Law Specialist, ILO, Geneva; ST Lee, PhD student at Birkbeck College, London; J Mascarenhas, PhD student at Merton College, Oxford University.

good reason that the Asia-Pacific region is so diverse and so large as to make such an exercise difficult in the extreme.[1] Rather, our object is to present a synopsis of recent developments in selected countries, viewed from the perspective of the framework established by the ILO in its Employment Relationship Recommendation, 2006 (No 198). Among other things, the chapter considers the tests utilized by courts to identify specific types of employment relationships, national statutory frameworks on which the various legal definitions of the employment relationship might hinge, the presence of specific administrative or tripartite machineries tasked with clarifying and identifying various working statuses (including employment), and finally the role and attitude of the social partners in the overall effort to assess and monitor the scope of the employment relationship.

What emerges from this overview is that a number of legal system are seeking to engage with the challenges posed by the emergence of new types of employment relationship, and by the increasingly perceived inadequacy of the traditional scope of application of employment protection legislation. However, these efforts are only partly led by a contiguous attempt to clarify the various notions of the employment relationship. At least in the countries considered here, Recommendation No 198 has not been the explicit object of any implementing measure. Many of the efforts that have been undertaken within these countries however clearly fall within the general framework established by the Recommendation, showing once again the signal importance of the instrument. Moreover, the different actions taken by states also illustrate the wide variety of practices in this field, a number of which had not been hitherto explored. But the chapter also reveals that, in spite of the many efforts and the various national approaches to clarifying the employment relationship, there is still a distinct need for statutory and collective regulation in this domain.

---

[1] Sean Cooney has pointed out that, while labour law systems in the Asia-Pacific region face similar challenges to those arising in other parts of the world, there is much greater diversity (of language, culture and legal tradition, among other things) than in some other regions of the world, particularly Europe, or North or South America: S Cooney, 'What Labour Law for the XXI Century? Labour Law Trends in the Asia Pacific Region' 2008, unpublished paper, copy on file with author—acknowledged as the source for material in A Bronstein, *International and Comparative Labour Law—Current Challenges* (ILO/Palgrave Macmillan, 2009) 232–40. On the similarities and diversity of labour law systems in East Asia, see S Cooney et al (eds), *Law and Labour Market Regulation in East Asia* (London, Routledge, 2002).

6.2 The Employment Relationship in Judicial Analysis

Judicial legal analysis can play a pivotal role in any national strategy aimed at guaranteeing an adequate level of employment protection in the labour market. It stands to reason that the test applied by courts to determine which workers are in an employment relationship can have a considerable impact on the actual coverage of employment protection legislation. For this reason alone, it is valuable to start with this aspect of how employment relationships are legally regulated in the countries under consideration. A further reason for doing so is that four of the six countries—Australia, India, Malaysia and Singapore—are either wholly or predominantly common law jurisdictions, as a result of their British colonial heritages.[2] For these four countries, their legal heritage dictates that the common law 'contract of service' is the starting point for how their legal systems conceptualize and regulate employment relationships. It follows that these legal systems have inherited some of the conceptual limitations that flow from a contract-based understanding of personal work relations, including that such an approach is often overly formalistic, and also that it is open to manipulation.[3]

This is of course not to say that many of the systems considered in this chapter have not developed a sophisticated range of legal tests and indices for identifying specific work relationships. However, there is no indication that any system has found, or chosen to adopt, a particular 'silver bullet' test, based on any particular presumption or set of presumptions. The common law jurisdictions under consideration appear to have continued with various approaches that have either maintained or effectively increased judicial discretion to a considerable degree. The same is not true of China or Viet Nam. There, by comparison with the common law jurisdictions, the role and influence of judge-made law are markedly different, at least in this context of establishing rules by which to identify who is a party to a legal employment relationship. In the case of China, judicial decisions have played a key role in determining the scope of the application of key employment and labour protection legislation. However, the same does not appear to be true of Viet Nam.

---

[2] While Malaysia has a well-developed common law system derived from that of the United Kingdom, it is a plural legal jurisdiction, in which both customary and Islamic also have spheres of operation.

[3] On the ease with which common law contracts might be drawn so as to ensure that workers fall one side or the other of the employee/independent contractor divide, see, for example, A Stewart, 'Redefining Employment? Meeting the Challenge of Contract and Agency Labour' (2002) 15 *Australian Journal of Labour Law* 235. While the argument developed there is made in the Australian context, it is of general application to many common law jurisdictions.

Australian jurisprudence on the employment relationship is typical of a common law legal system derived from the United Kingdom. Like many others, it has moved over time from an emphasis on the presence or absence of 'control' as the factor that determines whether or not an employment relationship exists, to a more complex, 'multi-factor test'. The range of factors to which courts and tribunals must have regard is established in several decisions of the High Court of Australia, the most recent of which is *Sweeney v Boylan Nominees Pty Ltd t/as Quirks Refrigeration*.[4] There the Court confirmed again that a multi-factor test is appropriate, and that judges should consider the sorts of factors to which the High Court had previously referred in *Hollis v Vabu Pty Ltd*,[5] and in *Stevens v Brodribb Sawmilling Co Pty Ltd*.[6] Judges will look at the 'totality of the relationship' between the parties, taking into account a range of factors relevant to the particular circumstances of the case.

The factors to which courts and tribunals will have regard in Australia include whether the putative employer has the legal power to exercise detailed control over the way the work is performed; the extent to which the worker is 'integrated' into the hirer's organization; whether the worker displays (on their clothes or equipment, for example) insignia that identify them as part of the hirer's organization; supply of tools and equipment; whether the worker is paid for completion of a task or for time worked; whether the worker bears some risk of losses or has potential to profit; whether the worker may work for others at the same time; whether the worker might subcontract or delegate the work to others; whether the hirer deducts taxation payments from the worker's remuneration at the time of payment; which party bears the responsibility of providing insurance for work-related injury; whether the worker is entitled to paid holidays and sick leave; and finally, the description of the worker's contractual status in the contract itself.[7] The difficulty with a multi-factor test is of course that it lacks precision—in the end it requires the court or tribunal to approach the identification of the legal nature of the work relationship in an impressionistic way.[8] Moreover, as noted in our introduction, these factors are open to manipulation: 'any competent employment lawyer knows how to "exploit" [the] indicia so as to arrive at the right result for their client.'[9]

---

[4] *Sweeney v Boylan Nominees Pty Ltd t/as Quirks Refrigeration* (2006) 226 CLR 161. For analysis, see D Rolph, 'A Carton of Milk, A Bump to the Head and One Legal Headache: Vicarious Liability in the High Court of Australia' (2006) 19 *Australian Journal of Labour Law* 294.

[5] *Hollis v Vabu Pty Ltd* (2001) 207 CLR 21.

[6] *Stevens v Brodribb Sawmilling Co Pty Ltd* (1986) 160 CLR 16.

[7] This list is based on the table at p 48 of A Stewart, *Stewart's Guide to Employment Law* (Sydney, Federation Press, 2008). The table is in turn based on the analysis of the Australian Industrial Relations Commission in *Abdalla v Viewdaze Pty Ltd* (2003) 122 IR 215.

[8] Stewart (n 3) 243.

[9] Stewart (n 3) 244.

As in many other jurisdictions, Australia has arrived at the use of the multi-factor test after many years of emphasis on the notion of 'control'. Historically, this was the touchstone by which English, and thus Australian courts determined whether a work relationship was one of employment.[10] Since the mid-1950s the approach has been to acknowledge that what matters is the legal *right* to control the manner of the performance of the work, as distinct from any actual or real ability to control or direct work in practice.[11] The legal question related to control was restated in recent years in an important decision of the Australian Industrial Relations Commission as being an inquiry into whether the 'putative employer exercises, or has the right to exercise, control over the manner in which work is performed, place of work, hours of work and the like'.[12] Despite the move to a multi-factor test in which the presence or absence of this type of control is merely one of the relevant indicia, the ability of the hirer to control the performance of the work can still play a more decisive role than some other factors in determining the legal nature of the work relationship in question: '[t]he more the worker is subject to direction, the more likely they will be seen as an employee.'[13]

In practice, the question whether the worker is subject to control can be difficult to answer in light of changes in employment practices and human resource management techniques in modern workplaces. The search for control in particular, and the multi-factor test in general, can be confusing in cases where high levels of worker autonomy are counterbalanced by strategic levels of control by the hirer. *Macro Investments Pty Ltd v Amor*,[14] for example, turned on the organization of the work of chicken boners, who had very high levels of autonomy. The chicken boners were able to decide whether or not they wanted to come to work, to determine certain operational elements of their job, and to appoint a spokesperson to represent them in discussions with management (which they did). On the other hand, Macro Investments took ultimate responsibility for quality-control in the

---

[10] The leading authority in Australian law for many years was the English case *Performing Rights Society Ltd v Mitchell & Booker Ltd* [1924] KB 762 (esp 767–68). The origins of the 'control' test in Anglo-Australian law might be traced to an earlier English authority, *Yewen v Noakes* (1880) 6 QBD 530. Arguably, the 'control' test as it developed was not only a misapplication of the rule in *Yewen v Noakes*, but also a basis on which courts came to decisions that had the effect of excluding many workers from early forms of employment protection legislation: A O'Donnell, "Non-Standard' Workers in Australia: Counts and Controversies' (2004) 17 *Australian Journal of Labour Law* 89, 108 (see in particular the sources referred to in fn 72).

[11] *Ziujs v Worth Bros* (1955) 93 CLR 561—the High Court arrived at this distinction in the context of a case brought by a circus performer seeking compensation for a work-related injury. The employer argued, among other things, that the artistic and unique nature of the performer's work was not subject to actual control, and that therefore the performer was not an employee.

[12] *Abdalla v Viewdaze Pty Ltd* (2003) 122 IR 215, 229.

[13] *Stewart's Guide to Employment Law* (n 7) 47.

[14] *Macro Investments Pty Ltd v Amor* [2004] SAIRComm 9.

production process, control over selection and performance, the monitoring of their attendance and of their production records. The Industrial Relations Commission of South Australia decided that the chicken boners' high level of autonomy was not inconsistent with an employment relationship. Rather, they were consistent with a 'self-directed work group, a recent industrial trend in which a group of employees is given authority to direct their own activities, raising matters with management only as a last resort'.[15]

In common with most other labour markets, the use of labour hire arrangements in Australia has received increasing attention in recent years.[16] During the first half of the 1990s, for example, the proportion of workers engaged through labour hire in Australia 'more or less doubled'.[17] As at this writing, the most recent statistics indicate that approximately 5 per cent of Australia's workers are placed in their jobs by recruitment or labour hire agencies.[18] This continuing trend in employment relations also poses challenges for the application of the prevailing multi-factor test, yet it must be used to identify the legal nature of the parties' obligations in multi-party work relationships. In one case, a tomato-picker supplied by an agency was held to be an employee of the agency. The picker worked regular hours, and was told when she could start and finish and also what work she was to do by the client (host business). The factors pointing towards a contract of employment with the agency were: the work did not involve special skills or qualifications; the worker had no right to delegate her work; the worker was paid by the hour; the worker did not have to supply equipment or invest in capital, and there was no scope to bargain for rates. The fact that the 'host' employer was entitled

---

[15] ibid [76].

[16] Labour hire arrangements have posed complexities for the legal regulation of employment relationships in Australia for some time. For comment on the high-profile litigation arising out of the activities of the labour hire agency, Troubleshooters, see C Fenwick, 'Shooting for Trouble? Contract Labour-hire in the Victorian Building Industry' (1992) 5 *Australian Journal of Labour Law* 237, and E Underhill and D Kelly, 'Eliminating Traditional Employment: Troubleshooters', available in the 'Building and Meat Industries' (1993) 35 *Journal of Industrial Relations* 398.

[17] Stewart (n 3) 251, referring to published work drawing from the 1995 Australian Workplace Industrial Relations Survey.

[18] Australian Bureau of Statistics, *Forms of Employment*, ABS Cat. 6359.0, November 2008. The conditions of work of labour hire workers and of independent contractors have been examined in a number of inquiries in recent years in Australia. See in particular: New South Wales, Labour Hire Task Force, *Final Report* (New South Wales Department of Industrial Relations, December 2001); G Stevens, *Review of the South Australian Industrial Relations System* (Adelaide, Workplace Services, October 2002); Economic Development Committee of the Parliament of Victoria, *Labour Hire Employment in Victoria* (Final Report), Parliament of Victoria, June, 2005; Parliament of the Commonwealth of Australia, *Making it work: Inquiry into contracting and labour hire arrangements*, Commonwealth of Australia, House of Representatives Standing Committee on Employment, Workplace Relations and Workforce Participation, Canberra, 2005.

under the agreement with the labour hire agency to exercise practical day-to-day control did not prevent the worker from being a casual employee of the labour hire company.[19]

Similar decisions have been delivered in other cases in which the contract between the labour hire agency and the client (host business) provides that the worker is to work at the direction of the host business. In *Drake Personnel Ltd v Commissioner of State Revenue*,[20] for example, the Victorian Court of Appeal considered whether Drake was the employer of the temporary staff that it arranged to work for its clients. Temporary workers on Drake's books were not bound to accept work, and were paid an hourly rate for time worked. They did not receive pay for long service, holiday or sick leave. Drake deducted income tax, paid workers' compensation premiums, payroll tax and superannuation (pension) contributions for their workers. The Court held that the workers were Drake's employees, rejecting the argument that a temporary worker could not be an employee of the labour hire agency because the work was done for the benefit of the labour hire agency's client. On the other hand, there is also long-standing authority that where the indicia to be considered under the multi-factor test are relatively evenly-balanced, then the parties are free, when acting honestly, to choose whether the work relationship should be one of employment or not. Thus, they may freely determine that the workers should be independent contractors, rather than employees of the labour hire agency concerned.[21]

India is another jurisdiction in which courts take the pragmatic approach of drawing, when necessary, from a broad arsenal of tests and indexes to identify the employment relationship. In *Workmen of Nilgiri Coop*, the Supreme Court of India expressly noted that 'No single test—be it control test, be it organization or any other test—has been held to be the determinative factor' and 'that it would not be prudent to search for a formula in the nature of a single test for determining the vexed question'.[22] The Court further argued that 'what is needed is an integrated approach meaning thereby integration of the relevant tests'.[23] As such we are told:

'[a] court is required to consider several factors which would have a bearing on the result : (a) who is appointing authority; (b) who is the paymaster; (c) who can dismiss; (d) how long

---

[19] *Country Metropolitan Agency Contracting Services Pty Ltd v Slater & Workcover/CGU Workers Compensation Insurance (SA) Pty Ltd* [2003] SAWCT 57 [22] (Cawthorne DPJ); [57, 61] (McCusker DPJ).

[20] *Drake Personnel Ltd v Commissioner of State Revenue* (2000) 2 VR 635.

[21] *Building Workers' Industrial Union of Australia v Odco Pty Ltd* (1991) 29 FCR 104; see further Fenwick (n 16).

[22] *Workmen of Nilgiri Coop. Mkt Society Ltd v State of Tamil Nadu & Ors* [2004] (101) FLR 137 [32].

[23] ibid.

alternative service lasts; (e) the extent of control and supervision; (f) the nature of the job, eg whether, it is professional or skilled work; (g) nature of establishment; (h) the right to reject.[24]

Lower jurisdictions accordingly adapted their approaches by sifting through various indexes and tests. In its 2007 decision in *Zee Entertainment Enterprises Ltd*, the Mumbai High Court, after considering a long list of judicial precedents, noted that:

> 'Recent case law suggests that the factors relevant to the process of identifying a contract of employment may usefully be listed as follows: (1) the degree of control exercised by the employer; (2) whether the worker's interest in the relationship involved any prospect of profit or risk of loss; (3) whether the worker was properly regarded as part of the employer's organization; (4) whether the worker was carrying on business on his own account or carrying on the business of the employer; (5) the provision of equipment; (6) the incidence of tax and national insurance; (7) the parties' own view of their relationship; (8) the traditional structure of the trade or profession concerned and the arrangement within it.'[25]

There is therefore a clear sense that, in the absence of any particular statutory instruction, the Indian judiciary is unwilling to commit to any particular legal reasoning or test.

While this approach is hardly a peculiarity of the Indian legal system, it leads to a rather lose and unpredictable framework, further exacerbated by the extremely fragmented, informal, and deregulated realities of the domestic labour market. For instance, while placing the burden of proof firmly on the 'the person who sets up a plea of existence of relationship of employer and employee'[26] is a common feature of most legal systems, it is often hard to expect workers in the informal economy to meet the required standards. Moreover, Indian judges are adamant that 'whether a contract is a sham or camouflage is not a question of law which can be arrived at having regard to the provisions of Contract Labour (Regulation and Abolition) Act, 1970',[27] and we know from cases such as *Municipal Corporation of Greater Mumbai*[28] that non-maintenance of records by the contractors was held to be not conclusive for determination as to whether the workmen were working under the contractor, and that the 'Court held that such disputed questions of fact cannot be gone into in a civil proceeding'.[29]

---

[24] ibid [37].

[25] *Zee Entertainment Enterprises Ltd v Gajendra Singh* [2008] (36) PTC 53 (Bom).

[26] *Workmen of Nilgiri Coop. Mkt.Society Ltd v State of Tamil Nadu & Ors* [2004] (101) FLR 137.

[27] ibid.

[28] *Municipal Corporation of Greater Mumbai v KV Sharamik Sangh and Others* (2002) 4 SCC 609.

[29] *Workmen of Nilgiri Coop Mkt Society Ltd v State of Tamil Nadu & Ors* [2004] (101) FLR 137.

Malaysia is also no exception to this progressive departure from tests ascertaining predominantly, if not exclusively, the control of the employer on the employee, to versions of the 'multiple test'. The criteria used in Malaysia are very similar to those employed by British judges, yet another testimony to the pervasive influence of common law reasoning in this region of the world. As was stated in *American International Assurance Co Ltd v Dato Lam Peng Chong and others*:[30]

> Broadly speaking, there are three tests for discerning the contract of employment/service, ie
>
> (1)   The 'traditional' or 'control' test;
>
> (2)   'organization' or 'integration' test; and
>
> (3)   'mixed' or 'multiple' test.
>
> No test can be conclusive. The weight to be attached may vary from case to case and the question whether or not there is a contract of service is a mixed one of law and fact. Since no test in conclusive the Courts will have to look at the following list of elements of the relationship which are important. . . .

The list of elements cited in the judgment are as follows:

1.   The employer's right of control.
2.   Integration.
3.   Chance of profit and risk of loss.
4.   Ownership of the instrumentalia and the onus to provide.
5.   Entitlement to exclusive service.
6.   Payment of fixed remuneration for a specific period.
7.   The power of selection and appointment.
8.   The power to suspend/dismiss the employee.
9.   The power to fix the place, time of work and the times at which holidays are taken.
10. The intentions and the agreement between the parties, especially where there is doubt or ambiguity.

The fact that Malaysian courts have not moved from this statement of the law in 1988 is shown by the fact that a 2007 Industrial Court award cited the exact passage from *American International Assurance,* quoted above.[31]

---

[30]   *American International Assurance Co Ltd v Dato Lam Peng Chong and others* [1988] 2 ILR 420 (hereinafter *American International Assurance*).

[31]   *Electrical Industry Workers' Union v Mitti Cables Mfg Sdn Bhd* [2007] 2 ILR 152. The Chairperson, however, cited a recent textbook as the source of the quote rather than the 1988 judgment. It is submitted that this must have been a slip.

In the 1988 case of *KL Mutual Fund Bhd v J B Leo*,[32] the Supreme Court expressed its view that the element of control was still the most important in determining whether a particular relationship is a contract of service. On the other hand, Lord Denning's 'organization test' (enunciated in *Stevenson, Jordan & Harrison Ltd v Macdonald*) was applied by Salleh Abas FJ in *Mat Jusoh Daud v Sykt Jaya Seberang Tahir Sdn Bhd*.[33] Also, the economic reality test appears in some recent Industrial Court awards. In some cases, such as *RM Top Holdings Sdn Bhd & Anor v Ahmad Md Yusoff*,[34] it is equated to the multiple test, whereas some Malaysian textbooks distinguish between the two.[35]

But the growing dissatisfaction of Malaysian courts with the traditional control test, is evidence by the decision in *Inchcape (M) Holdings Bhd v R B Gray*,[36] where Salleh Abas LP stated that for the purposes of construing who a 'workman' for the purposes of s 2 of the Industrial Relations Act 1967, the control test was not to be used, but rather, 'In construing the term "workman", the purpose for which a person is employed must be taken into consideration. In other words, the function and responsibility of an employee are the criterion and must be looked into.'

There is no single test that is considered to be definitive, and there are recent cases where several tests were applied to the facts.[37] On the other hand, in the Industrial Court award of *Electrical Industry Workers' Union v Mitti Cables Mfg Sdn Bhd*,[38] the chairman, Susila Sithamparam, noted that 'the recent trend is to apply the "economic reality" test to determine whether there is a contract of service or a contract for services'. Given that the more traditional elements of control and integration are incorporated into this multiple/economic reality test,[39] it is fair to say that although the older tests are still applied, they are now to be seen in this more articulate, if tortuous, framework.

Multi-party work relationships commonly manifest themselves in Malaysia in the form of labour suppliers or subcontractors. In the July 2007 case of *Hamden Sedi*

---

[32] *KL Mutual Fund Bhd v J B Leo* [1988] 2 MLJ 526.

[33] *Mat Jusoh Daud v Sykt Jaya Seberang Tahir Sdn Bhd* [1982] CLJ 562 (Rep); [1982] CLJ 366.

[34] *RM Top Holdings Sdn Bhd & Anor v Ahmad Md Yusoff* [2004] 1 ILR 1, citing *American International Assurance*.

[35] Tracing back the 'economic reality test' to the famous UK case of *Market Investigations* and the 'multiple test' to the equally well-known case of *Ready Mixed Concrete*. It is clear that the genesis of both tests are separate and should not be lumped together.

[36] *Inchcape (M) Holdings Bhd v R B Gray* [1985] 2 MLJ 297.

[37] eg *Tan Eng Siew & Anor v Dr Jagjit Singh Sidhu & Anor* [2006] 5 CLJ 175 where the control, integration and multiple tests were cited and applied.

[38] *Electrical Industry Workers' Union v Mitti Cables Mfg Sdn Bhd* [2007] 2 ILR 152.

[39] As noted above, there seems to be some confusion in the Malaysian courts as to the distinction between the 'multiple' and 'economic reality' tests.

& 12 Ors v Step Ahead Engineering Sdn Bhd & Anor,[40] an interim award was made regarding an application for one Lim Bok San to be joined as a party to the dispute. He had recruited the claimants to work for the respondents. In fact, the wages of the claimants were paid by the respondents into his account, and he then paid them on a daily basis. Surprisingly enough, the Industrial Court Chairman only applied the control test and concluded that it was the respondents who were the employers of the claimants and not Mr Lim, due to the fact that they 'decide on the work to be done, the claimants' daily wage rate and as to the time period by which they have to comply to complete the works'. This was regardless of the fact that Mr Lim was the one in direct supervision of their work. It was said that '[h]is non-independence in the supervision of the claimants is reflected by the instructions given to him by the company directors as to the manner of work, time schedule of work etc.'

In *Tan Eng Siew & Anor v Dr Jagjit Singh Sidhu & Anor*, a case involving vicarious liability, the issue was whether a hospital (the second defendant) was liable for the medical negligence of Dr Jagjit Singh (the first defendant), who was attached to the hospital. The control, integration and multiple tests were cited, but the reasons given for the eventual decision that the hospital was not the employer of Dr Singh were focused on the issue of control. It was stated that Dr Singh was a consultant with clients on his own, and had full control over the treatment, management and care of his patients. Also, although the hospital had proposed to the patient that he engage the services of Dr Singh, there was no obligation for Dr Singh to accept the recommendation. An independent contract was entered into between the doctor and the patient. In essence, Dr Singh was held to be an independent contractor using the hospital's facilities.

The legal academic Ravi Chandran has summarized the approach of the Singaporean courts as follows: 'The current position appears to be that while matters such as control and being an integral part of the employer's organization are important, no single factor is conclusive and the court has to look at all the relevant circumstances.'[41] Cases that evince this statement include *Kureoka Enterprise Pte Ltd v Central Provident Fund*[42] and *Koh Chin Chye v Promix Concrete Pte Ltd*.[43]

The control test in today's context does not always require the employer to determine for an employee the exact way services are to be performed. One clear example is the case of professional employees. In *Employees Provident Fund Board v MS Ally & Co Ltd*,[44] Wan Suleiman J stated that 'It seems to me the traditional control

---

[40] *Hamden Sedi & 12 Ors v Step Ahead Engineering Sdn Bhd & Anor* [2007] 2 LNS 1435.
[41] R. Chandran, *Employment Law in Singapore* (Singapore, LexisNexis, 2005) 5.
[42] Suit No 218 of 1991, Singapore High Court, Unreported.
[43] Suit No 973 of 1997, Singapore High Court, Unreported.
[44] *Employees Provident Fund Board v MS Ally & Co Ltd* [1975] 2 MLJ 89, 94.

test, based on the simpler socio-economic conditions of a bygone age must indeed be modified if it is to be valid'.

Among the factors that must be considered other than control and integration are:

(a) The method of payment (it is more likely that an employee will receive a regular salary rather than commissions, tips or piece-work, but this is not conclusive).[45]

(b) Restrictions on working for others (an employee would be obliged to work only for that employer. Nevertheless *cf Market Investigations*).

(c) Working hours (an employee would more likely have fixed working hours).[46]

(d) Overtime pay (non-employees do not usually receive overtime pay).

(e) Provident fund contributions (likely to be received by employees).[47] Whether such contributions were actually made is less important than whether there was a legal obligation to make such contributions.[48]

(f) Holidays (contractual right to holidays characteristic of contract of service).[49]

(g) Medical leave (more likely that employees contractually entitled to medical leave): *Market Investigations*.

(h) Right to dismiss (contractual right to dismiss would indicate that individual is an employee).[50]

(i) Power of selection (employer's choice of worker points towards that worker being an employee, but does not preclude there being a contract of service even if selection is left to someone else).[51]

(j) Mutuality of obligations (obligation to provide an accept work, especially relevant for temporary/casual workers).

(k) Authority to delegate work (such power would indicate an employment relationship).[52]

(l) Tools and equipment (employee unlikely to provide own).[53]

---

[45] *Kuala Lumpur Mutual Fund Berhad v J Bastian Leo & Anor* [1988] 2 MLJ 526. *cf Bata Shoe Company (Malaya) Ltd v Employees Provident Fund Board* [1967] 1 MLJ 120.

[46] *Kuala Lumpur Mutual Fund Berhad v J. Bastian Leo & Anor* [1988] 2 MLJ 526.

[47] *Chew Swee Hiang v Attorney General* [1990] 1 SLR 890.

[48] *Kuala Lumpur Mutual Fund Berhad v J. Bastian Leo & Anor* [1988] 2 MLJ 526, 529.

[49] *Kureoka Enterprise Pte Ltd v Central Provident Fund*, Suit No. 218 of 1991, Singapore High Court, Unreported.

[50] *Chew Swee Hiang v Attorney General* [1990] 1 SLR 890.

[51] *Chua Chye Leong Alan v Grand Paalce De-luxe Nite Club Pte Ltd* [1993] 3 SLR 449.

[52] *Employees Provident Fund Bord v MS Ally & Co Ltd* [1975] 2 MLJ 89.

[53] *Grand Palace De-luxe Nite Club Pte Ltd* (2004) 2 MLJ 75.

(m) Risk of loss and change of profit (employee's income normally in form of wages rather than profits).[54]

The application of these tests in practice is never too obvious an exercise. The case of *Kureoka Enterprises Pte Ltd v Central Provident Fund Board*[55] involved freelance hostesses who worked in a lounge. Here, the British case of *O'Kelly and Others v Trusthouse Forte PLC* was distinguished on the ground that the hostesses, although not contractually bound to report to work, had to provide good reasons for not doing so. This meant, according to the High Court, that they were in a continuous contract of employment. Alternatively, a separate contract of employment was formed each time a hostess turned up for work. While these two interpretations led to the same result in *Kureoka*, in other cases whether there is a single continuous contract of employment or a series of contracts would have an impact upon the issue of the applicability of certain rights conferred under the Employment Act, and which require continuity in service.[56] As for employment relations involving multiple parties, the case of *Construction Industry Training v Labour Force Ltd*[57] is instructive. In that case the respondents, Labour Force Ltd, was a supplier of labour in the construction sector. They struck up deals with building contractors whereby workmen would be supplied at certain rates. The contractors would pay the respondents, who would then pay the workers. The suppliers had no control over the work carried out by the workmen, however, and did not have authority to terminate the engagements. They also did not provide sick or holiday pay. Hence, although there was a contract between the suppliers and the workmen, it was not a contract of service. Also, it was held that neither were the workmen employees of the contractors. It is submitted that this is an unjust result.

Chandran rightly points out that 'the classification of a worker as an employee for one purpose may not always mean that he is an employee for all other purposes.'[58] What this means is that a person may be an employee in determining whether there is vicarious liability, but may not be so for the purpose of CPF contributions. This is something that, as evidenced by the treatise of the relevant statutes in the previous section, is not uncommon in other legal systems. However it adds to the sense of unpredictability and lack of legal certainty lamented so far, and that one would expect in what is undeniably a crucially important area of labour law.

---

[54] *Lee Keng Hiong T/A William Trade & Trans-Services v Ramlan bin Haron* [2002] 2 SLR 52.

[55] *Kureoka Enterprises Pte Ltd v Central Provident Fund Board (Suit No 218 of 1991,* Singapore High Court, Unreported).

[56] R Chandran, *Employment Law in Singapore,* 2nd edn (Singapore, LexisNexis, 2008) 14.

[57] *Construction Industry Training v Labour Force Ltd* [1970] 3 All ER 220.

[58] Chandran (n 56) 16.

We have already highlighted how the complexities of the employment relationship question often lead to the courts to adopting various versions of the 'multi-factor test'. As expressed by the Mumbai High Court:

> The most that profitably can be done is to examine all the factors that have been referred to in the cases on the topic. Clearly, not all of these factors would be relevant in all these cases or have the same weight in all cases. It is equally clear that no magic formula can be propounded, which factors should in any case be treated as determining ones. The plain fact is that in a large number of cases, the Court can only perform a balancing operation weighing up the factors which point in one direction and balancing them against those pointing in the opposite direction.[59]

Perhaps inevitably, this approach has led most systems to lean towards an overwhelmingly 'fact dominated' type of enquiry in deciding whether a contract is a contract of employment or another type of contractual, or non contractual, employment relationship. As put by the Allahabad High Court, Indian authorities are adamant that 'The question whether the relationship that exists between the parties is one of employer and employee *is purely one of fact*'.[60]

This approach is echoed in other jurisdictions. In Malaysia, the 2008 case of *Subramniam Mathaiah v Chin Heng Trading Sdn Bhd*, on the other hand, cited the 1996 case of *Hoh Kiang Ngan v Mahkamah Perusahaan Malaysia & Anor*[61] as 'the newest and most authoritative case on the meaning of the term "workman"'. Another 2008 case, *Aminah Zaiton Amir Dastan & Anor v Star RFM Sdn Bhd*, also cited *Hoh Kiang Ngan*, and the section quoted is instructive:

> In all cases where it becomes necessary to determine whether a contract is one of service or for services, the degree of control which an employer exercises over a claimant is an important factor, although it may not be the sole criterion. The terms of the contract between the parties must, therefore, first be ascertained. Where this is in writing, the task is to interpret its terms in order to determine the nature of the latter's duties and functions. Where it is not then its terms must be established and construed. But in the vast majority of cases there are facts which go to show the nature, degree and extent of control. These include, but are not confined, to the conduct of the parties at all relevant times. Their determination is a question of fact.[62]

---

[59] *Zee Entertainment Enterprises Ltd v Gajendra Singh* [2008] (36) PTC 53 (Bom).

[60] *United Provincial Transport Agency vs Presiding Officer Labour Court* [2005] RD-AH 1758 [14]. This was established earlier by the Supreme Court of India in *VP Gopala Rao v Public Prosecutor, Andhra Pradesh* [1970] 2 LLJ 59; AIR 1970 SC 66.

[61] *Hoh Kiang Ngan v Mahkamah Perusahaan Malaysia & Anor* [1996] 4 CLJ 687; [1995] 3 MLJ 364.

[62] *Aminah Zaiton Amir Dastan & Anor v Star RFM Sdn Bhd* [2008] 2 LNS 0105. My translation, original judgment in Bahasa Malaysia.

But while most courts are willing to portray their enquiry as an overwhelmingly, if not exclusively, fact-driven one, there is a sense that the various factors they focus on are partly derived by the conduct of the parties during the relationship, and partly contained in the letter of the contract. This is not to say that these jurisdictions are not familiar with the notion of sham contracts, and apply them to the contract of employment. Indian courts clearly provide a good list of legal precedents where sham contracts have been usefully unveiled, for instance in respect of sham 'multi-party' employment relationships. As put by the Supreme Court:

> There cannot be any doubt whatsoever that where a person is engaged through an intermediary or otherwise for getting a job done, a question may arise as the appointment of an intermediary was merely sham and nominal and rather than camouflage where a definite plea is raised in Industrial Tribunal or the Labour Court, as the case may be, and in that event, it would be entitled to pierce the veil and arrive at a finding that the justification relating to appointment of a contractor is sham or nominal and in effect and substance there exists a direct relationship of employer and employee between the principal employer and the workman. The decision of this Court in Hussainbhai, *Calicut* vs. *The Allath Factory Thezhilali Union, Kozhikode and Others* [(1978) 4 SCC 257] will fall in that category.[63]

However, there is a sense that, as in most common law systems, courts will be reluctant to interfere with the contractually agreed settlement, unless encouraged to do so by specific statutes. In that respect, Australia provides a good example. Courts look primarily at the facts of the relationship between the person and the putative employer in determining the existence of an employment relationship. The mere fact that the parties to the contract may expressly declare that the contract does not create an employer-employee relationship and that the party providing services is a self-employed independent contract is not sufficient to establish this as fact. The terms of the contract are relevant but it is clear that the parties cannot, by labelling the contract as an independent contract, alter what is in reality a contract of employment.[64] As stated by Justice Gray in *Re Porter, Re Transport Workers Union of Australia*,[65] on the question of whether truck owners were employees or contractors, 'the parties cannot create something which has every feature of a rooster but call it a duck and insist that everybody else recognize it as a duck'.[66] As we note below, reforms in Australia in 2006 introduced legislative provisions that make it

---

[63] *Workmen of Nilgiri Coop. Mkt Society Ltd v State of Tamil Nadu & Ors* [2004] (101) FLR 137.

[64] *Australian Mutual Provident Society v Allan* (1978) 52 ALJR 407, 409.

[65] *Re Porter, Re Transport Workers Union of Australia* (1989) 34 IR 179, 184.

[66] For a recent application of this principle, see the Full Federal Court decision in *Damevski v Giudice* (2003) 133 FCR 438.

unlawful to engage in 'sham' contracting arrangements, that is, treating persons who are really employees as independent contractors.

As in other countries, the application of Chinese labour law depends crucially on whether the parties are in an employment relationship. Legislation pertaining to labour protection, labour dispute resolution and collective labour relations generally applies only to the parties to such a relationship. Where a work relationship is not one of employment, the applicable legal rules will be derived from other sources, such as the general law governing contracts.[67] The general law of contracts does not apply to labour contracts, but it does cover independent contractor arrangements.

Notwithstanding the importance of the nature of the legal relationship, the texts of Chinese labour laws do not contain any detailed rules for distinguishing employment from other kinds of work relations. Nor has the only judicial body empowered to issue authoritative interpretations, the Supreme People's Court, provided extensive guidance on how to identify an employment relationship. It has however indicated that certain arrangements are *not* employment relationships. The question of how to characterize a work relationship in any single instance will therefore depend on the relevant body making the determination. That may include a court or arbitral tribunal (in the event of litigation), or an administrative body (such as a labour department).

One of the key considerations will be the nature of the work relationship itself. Chinese labour legislation such as the Labour Law and the Labour Contract Law applies where an employing unit enters into an employment relationship with a labourer.[68] This implies that, in order to establish an employment relationship, it is necessary not only to identify an employing entity but to identify a 'labourer'. This category is fairly broad, and China has not sought to narrow down the application of the labour law by reference to specific industries or wage thresholds. However, there are various categories of labourers which are generally treated as not falling with the scope of labour law.[69]

In an Interpretation issued in 2006, the Supreme People's Court listed several categories of dispute which are not 'labour disputes' and therefore do not fall within the jurisdiction of the labour dispute arbitration committees. They are to be treated

---

[67] And in particular the Contract Law of the People's Republic of China, c 15.

[68] See eg the formulation in art 2 of the Labour Law.

[69] See. generally, Ye Jingyi, *Twelve Lectures on the Chinese Labour Law Contracts* (China Legal Publishing House, 2007), 31–55; and Dong Baohua, *Research on Labour Contracts* (China Labour Law and Social Security Publishing House, 2005) 55–77.

as civil disputes by the courts.[70] The Court indicated that *any* disputes between the following parties are not to be treated as labour disputes:

— families/individuals and domestic workers;
— individual craftspeople and assistants or apprentices; and
— farm households and employees.

While the interpretation does not specifically state that labour legislation does not apply to these categories of workers, this would seem to be presupposed. These relationships are therefore considered to be work contracts regulated by the Contract Law.[71]

Aside from these categories, certain kinds of workers engaged directly by the State are not covered by the Labour Law. These consist of civil servants and analogous workers, and military officers. These are covered by a separate system of laws. However, most employees of the state sector (which still engages a large, though minority share of the Chinese industrial workforce) are not categorized as civil servants and therefore fall within the scope of the labour law. The relationship between these workers and the state enterprises is thus one of employment.

Chinese courts and labour tribunals set great store on written documentation. This has led some decision-makers to see a written employment contract as *constitutive* of an employment relationship. This view has the unfortunate effect of depriving those workers who are arguably most in need of legal protection— undocumented labourers—of the entitlements in the labour laws.[72] The Supreme People's Court made it clear in a 2001 interpretation that it did not accept this view, stating that a court has jurisdiction to hear a labour dispute where there was an undocumented labour relationship.[73] The reasoning behind this interpretation was not always observed, however. The Labour Contract Law has now made the position clear. It provides that an employment relationship can commence notwith-standing the absence of a labour contract,[74] and that an employee can claim double remuneration from an employer who has failed to enter into a written employment contract with the employee.[75]

---

[70] Interpretation of the Supreme People's Court on Several Issues Concerning the Application of Laws in Hearing Labour Disputes (II), Interpretation 6 of 2006.

[71] See Li Guoguang, *Supreme People's Court Interpretations on Labour Disputes* (Beijing, Law Publishing House, 2006), 87–90.

[72] A Halegua, 'Getting Paid: Processing the Labor Disputes of China's Migrant Workers' (2008) 26 *Berkeley Journal of International Law* 101, 119–23.

[73] See *Interpretation of the Supreme People's Court Concerning Several Issues Regarding the Application of Law to the Trial of Labor Dispute Cases* Interpretation 14 of 2001, art 1.

[74] art 10.

[75] art 82.

As appears further below, legal regulation of the employment relationship in Viet Nam has followed a similar trajectory in some respects to that of China, not least in the emphasis on establishing written labour contracts. More broadly, however, a key driver of legal change in each country has been government policy, the goal of which has been to establish a functioning labour market in some sectors of the economy. At the heart of this policy goal is the individual employment relationship—necessarily so, as it is both the basis for and the subject of exchange in such a market. The introduction of the Labour Code in 1994 brought with it important protections for the workers covered by its provisions, as might be expected of a comprehensive labour code. It follows of course that the effectiveness of these provisions depends, as in other systems, to a significant degree on the capacity of the legal system to identify which persons are parties to work relationships subject to the code. While the Code does provide some guidance about how to make such a determination in cases of doubt, it appears to provide relatively little scope for the judicial development of legal principles in this important respect. Indeed, the literature on Viet Nam and changes to its labour laws in recent years is strikingly devoid of any mention of the roles of courts or tribunals in the determination of the scope of the employment relationship, much less of particular decisions that might have been important in this respect.

The Labour Code of Viet Nam does provide for resolution of individual labour disputes in ways that may have the potential to produce jurisprudence on the nature of the work relationships that are to be covered by the Code. These disputes are to be resolved by the labour conciliation council of the enterprise, or by a conciliator; if those means are unsuccessful then they are to be resolved by the People's Court (art 165). At the same time, the Court can resolve certain types of dispute directly—that is, without them first going to conciliation. These include disputes about discipline and dismissal; disputes about payment of compensation for loss/damage, or severance at termination; a dispute between a domestic servant and an employer; and disputes concerning certain aspects of social insurance (art 166). Clearly a threshold issue in many such cases could be whether or not the worker is entitled to the benefit of the provision in question—that is, whether or not they are an 'employee'. To date, however, the available English language sources do not identify any key decisions in this area.

6.3 The General Legal Framework Sustaining the Employment Relationship

In this section we examine critically some recent statutory developments relating to the issues encompassed by Recommendation No 198. In some of the common law jurisdictions under consideration, there is a clear sense that some states, including Australia, India, and Singapore, have progressively explored ways of expanding the protections normally afforded to workers in standard employment relationships to other sectors of the labour force who are usually seen as falling outside the traditional scope of the application of employment protection legislation, or even social security or safety and health statutes. At the same time, these efforts have not always been accompanied by a conscious attempt to directly address and clarify the legal concepts and definitions of employment relationships upon which these new statutory provisions are premised.

Australia presents a somewhat confusing, but also intriguing example in this respect, particularly as concerns the most recent developments in its key federal statutes relating to employment and labour relations. These laws have undergone more or less continual revision and change since the late 1980s: major reforms were instituted in 1988, 1992/1993, 1996, 2006 and 2009, with many other amendments also enacted during this period. The most recent change, under the Australian Labor Party (ALP) Government elected in November 2007, was the transformation of the principal federal statute from the Workplace Relations Act 1996 (Cth) into the Fair Work Act 2009 (Cth).[76] What none of those changes did, however, was to enact any sort of statutory change to the underlying common law concept and legal definition of the employment relationship. Section 15 of the Fair Work Act 2009 (Cth), for example, refers to the 'ordinary meaning' of the terms 'employee' and 'employer' as including a reference to a 'person who is usually such an employee' and 'a person who is usually such an employer'.

Nor did the shift to the Fair Work Act 2009 (Cth) bring with it any changes to the Independent Contractors Act 2006 (Cth), which is one of the more remarkable enactments in recent years in the field of employment relations, certainly in Australia, and perhaps more widely as well. The Independent Contractors Act 2006

---

[76] On the changes in recent years leading to the passage of this statute, see A Forsyth and A Stewart (eds), *Fair Work: The New Workplace Law and the Work Choices Legacy* (Sydney, Federation Press, 2009).

(Cth) was enacted following an inquiry by a Committee of the House of Representatives of the Commonwealth Parliament in 2005.[77] As commentators have noted, however, the genesis of the legislation may be located somewhat earlier, in the policies of the Liberal Party of Australia, then the major partner in a coalition Government that had first been elected in March 1996. In advance of the federal election in 2004, the Liberal Party declared its intention to 'legislate to protect and enhance the freedom to contract and to encourage independent contracting as a wholly legitimate form of work'.[78]

Accordingly, the primary goal of the Independent Contractors Act 2006 (Cth) is to ensure that workers who wish not to be considered employees are able to have their work relations legally regulated as independent contractors. It represents, then, a determination to shift the legal regulation of such workers' working conditions from the realm of employment/industrial/labour law, to that of commercial law instead.[79] A key goal of the statute is therefore to exclude independent contractors from State and Territory laws that would otherwise extend various forms of employment protection to them.[80] This means that the Independent Contractors Act 2006 (Cth) operates to override the following sorts of State or Territory laws:[81] first, those laws that might operate generally to deem certain categories of contractors to be employees;[82] secondly, laws that establish a process under which a party to a contract for services might be deemed to be an employee;[83] thirdly, laws that require respect for rights equivalent or similar to those to which employees are entitled; and fourthly, laws that would allow a court or tribunal to review, vary or set aside the terms of a contract for services.[84] It can immediately be seen that this Act might be thought inconsistent with the goal of Recommendation No 198, which

---

[77] *Making it work* (n 18). For comment on this inquiry (and also that of the Victorian Economic Development Committee (n 18)), see E Underhill, 'Labour Hire and Independent Contracting in Australia: Two Inquiries, How Much Change?' (2006) 19 *Australian Journal of Labour Law* 306.

[78] Liberal and National Parties, *Protecting and Supporting Independent Contractors*, Liberal and National Parties, Canberra, quoted in A Stewart, 'Work Choices and Independent Contractors: The Revolution that Never Happened' (2008) 18 *Economic and Labour Relations Review* 53, 54.

[79] J Riley, 'A fair deal for the entrepreneurial worker? Self-employment and independent contracting post Work Choices' (2006) 19 *Australian Journal of Labour Law* 246, 254.

[80] A Forsyth, 'The 2006 Independent Contractors Legislation: An Opportunity Missed' (2007) 35 *Federal Law Review* 329, 330.

[81] The principal section to this effect is s 7.

[82] s 5(3) and sch 1 of the Industrial Relations Act 1996 (NSW) are examples: they have the effect of deeming certain types of workers, such as swimming pool supervisors, to be employees: Forsyth (n 80) 335.

[83] Such as s 275 of the Industrial Relations Act 1999 (Qld): Forsyth (n 80) 335.

[84] The State of New South Wales has for many years had such an 'unfair contracts' jurisdiction, under ss 105 to 109A of its Industrial Relations Act 1996 (NSW). Some of the cases from this jurisdiction have attracted significant attention—see Riley (n 79) 252, and the sources there referred to. The State of Queensland has for some time had a similar, although less notorious jurisdiction under s 276 of its Industrial Relations Act 1999 (Qld).

suggests that ILO member States consider implementing exactly the types of measures that the Independent Contractors Act 2006 (Cth) overrides.[85]

Yet the picture is much more complex than this initial description suggests. First, the Independent Contractors Act 2006 (Cth) only overrides State and Territory laws that deal with 'workplace relations' matters, as defined.[86] There are many topics that are excluded from the definition, including laws relating to child labour, discrimination, and occupational safety and health.[87] Secondly, certain State or Territory laws that might be overridden because they deal with 'workplace relations' matters, as defined, are expressly preserved. Thus, certain laws that have been enacted in recent years to provide protection to vulnerable home-workers (called 'outworkers' in Australian labour law parlance) in the textile, clothing and footwear industry are preserved.[88] So too are laws providing special protection for owner-drivers in the transport industry—except those in the State of Western Australia, which were enacted after the Independent Contractors Act 2006 (Cth) came into force.[89]

Another layer of complexity is added by those provisions in the Independent Contractors Act 2006 (Cth) dealing with so-called 'sham' contracts, and those concerning the federal jurisdiction to review the fairness of independent contracts covered by the Act. The provisions on 'sham' contracts were recommended by the federal parliamentary inquiry that preceded the enactment of the Independent Contractors Act 2006 (Cth).[90] Under them, a person who engages an employee must not misrepresent to that employee that they are engaged as an independent contractor. This prohibition only applies, however, if the hirer did not know that the person was actually engaged as an employee, and if the hirer is reckless in making the representation in question.[91] As Professor Andrew Stewart has pointed out, the

---

[85] See in particular art 11(b), which suggests that member States consider addressing these matters by means of a legal presumption of an employment relationship.

[86] The definition includes matters such as remuneration, leave, hours of work and industrial action: Independent Contractors Act 2006 (Cth) s 8.

[87] Independent Contractors Act 2006 (Cth) s 8.

[88] There are provisions in New South Wales, Queensland, South Australia and Victoria: see S Marshall, 'An Exploration of Control in the Context of Vertical Disintegration' and M Rawling, 'A Generic Model of Regulating Supply Chain Outsourcing', both in C Arup et al. (eds), *Labour Law and Labour Market Regulation* (Sydney, Federation Press, 2006) 542–60 and 520–41 (respectively); M Rawling, 'The Regulation of Outwork and the Federal Takeover of Labour Law' (2007) 20 *Australian Journal of Labour Law* 189; and I Nossar, R Johnstone and M Quinlan, 'Regulating Supply Chains to Address the Occupational Health and Safety Problems Associated with Precarious Employment: The Case of Home-Based Workers in Australia' (2004) 17 *Australian Journal of Labour Law* 137.

[89] The states of New South Wales and Victoria each have such laws: see Forsyth (n 80) 336.

[90] *Making it work* (n 18). See Riley (n 79) 257. First introduced into the then Workplace Relations Act 1996 (Cth), the provisions now form ss 357 to 359 of the Fair Work Act 2009 (Cth).

[91] Fair Work Act 2009 (Cth) s 357.

way these provisions are cast means that they will have no effect in cases where a business '*successfully* avoids or disguises an employment relationship, by carefully constructing an arrangement that at common law would be treated as a contract for services.'[92] Another section provides that an employer must not dismiss an employee in order to re-engage them as an independent contractor to do the same work.[93] This would appear to have been introduced in part as a response to a high-profile case in which, after the introduction of the 2006 WorkChoices laws, an abattoir dismissed some 29 employees and then offered them the same work as independent contractors.[94] The third provision on 'sham' contracting prohibits an employer from knowingly making a false statement to persuade a worker to agree to be engaged as an independent contractor, to do the same work that they do or formerly did as an employee.[95]

The provisions on 'sham' contracting are 'civil remedy' provisions, which may be enforced by the person affected by the contravention, by their union on their behalf, or by an inspector holding office under the Fair Work Act 2009 (Cth). The maximum penalty for contravention at the time of this writing is some A\$6,600 for an individual, or A\$33,000 for a corporation. As part of the changes made to create the Fair Work Act 2009 (Cth) the provisions were relocated within the statute among others that provide so-called 'general protections.' This means, among other things, that a person who is alleged to have contravened the provisions will be assumed to have acted with the impugned intention, unless they prove otherwise.[96] At least one important change has also been made to the 'sham' contracting provisions, by relocating them together with other general protections. As the 'sham' contracting provisions were originally enacted, an applicant was required to prove that an employer acted for the 'sole or dominant purpose' proscribed by the provisions.[97] As part of the general protections in the Fair Work Act 2009 (Cth),

---

[92] Stewart (n 78) 58.

[93] Fair Work Act 2009 (Cth) s 358.

[94] Forsyth (n 80) 345. The termination of the abattoir employees' employment was facilitated by changes made by WorkChoices to the laws concerning unfair dismissal from employment which, among other things, excluded businesses with fewer than 100 employees from the federal jurisdiction. On the termination of employment provisions in Australian law and changes to them in recent years, see A Chapman, 'The Decline and Restoration of Unfair Dismissal Rights', in Forsyth and Stewart (n 76) 207–28.

[95] Fair Work Act 2009 (Cth) s 359.

[96] Fair Work Act 2009 (Cth) s 361. On the general protections and their enforcement see C Fenwick and J Howe, 'Union Security after Work Choices', in Forsyth and Stewart (n 76) 164. Such reverse onus of proof provisions have a long history in Australian federal labour law: C Jessup, 'The Onus of Proof in Proceedings under Part XA of the Workplace Relations Act 1996' (2002) 15 *Australian Journal of Labour Law* 198.

[97] Forsyth (n 80) 345.

however, it is now only necessary to show that the impugned reason was one of the reasons for so acting, even if there were others.[98]

The final element of the package of provisions introduced by the Independent Contractors Act 2006 (Cth) is those dealing with unfair contracts. In their present form the provisions are relatively new, however they have a history in the federal law going back to 1992.[99] Under these sections a contractor may seek review of a contract on the ground that it is 'unfair' or 'harsh'—terms which will take their common law meanings.[100] The court will be required to consider, among other things, the relative bargaining strengths of the parties, and whether undue influence or unfair tactics were used to induce the worker to enter into the contract. The court will also be able to consider whether the remuneration provided for under the contract is less than that which would be paid to an employee performing similar work.[101] In what appears to be the only case to date under the provisions in their current form, the Federal Magistrates' Court ruled that contracts between three independent contractors who provided trucking services, and a supermarket transport company, were unfair. The court considered that the contract allowed the supermarket transport company to impose unilaterally and without making financial compensation a significant change to the equipment that the independent contractors used to provide their services. The court amended the contract to limit the power of the supermarket transport company to require that the contractors change the vehicles that they used to supply their trucking services.[102]

It is not easy to assess the Independent Contractors Act 2006 (Cth), and the associated provisions concerning sham contracting from the point of view of Recommendation No 198. The provisions on sham contracting offer some direct support for workers in employment relationships, as might be envisaged by the Recommendation. Moreover the scope of these provisions may have been broadened in recent times by the abolition of the 'sole and dominant' reason requirement. The provisions for review of unfair contracts (which have a long history) also can be considered a measure to protect workers who are economically vulnerable. Yet the centrepiece of the Independent Contractors Act 2006 (Cth) remains its provisions

---

[98] Fair Work Act 2009 (Cth) s 360. See A Stewart, 'A Question of Balance: Labor's New Vision for Workplace Regulation' (2009) 22 *Australian Journal of Labour Law* 3, 40.

[99] Stewart (n 78) 55; Forsyth (n 80) 338.

[100] Independent Contractors Act 2006 (Cth) s 12. See Forsyth (n 80) 339 as to the common law meanings.

[101] Independent Contractors Act 2006 (Cth) s 15. The criteria are similar to those in ss 51AB and 51AC of the Trade Practices Act 1974 (Cth), which prohibit unconscionable conduct by corporations in certain circumstances. It would appear that s 51AC would apply to any contract for less than A$3 million, in addition to the Independent Contractors Act 2006 (Cth): Riley (n 79) 261.

[102] *Keldote Pty Ltd & Ors v Riteway Transport Pty Ltd* [2008] FMCA 1167 (decision as to liability); [2009] FMCA 319 (decision as to remedy).

that invalidate state or territory laws that are also designed to provide protection to economically vulnerable workers. And while there are provisions for review of unfair contracts, Anthony Forsyth has noted how these federal provisions are weaker in several important ways than two of the key state laws that they over-ride.[103]

A question that is very difficult to answer is why successive federal governments have insisted on retaining the common law definitions of contracts of employment and independent contracting in major statutory regimes, including regimes that are designed to address in some ways the difficulties faced by some groups of workers. This cannot be explained away on the basis of ignorance. To take one important example: the Hancock inquiry, which led to the first of the many waves of major changes to Australian federal labour law in 1988, included recommendations about how to deal with emerging forms of employment relationships.[104] More generally, Australia's various conciliation and arbitration jurisdictions have been dealing with some of the challenges posed by evolving forms of employment relationships for over 100 years. Two recent examples of the outcomes of those processes will suffice to illustrate the point. First, in recent years both the federal arbitration jurisdiction and the South Australian jurisdiction developed model clauses to appear in industrial awards that would allow workers regularly and systematically engaged as casual employees to have a right in certain circumstances to convert their employment to permanent part-time or full-time employment.[105] Secondly, for many years, the federal arbitration system included special provisions in the award applying to the textile, clothing and footwear industry, in order to address the precarious and vulnerable position of outworkers.[106]

The regulation of working conditions for vulnerable workers in the clothing industry, through the arbitration system, in turn assisted in other innovative regulatory developments in recent years. In that period a number of State jurisdictions have enacted laws to address the situation of these workers. Moreover, they were also saved from some of the effects of the changes introduced by the *WorkChoices* changes, including some that had the effect of removing or reducing various minimum working conditions for many employees.[107] As noted, there are also special regimes in New South Wales, Victoria and Western Australia to deal with the

---

[103] The grounds for review are narrower in the federal law, excluding considerations such as the 'public interest'; the provisions of the federal law only apply as at the time the contract was made (as distinct from how it has evolved over time); and the remedies available are fewer (it is not clear, for example, whether orders for damages may be made under the federal law): Forsyth (n 80) 341–42.

[104] Stewart (n 78) 55.

[105] *Re Metals Award* (2000) 110 IR 247; *Clerks (South Australia) Award Casual Provisions* (2002) 118 IR 241.

[106] *Re Clothing Trades Award 1982* (1987) 19 IR 416.

[107] See the sources at n 88 above.

conditions of owner-drivers in the transport industry, and jurisdictions in New South Wales and Queensland enabling the terms of unfair contracts to be adjusted.

Furthermore, in recent years there have been many parliamentary and other inquiries into changes in the composition of the labour market, and the working conditions of certain vulnerable groups of workers.[108] According to the most recent statistics as at this writing, some 5 per cent of workers are hired through labour hire; 9.1 per cent are independent contractors, and 76.4 per cent get paid leave entitlements.[109] Earlier studies (which are not directly comparable with the methodology used most recently) have suggested that as many as 20 per cent of Australia's workforce are 'permanent casuals'—engaged regularly on an insecure basis, and without the right to paid leave.[110] Not surprisingly, the issue has also been widely addressed in academic literature,[111] and the failure of the federal statutes in recent years to address the hard issue of whether or not to continue with the common law definitions of employment and independent contracting— particularly in relation to the issue of disguised employment—has been lamented. [112] The literature also includes proposals for new means by which to define which workers are employees and independent contractors.[113]

The decision of the ALP Government to retain the Independent Contractors Act 2006 (Cth) has been attributed by Professor Andrew Stewart to the Government's desire not to offend the business community in Australia, and in particular to the influence of a business-backed lobbying group, the Independent Contractors' Association of Australia.[114] This might be thought to be in keeping with the priorities evidenced by the fact that, (as Stewart has also noted), the ALP Government was the first ever to establish a Ministerial portfolio for Small Business, Independent Contractors and the Service Economy.[115] Leaving aside political explanations, the outcome remains more or less the same. That is, the Independent Contractors Act 2006 (Cth) remains on the statute books, without any attempt to indicate, any more clearly than under the common law, which workers are to be

---

[108] See for example the inquiries noted above.

[109] Australian Bureau of Statistics (n 18). For critical analysis of the statistical categories that have been used over time to categorize information about the Australian labour market, see O'Donnell (n 10).

[110] O'Donnell (n 10).

[111] For a recent overview of changes in the Australian labour market see I Campbell, 'Australia: institutional changes and workforce fragmentation' in S Lee and F Eyraud (eds), *Globalization, flexibilization and working conditions in Asia and the Pacific* (ILO/Chandos, 2008) 115–52; and for a perceptive critical analysis of some important studies on workforce composition in Australia in recent times, see O'Donnell (n 10).

[112] Forsyth (n 80) (esp 347); Stewart (n 78) 59.

[113] Stewart (n 3).

[114] More information on this association is available at www.contractworld.com.au.

[115] Stewart (n 78).

considered as having this legal status.[116] Moreover, as Forsyth has pointed out, despite the former Government having supported the enactment of the Independent Contractors Act 2006 (Cth) on the basis that it would promote and protect workers' free choices, it does nothing to address the difficulties faced by workers who in reality have little or no such choice. In fact, it significantly reduces the level of protection available to some of these workers, by over-riding other laws intended to provide greater protection, in recognition of precisely these difficulties.[117] Not surprisingly, some have therefore questioned whether this law really offers a 'fair deal' for these workers.[118]

India has also recently enacted federal laws that deal with the difficulties and vulnerability that can result from the individual employment relationship, and in doing so it has attempted to engage with the issue of legal definitions at a substantive level. For instance The Unorganised Workers' Social Security Act 2008, recently approved by the Indian Parliament, contains a fairly detailed amount of definitions in an attempt to clarify its personal scope of application.[119] Section 2(b) of the Act, provides that 'home-based worker' means a 'person engaged in the production of goods or services for an employer in his or her home or other premises of his or her choice other than the workplace of the employer, for remuneration, irrespective of whether or not the employer provides the equipment, materials or other inputs'. Under s 2(k) 'self-employed worker' means 'any person who is not employed by an employer, but engages himself or herself in any occupation in the unorganized sector', though this is subject to a monthly earning of a specific amount that can be decided at state government level. Similar limits to the monthly earnings can be applied in respect of 'wage workers' that s 2(n) generously defines as 'person[s] employed for remuneration in the unorganized sector, directly by an employer or through any contractor, irrespective of place of work, whether exclusively for one employer or for one or more employers, whether in cash or in kind, whether as a home-based worker, or as a temporary or casual worker, or as a migrant worker, or workers employed by households including domestic workers'. It is noteworthy that these definitions do not shy away from the challenges posed by

---

[116] The Act applies to a 'contract for services' which is defined in s 5(1) as being a contract to which an independent contractor is a party, and that relates to the performance of work by the independent contractor. The provision also establishes a requirement for a certain 'constitutional connection': as the law is primarily supported by the federal government's power to regulate corporations, it basically applies to independent contractors whose businesses are incorporated.

[117] Forsyth (n 80) 346.

[118] Riley (n 79) 246.

[119] For an analysis of these definitional issues *cf* NCEUS, *Report on Definitional and Statistical Issues Relating to the Informal Economy*, (New Delhi, November 2008), available at http://nceus.gov.in/Report_Statistical_Issues_Informal_Economy.pdf.

labour intermediation practices, as also evidenced by the notion of 'employer' contained in s 2(a), meaning 'person or an association of persons, who has engaged or employed an unorganized worker either directly or otherwise for remuneration'. The Act seeks to 'provide for the social security and welfare of unorganized workers and for other matters connected therewith or incidental thereto'. It is therefore not concerned with extending to these categories of 'unorganized workers' the basic labour rights traditionally enjoyed by those employees with a standard contract of employment falling under the 'workman' definition contained in s 2(s) of the Industrial Disputes Act 1947. But this statute, for all its shortcomings, provides a good theoretical basis for recasting the personal scope of application of relevant statutes as to include a broad range of different employment relationships. For instance, it could very well serve as a conceptual basis for further elaboration on the very notion of 'workman', which is unduly confined to relationships where 'the main work of the employee is … manual or clerical'.[120] As it will become apparent in the reminder of this chapter, a particularly knotty issue, and one that somehow undermines the conceptual rationality of national labour law systems, is that different statutes often refer to different concepts of employment contract or relationship. India is hardly an exception to this general pattern and, as noted by Shrivastava, the Supreme Court 'has clarified that there is clear difference in the definition of "workman" under the Contract Labour (Regulation and Abolition) Act, 1970 and Industrial Disputes Act, 1947'.[121]

Other systems appear to be more reluctant to adopt more inclusive approaches in their recent labour law reforms. Malaysia for instance has maintained substantially unaltered the legal framework developed in the 1950s and 1960s with the Employment Act 1955 and the Industrial Relations Act 1967. Under the First Schedule of the Employment Act 1955, an 'employee'—the category of workers to which most of the employment protection rights apply—is primarily defined as 'Any person, irrespective of his occupation, who has entered into a contract of service with an employer under which such person's wages do not exceed one thousand five hundred ringgit a month'. Section 2 of the Industrial Relations Act 1967 define the concept of 'workman' as:

> any person, including an apprentice, employed by an employer under a contract of employ-ment to work for hire or reward and for the purposes of any proceedings in relation to a trade dispute includes any such person who has been dismissed, discharged or retrenched in

---

[120] HL Kumar, 'Workman Under the Industrial Disputes Act, 1947' (2005) *Factories and Labour Reports* 23.
[121] MP Shrivastava, '"Contract Labour" and "Principal Employer"—Its Implication for Industrial Disputes under Industrial Disputes Act, 1947' (2006) *Factories and Labour Reports* 39.

connection with or as a consequence of that dispute or whose dismissal, discharge or retrenchment has led to that dispute.

The explicit reference to 'contracts of service' recurs in the 'employee' definition of s 2 of the more recent Employees Provident Fund Act 1991.

In recent times Singapore has taken some very timid steps in the direction of a more inclusive personal scope of application for its core labour law statutes. Beginning on 1 April 2008, the Work Injury Compensation Act replaced the Workmen's Compensation Act.[122] The previous Act covered only all manual workers and non-manual workers with monthly earnings of $1,600 and below. The new Work Injury Compensation Act is applicable to all employees in general, both manual and non-manual workers and, most importantly, regardless of their level of earnings. However, there are categories of persons who are not covered under the Act. Schedule 4 explicitly excludes domestic workers, members of the Singapore Armed Forces, officers of the Singapore Police Force, the Singapore Civil Defence Force, the Central Narcotics Bureau and the Singapore Prisons Service from coverage under the Work Injury Compensation Act. Also, self-employed persons and independent contractors do not fall under the Act's provisions. The Employment Act, the core statute for the provision of labour rights in Singapore, was also subject to some amendments in recent times. Beginning on 1 January 2009,[123] the Act has been amended to cover staff in confidential positions[124] and managers and executives with monthly salaries of $2,500, albeit only in respect of non-payment of salary.[125] Also Part IV salary ceiling for non-workmen was raised from a basic monthly salary of $1,600 to $2,000,[126] and a salary ceiling of $4,500 for workmen was introduced, which may have some exclusive effects.[127] Part-time employees were redefined as those working 35 hours or less per week, as compared to 30 hours or less in the previous definition,[128] which effectively reduces the number of workers who are eligible for full protections under the Employment Act. Another amendment was made via the Employment Act (Amendment of First Schedule)

---

[122] This was via the Workmen's Compensation (Amendment) Act 2008 No 5 of 2008.

[123] The amending Act in question is the Employment (Amendment) Act 2008 No 32 of 2008.

[124] Definition of 'employee' in s 2 of the Act amended to remove the phrase 'does not include … any person employed in a … confidential position'.

[125] This was done via the insertion of s 2(2) EA, quoted above.

[126] Done via the amendment of s 35 EA, most importantly in this particular case (b).

[127] Done via the amendment of s 35 EA, most importantly in this particular case (a). The argument put forth by the government is that high-salaried workmen need not be protected as they are by themselves capable of negotiating favourable employment terms: Ministry of Manpower, *Changes to the Employment Act* (Singapore, Ministry of Manpower, 2008) 9.

[128] Done via the amendment of s 66A.

Notification 2008 No S 669/2008. It concerned the list of jobs classified specifically under the definition of 'workmen' in the First Schedule:

Prior to amendment	**After amendment**
1. Bus conductor	1. Cleaners
2. Lorry attendant	2. Construction Workers
3. Bus, lorry and van drivers	3. Labourers
4. Bus inspector	4. Machine operators and assemblers
5. Goldsmith and silversmith employed in the premises of the employer	5. Metal and machinery workers
	6. Train, bus, lorry and van drivers
	7. Train and bus inspectors
6. Tailor and dressmaker employed in the premises of the employer	8. All workmen employed on piece rates in the premises of the employer.
7. Harbour-craft crew	
8. All workmen employed on piece rates in the premises of the employer	

In China, the labour laws do not contain any detailed rules for distinguishing employment from other kinds of work relations. While there are no definitively authoritative rules for distinguishing an employee from an independent contractor, there are certain principles and approaches that appear to be used by various decision-makers.

Chinese labour law authorities place considerable emphasis on the nature of the employing enterprise. The key term used in the two most significant labour laws concerned with employee status—the Labour Law of 1994 and the Labour Contract law of 2007—is 'employing unit'. In the earlier law, the term included 'enterprises' and 'individual economic organizations', as well as 'state organs, institutions and public organizations'.[129] The later law uses a similar formulation, but extends it to cover 'private non-enterprise entities'. The Implementing Regulations for the Labour Contract Law clarify that partnerships, such as law and accountancy firms, and foundations also fall within this extension.[130]

The significance of the term 'employing unit' is that, in establishing whether a work relationship is one of employment, labour authorities need to consider whether the putative employer in fact fits into this category. Despite the apparent breath of the definition, this is not always straightforward. Under various PRC laws, employing units (other than state entities) will usually need to register as a business

---

[129] art 2.
[130] Implementing Regulations of the Labour Contract Law art 2.

or other entity.[131] Some judges and other officers administering the labour law have come to the conclusion that if an entity is not registered, then it is illegal and cannot be an 'employing unit' for the purposes of labour law.[132] This would have the perverse effect that workers performing services for an illegal business entity would be denied the protection of labour law.

In order to address this problem, the Labour Contract Law provides that a worker engaged by an illegal entity is entitled to receive remuneration and economic compensation for loss from the entity or its capital contributors.[133] While this is an improvement on the previous position, it does not equate to treating an unregistered entity as an employer, and so labour protections relating to working conditions other than pay (such as working time limits) may not be applicable to the work relationships.[134]

In Viet Nam, the employment relationship and its legal regulation have evolved significantly since the implementation of the *Doi moi* policies that were adopted by the Communist Party of Viet Nam at its Sixth National Party Congress in 1986.[135] Under *Doi moi*, Viet Nam 'is officially in transition from a centrally planned economy to a socialist-oriented market economy'.[136] This transition has led, among many other things, to the adoption of Viet Nam's first national labour laws, in the form of the Labour Code of 1994.[137] Indeed, a key reason for the adoption of the Code was to provide legal guidance on a labour policy oriented toward a market economy.[138] Within this framework, the policy of the Government of Viet Nam in the world of work has been for some time to promote the establishment of legally regulated individual employment relationships. The 1994 Code was amended in both 2002 and 2006, and it has been reported that the Code will be amended again by 2010. Changes that have been made already have altered the Code's provisions on 'labour contracts', and more are apparently planned.[139]

---

[131]   See, eg Implementing Regulations of the Labour Contract Law art 4.

[132]   Dong (n 69).

[133]   Labour Contract Law art 93.

[134]   Presumably the rationale here is that an illegal entity with poor working conditions should be shut down, rather than being directed to comply with the law. However, as illegal entities may operate for a considerable period of time prior to detection, it might be preferable to render an illegal entity responsible not only for pecuniary loss, but also for violations of labour standards generally.

[135]   *Doi moi* might be translated as 'renewal' or 'renovation': P Nicholson, 'Vietnam's labour market—Transition and the role of law' in Cooney et al (n 1) 123.

[136]   Nicholson (n 135) 122.

[137]   The Code was passed on 23 June 1994, and entered into force on 1 January 1995: L Qu, W Taylor and S Frost, 'Labour Relations and deregulation in Vietnam: Theory and Practice' (September 2003) Working Paper No 53, Southeast Asia Research Centre, City University of Hong Kong 7.

[138]   N Collins and Y Zhu, 'Vietnam's Labour Policies Reform' (2003) *Asia Pacific Labour Law Review* 375–385, 375.

[139]   VD Quang, 'Vietnam: workers in transition' in Lee and Eyraud (n 111) 383–411, 384.

From the point of view of the present inquiry, the introduction of the Labour Code in 1994 marked the most significant development in the legal regulation of the employment relationship in Viet Nam in quite some time:

> In the context of the economic transition to a market economy, the role of the Labour Code has been significant. In the past, only jobs in the collective sector were considered formal employment, but with the promulgation of the Labour Code, the definition of formal employment was expanded.[140]

Thus, the Labour Code of 1994 was intended to, and did have the effect of creating the very concept of an employment relationship, as well as its legal form and regulation, in a context in which this marked a significant departure from previous policy: '[t]his was the first time that the relationship between employees and employers and their rights and obligations had been officially recognized under government law'.[141] Perhaps not surprisingly, it may therefore appear that the legal regulation of the relationship is somewhat underdeveloped by comparison with other jurisdictions considered in this chapter, and indeed in other chapters in this book. Nor is it surprising to note that legal regulation of the employment relationship in Viet Nam is widely reported to be relatively ineffective in practice. This is perhaps only to be expected given that the overwhelming majority of workers in Viet Nam continue to be engaged in the informal economy, and therefore effectively beyond the reach of the Labour Code and its legal regulation of the employment relationship.[142]

Before *Doi moi,* all enterprises were officially owned and operated by the State, and all workers were assigned to work in enterprises through the operation of government labour bureaux. Neither those responsible for the management of enterprises nor those who worked in them were able freely to choose to participate in the relationship. While managers had some capacity to discipline those who worked in their enterprises, they 'did not have the authority to dismiss employees', who enjoyed work for life' (*bien che*). Once employees had been placed under the 'work for life' system, they continued to work until retirement.[143] Thus, before the introduction of *Doi moi,* there was no official labour market in Viet Nam: 'the

---

[140] Quang (n 139) 394.

[141] Collins and Zhu (n 138) 376. See also Qu, Taylor and Frost (n 137).

[142] In 2002 it was reported that some 80% of workers in Vietnam were engaged in household or own-account work, Nicholson (n 135) 126. In 2008 the figure was still around 70%: Quang (n 139) 391.

[143] Collins and Zhu (n 138) 378.

concept of labour supply and demand did not exist'.[144] While it is true that private sector economic activity began obviously to emerge from 1979,[145] neither in official policy nor in law was there a possibility of a free exchange of labour, regulated by the device of contract.

The Government of Viet Nam began its efforts to change these rules and their operation from 1987, when it introduced a requirement that state-owned enterprises (SOEs) should engage all new workers on contracts, following a standard form drawn up by the Government.[146] All those who were engaged before 1987, however, remained on the 'work for life' system.[147] From the introduction of the Labour Code in 1994, the use of labour contracts 'gradually became compulsory' in SOEs,[148] other than for very senior workers, and also became compulsory, in law at least, for the non-SOE sector.[149] Notwithstanding the expansion of the Government's policy of requiring workers to be engaged on labour contracts, as will appear directly, the Labour Code has always excluded certain workers from its coverage, and continues to do so today. Moreover, as noted, the implementation of the provisions in practice has been very limited, and has been further hampered by the fact that the vast majority of workers in Viet Nam are engaged in the informal economy.

The initial provisions of the Labour Code establish a wide scope for it, yet as will appear, with very few definitions that might assist in determining its application in practice.[150] The Code is to regulate 'the labour relationship between a wage earning worker and his employer' (art 1), and 'applies to all workers, and organizations or individuals utilizing labour on the basis of a labour contract in any sector of the economy and in any form of ownership' (art 2).[151] It also applies to Vietnamese citizens working for enterprises 'with foreign owned capital in Viet Nam', or for 'a

---

[144] N Collins, 'Economic reform and unemployment in Vietnam' in J Benson and Y Zhu (eds), *Unemployment in Asia* (London, Routledge, 2005) 176–193, 176.

[145] Nicholson (n 135) 125. (And for this reason it has been argued that *Doi moi* in significant measure represented a recognition rather than an introduction of private sector economic activity: ibid, 123).

[146] Collins and Zhu (n 138) 378.

[147] Collins and Zhu (n 138) 377 and 378.

[148] Collins (n 144) 181.

[149] Collins and Zhu (n 138) 378.

[150] All references to the text of the Labour Code of Vietnam are to the English language version, published by Australian law firm Allens Arthur Robinson in collaboration with the Vietnamese government, available at www.vietnamlaws.com. The text available there takes into account amendments made up until those of 2 March 2007.

[151] A Circular issued in February 1995 clarifies that labour contracts are required for workers engaged in certain 'cultural and service' activities, which includes 'dancing halls, karaoke or massage services, hotels, guest houses' and other forms of work in which women are frequently employed to serve and/or to entertain: Circular Providing Guidelines for Entering into Labour Contracts in Respect of a Number of Forms of Cultural and Service Activities, No 04-LDTBXH-TT, 12 February 1995.

foreign or international organization operating in the territory of Viet Nam' and to 'a foreigner who works in an enterprise or organization or for a Vietnamese individual operating in the territory of Viet Nam' (art 3).[152] Nevertheless, the Code also limits its application predominantly to the commercial sector—whether state-owned or otherwise. Indeed, by virtue of article 4, the Code expressly does not apply to the following categories of workers:

— state employees and officials;
— elected and appointed officials;
— members of units of the people's armed forces and police force;
— members of public organizations;
— members of other political and social organizations; and
— members of cooperatives.

A Decree issued in May 2003 gives further, detailed guidance on the application of the Labour Code. It reiterates the exclusions listed above, and it identifies in some detail the 'organizations and individuals employing labour' that are required to enter into labour contracts.[153]

The Labour Code gives an employer an express right 'to recruit labour' as well as to assign, discipline and manage as required (art 8). It also defines the nature of a 'labour relationship between an employer and an employee' in article 9 as being one that is:

> established and developed through negotiation and agreement on the principles of voluntary commitment, fairness, co-operation, mutual respect of legal rights and benefits, and full performance of undertakings.

In this respect, the description of the nature of the 'labour relationship' bears many similarities to the content of the contract of employment that is implied at common law in certain countries.

In its c III, on 'Employment', the Code provides that '[a]ny labour activity which creates a source of income and which is not prohibited by law shall be recognized as employment' (art 13). It is difficult in an exercise of this nature to be definitive about the purpose of this provision. On its face, it seems that it could have the effect of defining the scope of employment relationships. And this would be in

---

[152] Rules concerning the engagement of Vietnamese citizens by foreign enterprises, and the employment of foreign citizens in Vietnam, are also found in arts 131–33.

[153] Decree Making Detailed Provisions and Providing Guidelines for Implementation of a Number of Articles of the Labour Code with Respect to Labour Contracts, (No 44–2003-ND-CP, Hanoi, 9 May 2003) art 2.

keeping with certain other provisions in the c III. In particular, article 16 expressly provides for an employee's right to be employed in any location and to seek employment either directly from an employer or through an agency (para 1), and an employer's right to recruit employees either directly or through an agency, and to increase or reduce the number of employees (para 2). Nevertheless, it should be noted that other provisions in c III are concerned with general employment policy obligations of the Government, and it might be presumed that the definition of 'employment' also has work to do in that context.[154]

Chapter IV of the Labour Code contains numerous provisions relating to labour contracts. The first of these (art 26) defines a labour contract as:

> an agreement between the employee and the employer on the paid job, working conditions, and the rights and obligations of each party in the labour relationship.

A labour contract must be personal, and while an employee may enter into more than one labour contract, the employee must carry out the work tasks required and may not transfer that obligation to another without the permission of their employer (art 30). In this, there is a clear echo of one of the basic elements of the common law test for determining the existence of an employment relationship, and distinguishing it from an independent contract. There is also a similarity with article 13(a) of Recommendation 198, which refers to a characteristic of the work of an employee as being that it 'must be carried out personally by the worker'.

A labour contract might be for either an indefinite or a definite term, including for seasonal jobs of less than 12 months (art 27(1)). The Code also provides that a worker and an employer with a definite term labour contract may conclude another labour contract within 30 days of the expiration of the initial contract where work continues, and in default shall be presumed to have entered into an indefinite term contract on the terms of the initial contract (art 27(2)).[155] Labour contracts should be in writing, although they may be oral for 'certain temporary works which have a duration of less than three months, and in respect of domestic servants' (art 28). The Code provides for when a labour contract comes into force, and how it might

---

[154] See in particular the obligations to establish targets for numbers of jobs (art 14) and to 'establish national employment programmes and investment projects for economic and social growth' (art 15).

[155] This provision was introduced in 2002, along with a requirement in art 41 that if an employee accepts an employer's decision no longer to employ the employee, the two parties should agree on a sum of compensation: Quang (n 139) 395.

be amended (art 33). There is a significant amount of further detailed regulation of the formation and entry into force of contracts in other legal instruments.[156]

Certain matters must be included in a labour contract: definition of work to be performed; working hours and rest breaks; duration; occupational safety and health conditions; and social insurance for the employee (art 29(1)). Where a labour contract is inconsistent with the Code, an applicable collective agreement, or internal labour regulations of the enterprise, it must be amended (art 29(2)), and the labour inspectorate is responsible for advising on how to correct contracts that do not comply with the Code (art 29(3)).

The Code provides for trial periods and the parties' rights to terminate during that period (art 32), for the rights and obligations of employees and employers in the event of transfer of enterprise (art 31), circumstances in which an employer might temporarily re-assign an employee party to a labour contract (art 34) and cases in which a labour contract might properly be suspended (art 35). It provides also for when a labour contract might be terminated (art 36) and gives specific rights of unilateral termination (which might be withdrawn under art 40) in defined circumstances to both employees (art 37) and employers (art 38). There are certain limits on the ability of an employer to terminate (art 39),[157] and an employer is obliged to re-employ an employee in certain cases, or to provide the employee with compensation if the employee agrees with the employer's preference not to re-employ them. Upon termination of the labour contract of an employee who has served for more than 12 months, an employer must provide severance pay (art 42) and each party must ensure that any outstanding payments are made within a specified period (art 43). Again, more detail on these obligations appears in other instruments.[158]

Not surprisingly, given the purpose of the provisions of the Code dealing with labour contracts (that is, to introduce the individual employment relationship into the Vietnamese labour market and the associated legal landscape), the provisions just described deal with many of the topics that are usually addressed in laws regulating the employment relationship. There are provisions for creation and termination of employment relationships (labour contracts). There are procedural obligations, provisions about the formalities for the creation of labour contracts, and others protecting the rights of each of the parties in given circumstances. There

---

[156] Decree No 44–2003-ND-CP (n 153) art 2, and Circular Providing Guidelines for Implementation of a Number of Articles of Decree 44–2003-ND-CP of the Government dated 9 May 2003 with Respect to Labour Contracts, No 21–2003-TT-BLDTB&XH, 22 September 2003.

[157] As for example when an employee is ill or has been injured at work, or is on authorized leave, or is female.

[158] Decree No 44–2003-ND-CP (n 153) art 2, and Circular No 21–2003-TT-BLDTB&XH (n 156).

is a model contract provided in a non-legislative instrument, together with further details on the formalities that must attend the creation of a valid labour contract.[159]

There is not, however, any provision that expressly defines an 'employee', and there is very little in the Code to explain which types of work relationships are to be considered employment relationships as distinct from any other work relationship regulated by a contract. The only provisions that go any way in this direction appear to be that which describes the nature of the mutual obligations that are at the heart of an employment relationship (art 8), together with that which requires that work under a labour contract be performed by the individual worker party to the contract, other than with the permission of their employer (art 30).

Notwithstanding the significant level of detailed legal regulation of the employment relationship in the Labour Code, it is widely agreed that the Labour Code has had relatively little impact in practice in the Vietnamese labour market. This reflects a continuation of difficulties that the Government has encountered since the early phases of its policy to move toward a system of individual labour contracts. The changes introduced in 1987, for example, under which SOEs were required to engage all new workers on labour contracts were rather ineffective in practice. Very few SOEs did put newly engaged workers on contracts, and those that did used contracts only for some matters, such as formalization of wage payments. Moreover, all those who had been engaged before 1987 remained on the 'work for life' system.[160]

Moreover, the relatively recent introduction and development of the legal concept of an employment relationship—that is, a work relationship for wages regulated by a labour contract—means that the concept is little developed. In this, however, things seem to have changed as concerns the application of the law in practice. Nicholson reported in 2002 that there was very little use of labour contracts other than in foreign invested enterprises. More recently, Quang has drawn on surveys from the Ministry of Labour, Invalids and Social Affairs which suggest that the use of labour contracts in those enterprises is close to universal, whether they are required by law or not.[161] Nicholson had also reported a significant level of economic activity in the informal economy: '[b]y far the greatest number of Vietnamese (roughly 80 per cent) work in the non-state sector, largely in households, where they rely on family and village networks for social security and land.'[162] Putting it differently, she reported that unemployment was a major problem (albeit

---

[159] Circular No 21–2003-TT-BLDTB&XH (n 156).
[160] Collins and Zhu (n 138) 377 and 378.
[161] Quang (n 139) 392.
[162] Nicholson (n 135) 126.

one of which the Government was aware), especially given the absence of an unemployment benefit.[163] Challenges over the application of the labour law in practice in Viet Nam are bound to remain. The collective systems of industrial relations remain weak,[164] and there are many new labour market and legal concepts to be absorbed. As Collins has pointed out, for example, 'unemployment was only written into the law, with a formulated policy, in the amended Labour Code of 2002.'[165]

6.4 The Social Partners and the Employment Relationship

While it is possible to draw a number of common analytical patterns in the actions, omissions, and approaches adopted by the governments, legislators, and the judiciaries of the countries hitherto considered, tracing a common trajectory in respect of the stance adopted by the Australian, Indian, Malaysian and Singaporean social partners is far less obvious an exercise. Different trade union traditions, different systems of industrial relations, different constitutional and regulatory frameworks for trade union action, and different economic and industrial set ups, make for a rather complex and heterogeneous set of priorities, by workers' organizations and employers' associations alike.

Australian trade unions and employers have been very much alert to the challenges posed by the traditional approach towards the regulation and identification of the employment relationship in domestic labour law. There is continuing pressure by the labour movement, some labour state governments and other interested parties to remove situations of disguised employment relationships. As noted, there been several significant parliamentary inquiries in recent years, to which the social partners have made many and detailed submissions. Many of the proposed changes to federal labour law in recent years have also been the subject of inquiry by parliamentary committees (in particular in the Senate), and again, both employers and unions have participated actively in this process. Moreover, both employers and unions are represented in the National Workplace Relations Consultative Council, which includes also a Committee on Industrial Legislation.

---

[163] ibid 137.
[164] S Clarke, C-H Lee and DQ Chi, 'From Rights to Interests: The Challenge of Industrial Relations in Vietnam' (2007) 49 *Journal of Industrial Relations* 545.
[165] Collins (n 144) 176.

In addition to the independent role that unions play in pressing for changes to arbitrated awards and to legislation, they have for many years been active in seeking regulation of the conditions of vulnerable workers in collective agreements. Under the WorkChoices changes, many such clauses in collective agreements were outlawed as so-called 'prohibited content'. While these rules have now been changed with the transition to the Fair Work Act 2009 (Cth), the legal tests that have been introduced do leave open some difficult questions about how far unions and employers will be able to agree on such matters in agreements to be certified (and so made legally binding) by Fair Work Australia.[166]

On the other hand, state legislation, awards and industrial instruments continue to provide significant protection to certain categories of vulnerable workers, who are frequently deemed to be employees for particular statutory purposes, including workers' compensation[167] and payroll tax contributions.[168] (These are also examples of laws that are not over-ridden by the Independent Contractors Act 2006 (Cth)).[169] The interaction of these laws with the proposed new national system for industrial relations nevertheless remains to be worked out in detail: the implementation of a truly national scheme of labour law, at least for the private sector, remains a work in progress, and has only recently begun.

As for India, a system with a pluralist tradition of industrial relations, much of the social partners' attention has been inevitably catalyzed by the debate surrounding the preparation and adoption of the Unorganized Workers' Social Security Act 2008. However, unions have also directed their reformist attention towards other statutes that are more closely and directly related to the issues treated by Recommendation No 198. The Centre of Indian Trade Unions (CITU) for instance, has been lobbying the Government with the aim of amending the Contract Labour (Regulation & Abolition) Act 1970 and 'Redefining [the] employment relationship on the basis of the linkage between the final recipients of the gains of production, i.e., the principal employer, vis-à-vis the producer at the lowest rung of the production process deployed through various decentralized agencies'.[170] Several

---

[166] Stewart (n 98) 28–30.

[167] ACT: Workers Compensation Act 1951 ss 10(2), 11; NSW: Workplace Injury Management and Workers Compensation Act 1998 s 5, sch 1, cll 1, 2A; Qld: Workers Compensation Act 1985 s 8(1); WA: Workers Compensation Act & Rehabilitation Act 1981 s 5.

[168] ACT: Payroll Tax Act 1987, s 2; NSW: Payroll Tax Act 2007; s 13; QLD: Payroll Tax Act 1971, s 2; SA: Payroll Tax Act 2009, s 11; Tas: Payroll Tax Act 2008, s 13; Vic: Payroll Tax Act 2007, s 13; WA: Payroll Tax Act 2002, s 5.

[169] Independent Contractors Act 2006 (Cth) s 8(2).

[170] CITU 41st Indian Labour Conference, 27–28 April 2007, available at www.citucentre.org/monthly_journals/sub_topic_details.php?id=42.

trade union centres have submitted formal representations to the National Commission for Enterprises in the Unorganized Sector (NCEUS), many of which have been incorporated in the Commission's final reports. When in 2007 the NCEUS enquired about the 'Lack of uniformity in definitions' contained in labour statues and spelling out their personal scope of application,[171] both CITU and the employers' association FICCI-AIOE agreed about the necessity to harmonize the various existing definitions,[172] and the Hind Mazdoor Sangh (HMS) usefully suggested that in doing so 'It may also be useful to consider what definitions ILO uses in its conventions'.[173]

There is however a sense that the Indian social partners are far from reaching a consensus over the scope of the employment relationship and about the scope of application of the Indian statutes in need of reform. For instance, FICCI-AIOE would like to see the concept of 'workman' contained in section 2(s) of the Industrial Disputes Act amended as to exclude 'employees in the higher salary brackets in the organized sector, like Airlines, Bank, Insurance' and 'supervisors',[174] a stance that is unlikely to strike a chord with the union movement, or facilitate an agreement or a social pact in respect of the 'vexed question'.

The Malaysian Employers Federation has commonly cited matters such as 'flexibility' and 'competitiveness' as reasons for not supporting regulation of the employment relationships too stringently. At the National Labour Advisory Council (Malaysia's pre-eminent body for tri-partite negotiations), the MTUC has raised the issue numerous times. The Government, however, has not been receptive to their appeals. The reason given has been that such legislation would discourage investment in Malaysia's industries.

There do not seem to be any collective agreements or 'social pacts' in Malaysia which assist in the identification of a particular sort of employment relationship. With regards to collective agreements in general, migrant workers are technically in law supposed to be covered by such agreements. Also, although the Trade Union Act 1959 provides that any worker over 16 years of age is eligible to join a union,[175] the work permits granted to migrant workers by the Immigration Department provide that they do not have the right to join a union.

Also, there is at present no existing union that focuses on organizing 'atypical' workers. As for the unions that exist, a problem which has reared its head is the fact that it is the Government, and not the unions, who set the parameters as to who can

---

[171] NCEUS, *Labour Reforms in India—Background Note to the First Meeting of the Task Force on Labour Reforms*, (26 March 2007), 4. Available at www.iiaonline.in/doc_files/labour_revised.pdf.

[172] ibid 58–59.

[173] ibid 59.

[174] NCEUS (n 171) 68.

[175] s 26.

join which unions. During the union recognition procedure, a trade union must apply to represent a particular class of workers. As a result, it is commonly the case that each union in Malaysia represents a very specific set of workers, eg bank employees.

These restrictions on who may join which unions hinder some agency workers from joining any particular union because such workers may be working for a series of employers in different sectors. For example, an agency worker employed as a cleaner may work for an educational institution, then a bank, then a manufacturing plant. There would be confusion as to which union he or she may join, given that he or she has been employed in numerous industries, each with their own unions.

Singaporean social partners are perhaps even more reluctant to take any decisive steps in addressing the many problematic issues arising from Recommendation No 198. A preliminary issue that must be noted is that, for historical and political reasons that go beyond the scope of the present work, the social partners in Singapore work very closely in a co-operative, rather than adversarial or confrontational, manner. According to an official of the Singaporean National Trades Union Congress, interviewed by one of the present authors, its view is that outsourcing (a practice which is a fertile ground for disguised employment relationships) cannot be 'stopped' due to a need for companies to be competitive (a rather surprising, but perhaps pragmatic, view for a trade unionist). Hence, together with the other social partners it has endeavoured to encourage employers to adopt what they call responsible 'best sourcing' practices. Her description of this concept is as follows:

> [T]he key ideas under consideration include encouraging buyers to move away from headcount-based contracts to performance-based contracts; and lengthening the contract period so that it will provide income stability to contract workers and motivate service providers to invest in training and technologies, which will result in productivity gain and consequently, better wages for contract workers.

To date, there have been no collective agreements or social pacts which contain guidelines for identifying an employment relationship.

6.5 Administrative Solutions to the Challenges Posed by the Scope of the Employment Relationship

ILO Recommendation No 198 actively encourages a prominent role for national labour administrations, and for public and tripartite mechanisms in both monitoring and enforcing programmes related to the clarification of the employment relationship.[176] In the countries considered here, however, this encouragement appears to be trickling down at the national level at a disappointingly slow pace. In the common law jurisdictions, most of the national bite continues to rest with the judiciary. In China and Viet Nam, the administrative, legal and political structures would seem to leave considerable scope for administrative action to clarify the scope of the employment relationship. Nevertheless, there appear to have been relatively few developments in these jurisdictions in this respect.

Australia is one country that shows some signs of a different approach from the otherwise widespread trend, albeit one that is fairly circumscribed and limited in scope. Under the changes made in Australia in recent times, the Australian Industrial Relations Commission (AIRC) will be replaced by an institution called Fair Work Australia (FWA). Among FWA's responsibilities will be the exercise of jurisdiction in cases in which unfair dismissal from employment is alleged. In this it will continue to play an important role in superintending the boundaries of the employment relationship, for it is only those workers engaged as employees within the meaning of the common law tests discussed above who have access to this jurisdiction.[177]

FWA's primary responsibilities will also include resolution of conflicts about enterprise agreements between employers and employees, and their representatives, and the safeguarding of those minimum working conditions established by the AIRC in so-called 'modern awards', rather than in the terms of the Fair Work Act 2009 (Cth).[178] As we have seen, awards have traditionally played an important role in extending employment protections to certain categories of vulnerable workers. Not surprisingly, as part of the process of award modernization, the AIRC retained in some (but not all) modern awards, provisions that would allow regularly-engaged casual employees to elect to convert their work engagement to regular part-time or full-time employment.[179] Looking forward, FWA is required to review modern awards every four years,[180] and will therefore have regular opportunities at which to consider the ongoing need for these or other similar initiatives. In doing so, however, FWA will be constrained by the general terms of its powers in this function under the Fair Work Act 2009 (Cth).[181]

---

[176] cf paras 16–22 of ILO Recommendation No 198.

[177] On FWA's unfair dismissal jurisdiction see Chapman (n 94).

[178] On the complex interaction of contract, statute, awards and collective bargaining as sources of minimum working conditions in Australia, see J Murray and R Owens, 'The Safety Net: Labour Standards in the New Era', in Forsyth and Stewart (n 76) 40—74.

[179] See the Award Modernisation decision, [2008] AIRCFB 1000 [51] (available at: www.airc.gov.au/awardmod/databases/security/Decisions/2008aircfb1000.htm).

[180] Fair Work Act 2009 (Cth) s 156.

[181] See Stewart (n 98) 20–25 on the modern award system. On the changes to the scope of the powers of the AIRC in setting minimum conditions in awards over time, see for example C Fenwick, 'How Low Can You

Apart from the roles of the AIRC and FWA in establishing and maintaining award conditions, the Australian system also includes a high-profile enforcement agency. Under the Fair Work Act 2009 (Cth) this role is played by the Fair Work Ombudsman, who is responsible for investigating and prosecuting breaches of the Fair Work Act 2009 (Cth).[182] The rejuvenation of enforcement under the Australian system, however, goes back (somewhat ironically) to changes made by the Howard Government, which were widely perceived as having the effect of reducing protection for Australian employees.[183] Fair Work Inspectors have jurisdiction to investigate matters relating to independent contractors, including alleged sham contracting arrangements that would be in breach of sections 345–59 of the Fair Work Act 2009 (Cth). The Fair Work Ombudsman had launched two prosecutions for alleged sham contracting.[184] In the first of these cases, it was alleged that a company 'converted' eight employees to contractors, but continued to have them perform the same duties under the company's direction, leading to total losses to the workers concerned of more than $52,000 in wages and annual leave entitlements. In a media release at the time of the first prosecution, Mr Leigh Johns, (then) Chief Legal Counsel of the Workplace Ombudsman (as the enforcement agency was then known), said:

> Where we suspect sham contracting is occurring, we will look behind the often carefully drafted legal documents prepared by clever lawyers to determine the true state of affairs for affected workers ... We are very much alive to the inherent unfairness and indecency attached to these sham contracting arrangements when, as is often the case, employees do not feel as though they have any real choice in the matter.[185]

Other national debates suggest that there is a clear demand for an increased and specific involvement of national labour administrations in helping clarifying, monitoring and enforcing the correct application of labour statutes and the correct

---

Go? Minimum Working Conditions Under Australia's New Labour Laws' (2006) 16 *Economic and Labour Relations Review* 85; and R Owens, 'Working Precariously: The Safety Net after Work Choices' (2006) 19 *Australian Journal of Labour Law* 161.

[182] A significant amount of information about the functions, jurisdiction and enforcement approach of the Fair Work Ombudsman is available from its website: www.fwo.gov.au.

[183] On the evolution of enforcement in recent years, see T Hardy, 'A Changing of the Guard: Enforcement of Workplace Relations Laws Since Work Choices and Beyond', in Forsyth and Stewart (n 76) 75–98, and T Hardy and J Howe, 'Partners in Enforcement? The Rise of State Enforcement of Employment Standards and the Decline in the Regulatory Function of Trade Unions in Australia' (2009) 22/306 *Australian Journal of Labour Law* (forthcoming).

[184] See the list of current cases at www.fwo.gov.au/Legal-info-and-action/Pages/Current-cases.aspx.

[185] Workplace Ombudsman, *Watchdog launches first prosecution over sham contracting*, available at: www.fwo.gov.au/Media-centre/Pages/20090130–01.aspx.

definitions of employment relationship. In 2007, for instance, the Indian CITU clearly demanded that 'in the informal sector, where in majority of the cases the employment relationship is clouded and camouflaged (excluding the self-employment area), appropriate machinery should be put in place to save the workers from the anarchy of the employers and administration'.[186] These demands do run however contrary to the recent visible trend of progressive rationalization and demobilization of national labour inspectorates in a number of countries of the Asia-Pacific region.

6.6 Conclusions

The present chapter has looked at recent national debates surrounding some of the central issues addressed by ILO Recommendation No 198, in a selection of countries from the Asia-Pacific region. What emerges from this analysis is a rather contradictory set of conclusions. On the one hand it appears that no single system has either found or adopted a comprehensive strategy for clarifying, conceptually and legally, the scope of the employment relationship. This is so in spite of the fact that both doctrinal and judicial analysis, as well as policy debates in legislatures and between the social partners, suggest that the current state of the national frameworks sustaining the employment relationship is less than satisfactory. Thus we continue to observe, in the jurisdictions considered here, numerous commonly lamented deficiencies, including: (1) the inability of existing definitions to match the rapid and constant changes in labour markets and workplace organization; (2) the coexistence within each national system of various different definitions and personal scopes of application for labour and social statutes; (3) the dissatisfaction with, and unpredictability of, judicial tests and reasoning; (4) the less than clear approach in respect of relationships involving multiple parties; and (5) the conceptual and legal complexities surrounding sham and disguised employment relationships.

The relative lack of direct action in the field is of course testament to the complexity of the issues at hand. Nevertheless, the absence of greater clarity is quite striking in certain cases considered here. As we have noted, Australia has consciously overlooked the opportunity to clarify the legal scope of the employment relationship through numerous recent rounds of legislative revision. And in both

---

[186] NCEUS (n 171) 68.

China and Viet Nam, Governments have set out on no less a task than the introduction of individual employment relations as a key element in the planned transformations of their industrial relations systems and economies—but without adequately addressing this critical issue of definition.

Neither has any of the systems examined in this chapter explicitly and comprehensively sought to implement Recommendation No 198 in its domestic legislation. This is so despite the fact that the Recommendation is an instrument that was specifically conceived to provide practical solutions to the aforementioned problems. There are various suggestions in the instrument that states might consider, including for instance the use of legal presumptions, of tripartite administrative enforcement mechanisms, and gender mainstreaming approaches. To a very great degree, however, these appear to have been wholly ignored in national debates and practices.

In spite of this failure to act, there is a general perception that while the letter of Recommendation No 198 is not necessarily trickling down to the national level, many of the concepts embodied in the instrument are progressively emerging in the national policy debates. The current Australian Government has certainly modified the stance of the previous executive in respect of the nature and scope of the employment relationship, and might be thought to be pursuing a harder line vis-à-vis sham and disguised arrangements. Indian unions are increasingly aware of the importance of ILO instruments as a blueprint for the reforms currently being discussed at a domestic level. The Indian Government is also addressing important collateral issues such as the access of workers in the informal and unorganized economy to social security. Courts are increasingly adopting a factual approach in establishing the nature of employment relationships, and are less reliant on older tests, such as control, that may be ill-suited indicators for work relationship in modern workplaces.

There is hardly any doubt that, as noted by the Chinese Government delegate at the 2006 International Labour Conference, 'the establishment of an employment relationship was the most fundamental social relationship in a country's social and economic life and formed the basis of the labour market'.[187] It nevertheless seems that this awareness is yet to be translated into an actual strategy for some systems of the Asia-Pacific region.

---

[187] International Labour Conference (95th Session) Report of the Committee on the Employment Relationship (Geneva 2006) 21/6.

Protecting Workers in a Changing Workworld: The Growth of Precarious Employment in Canada, the United States and Mexico

7

JEFFREY SACK, EMMA PHILLIPS AND HUGO LEAL-NERI[*]

7.1 Introduction

Governments generally seek to ensure certain minimum protections for workers through labour legislation that applies to the employment relationship. As one Canadian court has stated, the purpose of labour standards legislation is 'to prevent the exploitation of those who, to earn a living, have no choice other than to follow the direction of the employer....'[1] In North America—as in other industrialized regions—however, the expansion of non-standard, precarious work over the past 25 years has become a subject of significant concern to policy-makers, trade unions, and academic observers. As employers call for greater 'flexibility' in the employment relationship, an increasing number of workers have been excluded from statutory labour standards and legislative benefits designed to protect full-time salaried workers. Both the causes and the consequences of the increase in non-standard, or 'atypical', work bear some resemblance to workers' experiences in other parts of the world. However, North American workers face certain unique challenges, in part as

---

* Jeffrey Sack QC is senior partner in the law firm Sack Goldblatt Mitchell, Toronto, Canada. Mr Sack is Co-Director of the Canadian Labour Law Association, and a member of the Executive Committee of the International Society for Labour and Social Security Law. Emma Phillips and Hugo Leal-Neri are associates in Sack Goldblatt Mitchell. Christine Davies, also an associate of the firm, contributed to the final version of this paper.
    [1] *Imperial Taxi Brandon (1983) Ltd v Hutchison* (1987) 46 D.L.R. (4th) 310, 313; 50 Man.R. (2d) 81 (Manitoba CA).

a result of the North American Free Trade Agreement ('NAFTA'), which has had a significant impact on the labour markets of the three signatory countries.[2]

This chapter will examine the changing nature of the employment relationship in Canada, the United States and Mexico. Specifically, it will look at the national laws, regulations and jurisprudence that define the existence of an employment relationship and the ways in which an increasing number of contractual arrangements are being designed to circumvent statutorily defined categories of employment. Of course, the legal rules governing work arrangements differ significantly in each of the three countries. In Canada and the United States, terms such as 'employee' and 'employer' are largely defined through tests developed by courts and arbitrators, although these may vary by jurisdiction and take their colour from the legislative context. In Mexico, by contrast, employment relationships in the private sector are largely governed by the Federal Labour Act (*Ley Federal del Trabajo*, or 'LFT' by its Spanish acronym),[3] or by Mexico's political Constitution (*Constitución Política de los Estados Unidos Mexicanos*),[4] and are therefore subject to a more unified, national interpretation. Moreover, the labour markets in the three countries also vary significantly—while Canada has a working population of 18.4 million,[5] Mexico has approximately 43.3 million workers,[6] and the United States has around 157 million.[7] And while the workforce in Canada and the United States is predominantly urban with a growing service industry, in Mexico the informal economy, manufacturing and micro-enterprise play a more significant role. Yet despite these differences, it is clear that in all three countries, traditional models of employment are coming under pressure, and new work arrangements are arising, with important consequences for the social welfare of many workers.

---

[2] E Tucker, '"Great Expectations" Defeated?: The Trajectory of Collective Bargaining Regimes in Canada and the United States Post-NAFTA' (2004) 26 *Comparative Labor Law & Policy Journal* 97.

[3] Ley Federal del Trabajo, *Diario Oficial de la Federación* (1° April 1970) ('LFT').

[4] Constitución Política de los Estados Unidos Mexicanos, *Diario Oficial de la Federación* (5 February 1917) ('Mexican Constitution'). Art 123 of the Mexican Constitution establishes a wide range of labour standards for workers—such as minimum wage, protection against dismissal except where just cause exists, maternity leave, severance pay, hours of work, days of rest, prohibitions on child labour, and housing standards—regardless of occupation or status.

[5] Statistics Canada, 'Labour force characteristics by age and sex.' Online: www.statcan.gc.ca/subjects-sujets/labour-travail/lfs-epa/t090904a1-eng.htm. According to the Arthurs Report (n 15) 8, based on 2005 Statistics Canada data, 8.4% of the Canadian workforce are employed by employers subject to federal jurisdiction.

[6] INEGI, 'Encuesta Nacional de Ocupación y Empleo (ENOE). Valores absolutos, Nacional, Total, Población ocupada, Por posición en la ocupación' (February 2009), online: http://dgcnesyp.inegi.org.mx/cgi-win/bdieintsi.exe/SER116096 ('INEGI, Total Working Population').

[7] US Census Bureau, 'Selected Economic Characteristics: 2008'. Online: http://factfinder.census.gov/servlet/ADPTable?_bm=y&-geo_id=01000US&-qr_name=ACS_2008_1YR_G00_DP3&-ds_name=&-_lang=en&-redoLog=false&-format=.

An examination of non-standard work in North America is particularly important in light of the ILO Employment Relationship Recommendation, 2006 (No 198). The Recommendation begins by noting

> ... the difficulties of establishing whether or not an employment relationship exists in situations where the respective rights and obligations of the parties concerned are not clear, where there has been an attempt to disguise the employment relationship, or where inadequacies or limitations exist in the legal framework, or in its interpretation and application, and

> ... that situations exist where contractual arrangements can have the effect of depriving workers of the protection they are due ...

To this end, Recommendation 198 recommends that national policies should be developed to clearly establish the existence of an employment relationship, distinguish between employed and self-employed workers, combat disguised employment relationships, implement standards applicable to all forms of contractual arrangements to ensure that employed workers have the protection they are due, and effectively enforce such standards to ensure employer compliance. This position is consistent with earlier ILO Recommendations, namely the Private Employment Agencies Recommendation, 1997 (No 188), the Home Work Recommendation, 1996 (No 184) and the Part-Time Work Recommendation, 1994 (No 182), and with the Fee-Charging Employment Agencies Convention (Revised), 1949 (No. 96).

The paper proceeds in four parts. The first part examines the characteristics of 'non-standard work', as well as the impact of NAFTA on the structure and organization of work in Canada, the United States and Mexico. The second part looks more closely at the definition and regulation of key aspects of the employment relationship in each country as well as at the changing nature of the employment relationship and the problem of enforcement. The third part examines a number of solutions that have been proposed to extend labour protections to non-standard workers, with particular reference to specific initiatives developed in North American jurisdictions. Finally, the chapter makes a number of concluding observations.

A Word on Terminology

Terms such as 'worker', 'employee' and 'employment contract' are used differently in Canada, the United States and Mexico, and in some cases are terms of art subject to statutory definitions and/or judicial interpretation. Indeed, the definition of such terms lies at the heart of any debate surrounding labour standards, since it is the scope of the terms which will determine the assignment of rights and benefits. For the sake of clarity, this paper will refer to 'worker' as a general term encompassing any individual who provides services for compensation, regardless of status. 'Employee' is used to refer to workers who have satisfied some statutory definition in their jurisdiction, and who are therefore subject to the relevant labour standards legislation. Similarly, 'work arrangement' is used to generally denote a relationship between an individual and another party in which the individual provides services in exchange for compensation; 'employment relationship' refers specifically to a work arrangement in which one party has been designated as the employee and another as the employer under the relevant legislation, so that the parties are subject to labour standards provisions. 'Contract of employment' is used to refer to contracts between individual non-unionized employees and employers. Finally, 'labour regulation' refers to the combined juridical and statutory sources which govern all employment relationships. Other terms will be defined as they are referred to.

7.2 Non-Standard Work in Canada, the United States and Mexico

The Characteristics of Non-Standard Employment

As will be discussed below, labour regulations are largely based on a model of employment in which an individual employee works in a 'full-time, full-year, permanent paid job'[8] for a single employer. A number of terms have been used to describe work that departs from this traditional employment model, including 'non-standard', 'atypical', 'contingent', and 'precarious' work. 'Non-standard', or 'atypical', work is an umbrella term, encompassing work situations 'which do not match the standard of full-time, salaried employment for an indefinite duration with a single, readily identifiable employer on company premises',[9] namely part-time employment, temporary employment,[10] own-account self-employment, and multiple jobholding.[11] Non-standard work may therefore include 'contingent work', which refers to 'any job in

---

[8]   LF Vosko, N Zukewich and C Cranford, 'Precarious jobs: A new typology of employment' (Oct 2003) 4(10) *Perspectives on Labour and Income* 16, 17, online: Statistics Canada, www.statcan.ca/english/freepub/75–001-XIE/75–001-XIE2003110.pdf ('Vosko, Zukewich and Cranford').

[9]   G Vallée, 'Towards Enhancing the Employment Conditions of Vulnerable Workers: A Public Policy Perspective' (2005) Canadian Policy Research Networks, Vulnerable Workers Series No 2, 2 ('Vallée').

[10]   Temporary employment includes 'term or contract, seasonal, casual, temporary agency, and all other jobs with a specific pre-determined end date.' Vosko, Zukewich and Cranford (n 8) 17.

[11]   H Krahn, 'Non-standard work on the rise' (Winter 1995) 7(4) *Perspectives on Labour and Income* 35, 35–42, cited in Vosko, Zukewich and Cranford (n 8).

which an individual does not have an explicit or implicit contract for long-term employment and one in which the minimum hours can vary in a non-systematic manner.'[12] Non-standard work may also be 'precarious' because workers in such unstable work arrangements are frequently unable to earn a sufficient income to maintain the worker and his or her dependants. The term 'precarious work' has also been advanced as an alternative to 'non-standard work'[13] in the face of criticisms that the dichotomy between 'standard (full-time, permanent) and non-standard (part-time and/or short-term) employment' no longer adequately reflects 'the complexities of work arrangements resulting from neoliberal economic and social reforms such as privatization and labour market de-regulation.'[14]

In sum, 'non-standard', 'atypical', 'contingent' or 'precarious' work generally refers to work arrangements in which the worker has little or no job security, enjoys no fringe benefits or pension, and is subject to varying hours of work which may fall below full-time. Moreover, the worker may be part of a triangular employment relationship where the ultimate beneficiary of his or her services is somebody other than the party who compensates the individual for the performance of the work.

Numerous studies have examined the causes and consequences of the rise in non-standard work.[15] Apart from the economic gain that accrues to employers from

---

[12] AE Polivka and T Nardone, 'On the definition of 'contingent work'' (1989) 112 (12) *Monthly Labour Review* 9, 11.

[13] Vosko, Zukewich and Cranford (n 8) 19.

[14] Oxfam Canada, 'Women and Precarious Work: A Framework for Policy Recommendations Based on Work of the Women and Work Policy Working Group' (3 February 2005) 3, online: Oxfam Canada, www.oxfam. ca/news-and-publications/publications-and-reports/women-and-precarious-employment-a-framework-for-policy-recommendations-2005/file.

[15] See eg A Kalleberg, 'Precarious Work, Insecure Workers: Employment Relations in Transition' (2009) 74 *American Sociological Review* 1–22; M Freedland and N Kountouris, 'Towards a Comparative Theory of the Contractual Construction of Personal Work Relations in Europe' (2008) 37(1) *Industrial Law Journal* 49–74 ('Freedland and Kountouris'); OVP Páez, 'La Precarización del Empleo en las Grandes Ciudades Latinoamericanas', in R Cordera, PR Kuri and A Ziccardi (eds), *Pobreza, Desigualdad y Exclusión Social en la Ciudad del Siglo XXI* (México, Siglo XXI: UNAM, Instituto de Investigaciones Sociales, 2008) 353; M Laparra, *La construcción del empleo precario. Dimensiones, causas y tendencias de la precariedad laboral* (Madrid, Fundación FOESSA, 2007); P Davies and M Freedland, *Towards a Flexible Labour Market: Labour, Legislation and Regulation since the 1990s* (Oxford, Oxford University Press, 2007); A Bernhardt, S McGrath and J DeFilippis, 'Unregulated Work in the Global City: Employment and Labor Law Violations in New York City' (2007) online: Brennan Center for Justice at New York University School of Law, www.brennancenter.org/dynamic/subpages/download_file_49436.pdf ('Brennan Center for Justice'); SF Befort, 'The Regulatory Void of Contingent Work' (2006) 10 *Employee Rights and Employment Policy Journal* 233; H Arthurs, *Fairness at Work: Federal Labour Standards for the 21st Century* (Human Resources and Skills Development Canada, 2006), online: HRSDC, www.hrsdc.gc.ca/eng/labour/employment_ standards/fls/pdf/final_report.pdf ('Arthurs Report'); E de la Garza and C Salas, (eds), *La situación del trabajo en México* (México, Universidad Autónoma Metropolitana, Plaza y Valdés et al, 2006); J Fudge, 'Beyond Vulnerable Workers: Towards a New Standard Employment Relationship' (2005) 12 *CLELJ* 145; J Fudge, E Tucker and L Vosko, 'Changing Boundaries in Employment: Developing a New Platform for Labour Law' (2003) 10 *CLELJ* 329 ('Fudge, Tucker & Vosko, 2003'); SN Houseman and M Osawa (eds), *Nonstandard Work in Developed Economies: Causes and Consequences* (New York, Routledge, 2003); Commission for Labor Cooperation, *The Rights of Non-Standard Workers: A North American Guide* (Commission Secretariat 2003), online: www.new.naalc.org/index.

the avoidance of benefits and protections that attach to standard employment, there are a number of operational advantages that result from alternative employment arrangements. Thus, employers increasingly rely on hiring temporary, part-time, and casual workers, as well as independent contractors and sub-contracted workers, for reasons of both numerical and functional flexibility.[16] For example, by hiring through temporary work agencies or subcontractors, employers may avoid the administrative and financial burden of worker turnover, as well as the transaction costs associated with termination.[17] This is particularly true in Mexico, where the high severance payments for dismissal without cause mandated by the Mexican Constitution and the LFT[18] are, some have suggested, an onerous feature of an outdated legal framework.[19]

Employers may therefore use contingent workers to more easily adjust the size of their workforce to meet the rapid fluctuations in production driven by an

---

cfm?page=165; S Deakin, 'The Many Futures of the Contract of Employment', in J Conaghan, M Fischl and K Klare, (eds), *Labour Law in an Era of Globalization: Transformative Practices & Possibilities* (Oxford, Oxford University Press, 2002) ('*Deakin*'); J Mangan, *Workers Without Traditional Employment: An International Study of Non-Standard Work* (Cheltenham, Edward Elgar Publishing, 2000); J O'Reilly and C Fagan, *Part-Time Prospects: An International Comparison of Part-Time Work in Europe, North America, and the Pacific Rim* (New York, Routledge, 1998); and Labour Canada, *Part-time Work in Canada: Report of the Commission of Inquiry into Part-time Work* (Ottawa, Minister of Supply and Services, 1983) ('Wallace Report').

[16] AB Sukert, 'Marionettes of Globalization: A Comparative Analysis of Legal Protections for Contingent Workers in the International Community' (Summer 2000) 27 (2) Syracuse Journal of International Law and Commerce 431, 438 ('Sukert').

[17] D Autor, 'Outsourcing at will: The contribution of unjust dismissal doctrine to the growth of employment outsourcing' (2003) 21(1) *Journal of Labor Economics*.

[18] An employee who proves dismissal without cause is entitled, according to the letter of the law, to elect between reinstatement or a compensation package in the terms established by the LFT (LFT (n 3) arts 48, 50). However, an employer is exempt from having to reinstate a dismissed employee if the employer pays the employee compensation in the amount established in the LFT, where the employee (a) has a length of service of less than one year, (b) holds a position of trust, (c) is a domestic worker, (d) is a casual worker, or (e) where it is shown that the normal performance of the employment relationship would be impossible given the nature of the work and the direct and permanent contact between the employer and the employee (Mexican Constitution(n 3) art 123(XXI)-(XXII); and LFT (n 4) arts 49(I) and 50(I)).

In this vein, an employee with a contract of employment for an *indefinite period of time* who is dismissed before a year from the date of hiring would be entitled to (i) the pro rata amount of 20 days' salary per year of service, (ii) three months' salary, and (iii) back pay from the date of the dismissal to the date on which all of the compensations are paid (LFT (n 4) art 50(II)-(III)).

Greater compensation would be owed to an employee employed for a *fixed period of time shorter than one year* who is dismissed without cause. Such an employee would be entitled to (i) the salaries pertaining to half the time the employee was under the employer's service, (ii) three months' salary, and (iii) back pay from the date of the dismissal to the date on which all of the compensations are paid (LFT (n 4) art 50(I), (III)). Similarly, an employee employed for a *fixed period of time longer than one year* who is dismissed without cause would be entitled to (i) an amount equal to six months' salary for the first year, and twenty days for each year of employment thereafter, and (ii) three months' salary, and (iii) back pay from the date of the dismissal to the date on which all of the compensations are paid (LFT(n 4)).

[19] MM Giugale, O Lafourcade and VH Nguyen (eds), *Mexico: A Comprehensive Development Agenda for the New Era* (Washington DC, World Bank, 2001) 15–16 ('Giugale, Lafourcade and Nguyen').

increasingly demanding consumer culture, or to fill in gaps while permanent workers are absent, for instance, during a medical leave of absence or maternity leave. Contingent workers also provide employers with 'functional flexibility' by providing employers with a pool of specialized expertise that can be utilized on demand, or drawn upon as a reliable hiring base for future full-time workers.[20]

Some workers may also benefit from non-standard work arrangements. Highly skilled workers, for example, may prefer the tax advantages of self-employment to any social welfare benefits received through full-time employment. Other workers, particularly those balancing family obligations, retirees, or students, may benefit from the flexible schedule associated with temporary, casual or part-time work. Similarly, workers may use non-standard work as a source of income while transitioning from one full-time employment situation to another.

Yet many non-standard workers would prefer full-time permanent work, or at least the job security and welfare benefits normally associated with full-time work.[21] Such workers experience neither the lifestyle advantage of a flexible schedule nor the financial benefits of self-employment status. Instead, they are coerced into work arrangements in which they are denied basic benefits and job security in order to confer a financial benefit on their employer. As the authors of a recent report on unregulated work in New York City observe, this category of work generally includes '[j]obs that are not legally covered by one or more employment and labor laws, but where the terms of employment are effectively dictated by an employer, contracting agency or industry regulation, and where conditions of work fail to meet one or more of the minimum standards of workplace regulation.'[22]

Generally, then, non-standard workers tend to fall into one of two categories. At one extreme, as noted, an increasing number of highly educated knowledge workers are voluntarily engaging in self-employment, often motivated by tax benefits or the desire for improved scheduling flexibility. At the opposite extreme, low-skilled, poorly paid workers are being involuntarily pushed into non-standard work arrangements such as 'triangular' contractual relationships (eg through temporary agencies or contracting-out), 'disguised' work relationships (in which the

---

[20] Sukert (n 16) 438. For a detailed discussion of the benefits of temporary workers, see JT Addison and CJ Surfield, 'Atypical Work and Pay' (2007) 73 (4) *Southern Economic Journal* 1038, 1039–41.

[21] In Canada, 'it appears that as many as 75% of temporary employees would prefer permanent employment, as would about 25% of own-account self-employed workers. About 25% of part-time workers would prefer full-time work.' Arthurs Report (n 15) 27.

In the United States, 4 million out of the 22 million part-time and contingent workers who laboured in the American economy in the mid-1990s (about two-thirds of whom were women) would have preferred full-time status. These workers earned approximately 62 cents of every dollar earned by a regular, full-time employee. RH Zieger and GJ Gall, *American Workers, American Unions: The Twentieth Century*, 3rd edn (Baltimore & London, The Johns Hopkins University Press, 2002) 242.

[22] Brennan Center for Justice (n 15) 5.

worker functions on a practical level as a full-time employee, but is labelled through a contractual arrangement as a self-employed worker), or part-time and/or casual work arrangements. Workers at this end of the spectrum also tend to fall into the category of 'precarious' or 'vulnerable' workers who work non-standard hours, have high job insecurity, and poor or no access to employment benefits such as vacation pay, medical care, unemployment insurance, or pensions. They tend to be disproportionately female and members of minority groups, leading to concerns about increasingly gendered and racialized disparities in access to employment benefits and protections.[23] Such precarious, non-standard work also tends to be associated with increased health and safety problems as the result of, for example, the contracting out of risky work.[24]

Mexico

While this description of non-standard work applies to all three countries, the character of non-standard work differs in each jurisdiction. Mexico's large informal sector and high proportion of microenterprises, for example, are key features setting Mexico's labour market apart from Canada and the United States. In the period 2000–04, 72 per cent of the total jobs created in Mexico were in enterprises employing five or fewer workers,[25] and 62 per cent lacked any social benefits.[26] Of Mexico's 43.3 million workers, 28.64 million are employed in the formal sector whereas 12.19 million are employed in the informal economy. Accordingly, about 28.12 per cent of Mexico's working population works in the informal economy.[27] 'Informal work' has been defined as 'those economic and productive activities that,

[23] S Fuller and L Vosko, 'Temporary Employment and Social Inequality in Canada: Exploring Intersections of Gender, Race and Immigration Status' (2008) 88 *Social Indicators Research* 31–50.

[24] K Lippel, 'Precarious Employment and Occupational Health and Safety Regulation in Quebec' in L Vosko (ed.) *Precarious Employment: Understanding Labour Market Insecurity* (Montreal, McGill-Queen's University Press, 2006).

[25] C Salas, 'Mexico Labor Report, 2001–2006' (9 March 2007) 8, online: Global Policy Network, www.gpn.org/data/mexico/mexico-eng.pdf ('Salas, 2007').

[26] ibid. In 2007, about 53% of young people in Mexico worked either in the informal economy or the service sector. The work life of 31 out of the approximately 44 million Mexicans between the ages of 25 and 50, has thus been characterized by low wages, high underemployment, virtually no savings, and lack of health care coverage. Only 26.2% of the 4.8 million Mexicans over the age of 65 have a pension or retirement benefits (Gobierno de los Estados Unidos Mexicanos, Presidencia de la República, *Plan Nacional de Desarrollo 2007–2012* (México, Talleres de Impresión de Estampillas y Valores, 2007) 74, 221, online: Plan Nacional de Desarrollo, http://pnd.calderon.presidencia.gob.mx/pdf/PND_2007–2012.pdf).

[27] INEGI (n 6); 'Valores absolutos, Nacional, Total, Trabajadores subordinados y remunerados, Sector de actividad económica' (February 2009), online: http://dgcnesyp.inegi.org.mx/cgi-win/bdieintsi.exe/SER118775; and 'Valores absolutos, Nacional, Total, Población ocupada en el sector informal' (February 2009), online: http://dgcnesyp.inegi.org.mx/cgi-win/bdieintsi.exe/SER163695.

without being of a criminal nature, take place on the margins of legality' or which are in non-compliance with the law.[28] Consequently, statutory labour standards are largely irrelevant to informal work.[29] And although micro-businesses absorb workers who would otherwise be unemployed,[30] the average wages and benefits are generally lower than those in medium and large companies.[31]

Low wages and lack of economic opportunities in Mexico, together with the increasing wage gap between Mexico and its NAFTA partners, have led to the migration of large numbers of workers to the higher-paying labour markets of the United States and Canada,[32] where they are often precariously employed. Benjamin Davis, Director of the AFL-CIO Solidarity Center in Mexico City, points out that '[w]hile Mexican-born workers make up 4.7 per cent of the US civilian labor force, 14 per cent of all Mexican workers now work in the United States.'[33] Mass migration has been accompanied by a steady cash flow back to Mexico, which has in turn resulted in heavy dependence on such remittances[34]—on the part of both workers' families, and the national economy as a whole.[35] While some workers participate in

---

[28] MP Cosmópolis, 'Contratos de trabajo, economía informal y empresas de mano de obra' ('Cosmópolis'), in PK Villalobos (ed), *Décimocuarto encuentro iberoamericano de derecho del trabajo* (México, UNAM, 2006) 70–71, online: Instituto de Investigaciones Jurídicas de la UNAM, Biblioteca Jurídica, www.bibliojuridica.org/libros/4/1950/7.pdf (translated by Hugo Leal-Neri) ('Kurczyn').

[29] Cosmópolis (n 28); A Sánchez-Castañeda, '¿Un régimen laboral diferenciado para la pequeña y mediana empresa?', in Kurczyn (n 28) 12–13.

[30] Salas (n 25) 9.

[31] Commission for Labor Cooperation, 'North American Labor Markets: Main Changes since NAFTA' (2003) 69, 72, online: Commission for Labor Cooperation, www.naalc.org/english/pdf/labor_markets_en_1.pdf.

[32] Benjamin Davis points to a number of studies in observing that '[u]nemployment is a negligible factor driving migration: nearly all Mexican immigrants to the United States were employed in Mexico.' B Davis, 'Workers' Freedom of Association Under Attack in Mexico' (August 2008) 8, n 16, online: Solidarity Centre website, www.solidaritycenter.org/files/pubs_policybrief_mexico.pdf ('Davis'). See for instance, R Kochhar, *Survey of Mexican Migrants*, Part 3, 'The Economic Transition to America' (Washington DC, Pew Hispanic Center, December 6, 2005), online: http://pewhispanic.org/files/reports/58.pdf; and Migration Policy Institute, 'Mexican-Born Persons in the US Civilian Labor Force' (November 2006), online: www.migrationpolicy.org/pubs/FS14_MexicanWorkers2006.pdf.

[33] Davis (n 32) 5.

[34] In 2008, Mexico was the third largest recipient of migrant remittances in absolute terms, with $26.3 billion (India came first and China came second). Remittances to Mexico represented 40.81% of total flows to Latin America in that year. See D Ratha et al, Migration and Remittances Team, Development Prospects Group, World Bank, 'Outlook for Remittance Flows 2009–2011: Remittances expected to fall by 7–10 per cent in 2009', Migration and Development Brief No 10 (13 July 2009), online: World Bank website, http://siteresources.worldbank.org/INTPROSPECTS/Resources/334934–1110315015165/Migration&DevelopmentBrief10.pdf; and companion 'Excel Data for Brief', online: http://siteresources.worldbank.org/INTPROSPECTS/Resources/334934–1110315015165/RemittancesData_July09(Public).xls.

[35] According to a Bank of Mexico (*Banco de México*) document, '[s]tudies regarding worker remittances' impact have found that those resources are mainly used to finance consumption, as well as to increase human capital (education and health expenditure).' Investment in human and physical capital 'has a direct impact on economic growth, while consumption expenditure affects GDP indirectly through increasing aggregate demand.' Furthermore, some studies have found that remittances reduce family income volatility during

official 'seasonal worker' programmes, most of them work as undocumented labourers, predominantly in the agricultural, construction, and service industries. Whether documented or not, these migrant workers represent some of the most vulnerable workers in North America, without access to the labour standards which otherwise apply in the relevant jurisdiction, and are subject to frequently exploitative work practices and hazardous working conditions.

Canada

In Canada, which in 2008 accepted almost 200,000 temporary foreign workers, there is pressure on the federal government to issue regulations which will punish employers who exploit foreign workers and prevent employers who repeatedly violate labour laws from being allowed to bring in foreign workers. On 10 October 2009, new amendments to the regulations under the federal Immigration and Refugee Protection Act (IRPA) came into force. While these new regulations preclude employers who have acted exploitatively from bringing more foreign workers into Canada, they do not otherwise provide for enhanced enforcement or compliance.

Under the Seasonal Agricultural Workers Programme ('SAWP'), which is just one stream of Canada's temporary foreign worker programme, 18,000 Mexican workers are annually employed in Canada during the fruit-picking season. Following completion of a trial period of employment,[36] these 'temporary'[37] workers can be prematurely repatriated for non-compliance with the employment agreement, refusal to work, or 'any other sufficient reason.'[38] Unlike Canadian workers whose freedom of mobility is guaranteed by s 6 of the Canadian Charter of Rights and Freedoms, seasonal workers can work only for the employer with whom their

---

economic crises, and suggest 'that members of recipient households have fewer incentives to search for alternative sources of income'. Banco de México, 'Remittances and Development: The Case of Mexico' (28 June 2005) at 13–14, online: Inter-American Development Bank, WEB-IDBdocs, http://idbdocs.iadb.org/wsdocs/getdocument.aspx?docnum=561166.

[36] Fourteen actual working days from the date of arrival at the place of employment ('Agreement for the Employment in Canada of Seasonal Agricultural Workers from Mexico—2007' at I(4), online: Human Resources and Skills Development Canada, www.rhdsc.gc.ca/en/epb/lmd/fw/forms/2007mexicansawp-e.pdf ('SAWP Agreement Mexico')).

[37] Labour lawyer Veena Verma notes that SAWP allows employers to hire seasonal agricultural workers on a seasonal basis for the period of 1 January to 15 December each year (V Verma, paper presented to the Conference of the Canadian Association of Labour Lawyers, Yellowknife, Canada, June 29, 2007(unpublished)); and SAWP Agreement Mexico (n 36) I(1)(c). For additional background on SAWP's, see V Verma, 'The Mexican and Caribbean Seasonal Agricultural Workers Program: Regulatory and Policy Framework, Farm Industry Level Employment Practices, and the Future of the Program under Unionization' (December 2003), online: The North-South Institute, www.nsi-ins.ca/english/pdf/csawp_verma_final_report.pdf.

[38] SAWP Agreement Mexico (n 36) X(1).

employment agreement was signed, and only in the occupation specified by the employment agreement. Most workers live on the employer's property, so that if the employer decides to terminate the employment agreement, the worker also immediately loses his or her shelter. To this point, unionization of foreign workers has met with strong resistance from employers. However, the employers' position—which is that provincial collective bargaining laws do not apply to foreign nationals working under the federal SAWP—has been rejected by the British Columbia Labour Relations Board.[39]

In his 2006 Federal Labour Standards Review, Professor Arthurs recommends that foreign agricultural workers should be protected by mandatory agreements with their employer specifying that they will receive wages equal to those of locally recruited workers, rest and meal breaks, and weekly rest periods, protection against unauthorized deductions from pay, and access to an informal and expedited hearing in the event they are dismissed and liable to repatriation. They should receive information concerning legislative protections, and be given access to toll-free numbers for advice and assistance. Inspections should be conducted, and employers who repeatedly or systematically violate labour standards or the terms of employment agreements should be denied future access to workers under the foreign worker programme for a period of not less than one year. (See Arthurs Report (n 15) 243–45.)

While labour advocates in Canada have fought for the right of agricultural workers to unionize, this battle has not been finally resolved. In the landmark case of *R v Dunmore*,[40] decided in 2001, the Supreme Court of Canada held that the exclusion of agricultural workers from representation by a union under the Ontario Labour Relations Act, 1995 breached the guarantee of freedom of association under the Canadian Charter of Rights and Freedoms. However, the Court stopped short of finding that the Charter guaranteed the workers a right to collectively bargain, and while this principle was subsequently established in 2007 by the Supreme Court of Canada in the *Health Services* case,[41] and in 2008 the Ontario Court of Appeal applied that ruling to agricultural workers in the *Fraser* case,[42] an appeal by the employer is pending before the Supreme Court of Canada. In the meantime, however, despite the uncertain scope of a union's associational rights, the Manitoba Labour Board has ordered the certification of a union for a bargaining unit, the vast majority of whose members were foreign seasonal agricultural workers

---

[39] *Greenway Farms Ltd v United Food and Commercial Workers International Union, Local 1518*, [2009] BCLRBD No 135 (QL).

[40] *Dunmore v Ontario (Attorney General)* [2001] 3 S.C.R. 1016; 2001 SCC 94.

[41] *Health Services v British Columbia* 2007 SCC 27; [2007] SCJ No 27 (SCC) (QL).

[42] *Fraser v Ontario* [2008] ONCA 760; [2008] OJ No 4543 (Ontario CA) (QL).

from Mexico employed pursuant to the SAWP.[43] Inter alia, the Labour Board rejected the employer's argument that the workers were not 'employees' under Manitoba's Labour Relations Act. Whether citizens of Canada or not, the Board held, foreign workers are employees under the Labour Relations Act.[44] On 9 December 2009, the Ontario government enacted amendments to employment standards legislation to address the problem of unscrupulous recruiters of foreign workers. The legislation addresses a number of concerns with respect to recruitment agencies which provide services to foreign nationals, including those working as live-in caregivers. For example, the amendments ban fees charged to live-in caregivers and others by recruiters, prohibit employers from recovering recruitment and placement costs from live-in caregivers, and proscribe reprisals against caregivers for exercising their rights. The federal government has also recently implemented changes to improve the Federal Live-in Caregiver Program. Included in these changes are requirements that employers of live-in caregivers pay for their travel costs to come to Canada and medical insurance until they are eligible for provincial coverage.

In Canada, more and more workers are engaged in non-standard work. Currently, about 32 per cent of Canadian workers—up from about 25 per cent at the end of the 1980s—work in temporary or part-time jobs, or are self-employed, with the last group accounting for 16 per cent, a relatively high proportion by international standards.[45] It is estimated that in 2000 only 34.6 per cent of self-employment was performed by genuine business entrepreneurs who hired employees of their own.[46] Certain occupations and sectors tend to be organized around non-standard work arrangements—such as food service, domestic work, the garment industry, light manufacturing, and building maintenance. Women, young people, and members of disadvantaged minorities are over-represented in these occupations, and account for a disproportionately high proportion of vulnerable workers.

---

[43] *United Food and Commercial Workers Union, Local No 832 v Mayfair Farms (Portage) Ltd* (2007) MLB Case No 595/06/LRA.

[44] The Labour Board also rejected the employer's argument that the provincial Labour Board did not have jurisdiction because SAWP is a federal worker programme (while regulation of labour is a provincial matter) and that Canada and Mexico were the real employers, not the individual farm owners. Ibid. In Canada, legislative jurisdiction over labour is divided: the provinces have been held by the courts to enjoy primacy, while the federal government is limited to jurisdiction over workers in federally regulated sectors, eg interprovincial transportation and communications, banking, nuclear energy, etc. The United States and Mexico are, like Canada, also federal states, but jurisdiction over labour is in those countries largely federal.

[45] Statistics Canada, 'Self-employment, historical summary.' Online: self-employment www40.statcan.gc.ca/l01/cst01/labor64-eng.htm; Statistics Canada, 'Full-time and part-time employment by sex and age group'. Online: www40.statcan.gc.ca/l01/cst01/labor12-eng.htm; Statistics Canada, 'Labour force characteristics'. Online: www40.statcan.gc.ca/l01/cst01/econ10-eng.htm.

[46] Fudge, Tucker & Vosko (n 83) 99–100.

United States

The percentage of non-standard workers in the United States has similarly increased over the past 25 years. In the early 1980s, the number of temporary workers increased by as much as 70 per cent in large companies. The number of workers in 'alternative work arrangements' increased from an estimated 12.5 million in 1997[47] to 14.8 million as of February 2005.[48] Workers in alternative arrangements amounted to almost 11 per cent of the 138,952,000 employed workers in the United States that year.[49] Also in 2005, there were approximately 25 million part-time workers[50] and 10.5 million unincorporated self-employed workers[51] in the United States. Seven and a half million workers were multiple jobholders, 1.7 million of whom held two part-time jobs.[52] Non-standard workers received significantly lower wages and benefits than full-time workers with similar skills and qualifications; for example, 22 per cent of part-time workers received health insurance, as compared to 78 per cent of full-time workers.[53]

The Impact of Neoliberal Policies and the North American Free Trade Agreement

Numerous studies have tied the growth of non-standard work to policies of economic restructuring pursued by most industrialized countries over the past 25 years.[54] As a result of economic restructuring, during the 1980s and 1990s a growing

---

[47] Suker (n 16) 433.

[48] The breakdown of the 14,826,000 workers with alternative arrangements is as follows: 10,342,000 independent contractors, 2,454,000 on-call workers, 1,217,000 temporary help agency workers, and 813,000 workers provided by contract firms. US Census Bureau, 'Table 594. Employed Workers With Alternative and Traditional Work', online: US Census Bureau, The 2007 Statistical Abstract: The National Data Book, www. census.gov/compendia/statab/tables/07s0594.xls ('US Census, Table 594').

[49] ibid.

[50] ibid.

[51] US Census Bureau, 'Table 591. Self-Employed Workers by Industry and Occupation: 2000 to 2005', online: US Census Bureau, The 2007 Statistical Abstract: The National Data Book, www.census.gov/ compendia/statab/tables/07s0591.xls ('US Census, Table 591').

[52] The US Census Bureau defines 'multiple jobholders' as 'employed persons who, either 1) had jobs as wage or salary workers with two employers or more; 2) were self-employed and also held a wage and salary job; or 3) were unpaid family workers and also held a wage and salary job.' US Census Bureau, 'Table 595. Multiple Jobholders: 2005', online: US Census Bureau, The 2007 Statistical Abstract: The National Data Book, www. census.gov/compendia/statab/tables/07s0595.xls ('US Census, Table 595'). For statistics on part-time workers, see US Bureau of Labor Statistics, "Employment and Earnings Online', online: US Census Bureau, www.census. gov/compendia/statab/tables/09s0582.pdf.

[53] Sukert (n 16) 434.

[54] Brennan Center for Justice (n 15).

number of workers in the United States were engaged in non-standard forms of employment. In a recent study of unregulated work in New York City, Bernhardt, McGrath and DeFilippis argue that:

> The story of unregulated work has unfolded against a backdrop of three decades of economic restructuring in the American labor market. Since the mid-1970s, globalization, deindustrialization, deunionization and a deteriorating social contract have reshaped how and where work is performed, and what it is paid. Throughout the US economy, researchers have identified a pronounced shift in firms' competitive strategies, with growing numbers of employers focused on cutting wage and benefit costs and achieving greater flexibility in how work is organized. The symptoms of this shift are well documented. For example, the US wage distribution has grown significantly more unequal; workers increasingly find themselves stuck in contingent, non-standard and low-wage jobs; employers are reducing their provision of health and pension benefits, and investing less in the skills and long-term careers of their workers.[55]

These policies of deregulation have also been influential in Canada and Mexico, where economic policies have been similarly characterized by expenditure cut-backs, removal of trade barriers and subsidies, the privatization of publicly-owned enterprises, limited intervention in the market, and increased labour market flexibility.

Most significantly, on 1 January 1994, Canada, the United States and Mexico entered into NAFTA, a quintessentially neoliberal international instrument. Through the lowering of trade barriers, increases in labour mobility, and the harmonization of environmental protection laws, among other measures, NAFTA has brought the three countries into a relationship of unprecedented economic integration. Without question, the passage of NAFTA has had a profound impact on the organization, movement, and regulation of work across the continent.

The causal relationship between neoliberal pressures and the deregulation of work in North America, especially since NAFTA, is clear, particularly with regard to Mexico. For example, according to its proponents in the Clinton administration, NAFTA's main purpose 'was to lock these [IMF-dictated structural] reforms in place within Mexico to provide a more stable environment for continued integration.'[56] Labour flexibility and deregulation have been among the most important structural reforms imposed on Mexico by international financial

---

[55] ibid 28.

[56] RE Scott, 'NAFTA's Legacy: Rising Trade Deficits Lead to Significant Job Displacement and Declining Job Quality for the United States' ('Scott'), in Economic Policy Institute, 'Revisiting NAFTA: Still Not Working for North America's Workers', Economic Policy Institute Briefing Paper No. 173 (28 September 2006) at 18, online: Economic Policy Institute, www.epinet.org/briefingpapers/173/bp173.pdf ('Economic Policy Institute').

institutions. A 2006 IMF country report on Mexico refers to labour regulations in Mexico as an obstacle to the efficient allocation of labour and productivity. Restrictive hiring and firing modalities (eg that employment relationships are permanent and severance payments are high) add considerably to the cost of labour. This, in turn, is said to result in low turnover and to have a negative effect on productivity, and also on informality in the labour market. A 2006 staff report following consultations between the IMF and the Mexican Government thus reported that Mexico's economic growth is being held back in part by overly-rigid labour regulation, and that 'medium-term growth will depend on structural reforms'. The IMF staff representatives endorsed the Mexican Government's emphasis on steps 'to remove barriers to labour market flexibility' on the grounds that 'to spur productivity, growth, labor market flexibility and competitive forces in general need to be given more room'.[57] Some Mexican labour activists have resisted the neoliberal logic underpinning such structural reforms, arguing, for example, that 'transnationals talk about making working practices more "flexible", when the reality of this so-called flexibility is that people are forced to work on contracts of only 28 days, with low pay, no social security, no pensions, and no union protection. The contracts are often illegal in themselves, and then even these are not respected.'[58]

While debates around the relative benefits brought by NAFTA continue, it is clear that the treaty has had a severe impact on labour markets in each of the three countries and caused significant displacement of work. In the United States, for example, since NAFTA came into force, the trade deficit with Canada and Mexico has grown rapidly—increasing by $107.3 billion from 1993 to 2004—thus resulting in significant employment displacement.[59] US workers with less than a college education, workers in the manufacturing industry, and workers in the apparel industry, were especially hard hit.

---

[57] IMF Staff Representatives for the 2006 Consultation with Mexico, 'Mexico: 2006 Article IV Consultation—Staff Report; Staff Statement; Public Information Notice on the Executive Board Discussion', IMF Country Report No 06/352 (October 2006) 29–30, para 69, online: IMF, www.imf.org/external/pubs/ft/scr/2006/cr06352.pdf. In a similar vein, the authors of a World Bank-sponsored book on development in Mexico suggest that in order for Mexican employers to be able to 'extract the most out of their human capital', a wide range of traditional employment protections should be 'phased out', including '[t]he current system of severance payments; collective bargaining and industry-binding contracts (*contratos-ley*); obligatory union membership (*cláusula de exclusión*); compulsory profit-sharing; restrictions to temporary, fixed-term and apprenticeship contracts; requirements for seniority-based promotions; registration of firm-provided training programs, and liability for subcontractors' employees (*patrón indirecto*)' (Giugale, Lafourcade and Nguyen (n 19) 16).

[58] Sergio Cobo, Director of the Mexican NGO Fomento (CAFOD, 'Clean Up Your Computer: Working Conditions in the Electronics Sector' (January 2004) 28, online: CAFOD, www.cafod.org.uk/var/storage/original/application/phpYyhizc.pdf ('CAFOD Report')).

[59] Scott (n 56) 5.

In Canada, precarious employment has grown since NAFTA came into force, key elements of social welfare policy have been continuously eroded, and economic dependence on the United States has increased significantly.[60] Real income has virtually stagnated while continued emphasis on improving the competitiveness of Canadian enterprises has motivated tax cuts and small government agendas.[61] Both government transfers to individuals and overall programme spending (with the exception of military spending) have dropped.[62] As Bruce Campbell and Andrew Jackson observe, since NAFTA came into effect in Canada, 'displaced workers in the trade sectors have moved to the lower-skill, lower-wage jobs in the services sector. Precarious forms of employment (part-time, temporary, and self-employment) have also increased, disproportionately impacting women and workers of colour.'[63]

In Mexico, a turn towards open-market economic policy, accentuated by NAFTA, 'has resulted in the poor performance of the national economy in terms of creating quality jobs and addressing the erratic and feeble growth of labor income.'[64] Carlos Salas argues that the race to the bottom brought about by low wages for the majority of Mexican workers 'has brought benefits solely to large companies, the financial sector, and a reduced layer of administrative and professional workers earning high salaries.'[65] Between 2000 and 2004, 23 per cent of new salaried positions created in Mexico had no social benefits, while only 37 per cent of new jobs had full social security benefits. In 2004, approximately 43 per cent of the total number of salaried employees worked under a verbal contract, and 86 per cent of them received no social benefits. Although employment increased overall, most of the new, non-agricultural jobs were precarious, many of them in low-wage *maquiladoras*.[66]

The agricultural sector has experienced one of the greatest losses of employment in Mexico: between 1991 and 2000, 1.013 million jobs were lost among corn producers, and 142,000 among flower and fruit growers. This dramatic loss of jobs

---

[60] A Jackson, *Work and Labour in Canada: Critical Issues* (Toronto, Scholars Press, 2005), cited in B Campbell, 'Backsliding: The Impact of NAFTA on Canadian Workers', in *Economic Policy Institute* (n 56) 53.

[61] ibid at 57.

[62] ibid at 58.

[63] ibid at 55.

[64] C Salas, 'Between Unemployment and Insecurity in Mexico: NAFTA enters its second decade' ('Salas, 2006'), in *Economic Policy Institute* (n 56) 33.

[65] ibid 33.

[66] ibid 33, 43–44. *Maquiladoras*, manufacturing or export assembly plants, largely non-unionized, located on the border between the US and Mexico. See: http://geography.about.com/od/urbaneconomicgeography/a/maquiladoras.htm

has been directly linked to NAFTA, which mandated the liberalization of agricultural trade.[67] Ultimately, Jeff Faux, founder of the Economic Policy Institute, points out, '[t]he continued willingness every year of hundreds of thousands of Mexican citizens to risk their lives crossing the border to the United States because they cannot make a living at home is in itself testimony to the failure of NAFTA to deliver on the promises of its promoters.'[68]

Although proponents of NAFTA have argued that NAFTA benefits workers by, for example, allowing them to work in businesses in the other participating jurisdictions without a visa, at a minimum the treaty has had a severe impact on the location, structure and remuneration of work with respect to the great majority of workers in all three countries. Moreover, while the three signatory countries also signed a 'side agreement' on labour as part of the NAFTA negotiations—the North American Agreement on Labor Cooperation ('NAALC')—the labour protections it promised have proved illusory. One of the NAALC's objectives is the promotion of a series of guiding labour protection principles,[69] but these are 'subject to each Party's domestic law' and do not establish 'common minimum standards for their domestic law.'[70]

The aim of the NAALC (under art 3) is to encourage the governments that are party to it to enforce their own labour laws. With respect to that purpose, the administrative structure under the NAALC consists of a Commission for Labour Cooperation, governed by a council of labour ministers, and assisted by a secretariat, with a National Administrative Office (NAO) in each country.[71] However, apart from co-operation in technical matters,[72] the NAALC has been ineffectual. While non-governmental organizations can initiate complaints to the appropriate NAO (under art 16), they cannot by themselves pursue a complaint beyond that stage; it is only at the option of the governmental parties themselves (under arts 23, 27 and 29) that a complaint can proceed further, to expert evaluation, council

---

[67] ibid 43.

[68] *Scott* (n 56) 2.

[69] These principles are: (1) freedom of association and protection of the right to organize, (2) the right to bargain collectively, (3) the right to strike, (4) prohibition of forced labour, (5) labour protections for children and young persons, (6) minimum labour standards, (7) elimination of employment discrimination, (8) equal pay for women and men, (9) prevention of occupational injuries and illnesses, (10) compensation in cases of occupational injuries and illnesses, and (11) protection of migrant workers (Annex 1 to the North American Agreement on Labour Cooperation (NAALC) Between the Government of Canada, the Government of the United Mexican States and the Government of the United States of America 1993 (13 September 1993) ('Annex 1 to NAALC')).

[70] ibid.

[71] North American Agreement on Labour Cooperation between the Government of Canada, the Government of the United Mexican States and the Government of the United States of America 1993 (13 September 1993).

[72] ibid art 20.

consideration and ultimately arbitration, and then only with respect to a truncated list of matters (occupational health and safety, child labour and minimum wage standards).[73] As a result, proceedings under the NAALC have typically resulted only in inter-ministerial consultations and educational seminars and programmes. The NAALC has had little if any direct effect in moving the Governments of the three signatory countries to protect workers' rights.

As Professor Eric Tucker has observed in an article on collective bargaining post-NAFTA:

> The results of the complaints process have been disappointing, to say the least. As one commentator noted, 'up to now all cases have ended with ministerial consultations and … joint agreement [on] action programmes that have not produced visible changes in the legal practices of the countries concerned.' In part this is a function of the NAALC's design, since complaints about freedom of association, collective bargaining, and the right to strike cannot go past the first stage of ministerial consultations. The result is that disputes are resolved at the political level in a context in which no government has an interest in pursuing high intensity conflict strategies. Not surprisingly, activists are losing interest in using the NAALC and few new submissions are being filed.[74]

A labour struggle that took place between 1997 and 2000 at the Han Young Factory, a contractor for car manufacturer Hyundai, in Tijuana, Mexico, is a good example. The main issues were freedom of association and health and safety standards. As part of the strategy adopted by the myriad of labour organizations involved both in Mexico and the United States, a petition for a hearing was filed with the United States NAO.[75] The NAO's report 'laid out damning verdicts on the government's behavior', and criticized the Mexican labour adjudicators by stating that 'the

---

[73] An NAO may request consultations with another NAO ('in relation to the other Party's labour law, its administration, or labor market conditions in its territory'; ibid arts 15(1), 21(1)) as well as ministerial consultations (ibid art 22). The establishment of an Evaluation Committee of Experts (ECE) may be requested where a matter has not been resolved after ministerial consultations (ibid art 23(1)). Once the ECE has issued its final report, a request can be made for a consultation with any other Party on 'whether there has been a persistent pattern of failure by that other Party to effectively enforce such standards in respect of the general subject matter addressed in the report' (ibid art 27(1)). If the Parties are unable to resolve the matter through consultations, a special session of the Commission for Labor Cooperation's Ministerial Council may be requested (ibid art 28(1)). If the matter has not been resolved within 60 days after the Council has convened, 'the Council shall, on the written request of any consulting Party and by a two thirds vote, convene an arbitral panel to consider the matter where the alleged persistent pattern of failure by the Party complained against to effectively enforce its occupational safety and health, child labor or minimum wage technical labor standards is: (a) trade-related; and (b) covered by mutually recognized labor laws' (ibid art 29(1)).

[74] Tucker (n 2) 145.

[75] HL Williams, 'Of Labor Tragedy and Legal Farce: The Han Young Factory Struggle in Tijuana, Mexico' 1, 2, 12 (paper presented to the conference 'Human Rights and Globalization: When Transnational Civil Society Networks Hit the Ground', University of California at Santa Cruz, 1–2 December 2000), online: University of California at Santa Cruz, www2.ucsc.edu/globalinterns/cpapers/williams.pdf ('Williams').

conciliation and arbitration boards have not been consistent and have not applied uniform criteria in adjudicating disputes between established unions aligned with the ruling political party, or PRI, and independent unions.'[76] However, by the time the NAO released its report,[77] 'the Han Young factory had already moved its installations and fired the last of the insurgent workers.'[78]

Professor Heather Williams argues that, ironically, the NAALC, 'which was supposed to have provided a real governmental incentive for all trading parties to curb or even prevent industry abuses', probably exacerbated the situation in the Han Young case. After the NAO hearing but before the release of the NAO's official report on the case, 'Han Young's management announced that it would close the factory and began firing the last of the insurgent workers remaining at the plant.'[79] In response, and despite findings 'that technically empowered the US Department of Labor to assess monetary sanctions on the Mexican Government for failure to enforce its health and safety laws', the NAO recommended only 'ministerial consultations' as a remedy.[80]

The outcome was no different in a complaint against Mexico heard by the Canadian NAO arising from a denial of the right to organize and a failure to protect workers from asbestos pollution at a Mexican plant operated by a subsidiary of Hayes Dana, a US multinational.[81] Indeed, of the fewer than 30 complaints submitted under the NAALC, as Arturo Bronstein points out, none led to expert evaluation, let alone arbitration, and penalties for breach of the NAALC have never been imposed. 'At present', Bronstein notes, 'the Canadian trade unions have decided not to submit new complaints under NAALC as they do not want to give credibility to what they consider a meaningless procedure.'[82]

7.3 The Changing Nature of Employment

Determining whether a particular work arrangement constitutes an 'employment relationship' is of central importance, since employee status is the gateway to most

---

[76] ibid 24–25.

[77] US Department of Labor, US National Administrative Office Bureau of International Labor Affairs, Public Report of Review of NAO Submission No 9702.

[78] Williams (n 75) 24.

[79] Williams (n 75) 26.

[80] ibid.

[81] Public Communication, Canadian NAO 98–1 (Secretariat of the Commission for Labour Co-operation).

[82] A Bronstein, *International and Comparative Law: Current Challenges* (Geneva, ILO, 2009) 105.

employment protections under labour standards laws. At the core of any work arrangement is the basic exchange of services for compensation. The employment relationship, however, adds two further ingredients to this exchange: subordination in return for security. In this classical conception of the employment relationship, an employer can expect not only that the employee will provide the specific services contracted for, but also that the employer can control the means, location and schedule by which those services are provided. In exchange for losing his or her ability to direct the labour process, the employee is entitled to remuneration and security.[83] The self-employed worker, according to this model, retains autonomy over his or her labour, and thus does not need the relatively substantial protections of labour standards legislation. As Fudge, Tucker and Vosko explain in a 2002 report to the Law Commission of Canada:

> In the conventional legal narrative, what distinguishes an employee from an independent contractor who also performs personal services is the degree of control exercised by the purchaser over the labour of the person performing the service. The importance of control, understood as authority to direct the labour process, is attributed both to the historical legacy of master and servant law with its emphasis on subordination and the nature of early production processes in which masters could directly supervise workers.[84]

While numerous scholars have demonstrated that the historical origin of the distinction between employees and self-employed workers is largely a legal fiction, it nevertheless remains a powerful narrative which continues to influence the regulation of the employment relationship.[85] And although the juridical sources governing employment relationships vary significantly in Canada, the United States and Mexico, the employee/self-employed dichotomy is a central feature of all three regulatory regimes, with subordination of the worker being a key litmus test.

What Makes an Employee? Subordination versus Autonomy

Canada and the United States

Despite its importance, the term 'employee' has been largely undefined in Canadian and United States law, and it has been left to courts and tribunals to give it content.

---

[83] RH Coase, 'The Nature of the Firm' (1937) 4 *Economica* (NS) 386, JH Goldthorpe, *Social Mobility and Class Structure in Modern Britain* (Oxford, Clarendon Press, 1980), and H Simon, 'A Formal Theory of the Employment Relation' (1951), 19 *Econometrica* 293, as cited in Fudge, Tucker and Vosko, 2003 (n 15) 331, n 5.

[84] J Fudge, E Tucker, and L Vosko, *The Legal Concept of Employment: Marginalizing Workers*, (Ottawa, Report for the Law Commission of Canada, 2002) ('Fudge, Tucker and Vosko, 2002').

[85] ibid 29.

As a result of the ad hoc nature of judicial decision-making, as well as the variation between jurisdictions, there is a lack of predictability, consistency and clarity in the interpretation of the term. In both Canada and the United States, four general tests are typically applied to determine if a worker meets the definition of 'employee'. The 'control' test was initially used to determine who, as between the worker and purchaser of the worker's services, controlled the tools of production, relying on a highly Marxian conception of class and labour. However, in the 1940s, courts began to develop more nuanced tests of employee status in recognition of 'the more complex conditions of modern industry'.[86] The 'entrepreneur test', for example, looks at control, ownership of tools, chance of profit, and risk of loss.[87] With the increase in skills and the exercise of autonomous judgment by employees, attention is currently also being paid to the 'business organization' test[88]—which asks whether the worker has been integrated into the organization—and the 'allocation of risks' test.[89]

In the face of this multiplicity of tests, both the Canadian and United States Supreme Courts have attempted to articulate a more coherent approach to determining employee status. While the two courts have developed somewhat different approaches—the United States Supreme Court has emphasized the 'right to control' test, while the Canadian Supreme Court has adopted a more purposive approach—both courts have held that the number of indicia applied is not limited, and no one criterion is determinative.

In the 1992 case *Nationwide Mutual Insurance Company v Robert T Darden*,[90] the United States Supreme Court held that, where the term 'employee' is not expressly defined by statute (or when the definition 'explains nothing'—eg 'an employee is a person employed by an employer'), the common-law 'right to control' test will apply. While employee status is to be determined on a case-by-case basis, assessing all factors, a court should ask whether the hiring party had a 'right to control the manner and means by which the product is accomplished'. Relevant factors to be considered include:

---

[86] *Montreal v Montreal Locomotive Works Ltd* [1947] 1 DLR 161 (PC) 169 ('*Montreal Locomotive*').

[87] This test was first set out by WO Douglas (later Justice) in 'Vicarious Liability and Administration of Risk' (1928–1929) 38 *Yale Law Journal* 584, and applied by Lord Wright in *Montreal Locomotive* (n 86).

[88] See *United States v Silk*, 331 US 704 (1947); 1947–2 CB 167; *Stevenson Jordan and Harrison, Ltd v Macdonald* [1952] 1 The Times L.R. 101 (CA) 111.

[89] This test posits that the employer should be vicariously liable because (1) he/she controls the activities of the worker; (2) he/she is in a position to reduce the risk of loss; (3) he/she benefits from the activities of the worker; (4) the true cost of a product or service ought to be borne by the enterprise offering it.

[90] *Nationwide Mutual Insurance Company v Robert T Darden* 503 US 318; 112 SCt. 1344 (1992) ('*Darden*').

— the skill required;
— the source of tools and instrumentalities;
— the location of the work;
— the duration of the relationship between the parties;
— the hiring party's right, or lack thereof, to assign additional projects to the hired party;
— the hired party's discretion over when and how long to work;
— the method of payment;
— the hired party's role in hiring and paying assistants;
— whether the work is part of the hiring party's business;
— whether the hiring party is in business;
— whether employee benefits are provided; and
— the tax treatment of the hired party.[91]

Significantly, the Court expressly rejected the 'economic realities' test, which considers the economic dependency of the individual on the employer.[92] Subsequent to the *Darden* decision, the 'right to control' test has been applied to the Americans with Disabilities Act, the Age Discrimination in Employment Act, and Equal Employment Opportunity laws, among other labour protection laws. The *Darden* reasoning has been criticized by some American labour lawyers, however, for expressly rejecting the view that the remedial purpose of the legislation may affect the definition of 'employee' for the purposes of that statute. Marc Linder notes, for example, that '[i]n the wake of *Darden* . . . statutory purpose became irrelevant and control became [t]he most important question'.[93]

---

[91] ibid 323–24.

[92] One formulation of this test was given in *Spirides v Reinhardt* 613 F2d 826 (DC Cir 1979), in which the Court of Appeals for the District of Columbia addressed the meaning of 'employee' under the Fair Labor Standards Act (FLSA). The Court applied a hybrid approach, examining the 'economic realities' of the work relationship, while emphasizing 'the employer's right to control the 'means and manner' of the worker's performance.' In *Darden,* the Supreme Court distinguished the test applied under the Fair Labor Standards Act, on the ground that it defines 'employ' more broadly to mean 'suffer or permit to work'. Because the Employee Retirement Income Security Act (ERISA) lacks a similar provision, the Court reasoned that the 'economic realities' test under the FLSA was not the intended standard under ERISA (*Darden* (n 90) 326).

[93] M Linder, 'Dependent and Independent Contractors in Recent US Labor Law: An Ambiguous Dichotomy Rooted in Simulated Statutory Purposelessness' (1999–2000) 21 *Comparative Labour Law & Policy Journal* 187, 196. Linder refers to this as the 'purposelessness' approach of the *Darden* court (ibid. 195). Despite the uniform approach mandated by *Darden,* the purposive approach has also had some influence in the United States. In the recent case *D'Annunzio v Prudential Insurance Co* No A-119–2005 (July 25, 2007), the New Jersey Supreme Court ruled that in certain circumstances, an independent contractor may constitute an employee under New Jersey's whistleblower statute, the Conscientious Employee Protection Act (CEPA), and thus be entitled to pursue a statutory wrongful termination claim. In reviewing the lower courts' decisions analyzing employee status under CEPA, the New Jersey Supreme Court considered the public policy rationale behind the legislature's enactment of the statute. The Court recognized that workers performing duties independently may nevertheless require whistleblower protection against retaliatory action. Moreover, the Court believed that CEPA's deterrent

It is precisely this *purposive* approach that has been adopted by the Canadian Supreme Court, which held that the definition of 'employee' will largely depend on the particular legislative scheme at issue and that, while control is an important test, no one test or set of factors will be determinative.[94] As the Court noted: 'The central question is whether the person who has been engaged to perform the services is performing them as a person in business or on his own account.' Despite the uncertainty of result in any given case, there is a general consensus among Canadian adjudicators that the determination of whether a worker is an 'employee' should focus on the substance of the arrangement, and not the form. As the Federal Court of Appeal stated in an early case on the determination of employee status in the context of taxation, the 'surface arrangement' between the worker and the payor is 'not necessarily expressive of their intrinsic relationship'.[95] The parties' intentions cannot, however, be entirely disregarded.[96]

While the purposive approach adopted by Canadian courts generally advances the protective goals of labour standards legislation, it also means that the issue may be decided differently according to the specific purpose or context of the inquiry, ie according to whether the question arises under legislation relating to taxation, employment insurance, pension and disability law, labour relations, labour standards, health and safety, or wrongful dismissal. In other words, while a worker may be an 'employee' for the purposes of one statute, he or she may be 'self-employed' for another. This creates a situation in which some workers may fall through the 'cracks' of labour regulation.

Mexico

By contrast to the highly varied definition of employee in Canada and the United States, in Mexico the term 'worker' is defined by the LFT as the natural person who

---

function would be undermined if individuals labelled as independent contractors were ineligible for coverage under it.

The Court explained that, in fulfilling CEPA's remedial purpose, the test used for determining employment status under CEPA must be adjusted to the specialized and non-traditional worker who is nevertheless integral to his or her employer's business interests. Although *D'Annunzio* does not per se extend the CEPA's protections to all independent contractors, the decision is significant in that the Court expanded the potential class of individuals who, their title notwithstanding, may be entitled to CEPA's statutory protections.

[94] *671122 Ontario Ltd v Sagaz Industries Canada Inc* [2001] 2 SCR 1983; *Rizzo & Rizzo Shoes Ltd (Re)* [1998] 1 SCR 27 (Supreme Court of Canada).

[95] *Wiebe Door Services Ltd v MNR* [1986] 3 FC 553 (Federal Court of Appeal).

[96] *Royal Winnipeg Ballet v Canada (Minister of National Revenue—MNR)* [2006] FCJ No 339 (Federal Court of Appeal).

provides personal, subordinate work to another person, either natural or legal.[97] Given that there is no distinction between labour and employment law along unionization lines under Mexican labour law, there are only 'workers' (*trabajadores*) in the private sector, regardless of whether they are unionized. The term 'employee' is usually reserved for public sector workers.

The LFT defines the employment relationship as 'the provision of personal, subordinated work to a person in exchange for the payment of a salary, regardless of the act that gave it origin',[98] and establishes that in order for an employment relationship to exist, the provision of work must be (i) personal, (ii) subordinated, and (iii) remunerated. The LFT defines 'work' as 'any intellectual or material human activity, regardless of the degree of technical training required for each profession or trade.'[99] The element of subordination is considered to be an essential element of the employment relationship. It is key to determining whether an employment relationship exists, and distinguishes a contract of employment from civil contracts such as a contract for the provision of professional services. According to the jurisprudence, subordination means, with respect to the employer, 'a legal power of control, correlative to a duty of obedience on the part of the person who provides the service.'[100] The presence of subordination is sufficient to establish an employment relationship, even in the absence of a contract of employment.[101]

Contracts for the provision of professional services, which are governed by the Civil Code of the relevant jurisdiction, are generally not considered contracts of employment due to the absence of subordination. However, the Mexican Supreme Court of Justice has recognized that subordination may exist even where outward signs indicate a civil or commercial contractual arrangement. Thus the Mexican Supreme Court of Justice has held that the services of a professional will constitute employment where there is control, ie a 'legal possibility that the employer may avail itself of the [professional's] work, even if technical direction is not in fact being exercised.'[102] 'Legal possibility' refers to what more recent jurisprudence calls 'legal subordination':

---

[97] LFT (n 3) art 8.

[98] ibid art 20.

[99] ibid art 8.

[100] 'Subordinación. Elemento Esencial de la Relación de Trabajo.' Cuarta Sala de la Suprema Corte de Justicia de la Nación, *Apéndice al Semanario Judicial de la Federación 1917–2000*, Vol 1, Material del Trabajo, Tomo V, p 494 n°. 608.

[101] R Charis Gómez, 'El Contrato Individual y la Relación de Trabajo en México' ('Charis'), in P Kurczyn Villalobos and CA Puig Hernández (eds), *Estudios Jurídicos en Homenaje al Doctor Néstor de Buen Lozano* (México, UNAM, 2003) 224, online: Instituto de Investigaciones Jurídicas de la UNAM, Biblioteca Jurídica, www.bibliojuridica.org/libros/3/1090/13.pdf ('Kurczyn & Puig'); and LFT (n 3) art 134(III).

[102] 'Profesionistas, Características de la Relación Laboral Tratándose de, Sexta Época', Quinta Parte, vol XCII, amparo directo 3339/64, 1 February 1965, 33.

The provision of a personal and direct service by one person to another is not enough to give rise to an employment relationship, since that provision must have legal subordination as its main requirement, which entails that the employer has the possibility at all times of availing itself of the physical and/or mental efforts of the employee, depending on the relationship agreed upon; that is, that there must be a legal power of control on the part of the employer, correlative to a duty of obedience on the part of the person who provides the service; that relationship of subordination must be permanent during the work day and entails being under the direction of the employer or its representative.[103]

In other words, where a party exerts control over an individual's time and efforts, regardless of any surface contractual arrangement, this may be an indication that the individual is in an employment relationship, rather than a civil or commercial arrangement. The concept of legal subordination has thus acquired much the same meaning in Mexico as the 'right to control' in the United States.

Economic Dependence: the Grey Zone between Employee and Entrepreneur

Control over the labour process has thus played a central role in determining employee status in Canada, the United States and Mexico. In all three countries, however, there has also been increasing recognition by academic commentators that the strict dichotomy between 'employees' and 'self-employed entrepreneurs', or 'independent contractors', has broken down, if it ever existed at all. For example, Fudge et al note that in Canada, as in several other countries, the Organisation for Economic Co-operation and Development ('OECD') has reported a steady increase since the mid-1970s in the number of self-employed workers who work for just one company.[104] According to the OECD, this indicates that self-employment status 'may be little more than a device to reduce total taxes paid by the firms and the workers involved.'[105] In short, while some workers may on the surface bear the indicia of independent contractors, in reality they may be economically dependent on a single payor. Similarly, while some workers may be engaged under short,

---

[103] 'Relación Laboral Requisito de la, su Diferencia con la Prestación de Servicios Personales.' Tribunales Colegiados de Circuito, *Semanario Judicial de la Federación,* Época 8ᵃ, Tomo XII p 945.

[104] OECD, 'Partial Renaissance of Self-Employment', *OECD Employment Outlook* (Paris, OECD, 2000), cited in Fudge, Tucker and Vosko, 2003 (n 15) 339, n 38 ('OECD')

[105] Significantly, in Canada and Germany, the two OECD countries where self-employment grew most, *employer* self-employment fell sharply; in other words, the growth in self-employment was largely comprised of single individuals working for own-account, not self-employed persons who hired other paid employees (OECD, ibid). As Fudge et al note, countries with a high proportion of self-employed employers generally experience greater job growth than those with a high proportion of own-account self-employment, and thus the rise in self-employment 'is not necessarily linked to entrepreneurship' (Fudge, Tucker and Vosko, 2003 (n 15) 339–41).

fixed-term contracts with a company, as part of 'consulting', 'freelancing' or 'subcontracting' arrangements, these fixed-term contracts may be renewed consistently over a period of time, so as to effectively create a relationship of economic dependence.[106]

Canada and the United States

Of all three countries, Canada has taken the most significant steps towards recognizing an intermediate category between 'employee' and 'independent contractor.' A number of provinces, as well as the federal government in the Canada Labour Code, have deemed 'dependent contractors' to be employees under labour relations legislation in order to recognize that certain workers who do not fit the classic definition of 'employee' should still be entitled to collective bargaining rights. For example, the Ontario Labour Relations Act specifically deems 'dependent contractors' to be 'employees' and defines a dependent contractor as

> A person, whether or not employed under a contract of employment, and whether or not furnishing tools, vehicles, equipment, machinery, material or any other thing owned by the dependent contractor, who performs work or services for another person for compensation or reward on such terms and conditions that the dependent contractor is in a position of economic dependence upon, and under an obligation to perform duties for, that person more closely resembling the relationship of an employee than that of an independent contractor;[107]

Some labour boards have considered the following factors as relevant to the determination of dependent contractor status: the worker's ability to exercise independent judgment in the course of providing services, including suggesting changes to the services being provided to a client; control over scheduling; method of payment (eg bidding for work contracts); whether the worker negotiates the rate of pay; the degree to which the worker's services are integrated into the essential operations of the enterprise; opportunity for profit or loss; compliance with employee manuals and associated evaluations and/or discipline.[108]

In one case assessing the work relationship between snack food distributors and the snack food company, with consequences for the distributors' ability to seek union representation under the relevant Labour Relations Code, the British Columbia Court of Appeal noted that, in determining dependent contractor status, it was

---

[106] Arthurs Report (n 15).
[107] Ontario Labour Relations Act 1995 SO 1995 c 1 Sch A s 1(1).
[108] *Huntsville District Memorial Hospita,* [1998] OLRB Rep November/December 968.

important to assess the 'substance of a relationship, not merely its form.' The Court found that the workers were dependent, rather than independent contractors, taking specific account of the fact that the company effectively governed the distributors' remuneration and that the distributors were a necessary part of the company's system of product sales and distribution.[109]

Building on the recognition of dependent contractors in collective bargaining legislation, Canadian labour expert Harry Arthurs has called on the Canadian governments to formally recognize, for the purposes of labour standards protection, a category of 'autonomous workers' who 'inhabit some of the same workplaces and labour markets' as employees, and who 'must deal with many of the same practical and contractual issues.'[110]

For Arthurs, extending certain labour standards protections to autonomous workers is a matter of fundamental decency in the workplace. To quote from the Federal Labour Standards Review, which he conducted and which concluded in a 2006 report:

> Labour standards should ensure that no matter how limited his or her bargaining power, no worker in the federal jurisdiction is offered, accepts or works under conditions that Canadians would not regard as 'decent.' No worker should therefore receive a wage that is insufficient to live on; be deprived of the payment of wages or benefits to which they are entitled; be subject to coercion, discrimination, indignity or unwarranted danger in the workplace; or be required to work so many hours that he or she is effectively denied a personal or civic life. (p x)

Arthurs argues: 'If Canadians do not consider that certain kinds of working conditions are decent when experienced by employees, they are unlikely to consider

---

[109] *Old Dutch Foods Ltd v Teamsters, Local Union No 213* [2006] BCJ No 3127 (BCCA).

[110] Arthurs Report (n 15) at 61. In the 2006 report concluding his Federal Labour Standards Review, Arthurs uses the example of truck drivers to demonstrate the need for such a category: 'In some cases, "owner-operators" drive regularly for a particular trucking firm, in others they make themselves available directly or through brokers to a number of firms; in some cases, they operate their own trucks, in others they drive trucks owned by the employer or third parties; in some cases, the trucks carry their own insignia, in others, they bear the markings of a fleet operator; in some cases, they work alone, in others they may hire one or two drivers regularly or occasionally to handle assignments; in some cases, they are paid hourly rates, in others on a mileage basis, and in still others on the basis of a fixed price for a specific job.

These differences are all material to determining whether these owner-operators—and more generally, own-account self-employed persons—enjoy the legal status of "employees" under Part III, or whether they are excluded from it because they are "independent contractors." However, in real life terms, it is extremely difficult to distinguish among the variety of persons encountered in the workplace. In many cases, members of the two groups work for the same trucking firm, undertake similar assignments, drive vehicles that are visually indistinguishable, and are subject to comparable degrees of managerial control; indeed individuals move back and forth from one status to the other.' (ibid 61–62)

those same conditions acceptable if experienced by other persons.'[111] Furthermore, Arthurs points out, the pay and working conditions of non-employees will likely influence the labour standards enjoyed by those who are clearly 'employees'.[112]

Arthurs recommends that 'autonomous workers' should be defined by Ministerial regulation as including persons who perform services comparable to those provided by employees and under similar conditions, but whose contractual arrangements with the employer distinguish them from 'employees.' To the extent necessary to protect their basic right to decent working conditions, and to protect the interests of employees from unfair competition based on their exploitation, 'autonomous workers' should be entitled to limited labour standards protections on a sector-specific basis.

The category of dependent contractor as a distinct classification does not exist in the United States. According to a US Department of Labor report, 'over half of all the self-employed call themselves independent contractors, independent consultants, or freelancers'. However, '[n]o legal meaning attaches to such descriptions as dependent contractor, permanent employee, regular employee, temporary employee, and the like. There are only employees entitled to a modest suite of rights, and independent contractors entitled to fewer.'[113] Significantly, the Commission on the Future of Worker-Management Relations (commonly known as the Dunlop Commission) recommended in its 1995 report that the 'economic realities' test also be applied to define the coverage of all federal labour statutes.[114] As discussed above, this approach was expressly rejected in 1992 by the United States Supreme Court in *Darden*.

Mexico

As in the United States, in Mexico there is no distinct legal category of dependent contractor. Working persons who do not fall within the above-mentioned definition of 'worker' are self-employed persons not protected by Mexican labour law. As

---

[111] ibid 61.

[112] ibid 61–62.

[113] SN Houseman, 'Flexible Staffing Arrangements: A Report on Temporary Help, On-Call, Direct-Hire Temporary, Leased, Contract Company, and Independent Contractor Employment in the United States' (August 1999), online: www.dol.gov/oasam/programs/history/herman/reports/futurework/conference/staffing/flexible.htm.

[114] Commission on the Future of Worker-Management Relations (Dunlop Commission), *Report and Recommendations* (December 1994), cited in A Hyde, 'Classification of U.S. Working People and Its Impact on Workers' Protection' (6 January 2000) 80, online: International Labour Organization, Social Dialogue, Labour Law and Labour Administration Department, www.ilo.org/public/english/dialogue/ifpdial/downloads/wpnr/usa.pdf.

discussed, 'subordination' is the key factor in determining whether a worker is self-employed or not. Some Latin American commentators have, however, begun to push for the recognition of alternatives to subordination. For example, Uruguayan professor Óscar Ermida Uriarte and Venezuelan professor Óscar Hernández Álvarez suggest that an employee's economic dependence, or 'economic subordination', should be an influential factor where it is difficult to establish legal subordination. Although economic dependence is not an absolute indicator, Ermida and Hernández favour it because it is harder to hide, and because it is consistent with labour law's primary function of protecting workers as economically weak actors.[115]

Ermida Uriarte and Hernández Álvarez conclude that, as the law stands today, the dominant criteria for the determination of an employment relationship are both subordination and '*ajenidad*', meaning an employee's provision of services *for the benefit of an employer* who, even where the work is performed outside [the employer's] physical premises'[116], assumes any liabilities that may derive from the work. Ermida Uriarte and Hernández Álvarez argue that subordination and *ajenidad* are two sides of the same coin.[117] This approach is consistent with the Italian concept of 'parasubordination', which aims at covering those autonomous workers who, although not legally subordinated, are engaged in a continuous, coordinated collaboration with an enterprise, and experience inequality of bargaining power, regardless whether they are physically present at the workplace during working hours.[118]

---

[115]   Panama's Labour Code (*Código de Trabajo*) has embraced this notion by expressly defining the concept of economic dependence, which exists in any of the following cases:

'1.   Where the sums that the natural person who provides the service or performs the work receives constitute the only or main source of his or her income;

2.   Where the sums to which the previous paragraph refers come directly or indirectly from a person or enterprise, or are the consequence of his or her activity;

3.   Where the natural person who provides the service or performs the work does not enjoy economic autonomy, and is economically linked to the line of activity that the person or enterprise deemed to be the employer carries on....'

Where doubt exists, proof of economic dependence is determinative of an employment relationship under Panamanian law. In contrast, when a 1985 labour bill from Venezuela attempted to define economic dependence as the situation that exists 'where the remuneration obtained for the provision of the service constitutes the basis for the economic sustenance of the worker and his or her family, or at least a part of it', the reference to economic dependence was strongly opposed by the entrepreneurial sector in that country, and was ultimately eliminated on the Senate's recommendation. See Ó Ermida Uriarte and Ó Hernández Álvarez, 'Crítica de la subordinación' ('Ermida and Hernández'), in Kurczyn and Puig (n 101) 273–74, 288–89, and *Código de Trabajo de Panamá* art 65 [translated by Hugo Leal-Neri].

[116]   ibid 295.

[117]   Ermida Uriarte and Hernández Álvarez 285–86.

[118]   ibid 290.

Jeffrey Sack, Emma Phillips and Hugo Leal-Neri

Who Is the Employer? Triangular Relationships

Frequently, the necessity arises of determining in any work arrangement if the purchaser of an individual's services is an 'employer'. Generally, if a worker is deemed, through application of the tests described above, to be an employee, then the party paying for his or her services is by definition the employer, and has all the concomitant legal obligations. Indeed, this is how the 'employer' is typically defined in Canada and the United States—as the party who employs the employee. In Mexico, 'employer' is defined as the 'natural or legal person who uses the services of one or more workers' and a finding to that effect depends on whether an employment relationship or contract of employment exists.[119]

Where the determination of 'employer' becomes more complicated, however, is in the case of 'triangular' work arrangements in which the worker is hired by an intermediary (such as a temporary agency or contractor) for the provision of services to a third-party or 'user enterprise.' In Canada, about 13 per cent of the labour force, or 1.7 million workers, are temporary, performing seasonal or casual work. Currently, one in five new hires is a temporary worker, compared to one in ten in 1989.[120] In Ontario alone, there are an estimated 1,300 employment agencies, and the industry continues to grow. In Mexico, in 2004 1,399,264 employed workers were not dependent on the enterprise where they worked, but had been hired by a third party.[121] The largest number of these workers (338,442) were employed in the manufacturing sector, followed by those in the retail sector (241,409).[122] In contrast, in the United States there were 1,217,000 temporary help agency workers and

---

[119] LFT (n 3) art 10.

[120] 'MPPs Target "Temp" Boom', December 8, 2006, *The Toronto Star*.

[121] Employed workers not dependant on the enterprise where they work (*personal ocupado no dependiente de la razón social*) included those persons 'who worked for the economic unit, but who were foreign to the enterprise and who performed substantive work, such as: production, commercialization, provision of services, administration, accounting, among others; covering at least a third of the economic unit's work day.' INEGI, 'Metodología de los Censos Económicos 2004' 57, online: INEGI, www.inegi.gob.mx/est/contenidos/espanol/metodologias/censos/metodo_ce2004.pdf [translated by Hugo Leal-Neri].

[122] INEGI, 'Personal ocupado en las unidades económicas por sector de actividad', *Censos Económicos 2004*, online: INEGI, Censos económicos 2004, www.inegi.gob.mx/est/contenidos/espanol/rutinas/ept. asp?t=gen03&c=6538. According to INEGI, Mexico's working population as of the second trimester of 2003 amounted to 40,633,197. A caveat must be noted that this figure—contained in the National Employment Survey 2003—is not parallel in terms of its census universe to the figures in the Economic Census 2004 (which pertains to 2003), for they follow different statistical methodologies. For instance, 6,813,644 workers out of the 40,633,197 cited above were employed in the rural sector, most of whose activities were excluded from the universe used in the Economic Census. See INEGI, 'Población ocupada por sexo y grupos de ocupación, Cuadro 8, Parte 1', *Encuesta Nacional de Empleo 2003*, online: INEGI, Encuesta Nacional de Empleo 2003, www.inegi.gob. mx/est/contenidos/espanol/sistemas/ene/ene_2003/datos/tabulados/ocupada.xls. The Economic Census 2009 has now been released and is available at http://www.inegi.org.mx/est/contenidos/espanol/proyectos/ censos/ce2009/default.asp?s=est&c=14220.

813,000 workers provided by contract firms as of February 2005, totalling about 1.46 per cent of the workforce.[123]

Determining who is the 'employer' in triangular work arrangements may have significant consequences for a worker's status, health benefits, vacation entitlements, overtime pay, collective bargaining rights, severance pay, and access to national social security and unemployment insurance plans. While occupational health and safety statutes and anti-discrimination statutes generally apply equally to temporary and non-temporary workers, eligibility requirements based on length of service often exclude temporary workers from substantial labour protections. For example, in Canada, laws providing rights to severance pay, pay in lieu of notice of termination, protection against unjust dismissal, and entitlement to maternity/parental leave do not apply to temporary workers upon termination because they do not meet the eligibility requirements. Similarly, in the United States, such eligibility requirements effectively exclude most temporary workers from family and medical leave benefits, as well as from unemployment compensation. In Mexico, eligibility requirements operate to exclude many workers from the national social security regime. For example, the accrual rules of the Social Security Act (*Ley del Seguro Social*), which governs the social security regime applicable to private sector workers, are linked to active employment and impose lengthy waiting periods.[124]

In Canada and the United States, employers are generally permitted to pay temporary or part-time workers less than permanent ones for equal work.[125] In Mexico, the LFT enshrines a general labour principle whereby equal work, performed under similar conditions, must be remunerated through equal salary.[126] This

---

[123] US Census, Table 594 (n 48).

[124] The accrued rights to life, retirement and old age insurance of insured workers who lose their employment are preserved for only a period of one-fourth of the time covered by their weekly contributions, or 12 months, whichever is greater. The worker's accrued rights will not be recognized until he or she returns to work. If the worker returns to work before the expiry of the preservation of contributions period mentioned above, no waiting period will apply and the worker's contributions will be recognized immediately upon return. Otherwise, a waiting period will apply pursuant to the following rules: If the worker returns to work after an interruption in the payment of contributions of *not more* than 3 years, all of the worker's contributions will be recognized upon re-registering. However, if the worker returns to work after an interruption in the payment of contributions of *more* than three years but less than six, the worker will face a 26-week waiting period upon resumption of contributions. If the interruption is longer than six years, there will be a 52-week waiting period. *Ley del Seguro Social*, Nueva Ley publicada en el Diario Oficial de la Federación el 21 de diciembre de 1995) arts 150 and 151.

These rules seem to be aimed at forcing the worker to rejoin the workforce as soon as possible even though obtaining employment is subject to numerous externalities beyond the worker's control. The effect of these provisions is to penalize workers who have been unable to secure new, formal employment or to pay for the contributions themselves, regardless of the circumstances, and have particularly severe consequences for temporary or casual workers.

[125] With the exception of the provinces of Saskatchewan and Quebec, where employers are required to provide pro-rated benefits to part-time workers, benefits are provided to those working full-time hours.

[126] LFT (n 3) art 86.

provision extends to employees hired by an intermediary company; they have a right to the same terms and conditions of employment as the direct employees of the user enterprise.[127] The LFT even guarantees that part-time workers are entitled to, for instance, the proportional part of their seventh day[128] and that casual and seasonal workers are entitled to annual vacation in proportion to the number of days worked during the year.[129] Despite these strong protections, however, enforcement is a problem and, as will be discussed below, such labour standards are rarely respected.

In all three countries, working conditions for temporary and casual workers are frequently unsafe, and workers often have difficulty enforcing what employment protections they do have, such as overtime or statutory holiday pay. These working conditions have caused one Canadian union leader to comment, 'we are struck by the similarities of the conditions faced by some temp workers today to the sweatshops we first started organizing over a century ago.'[130] Worker advocates have also raised concerns about the growth of a permanent, 'second-class' tier of workers who labour alongside full-time, permanent employees, but without the same benefits. In the United States, these workers have sometimes been referred to as 'permatemps', a term that refers to workers whose status is somewhere between a permanent employee and a temporary one.

Canada and the United States

In Canada, the determination of 'employer' status usually arises in the labour relations context. For example, provincial labour relations statutes in Canada generally provide that associated companies may be considered as one employer or as a common employer for the purposes of bargaining. Thus, the Canada Labour Code provides in s 35(1) that, where associated or related federal works, undertakings or businesses are operated by two or more employers having 'common control or direction', the Board may declare that they are a 'single employer'.[131] Generally, the determination of employer status is made on the basis of the same factors that apply to the definition of 'employee' for labour relations purposes, by asking:

---

[127] ibid art 14.I.

[128] art 72 of the *LFT* reads: 'Where the worker does not provide his or her services during all the working days in a given week, or where in the same day or in the same week he or she provides his or her services to several employers, he or she will have the right to be paid the proportional part of the salary for the days of rest, calculated on the basis of the salary for the days in which he or she worked or on the basis of the salary received from each employer' [translated by Hugo Leal-Neri].

[129] LFT (n 3) art 77.

[130] Comments of Alex Dagg, Ontario Director of UNITE HERE, to Standing Committee of the Ontario Legislative Assembly on 3 May 2007.

[131] Canada Labour Code, RSC 1985 c L-2 s 35(1).

1. who bears the burden of remuneration;
2. who imposes discipline;
3. control over hiring the worker;
4. authority over dismissing the worker;
5. the worker's own perception of who the employer is;
6. the existence of an intention to create the relationship of employer and employee; and
7. day-to-day direction and control over the worker.[132]

In the United States, where two entities co-govern the essential terms and conditions of work, the two organizations can be treated as 'joint employers.' However, despite this joint employer doctrine, it was generally held that workers employed by a staffing company were the employees of the staffing company and not of the client company.[133] More recently, following *Vizcaino v Microsoft Corp*,[134] the joint employer doctrine has been applied to treat temporary agency workers as employees of both the agency and the client company for the purposes of certain labour protection laws, including anti-discrimination and occupational health and safety laws, and pension regulations. *Vizcaino* involved a class action lawsuit against Microsoft by thousands of current and former employees who had been classified as temporary and freelance workers, and therefore excluded from participating in Microsoft's 401K retirement plan. Stating that 'large corporations have increasingly adopted the practice of hiring temporary employees or independent contractors as a means of avoiding payment of employee benefits and thereby increasing their profits', the Ninth Circuit Court of Appeals held that the Employment Retirement Income Security Act ('ERISA') entitled all of Microsoft's employees, including temporary workers, to participate in Microsoft's retirement plans.

Trade unions have also fought to have client companies recognized as the employer of temporary workers in order to include temporary workers in the client's bargaining unit. In *Nike Canada Ltd,*[135] for example, the Ontario Labour Relations Board relied on the seven factors listed above and found that Nike was the 'real

---

[132] Generally, the seven-part test from *York Condominium Corp.* is applied: [1977] OLRB Rep 645 (OLRB). More recently, in *CAW-Canada v National Waste Services Inc* (2009), Lancaster's *Labour Law E-Bulletin*, Issue No 9 (OLRB, June 8, 2009), the Ontario Labour Relations Board reiterated its view that indicators of control are more important than the perception of the employee or the intention of the parties.

[133] Indeed, a 1996 legislative change in the definition of 'leased employee' under the Internal Revenue Code was intended to clarify that a worker could perform services under the 'primary direction or control' of a client company and still not be the client company's common-law employee.

[134] *Vizcaino v Microsoft Corp* 173 F3d 713 (9th Cir 1999).

[135] *Nike Canada Ltd* [2006] OLRD No 2482.

employer' of the temporary workers. Although the workers were nominally controlled by the temporary staffing agency, it was Nike which set the rate of pay and decided whether certain workers should receive pay increases, and it was Nike which informally admonished workers for lateness and ineptitude, assessed the workers' performance, and sent them back to the employment agency if they were incompetent.

The approach in *Nike Canada* is consistent with that articulated in 1997 by the Supreme Court of Canada in *Pointe-Claire (City)*, which held that temporary workers supplied to a unionized employer by an agency became 'employees' of that employer for the purposes of collective bargaining, because 'it is essential that temporary employees be able to bargain with the party that exercises the greatest control over all aspects of their work—and not only over the supervision of their day-to-day work.'[136]

Because the status of temporary workers is left to judicial interpretation, rather than statutory regulation, the determination of employer status remains somewhat ad hoc, and labour arbitrators, determining grievances under collective agreements, have arrived at contrary outcomes.[137] Furthermore, these decisions typically relate only to the issue of inclusion of temporary or subcontracted workers in collective bargaining regimes; there is no general regulation in Canada providing workers in triangular work arrangements with labour standards and other employment protections available to 'standard' full-time employees.

On 6 November 2009, Bill 139, the Employment Standards Amendment (Temporary Help Agencies) came into force. The Act amends the Employment Standards Act to protect the more than 700,000 workers employed in the province by temporary help agencies. So-called 'elect-to-work' employees of temporary help agencies will no longer be excluded from entitlement to public holiday pay and (as of 2012) from entitlement to termination and severance pay. Temporary employees may not be unfairly prevented from accessing permanent jobs when employers want to hire them from agencies, they must be provided with information about work assignments, and have access to information about their statutory rights. Finally, temporary help agencies may not charge fees to workers for things such as resume

---

[136] *Pointe-Claire (City) v SEPB Locale 57* [1997] 1 SCR 1015 (Supreme Court of Canada) [48] ('*Pointe-Claire*').

[137] Compare, eg, *Canadian Union of Public Employees, Local 4000 v Ottawa Hospital* [2006] OLAA No 378 (Briggs, Chair) (housekeeping staff considered employees not of the hospital, but rather of the supplier of labour) and *Ontario Public Service Employees' Union v Ontario Property Assessment Corporation* unreported, 6 October 2006 (MacDowell, Chair) (temporary workers deemed employees of the client company, not of the staffing agency).

writing and interview preparation. Bill 139 does not, however, institute a licensing regime to regulate the temporary staffing industry.[138]

Mexico

The regulation of intermediaries is significantly different in Mexico, where article 10 of the LFT clarifies how the employer is to be identified, establishing that '[i]f the worker, pursuant to what has been agreed upon or to custom, uses the services of other workers, the employer of the former shall also be the employer of the latter.' Thus, according to this and other LFT provisions, an employer cannot escape its employment obligations by 'contracting out' work, or by resorting to a temporary agency.

The LFT refers to a person who hires or participates in the hiring of employees for the provision of services to an employer as an 'intermediary.'[139] According to one appellate court decision, an intermediary is a person who does not benefit from the work provided to another.[140] Employers who use intermediaries to hire workers are responsible for fulfilling the obligations contained in the LFT and for the services provided. Moreover, the workers provided by an intermediary will have the same rights and working conditions as the workers performing similar work in the user enterprise.[141]

While some intermediaries provide 'specialized services different from the core activity of the user enterprise',[142] thus becoming the user enterprise's subcontractors, many others provide permanent personnel to a user enterprise, under the guise of temporariness, thus eliminating the possibility of direct hiring of those workers by the user enterprise.[143] This is an increasing problem, with the number of companies in Mexico hiring personnel through another firm rising by 41.5 per cent

---

[138] In his 2006 Federal Labour Standards Review, Professor Arthurs recommends that, with a view to protecting the 45,000 temporary workers in federally regulated enterprises—about 5 per cent of the federal workforce—such enterprises should be made jointly and severally liable with temporary employment agencies for non-payment of wages and benefits, and temporary employees who have worked for one year should be entitled to be considered for permanent employment on the same basis as probationers, and receive access to the same pay as other employees with equivalent jobs, length of service and abilities. See Arthurs Report (n 15) 233–37. For ILO policy on temporary work and private employment agencies, see Arturo Bronstein (n 82) 38–43.

[139] LFT (n 3) art 12.

[140] 'Intermediario. Responsabilidad solidaria del.' Tribunales Colegiados de Circuito, Octava Época, *Semanario Judicial de la Federación*, XIV, Julio de 1994, 638.

[141] LFT (n 3) art 14.

[142] Cosmópolis (n 28) 81.

[143] ibid.

between 1998 and 2003.[144] The highest demand came from the manufacturing industry and retail sector which absorbed, respectively, 25.9 per cent and 30.8 per cent of this type of personnel.[145]

Peruvian law professor Mario Pasco Cosmópolis argues that the triangulation of the employment relationship typical of the regime of intermediation or contracting out makes it difficult for workers to know with certainty who their true employer is, and in particular 'who must ultimately be responsible for their rights, given that often [the intermediaries] … are barely a formal façade, without the capital assets (buildings, machinery, equipment, tools, etc.) that tend to guarantee the [workers'] rights.'[146] The LFT deals with this issue as follows:

> Article 712: When the worker is ignorant of the name of the employer or the business or firm name of the place where he works or worked, in his statement of claim he shall indicate at least the address of the enterprise, establishment, office or place in which he performed or performs the work, and the activity carried on by the employer.
>
> The mere filing of the statement of claim in the terms expressed in the previous paragraph suspends the running of the limitation period with respect to whoever may turn out to be the employer of the worker.

If the defendant employer fails to file a statement of defence, it is incumbent upon the conciliation and arbitration board to ascertain the identity of the employer before making an award against it. The level of responsibility of both the user enterprise and its contractor or subsidiary will depend not only on whether the contractor or subsidiary has sufficient material means of its own to perform the work and satisfy its obligations to its workers, but also on whether the contractor or subsidiary performs work or services for the user enterprise in an exclusive and principal manner.

If the contractor has sufficient material means as defined above, the contractor is deemed to be the employer of the workers, rather than an intermediary between the user enterprise and the workers.[147] If it does not, however, the contractor and the user enterprise will be jointly and severally liable for the obligations owed to the workers.[148]

---

[144] INEGI, 'Censos Económicos 2004: ¡El quehacer económico en números! Resultados generales' (July 2005) 7, online: INEGI, www.inegi.gob.mx/est/contenidos/espanol/proyectos/censos/ce2004/pdfs/resultados_grals.pdf ('translated by Hugo Leal-Neri') ('INEGI, Economic Census 2004').

[145] ibid.

[146] Cosmópolis (n 28) 81.

[147] LFT (n 3) art 13.

[148] ibid art 13.

On the other hand, if an enterprise (for instance, a subsidiary of the user enterprise) performs work or services for the user enterprise in an exclusive and principal manner and does not have sufficient means to guarantee its obligations to the workers, the subsidiary and the user enterprise will be jointly and severally liable for the obligations owed to the workers provided by the subsidiary.[149] Further, the subsidiary's workers have a right to enjoy terms and conditions of employment proportional to those enjoyed by workers performing similar work in the user enterprise.[150]

Federal courts have been consistent in holding that the user enterprise has the burden of proving the economic solvency of its contractor in order to free itself from joint and several liability.[151] For example, in a 1994 decision, an appellate court found the Mexican Institute of Social Security (*Instituto Mexicano del Seguro Social*, IMSS) to be the direct beneficiary of the services provided by its co-defendant, a construction contractor to which the character of employer of the plaintiff was imputed. Since IMSS failed to prove the economic solvency of the contractor, both defendants were held jointly and severally liable under article 13 of the LFT with respect to the obligations owed to the plaintiff employee. The court went on to say that, before entering into the contract, IMSS as the user enterprise should have

---

[149] ibid arts 13, 15.I.

[150] ibid arts 13, 15.II.

[151] See, for instance, 'Responsabilidad solidaria del beneficiario de una obra. A él le corresponde la carga de la prueba para acreditar que el contratista cuenta con recursos suficientes para responder de la relación laboral con los trabajadores o que no le prestó sus servicios de manera exclusiva o principal.' Segundo Tribunal Colegiado del Noveno Circuito, Novena Época, *Semanario Judicial de la Federación y su Gaceta*, XXIII, Enero de 2006, Tesis: IX.2o.25 L, p 2477, Registro No 176130; 'Intermediarios, la carga de la prueba de su solvencia corresponde al beneficiario de la obra o servicio.' Segundo Tribunal Colegiado del Sexto Circuito, Octava Época, *Semanario Judicial de la Federación*, XIV, Julio de 1994, p 639, Registro No 211564; and 'Intermediario, solvencia del. Carga de la prueba.' Segundo Tribunal Colegiado del Sexto Circuito, Octava Época, *Semanario Judicial de la Federación*, IX, Abril de 1992 p 527, Registro No 219759.

Significantly, the employee does not have the onus of proving the insolvency of the intermediary. Having pleaded that his or her employer (ie the intermediary) does not have sufficient economic elements to cover the compensation sought, the employee is relieved from proving this assertion of fact and the burden of proof shifts to the user enterprise. This is because a worker will not generally have the means necessary to demonstrate the insolvency of his or her direct employer, since he or she would not have 'access to the documents or elements that reveal the administration and pecuniary balance of the subject with whom he has entered into an employment relationship.' 'Autoridades ejecutoras, negación de amparo contra ordenadoras. Amparo Directo 382/88. Instituto Mexicano del Seguro Social.' Segundo Tribunal Colegiado del Sexto Circuito, Octava Época, *Semanario Judicial de la Federación*, Tomo XIV, Agosto de 1994, p 312, Registro No 2079 [translated by Hugo Leal-Neri]. See also, 'Intermediarios, la carga de la prueba de su solvencia corresponde al beneficiario de la obra o servicio.' Segundo Tribunal Colegiado del Sexto Circuito, Octava Época, *Semanario Judicial de la Federación*, XIV, Julio de 1994, p 639, Registro No 211564; and 'Intermediario, solvencia del. Carga de la prueba.' Segundo Tribunal Colegiado del Sexto Circuito, Octava Época, *Semanario Judicial de la Federación*, IX, Abril de 1992, p 527, Registro No 219759.

satisfied itself of the economic solvency of the construction contractor in order to avoid liability in the event of a labour dispute.[152]

Unfortunately, although Mexico's provisions governing the use of intermediaries appear to be more advanced than those of Canada and the United States, enforcement remains a problem. For example, the use of employment agencies as intermediaries in the recruitment process is central to the electronics industry in Guadalajara, where there is a high concentration of *maquiladoras* or contract manufacturers of computers and other electronics for multinational corporations such as IBM, Hewlett Packard or Dell. In a report on working conditions in the electronics industry in Mexico and elsewhere, the London-based Catholic Agency for Overseas Development (CAFOD) observes that manufacturers do not employ many employees directly as they outsource recruitment to employment agencies.[153] These agencies, in turn, avoid the obligations incumbent on the ultimate employer by registering themselves as 'manufacturing subcontractors' rather than as intermediaries. These agencies then '[employ] workers on significantly worse terms than those of direct employees of the company, cutting employment costs by 10 to 40 per cent.'[154] Furthermore, as a result of having been engaged under a number of short-term contracts, the CAFOD report points out, 'workers with many periods of short employment find it difficult to acquire the right to a pension or to housing benefits', or even to holidays and compassionate leave.[155] Those who are terminated are ineligible for 'length of service' payments to which permanent workers are entitled.[156]

The Problem of Enforcement: Misclassification and Inadequate Resources

The legal scope of labour protections is, of course, only as good as the mechanisms which enforce them—and poor enforcement is a problem identified by workers' advocates in all three countries as a major contributor to the growth of non-standard work. As Arthurs notes in his Federal Labour Standards Review, completed in 2006:

---

[152] 'Autoridades ejecutoras, negación de amparo contra ordenadoras. Amparo Directo 382/88. Instituto Mexicano del Seguro Social.' Segundo Tribunal Colegiado del Sexto Circuito, Octava Época, *Semanario Judicial de la Federación*, Tomo XIV, Agosto de 1994, p 312, Registro No 2079.
[153] CAFOD Report (n 58) 23, 27.
[154] ibid 26.
[155] ibid 28.
[156] ibid 26.

Compliance may be the single most important issue confronting this review. To put the matter succinctly, if employers do not comply with Part III [of the *Canada Labour Code*],[157] if workers do not receive the protections it promises, if government is not prepared to ensure that it is having the intended results, there is not much point in having labour standards legislation at all.[158]

Because of the pervasive nature of the problem of enforcement, this section will approach the issue thematically, rather than regionally.

While some workers enter into self-employment understanding the legal consequences, many others do so in ignorance of the fact that they have been classified as 'independent contractors', the ramifications of such a classification, or their rights under the law. Even where workers are informed of their classification, inequality in bargaining power may result in the worker accepting unfavourable work terms. The problem of 'disguised work relationships', or misclassification, has thus become a common one.

In the United States, the case of *Vizcaino v Microsoft*, described above, is paradigmatic. In that case, Microsoft misinformed its employees that they were independent contractors, requiring them to sign an agreement stating that 'as independent contractors to Microsoft, [they were] responsible to pay all their own insurance benefits.'[159] The Internal Revenue Service, however, had classified the workers as employees, pursuant to both the 'agency', ie control test, and the 'economic realities' test.[160] The workers brought a class action suit which Microsoft ultimately settled out of court. In the course of long and complicated litigation, however, the United States Court of Appeals in San Francisco held that as many as 15,000 temporary agency workers assigned to Microsoft in specified positions were 'presumptively' common law employees of Microsoft and were therefore 'presumptively' entitled to receive retroactive benefits under the company's employee stock purchase plan.

Disguised employment practices are also common in Mexico. Although article 20 of the LFT specifically provides that the existence of a contract of employment is not contingent on 'its form or denomination', precisely in order to address the common employer practice of disguising employment relationships, this provision has proven to be ineffective. As Mexican labour lawyer Carlos de Buen Unna asserts, it is common for a contract of employment to be given 'other names such as a

---

157 Federal labour law in Canada is largely contained in the Canada Labour Code. Part I deals with industrial relations, Part II with health and safety, and Part III with labour standards.

158 Arthurs Report (n 15) 190.

159 FL Perkins, '*Vizcaino v Microsoft Corp.*: Are Independent Contractors Eligible for Employee Benefits?' (1997–1998) 21 *American Journal of Trial Advocacy* 205, 206.

160 *Vizcaino v Microsoft* 120 F3d 1010 (Ninth Cir 1997).

contract for the provision of professional services, a commercial agency contract or even a joint venture agreement, with a view to feigning [the existence of] less constraining relationships than the employment relationship.'[161] For example, home work—which has been on the rise in recent years in economic sectors related to exports—is often disguised as a contract for sale of supplies and purchase of finished products.[162] Similarly, it is an ingrained practice among public sector employers to hire workers on contract for the provision of professional services even though such workers are not professionals, or the job may not be one that only a professional can perform. According to Claudia de Buen Unna, this arrangement 'has been ratified by federal labour tribunals in their decisions, even though it is contrary to the fundamental principles governing the Mexican legal system.'[163]

To combat the problem of disguised relationships, Arthurs argues that not only should the Canadian government clearly define who is an employee for the purposes of labour protections, but also that legislation should be passed requiring employers to notify workers of their status—employee, autonomous worker, or independent contractor—in writing. If no such notice is provided, the worker would be presumed to be an employee. Furthermore, it would be a violation of the Canada Labour Code for an employer to exercise coercion or use misrepresentation or undue influence in order to obtain a worker's consent to a particular status.[164]

To a limited degree, this kind of 'legal presumption' of employee status is already in use in Mexico, insofar as the LFT establishes that the provision of work is sufficient to create an employment relationship, even if the employee does not have complete knowledge of the terms and conditions of employment or the identity of the employer, and regardless of whether the employer intends the interaction to give rise to an employment relationship.[165] The absence of a written contract of employment 'does not deprive the employee of the rights derived from the labour rules and the services rendered, since the lack of formality shall be imputed to the employer.'[166]

---

[161] C de Buen Unna, *Ley Federal del Trabajo, comentada* (Mexico City, Themis, 2000) 21 [translated by Hugo Leal-Neri], cited in Charis (n 101) 222.

[162] SR Lugo, 'La relación de trabajo, mercado de trabajo, protección, equidad y adaptabilidad. Cuestionario para la preparación del informe nacional' (August 2006) at 8, online: OIT, Centro Internacional de Formación, http://training.itcilo.org/americas/relacion_trabajo/doc_base/CUESTIONARIOS/MEX%20Rodriguez.pdf. Art 312 of the *LFT* attempts to address this problem by stating: 'The agreement whereby an employer sells raw materials or objects to a worker, for the worker to transform or manufacture at home and later sell to the same employer, and any other similar agreement or operation, constitutes home work.' [translated by Hugo Leal-Neri].

[163] C de Buen Unna, 'El contrato de prestación de servicios profesionales, vía de fraude laboral', in Kurczyn and Puig (n 101) 168.

[164] Arthurs Report (n 15) 66.

[165] F Arciniega, 'El Contrato de Trabajo', in Kurczyn and Puig (n 101) 85.

[166] LFT (n 3) art 26.

Another protective measure built into Mexican labour law consists of restrictions on when an employer can use fixed-term contracts. Under the LFT, for example, employment relationships are deemed to be indefinite unless the parties contract for a specific term.[167] Moreover, pursuant to article 37 of the LFT, the parties are allowed to enter into a contract of employment for a fixed or predetermined period of time only in the following circumstances:

— where the nature of the work to be provided requires it;
— where the purpose of the employment relationship is to temporarily replace another worker;
— where the purpose of the employment relationship is to exploit mines without profitable minerals or to restore abandoned or paralysed mines (art 38 LFT);
— in the agricultural, livestock raising, or forestry industries (art 280 LFT); or
— in any other instances where the LFT allows it.

Such restrictions function, at least on paper, to limit employer use of fixed-term contracts to avoid hiring permanent employees. Despite these protective provisions, however, the fashioning of contracts for a specified term is a pervasive employer practice in Mexico. For instance, fixed-term contracts are part and parcel of human resources practices in Guadalajara's electronics industry. The electronics sector is the most volatile in that city: 'This is partly due to the instability of the sector, with all the hiring and firing that goes on as big orders, or even entire companies, come and go.'[168] Electronics workers are vulnerable and are not unionized. The majority are poor, young women between the ages of 18 and 25; many of them are single mothers.[169] They are generally employed on consecutive short-term contracts of between 28 days and three months, and may remain on such contracts for several years.[170] The CAFOD report on the electronics industry in Guadalajara found that such short-term contracts are particularly harmful to women, 'because they are used as a mechanism to avoid paying maternity benefits: when a woman becomes pregnant, her contract is simply not renewed.'[171] The LFT provides that upon expiry of a fixed-term contract of employment, the employment relationship will continue for as long as the object of the work subsists.[172] Of course, this provision presupposes that the fixed-term contract of employment has been entered into in compliance with the LFT.

---

[167] ibid art 35.
[168] CAFOD Report (n 58 at 26.
[169] ibid 23.
[170] ibid 26.
[171] ibid.
[172] LFT (n 3) art 39.

Enforcement of existing labour standards laws is also severely hampered in Canada, the United States and Mexico by inadequate resources, together with a generalized lack of political will. A report on unregulated work in New York City, for example, notes that the number of workplace investigations by the US Department of Labor declined by 14 per cent between 1975 and 2004, at the same time as the number of covered workers grew by 55 per cent and the number of covered establishments grew by 112 per cent.[173] The report notes that this weakening of enforcement is not only a matter of inadequate staffing, but also a lack of administrative will:

> . . . between 1996 and 2004 . . ., the agency was settling workers' claims for less than what the workers were owed, as well as failing to seek full penalties available under the law. Additional problems . . . include: failure to investigate a full workplace when an individual complaint is received; multi-year delays in pursuing and processing claims; lack of translation services so that immigrant workers can file complaints; and in general, waiting for complaints to be filed instead of aggressively investigating low-wage industries . . .[174]

Penalties for employers who violate labour standards are generally weak and criminal sanctions are rarely pursued.[175]

In his 2006 Federal Labour Standards Review, Harry Arthurs notes that in the federal employment sector in Canada, there is a 'significant discrepancy between the very low level of formal complaints and findings of violation on the one hand, and widespread self-reported non-compliance on the other.'[176] This discrepancy, he suggests, is largely due to under-reporting of labour standards violations:

> Workers may not complain because they are ignorant of their rights under Part III, because they fear employer reprisals, or because they lack the stamina or means to pursue their remedies. Difficulties within the enforcement agency may compound the problem. Understaffing may slow the response time of inspectors and lead them to focus on resolving individual complaints, rather than taking the initiative to seek out non-compliance or trying to eradicate systemic patterns of violation. Lack of appropriate legal powers may hamper their search for evidence, and awkward legislative language may make it difficult for them to prove violations. Such difficulties may not only dissuade complainants from coming forward, but may also tempt employers to ignore the law as they take note of the long odds against being caught.[177]

---

[173] Brennan Center for Justice (n 15) 31.
[174] ibid 32.
[175] ibid.
[176] Arthurs Report (n 15) 192.
[177] ibid.

Relying on formal complaints may also skew our perception of the nature of the violations. For example, Arthurs found that 92 per cent of all complaints under Part III of the Canada Labour Code were filed by workers who were no longer employed in the same workplace, suggesting that 'some workers are so concerned that they will be fired that they abandon their statutory rights.'[178] Furthermore, formal complaints tend to relate to key conditions of work, such as non-payment of wages, benefits or overtime. Yet survey evidence suggests that a much broader range of violations of the Canada Labour Code occur, such as failure to comply with vacation entitlements, failure to provide overtime compensation rather than time off, and failure to establish a sexual harassment policy, as required by law.[179]

In Mexico, a lack of resources is also exacerbated by the large number of micro-enterprises. In 1993, for example, 22,546 garment manufacturing centres were registered, 73 per cent of which had two employees or less.[180] In a study of the garment industry in the three NAFTA countries, the Commission for Labor Cooperation made the following observations regarding the effectiveness of labour inspections when faced with a great number of small establishments:

> The large number of establishments makes it more difficult for public inspectors to verify compliance with labor standards through on-site visits. In fact, given the number of inspectors employed by governments to oversee compliance with labor legislation, the probability of a company being inspected decreases with the number of establishments and firms existing in the industry. It is therefore important that this aspect of administration of the labor laws be reinforced by other measures which appeal to the dynamic strengths of the industry.[181]

In 1995, the US Department of Labor adopted a new approach to labour inspections, which some would argue is a model worth considering for Mexico. This approach is aimed at 'getting the major industry players to cooperate actively in achieving ongoing compliance with labor standards' by making compliance with labour standards 'part of the normal business relationship between manufacturers and contractors as well as between contractors and major retailers.'[182] That expectation is turned into a contractual obligation through the signing of two sets of contracts: one between the Department of Labor and the clothing manufacturers,

---

[178] ibid 192–93.

[179] ibid 193.

[180] Commission for Labor Cooperation, '"Standard" and "Advanced" Practices in the North American Garment Industry' (2000) 40–41, online: www.naalc.org/english/pdf/study3.pdf ('North American Garment Industry').

[181] ibid 26.

[182] ibid 23.

and the other between the manufacturers and their contractors. The contract between the Department of Labor and the manufacturer typically imposes the following obligations on the manufacturer or user enterprise:

— to include a set of specific labor standards in its written agreement with its contractors;
— to require its contractors to submit regular reports to the manufacturer;
— to conduct an assessment of a contractor prior to giving that contractor an initial order: 'In particular, the manufacturer and the contractor must assess the contractor's ability to deliver the order at the agreed-upon price while complying with labor standards';
— to visit its contractors' sites 'to audit their books and ensure that their accounting records reflect what is actually going on in their factories. The manufacturer must also have discussions with the contractors' employees'; and
— to alert the Department of Labor when violations of labour standards are discovered.[183]

Of course, compliance with these provisions itself requires monitoring.

While Mexico has perhaps some of the most comprehensive labour protections in its Constitution and national labour laws, enforcement of these protections is severely hindered by the lack of neutral, independent labour bodies. Charges of corruption, bias and lack of independence are recurrently levelled against conciliation and arbitration boards at both the federal and the local levels, as well as at the Labour Inspectorate (*Inspección del Trabajo*), a department within the Ministry of Labour.[184] Members of Mexico's political opposition have argued that the independence of the Labour Inspectorate will be compromised until an autonomous, independent, and impartial Federal Institute for Labour Inspection is created. In the preamble to a private member's bill calling for the establishment of an independent institution, opposition party member Franco Hernández declared that in Mexico 'the Labour Inspectorate has been reduced to almost zero importance due to corruption, lack of professionalism, lack of resources, and partiality in the performance of their duties: the employers pretend to comply and the labour authorities pretend to inspect.'[185]

---

[183] ibid 26.
[184] LFT (n 3) art 540(I).
[185] 'Iniciativa con proyecto de decreto por el que se adiciona un último párrafo a la fracción XXXI del apartado A del artículo 123 de la Ley Fundamental, así como se reforman y derogan diversas disposiciones de la Ley Orgánica de la Administración Pública Federal, de la Ley Federal del Trabajo y de la Ley del Seguro Social, presentada por el diputado Pablo Franco Hernández, del grupo parlamentario del PRD, en la sesión de la Comisión Permanente del miércoles 21 de junio de 2006', Gaceta Parlamentaria 2036 (26 June 2006) 2, online: Senado de la República, www.senado.gob.mx/iilsen/docs/reforma_estado/1_6_gar_soc/art_123/in_123_260606d.doc [translated by Hugo Leal-Neri].

In 2001 the independent National Union of Workers (*Unión Nacional de Trabajadores*, UNT) presented a proposal for the amendment of the LFT to then-Minister of Labour Carlos Abascal. In particular, the UNT proposed that federal and local conciliation and arbitration boards be replaced by federal judges specialized in labour law. An amendment of this sort would transfer the locus of the administration of labour justice from the executive to the judicial power. This proposal would promote greater consistency in decision-making, as well as the professionalization of labour adjudicators, their clerks and staff.[186]

7.4 Reregulating the Employment Relationship

Since the growth of non-standard work was first identified in the 1980s, legislators, academics and labour activists have debated a range of new approaches to the regulation of labour. As conventional regimes of employment have broken down, the disjunction between statutory models of employment and the nature of work 'on the ground' has become increasingly clear. Faced with the pressing question of how to provide broader access to labour protections, policymakers have been faced with a series of questions: what are the appropriate criteria for determining entitlement to the rights and benefits traditionally associated with the employment relationship? Should the employment contract remain a central axis for the regulation of work, or should labour law be replaced by a broader, more comprehensive 'social law'? What is the relationship between regulation and labour market change? What is the appropriate balance between employer 'flexibility' and employee security, and how can this be achieved?

The debate has largely centred around the utility of maintaining the employment contract as the 'platform'[187] for the provision of social welfare benefits.[188] British scholar Mark Freedland, for example, suggests shifting our focus from the contract of employment to the 'personal work contract' to determine the worker's level of subordination or autonomy, and, by implication, the necessity and/or

---

[186] Unión Nacional de Trabajadores, 'Carta a Lic. Abascal: Reformas a la Constitución en materia laboral' (30 July 2001), online: Unión Nacional de Trabajadores, www.unt.org.mx/lft/antref.htm.

[187] This term is a metaphor for the relationship between conventional models of employment and the provision of social welfare benefits: B Langille, 'Labour Policy in Canada—New Platform, New Paradigm' (2002) 28 *Canadian Public Policy* 133 ('Langille'). For a discussion of the historical development of the employment contract from master and servant law in common law countries, see Fudge, Tucker and Vosko, 2003 (n 15) 18–29.

[188] Fudge, Tucker and Vosko, 2003 (n 15); *Langille* (n 187); and *Deakin* (n 15).

relevance of statutory employment protections.[189] By examining each individual's 'personal work nexus', Freedland aims to develop a regulatory framework which can take into account the movement between, or overlap of, different work arrangements, including voluntary and unpaid work commitments, and which more accurately accounts for the non-contractual nature of some arrangements. French jurist Alain Supiot has advocated a test for granting social rights based on a more fluid conception of occupational status, rather than categorical conceptions like 'employee' or 'self-employed'. In his widely distributed report on the future of labour law in Europe,[190] Supiot advocates recognizing 'work' as a broad concept defined more by social utility than by compensation, including non-standard forms of work such as rearing children or volunteer activities. To facilitate the movement from one occupational status to another, Supiot suggests establishing a series of 'social drawing rights', such as time savings accounts, unemployment assistance and training vouchers, which individuals could draw upon to facilitate transitions in labour force membership.

A 'lifecycle' approach has also been urged by many European policymakers, although with a greater emphasis on increasing workforce 'flexibility'. The thrust of the 'flexicurity' model is to pair weaker job security regulations with strong short-term unemployment insurance and training programmes, on the premise that it is through well-designed unemployment benefit systems that transitions between workplaces can be smoothed out.[191] As others have pointed out, however, the danger in this approach is that in many cases 'flexibility proceeds apace, but security remains a rhetorical gesture.'[192] The result may be an increasingly precarious

---

[189] According to Freedland, this can be determined through an assessment of the continuity, mutuality or bindingness of the work arrangement, the 'personality' or substitutability of the worker, and the purpose or mode of the contractual relationship. By 'personality' or 'personal-ness', Freedland refers to the degree to which the work contract 'insists, and in practice ensures, that performance of the work or provision of the services or securing of the outcome in question be carried out by the contracting person him or herself.' M Freedland, 'From the Contract of Employment to the Personal Work Nexus' (2006) 35 *Industrial Law Journal* 1, 10–11, 14–15. See also M Freedland, 'Application of labour and employment law beyond the contract of employment' (2007) 146 *International Labour Review* 1–2 and, more recently, Freedland and Kountouris (n 15) 49–74.

[190] A Supiot, *Beyond Employment: Changes in Work and the Future of Labour Law in Europe* (New York, Oxford University Press, 2005); See, also, A Supiot, 'Au-delà de l'emploi: transformations du travail et devenir du droit du travail en Europe : rapport pour la Commission des communautés européennes avec la collaboration de l'Université Carlos III de Madrid' (Paris, Flammarion, 1999).

[191] For one articulation of the flexicurity approach, see for instance, Commission (EC), 'Modernising Labour Law to Meet the Challenges of the 21st Century' (Green Paper) COM 79 final, 22 November 2006. Online: http://ec.europa.eu/employment_social/labour_law/docs/2006/green_paper_en.pdf.

[192] S Fredman, 'Women at Work: The Broken Promise of Flexicurity' (2004) 33 *Industrial Law Journal* 299. Fredman further points out that the flexicurity model undermines the traditional exchange between employer and employee: 'An employment relationship which gives the worker the apparent freedom to choose not to take on a particular task at a particular time, need not give rise to responsibilities on the part of the employer.' See also S Fredman, 'Precarious Norms for Precarious Workers' in J Fudge and R Owens (eds), *Precarious Work, Women and the New Economy* (Oxford, Hart, 2006) 177.

workforce. For this reason, some labour advocates argue that the basic exchange at the heart of the employment relationship—subordination in return for security—has broken down to such a degree that the workplace is no longer an appropriate mechanism for the assignment of rights and entitlements. On this view, social welfare benefits should be disaggregated from the workplace entirely, and replaced by universal, state-administered programmes centred around other kinds of status such as citizenship or residency. In its most radical form, this approach advocates the establishment of a state-secured minimum income, thereby removing the provision of social welfare entitlements from employment status altogether.[193]

In practice, however, employment status often continues to influence the distribution of social welfare benefits. In the province of Quebec, for example, the only jurisdiction in North America which has established a 'universal' drug insurance plan, if an individual's workplace offers membership in a private drug plan, the individual is required to enter into that plan.[194] This kind of hybrid model has particular appeal to governments because it provides a means of ensuring universal access to social benefits while taking into account limited public resources. However, because such hybrid programmes reflect differences in employment opportunities, a disparity in benefit levels may persist between private benefit programmes available at the workplace and those provided by state-administered programmes.

Given the seemingly inevitable link between work and the distribution of social benefits, a third proposal for the extension of labour protections to non-standard workers is to improve access to collective representation and collective bargaining for non-standard workers. Rather than depend on government-implemented statutory reforms, some labour experts argue that it is only by decreasing the power imbalance between workers and employers that working conditions will be improved.[195] Such an approach faces significant difficulties on the

---

[193] See, for instance, A Jeammaud, cited in Vallée (n 9) 4.

[194] s 16 of An Act respecting prescription drug insurance, RSQ, c A-29.01 provides: 'All eligible persons … who by reason of current or former employment status, profession or habitual occupation qualify for membership in a group to which a group insurance contract or employee benefit plan including coverage for the cost of pharmaceutical services and medications applies, must become members of that group for at least the basic plan coverage.' See also Vallée (n 9) 5–6.

[195] Guylaine Vallée, for example, envisions an enhanced system of collective representation which stitches together a collective representation framework for self-employed and other non-standard workers, and the increased use of judicial power to extend collective agreements to a given occupational field or geographic area. See Vallée (n 9) 39.

ground, however, given the considerable legal and structural barriers to the extension of collective representational rights in the United States and Mexico, and to a lesser extent in Canada.[196]

Faced with the exclusion of increasingly large numbers of 'non-standard workers' from labour protections, one obvious reform is to expand the definition of 'employee' to include those workers who need the benefit of labour protections. This may, as Arthurs proposes, require the recognition of a new category of 'autonomous workers' who bear some of the outward indicia of autonomy, but who function in many ways as employees. It may also involve the extension of labour standards protections to those who work on a less than full-time basis, or to temporary workers where they function as employees of the client company. Pursuant to the Saskatchewan Labour Standards Act, for example, employers must give pro-rated benefits to part-time workers where they provide benefits to those working full-time hours, if a qualifying period is satisfied.[197] The Yukon Employment Standards Act includes 'contract workers'[198] within its definition of employee,[199] thereby extending its labour standards protections to these non-standard workers.

A view that is gaining increasing support in all three countries is that statutory definitions of 'employee' should be expanded to take into account the economic dependence of the worker. As noted, the US Dunlop Commission recommended in 1992 the adoption of the 'economic realities' test for the determination of employee status for all federal regulations, thereby putting the economic dependence of the

---

[196] In Mexico, for example, while the right to unionize is enshrined in the Mexican constitution and the LFT states that workers have the right to form a union, trade unions and their leaders are required to register with the Ministry of Labour or the relevant Conciliation and Arbitration Board in a procedure known as 'taking note' (*toma de nota*). Recognition by the labour authority may be denied if prescribed requirements are not fulfilled. This procedure may result in abuse where labour authorities favour the registration of government-controlled unions, or engage in the politically motivated cancellation of a union's registration. Furthermore, workers' freedom to unionize may be hampered by the widespread employer practice of 'protection contracts', namely collective agreements entered into with unrepresentative trade unions in exchange for a monthly or annual fee. See *Constitucion Politica de los Estados Unidos Mexicanos* art 123 A XVI; LFT arts 357, 365–70.

[197] Labour Standards Act, Revised Statutes of Saskatchewan 1978, c L-1 ss 45.1, 84(1)(e.8); and Labour Standards Regulations 1995 ss 25–26. In his Federal Labour Standards Review, Professor Arthurs recommends that part-time workers in federal jurisdiction—of whom there are 100,000, or 12% of the federally regulated workforce—should receive the same pay as full-time workers with equivalent jobs. See Arthurs Report (n 15) 237.

[198] s 1(1) of the Yukon's Employment Standards Act defines 'contract worker' as 'a worker, whether or not employed under a contract of employment, and whether or not furnishing tools, vehicles, equipment, machinery, material, or any other thing owned by the worker, who performs work or services for another person for compensation or reward on such terms and conditions that:
(a) the worker is in a position of economic dependence on, and under an obligation to perform duties for, that person, and
(b) the relationship between the worker and that person more closely resembles the relationship of employee to employer than the relationship of an independent contractor to a principal or of one independent contractor to another independent contractor.

[199] Employment Standards Act, Revised Statutes of the Yukon 2002 c 72 s 1(1).

worker at the heart of labour protections. In Mexico, as in other Latin American countries, academics and practitioners have vigorously proposed the concepts of economic dependence, economic subordination and parasubordination as criteria complementary to legal subordination.[200] One author has argued that, in those situations where it is difficult to establish the existence of legal subordination, 'the case is easily solved by finding economic dependence, provided that the remuneration ... is earned in consideration for a typical and simple provision of personal services.'[201] Similarly, parasubordination—as the partial or indirect subordination of an economic character—is suitable for those forms of atypical employment where higher specialization results in a reduced degree of subordination.[202] Nevertheless, these alternative criteria have yet to be embraced by Mexican labour law.

In Canada, the emphasis on economic dependence has led to the recognition of 'dependent contractors' in the collective bargaining legislation of a number of Canadian jurisdictions.[203] However, in a 2002 report to the Law Commission of Canada, Fudge, Tucker and Vosko propose an even broader extension of the definition of employee, suggesting that 'all dimensions of labour regulations should be extended to all workers, defined as persons economically dependent on the sale of their working capacity, unless there is a compelling reason for not doing so.'[204] Under this proposal, not only would employees and dependent contractors be covered, but also those independent contractors who perform the work personally. Only those workers who do not depend on the sale of their 'working capacity' for their survival would be excluded from employment protections.[205]

The 'dependent contractor' approach has more recently been espoused by Stephen Befort and John Budd who, based upon experience in Europe and Canada,

---

[200] Ermida and Hernández (n 114) 290, 292–93, 295–96; and A de los Heros Pérez Albela, 'La frontera entre el trabajo subordinado y el trabajo independiente', in Kurczyn and Puig (n 101) 408, 410, 414.

[201] R Caldera, *Derecho del Trabajo* (Caracas-Buenos Aires, Editorial el Ateneo, 1961) 271, cited in Ermida and Hernández (n 115) 288.

[202] RJ Ortiz Escobar, 'Breves reflexiones sobre el contrato de trabajo', in Kurczyn and Puig (n 101) 594–95.

[203] The idea germinated, in Canada, in an article published by Professor Harry Arthurs in 1965: see HW Arthurs, 'The Dependent Contractor: A Study of the Legal Problems of Countervailing Power' (1965), 16 *University of Toronto Law Journal* 89.

[204] Fudge, Tucker and Vosko, 2002 (n 15) 124.

[205] The Quebec expert committee responsible for studying social protection needs of persons in non-traditional work situations (the 'Bernier Report') makes a similar recommendation, suggesting the following statutory definition for the concept of employee: (1) a person who works for another person in exchange for remuneration; (2) whether this person is salaried or not under an employment contract; (3) and who is obliged to personally do work for that other person in such context or under such terms and conditions that he or she is made economically dependent on that person. J Bernier, G Vallée and C Jobin (the Expert Committee), 'Social Protection Needs of Individuals in Non-Standard Work Situations. Synopsis of Final Report' (2003) 431, online: Ministère du Travail du Québec, www.travail.gouv.qc.ca/actualite/travail_non_traditionnel/Bernier2003/RapBernier7a.pdf ('Bernier Report'). See Vallée (n 9) 9.

advocate the extension of employee protection statutes to 'employee-like' workers in the United States.[206] The approach suggested by Befort and Budd has been adopted in Germany, but is more limited; it treats dependent contractors like employees for certain purposes, by extending to them the protection of those statutes that serve 'core societal goals', such as anti-discrimination statutes and occupational health and safety legislation. However, it would not extend pension or extended health benefits to dependent contractors. In short, while this proposal recognizes the utility of expanding the legal definition of 'employee' to recognize the economic reality that many contractors are, in fact, economically dependent and therefore vulnerable and deserving of employee-like legal protections, it takes a fragmented approach that is likely to be confusing to the workers themselves and therefore harder to enforce.

Ultimately, the question of how to ensure the protection of vulnerable workers is inextricably tied to the question of who should make such a determination. Is this the role of legislatures, through the establishment of new categories of employment or the introduction of universal social benefits? Or is it the purview of courts or administrative tribunals which, through incremental decision-making, may develop appropriate tests more sensitive to the realities of economic relationships on the ground?

The answer will, of course, depend on the particular nature of the labour institutions, culture of labour relations, and legal tradition of each jurisdiction. For example, Professors Freedland and Kountouris note the distinction between the 'regulated self-designed contract' approach associated with liberal market economies, such as the common law-based United Kingdom, and the 'standardized contract typology' approach associated with more interventionist co-ordinated market economies, such as civil law-based Germany and Italy.[207] However, as Freedland and Kountouris acknowledge, citing European experimentation with 'flexicurity' as

---

[206] SF Befort and JW Budd, *Invisible Hands, Invisible Objectives: Bringing Workplace Law & Public Policy Into Focus* (Stanford, Stanford University Press, 2009) 171.

[207] M Freedland and N Kountouris, 'Towards a Comparative Theory of the Contractual Construction of Personal Work Relations in Europe' (2008) 37 *Industrial Law Journal* 49. In this paper, the authors point out 'a divergence, in particular, between institutional versions of the contract of employment in which norms derived from social legislation and/or collective bargaining are strongly integrated into the contract of employment and other versions in which such norms are weakly or superficially integrated.' In their view, this divergence implies a 'dual typology of institutional models of the contract of employment within European states', with one approach giving rise, in Anglo-Saxon common law-based states, to 'regulated self-designed contracts', and the other giving rise to a 'standardized contract typology.' Applying neo-institutional theory, and ideas regarding 'varieties of capitalism', Freedland and Kountouris suggest that the 'regulated self-designed contracts' approach might be considered as an example of the liberal normative regulation associated with 'liberal market economies' and the 'standardized contract typology' approach as an instance of 'the more interventionist or controlling normative regulation associated with co-ordinated market economies.'

an example, legal institutions are not immutable. In Canada, 'institutional adaptability' has been amply demonstrated by the courts in recent decisions involving the constitutional status of collective bargaining. Thus, reversing the position after a 20-year period in which it effectively abstained from oversight of governmental restrictions on labour rights, the Canadian Supreme Court, taking its cue from international law and in particular ILO standards, has applied the guarantee of freedom of association in Canada's Charter of Rights (part of its constitution) to protect workers' rights to bargain collectively.[208] In yet other jurisdictions, representatives of both unions and management have been able to come together to develop a consensual 'code of good practice' regarding the definition of employee.[209]

In this regard, international norms are of significance. The International Labour Conference of the ILO moved in 2006 to adopt Employment Relationship Recommendation No 198, urging Member States to 'guarantee effective protection for workers who perform work in the context of an employment relationship', and advising that national policies should include measures to, among other things, 'combat disguised employment relationships' that hide the true legal status of employees, given that 'situations can arise where contractual arrangements have the effect of depriving workers of the protections they are due.'[210]

---

[208] For example, in *Dunmore v Ontario* (n 40), when the Ontario provincial government sought to exclude agricultural workers from legislation protecting the right to collective representation and collective bargaining, the Supreme Court of Canada struck down the relevant legislation, finding that it violated the workers' constitutionally-protected right to freedom of association. More recently, in *Health Services and Support—Facilities Subsector Bargaining Assn. v British Columbia* 2007 SCC 27, the Supreme Court struck down British Columbia legislation curtailing a union's right to collectively bargain protections against contracting out the work of hospital support staff.

[209] See, for example, the South African *Code of Good Practice: Who is An Employee*, 498 Government Gazette No 29445 (Notice 1774, December 1, 2006). See also the Irish *Code of Practice for Determining Employment or Self-Employment Status of Individuals* (Dublin, July 2001): www.entemp.ie.

[210] The Recommendation has been followed by an annotated guide which sets out methods for guiding workers and employers as to the determination of the existence of an employment relationship. See ILO, 'The employment relationship: An annotated guide to ILO Recommendation No. 198', Paper No 18 (March 2008); and see, more generally, A Bronstein (n 82) 44–68. Comparative labour law is also instructive. In Europe, Member States of the European Union have adopted a variety of strategies to deal with the 'economically dependent worker', including 'treating them as employees and therefore falling within the scope of employment protection legislation, extending protection to specified categories of such workers and listing criteria that enable identification of the workers as either employees or self-employed'. Eurofound, 'Economically Dependent Workers', in *European Industrial Relations Dictionary* (Dublin). See also EC Council Directives 97/81/EC on part-time work (December 15, 1997), 99/70/EC on fixed-term work (June 28, 1999), and 2008/104/EC (proposed) on temporary agency work (November 19, 2008). The first two directives provide that part-time and fixed-term workers may not be treated in a less favourable manner than comparable full-time or permanent workers solely because they work part-time or have a fixed-term contract, unless different treatment is justified on objective grounds. The directive on temporary agency work provides that temporary workers assigned to user undertakings should be subject to the same essential working and employment conditions as workers recruited directly by the undertaking.

In the end, given the changing political and economic realities shaping employment relationships, the solution is unlikely to lie in any one particular model or approach. Rather, the extension of labour protections to non-standard workers will require a combination of approaches, involving statutory reform, judicial creativity, and the strengthening of codes of practice and collective bargaining regimes.

7.5 Conclusions

From the foregoing, it may be observed that Canada, the United States and Mexico have all experienced significant growth in various forms of non-standard work. However, while this development is common to all three countries, and has, if anything, accelerated as a result of the deregulation following upon the signing in 1994 of NAFTA, the responses of the legal regimes in the three countries have differed substantially.

In Mexico, with an extensive informal economy beyond the law's reach, the growth in non-standard work has continued unimpeded. Although Mexico exhibits a high degree of labour regulation, the regulatory regime is neutralized by a low level of enforcement of basic labour laws. Moreover, the federal government has repeatedly sought to 'flexibilize' the employment relationship through the introduction of legislative 'reforms' (which have so far failed to obtain the approval of Congress). 'In the United States, whose "liberal market economy" is conducive to a "self-designed contract" approach, prior to the election of the Obama Administration' few initiatives were taken by the federal government to prevent the use of alternative arrangements to avoid employment obligations, and nothing was done by it to clarify the 'grey area' between labour law and commercial law created by the expansion of 'economically dependent' work. However, on 22 April 2010, the Employee Misclassification Prevention Act (EMPA) was jointly introduced in the Senate and the House. The Act will, among other things, require records to be kept of non-employees who perform labour or services for remuneration and will impose a penalty for the misclassification of employees as non-employees.

Of particular interest in this respect is Canada. A liberal market economy, but possessed of a tradition of progressive labour legislation and openness to international norms, it has pioneered in extending collective bargaining rights to economically 'dependent contractors.' Indeed, a recent report by noted labour law scholar Harry Arthurs on federal labour standards amounts to a virtual blueprint for legislative action to remedy the problems associated with vulnerable workers. Not only does it recommend the establishment of a new category of 'autonomous workers' who would be entitled to labour standards protection, but it also urges enhanced protections for part-time, temporary, disabled, younger and older workers. The Arthurs Report is currently under consideration by the government of the day, but regardless of the immediate outcome—the current Conservative government is likely to be unreceptive—it is probable, if not inevitable, that at some point many of its recommendations will find their way into legislation.

Bibliography

Addison, JT and Surfield, CJ, 'Atypical Work and Pay' (2007) 73(4) *Southern Economic Journal*, 1038–1065.

Alonso, O, *Introducción al Derecho del Trabajo*, 5th edn (Madrid, Civitas, 1994).

Arthurs, HW, 'The Dependent Contractor: A Study of the Legal Problems of Countervailing Power' (1965) 16 *The University of Toronto Law Journal*, 89–117.

—— *Fairness at Work: Federal Labour Standards for the 21st Century* (Human Resources and Skills Development Canada, 2006), online: http://www.hrsdc.gc.ca/eng/labour/employment_standards/fls/pdf/final_report.pdf.

Asakura, M, *Workers' Protection in Japan* (Geneva, ILO, 1999) available at http://www.ilo.org/public/english/dialogue/ifpdial/downloads/wpnr/japan.pdf.

Autor, D, 'Outsourcing at will: The contribution of unjust dismissal doctrine to the growth of employment outsourcing' (2003) 21(1) *Journal of Labor Economics*, 1–42.

Ballestrero, MV, 'L'ambigua nozione di lavoro parasubordinato', (1987) *Lavoro e diritto*, 41.

Barbagelata, H, 'El futuro del Derecho del Trabajo', X Congreso Iberoamericano de Derecho del Trabajo y de la Seguridad Social, Montevideo, 1989.

—— *Derecho del Trabajo*, 3rd edn (Montevideo, FCU, 1999) book 1, vol 2.

Barrett, J, *Organising in the informal economy: A Case Study of the Mini-bus Taxi Industry in South Africa* (Geneva, ILO, 2003).

de Barros, AM, *Curso de Direito do Trabalho,* 2nd edn, (Sao Paolo, LTR, 2006).

Befort, SF, 'The Regulatory Void of Contingent Work' (2006) 10 *Employee Rights and Employment Policy Journal* 233.

—— and Budd, JW, *Invisible Hands, Invisible Objectives: Bringing Workplace Law and Public Policy Into Focus* (Stanford, Stanford University Press, 2009).

Benjamin, P, 'An Accident of History: Who Is (and Who Should Be) an Employee under South African Labour Law' (2004) 25 *Industrial Law Journal* 791.

—— 'Beyond the Boundaries: Prospects for Expanding Labour Market Regulation in South Africa' in G Davidov and B Langille (eds), *Boundaries and Frontiers of Labour Law: Goals and Means in the Regulation of Work* (Oxford, Hart, 2006).

Bennett, M, *Organising in the informal economy: A Case Study of the Clothing Industry in South Africa* (Geneva, ILO, 2003).

Bernhardt, A, McGrath, S and DeFilippis, J, 'Unregulated Work in the Global City: Employment and Labor Law Violations in New York City' (2007) online: Brennan Center for Justice at New York University School of Law, http://www.brennancenter.org/dynamic/subpages/download_file_49436.pdf.

Bernier, MJ et al, 'Les Besoins de Protection Sociale des Personnes en Situation de Travail non Traditionnelle' (2003), available at http://www.travail.gouv.qc.ca/actualite/travail_non_traditionnel/Bernier2003/BernierReportChap4.pdf.

Blanchard, O and Tirole, J *Protection de l'emploi et procédures de licenciement* (Paris, La Documentation française 2003) available at http://lesrapports.ladocumentationfrancaise.fr/BRP/034000592/0000.pdf.

Bologna, S, and Fumagalli, A, *Il lavoro autonomo di seconda generazione* (Milano, Feltrinelli, 1997).

Bibliography

Borzaga, M, 'Subordinazione e diritto della sicurezza sociale: le riforme fallite nella Repubblica Federale Tedesca', (2002) *Diritto delle Relazioni Industriali*, 655–683.

Bosh, R, 'Who is an Employee' (2003) 3(18) *Labour Law Updates* 1, available at http://www.law.wits.ac.za/cals/2003.vol.3%20no.18.pdf.

Brassey, M, 'The Nature of Employment' (1990) 18 *Industrial Law Journal*.

—— *Employment and Labour Law* (Cape Town, Juta, 1997).

Bronstein, A, *International and Comparative Labour Law: Current Challenges*, (Geneva, ILO/Palgrave Macmillan, 2009).

Buckley, GJ and Casale, G, *Social Dialogue and Poverty Reduction Strategies* (Geneva, ILO, 2006).

Cahuc P and Kramarz, F, *De la précarité à la mobilité : vers une Sécurité sociale professionnelle* (Paris, La Documentation française 2004), available at http://lesrapports.ladocumentationfrancaise.fr/BRP/054000092/0000.pdf.

Campbell, B, 'Backsliding: The Impact of NAFTA on Canadian Workers', Economic Policy Institute, N.22 (2006).

Campbell, I, 'Australia: Institutional changes and workforce fragmentation' in S Lee and F Eyraud (eds), *Globalization, flexibilization and working conditions in Asia and the Pacific*, (Geneva, ILO/Chandos, 2008).

Carinci F, De Luca Tamajo R, Tosi T and Treu T, *Diritto del lavoro, 2 – Il rapporto di lavoro subordinato*, (Torino, Utet, 2006).

Casale, G and Arrigo, G, *Glossary of Labour Law and Industrial Relations* (Geneva, ILO, 2005).

Chandran, R, *Employment Law in Singapore,* 2nd edn (Singapore, LexisNexis, 2008).

Cheadle, H and Clarke, M, 'National Studies on Worker's Protection: South Africa', Paper prepared for Meeting of Experts on Workers in need of Protection, Geneva, 2000.

Clarke, S, Lee, C-H and Do Quynh Chi, 'From Rights to Interests: The Challenge of Industrial Relations in Vietnam' (2007) 49 *Journal of Industrial Relations* 545.

Coase, RH, 'The Nature of the Firm' (1937) 4 *Economica* (NS) 386.

Cobo, S, 'Clean Up Your Computer: Working Conditions in the Electronics Sector' (January 2004), online: CAFOD, http://www.cafod.org.uk/var/storage/original/application/phpYyhizc.pdf.

Collins N, 'Economic reform and unemployment in Vietnam' in J Benson and Y Zhu (eds), *Unemployment in Asia* (London, Routledge, 2005).

—— and Zhu Y, 'Vietnam's Labour Policies Reform' (2003) in Frost S et al, (eds), *Asia Pacific Labour Law Review: Workers' Rights for the New Century*, Hong Kong: Asia Monitor Resource Center Ltd, 375–388.

Cooney S, et al (eds), *Law and Labour Market Regulation in East Asia* (London, Routledge, 2002).

Córdova, E, *Evolución del Pensamiento Juslaboralista—Estudios en Homenaje al Prof Héctor-Hugo Barbagelata, 'El papel de la industrialización y el principio de subordinación en la evolución de la legislación laboral'*, (Montevideo, FCU, 1997).

Cosmópolis, MP 'Contratos de trabajo, economía informal y empresas de mano de obra', in PK Villalobos (ed), *Décimocuarto encuentro iberoamericano de derecho del trabajo* (México, UNAM, 2006) online: Instituto de Investigaciones Jurídicas de la UNAM, Biblioteca Jurídica, http://www.bibliojuridica.org/libros/4/1950/7.pdf.

Creighton and Mitchell, R, 'The Contract of Employment in Australian Labour Law' in L Betten (ed), *The Employment Contract in Transforming Labour Relations* (The Hague, Kluwer, 1995).

Davidov, G, 'Who is a Worker?' (2005) 34 *Industrial Law Journal*, 57–71.

—— 'The Reports of My Death are Greatly Exaggerated: "Employee" as a Viable (Though Overly-Used) Legal Concept', in G Davidov and B Langille (eds), *Boundaries and Frontiers of Labour Law: Goals and Means in the Regulation of Work* (Oxford, Hart, 2006), available at http://papers.ssrn.com/sol3/papers.cfm?abstract_id=783484.

Davies, ACL, *Perspectives on Labour Law* (Cambridge, Cambridge University Press, 2004).

Davies, P and Freedland, M, *Towards a Flexible Labour Market: Labour, Legislation and Regulation since the 1990s* (Oxford, Oxford University Press, 2007).

De Stefano, V, *Smuggling-in flexibility: temporary work contracts and 'the implicit threat' mechanism Reflections on a new European path* (Geneva, ILO, 2009), LAB/ADMIN working document No 4.

Deakin, S, 'The Many Futures of the Contract of Employment' (2001) CBR Working Paper No 191, December 2001, available at http://www.cbr.cam.ac.uk/pdf/wp191.pdf.

—— 'The Many Futures of the Contract of Employment', in J Conaghan, M Fischl and K Klare (eds), *Labour Law in an Era of Globalization: Transformative Practices and Possibilities* (Oxford, Oxford University Press, 2002).

—— 'Autonomia, subordinazione e lavoro economicamente dipendente' (2004) *Diritto delle relazioni industriali* 599.

—— and Morris, G, *Labour Law* (London, Routledge, 2001).

—— and Wilkinson, F, *The Law of the Labour Market: Industrialization, Employment and Legal Evolution* (Oxford, Oxford University Press, 2005).

Del Punta, R, 'La scomparsa dei co.co.co.' (2003), available at http://www.lavoce.info/articoli/pagina488.html.

Department of Labour 'Synthesis Report: Changing Nature of Work and "Atypical" forms of Employment in South Africa' (unpublished, Pretoria, 2004).

Edgren, G, *How Different is the SA Labour Market? International Perspectives and Parallels* (HSRC/Sida, 1995).

Ermida Uriarte, O and Hernández Álvarez, O, 'Crítica de la subordinación' (2003) XLV(206) *Revista Derecho Laboral*.

Federal Association of Insurance Intermediaries (BVK), the German Direct Selling Association, the National Federation of German Trade Associations for Commercial Agencies and Distribution (CDH), the German Association of Chambers of Industry and Commerce (DIHK), *Practical experience report on economically dependent work/Parasubordination: Legal, social and economic aspects* (Bonn/Berlin, 2002).

Fenwick, C, 'Shooting for Trouble? Contract Labour-hire in the Victorian Building Industry' (1992) 5 *Australian Journal of Labour Law* 237.

—— 'How Low Can You Go? Minimum Working Conditions Under Australia's New Labour Laws' (2006) 16 *Economic and Labour Relations Review*, 85.

Flammand, FA and Morin, ML, 'L'activité professionnelle indépendante: quelle protection juridique?' (2001) *Le Notes du Lirhe* 6 Also available on http://www.univ-tlse1.fr/lirhe/publications/notes/346–01.pdf.

Forsyth, A, 'The 2006 Independent Contractors Legislation: An Opportunity Missed' (2007) 35 *Federal Law Review*, 328–346.

Fredman, S, 'Women at Work: The Broken Promise of Flexicurity' (2004) 33 *Industrial Law Journal* 299.

Freedland, M, 'The role of the contract of employment in modern labour law', in L Betten (ed), *The Employment Contract in Transforming Labour Relations* (The Hague, Kluwer, 1995).

—— 'Sur l'application du droit du travail et de l'emploi au delà du contrat de travail' (2007) 146(1–2) *Revue Internationale du Travail* 3.

—— *The Personal Employment Contract* (Oxford, Oxford University Press, 2003).

—— 'From the Contract of Employment to the Personal Work Nexus' (2006) 35 *Industrial Law Journal*, 1–29.

Bibliography

—— 'Application of Labour and Employment Law Beyond the Contract of Employment' (2006) *Oxford University Comparative Law Forum* 4, available at http://ouclf.iuscomp.org/articles/freedland.shtml.

—— 'Application of labour and employment law beyond the contract of employment' (2007) *International Labour Review* 146, 3–20.

—— and Countouris, N, 'Towards a Comparative Theory of the Contractual Construction of Personal Work Relations in Europe' (2008) 37(1) *Industrial Law Journal*, 49–74.

Fudge, J, 'The Legal Boundaries of the Employer, Precarious Workers, and Labour Protection' in G Davidov and B Langille (eds) *Boundaries and Frontiers of Labour Law* (Oxford, Hart Publishing, 2006).

—— and Owens, R (eds), *Precarious Work, Women and the New Economy* (Oxford, Hart, 2006).

—— Tucker, E and Vosko, L, *The Legal Concept of Employment: Marginalizing Workers*, (Ottawa, Report for the Law Commission of Canada, 2002).

Fuller, S and Vosko, L, 'Temporary Employment and Social Inequality in Canada: Exploring Intersections of Gender, Race and Immigration Status' (2008) *Social Indicators Research* 88, 31–50.

Garmendia, MM and Burastero, PB 'Trabajadores parasubordinados', in *Cuarenta y dos Estudios sobre la descentralización empresarial y el derecho del trabajo* (Montevideo, FCU, 2000).

Ghera, E, *Diritto del Lavoro* (Bari, Cacucci, 2000).

—— 'Subordinazione, statuto protettivo e qualificazione del rapporto di lavoro' in D Garofalo and M Ricci (eds), *Percorsi di Diritto del Lavoro* (Bari, Cacucci, 2006).

Ghezzi, G, 'Del contratto di agenzia', (1970) *Commentario del Codice Civile* (ed. A. Scialoja and G. Branca) (Bologna-Roma, Zanichelli editore- Soc. ed. del Foro Italiano).

Giugale, MM, Lafourcade, O and Nguyen, VH (eds), *Mexico: A Comprehensive Development Agenda for the New Era* (Washington DC, World Bank, 2001).

Giugni, G, 'Diritto del Lavoro (voce per una enciclopedia)'(1979) 1 *Giornale di Diritto del Lavoro e di Relazioni Industriali*.

Godfrey, S and Clarke, M 'The Basic Conditions of Employment Act amendments: More questions than answers' (2002) 6 *Law Democracy and Development* 1.

—— Maree, J, du Toit, D, and Theron, J, *Collective Bargaining in South Africa: Past, Present and Future* (Cape Town, Juta, 2010).

Goldín, A, 'El concepto de dependencia laboral y las transformaciones productivas' (1996) II(14) *Relaciones Laborales y Seguridad Social*, 131–142.

Goldman, T, *Organizing in the informal economy: A case study of the building industry in South Africa* (Geneva, ILO, 2003).

Goldthorpe, JH, *Social Mobility and Class Structure in Modern Britain* (Oxford, Clarendon Press, 1980).

Gómez, RC, 'El Contrato Individual y la Relación de Trabajo en México', in PK Villalobos and CA Puig Hernández (eds), *Estudios Jurídicos en Homenaje al Doctor Néstor de Buen Lozano* (México, UNAM, 2003), online: Instituto de Investigaciones Jurídicas de la UNAM, Biblioteca Jurídica, http://www.bibliojuridica.org/libros/3/1090/13.pdf.

Grunsky, W, *Arbeitsgerichtsgesetz Kommentar*, 3rd edn (Munich, Verlag F. Vahlen, 1980).

Hepple, B, 'The Future of Labour Law' (1995) 24 *Industrial Law Journal* 305.

Hoeland, A, 'A Comparative Study of the Impact of Electronic Technology on Workplace Disputes: National Report on Germany' (2005) *Comparative Labor Law and Policy Journal*, 147–176.

Houseman, SN, 'Flexible Staffing Arrangements: A Report on Temporary Help, On-Call, Direct-Hire Temporary, Leased, Contract Company, and Independent Contractor Employment in the United States' (August 1999), online: www.dol.gov/oasam/programs/history/herman/reports/futurework/conference/staffing/flexiblehtm.

——— and Osawa, M (eds), *Nonstandard Work in Developed Economies: Causes and Consequences* (New York, Routledge, 2003).

Ichino, P, *Il tempo della prestazione nel rapporto di lavoro*, I (Milano, Giuffrè, 1985).

——— *Il contratto di lavoro* (Milano, Giuffrè, 2003).

International Labour Organization (ILO), 'Contract labour', Report V(1), International Labour Conference, 85th Session (Geneva, 1997).

——— 'Contract labour', Report V(2A), International Labour Conference, 85th Session (Geneva, 1997).

——— 'Contract labour', Report V(2B), International Labour Conference, 85th Session (Geneva, 1997).

———'Contract labour', Report V(1), International Labour Conference, 86th Session (Geneva, 1998).

———'Contract labour', Report V(2A), International Labour Conference, 86th Session (Geneva, 1998).

———'Contract labour', Report V(2B), International Labour Conference, 86th Session (Geneva, 1998).

———'Contract labour', Report V(2B) Addendum, International Labour Conference, 86th Session (Geneva, 1998).

——— 'Report of the Conference, 16th International Conference of Labour Statisticians', document ICLS/16/1998/V, appended to Governing Body document 273/STM/7 (273rd Session, Geneva, November 1998).

———'Country studies on the social impact of globalization: Final report, Working Party on the Social Dimensions of the Liberalization of International Trade', Governing Body document GB.276/WP/SDL/1 (276th Session, Geneva, November 1999).

——— 'Meeting of Experts on Workers in Situations Needing Protection (The employment relationship: Scope)', Basic technical document (Geneva, 2000).

——— 'Report of the Meeting of Experts on Workers in Situations Needing Protection', document MEWNP/2000/4(Rev), appended to Governing Body document GB.279/2 (279th Session, Geneva, November 2000).

———'Decent Work in the Informal Economy', Report VI, International Labour Conference, 90th Session (Geneva, 2002).

———*The Scope of the Employment Relationship* (Geneva, 2003).

———*A Fair Globalization: Creating Opportunities for All,* World Commission on the Social Dimension of Globalization, Final Report (Geneva, 2004).

———'Report of the Working Party on the Social Dimension of Globalization: Overall reactions by the Working Party to the work of the World Commission', Governing Body document GB289/16 (289th Session, Geneva, March 2004).

——— 'Provisional Record No 21', Fifth item on the agenda: The employment relationship (single discussion), Report of the Committee on the Employment Relationship, International Labour Conference, 95th Session (Geneva, 2006).

———Recommendation concerning the employment relationship, International Labour Conference, 95th Session (Geneva, 2006).

———'The Employment Relationship', Report V(1), International Labour Conference, 95th Session (Geneva, 2006).

———'The Employment Relationship', Report V(2A), International Labour Conference, 95th Session (Geneva, 2006).

———'The Employment Relationship', Report V (2B), International Labour Conference, 95th Session (Geneva, 2006).

——— *The Employment Relationship: An annotated guide to ILO Recommendation No 198* (Geneva, 2008).

Bibliography

IRES, 'Il Lavoro Para-Subordinato A Rischio Di Precarietà: tra Scarsa Autonomia, Dipendenza Economica e Mancanza di Prospettive' (2006) available at www.ires.it/files/rapporto_compl_nidil_26ott2006.pdf.

Jackson, A, *Work and Labour in Canada: Critical Issues* (Toronto, Scholars Press, 2005).

Jauch, H, 'Labour Markets in Southern Africa' (Labour Resource and Research Institute, 2004), available at www.larri.com.na/ . . ./Labour%20Markets%20in%20Southern%20Africa.doc.

—— 'Namibia's Labour Hire Debate in Perspective' (Windhoek, Friedrich Ebert Stiftung (FES), 2010).

Jeammaud, A, 'L'avenir sauvegardé de la qualification du contrat de travail : à propos de l'arrêt Labbane' (2001) 3 *Droit Social*.

Jessup, C, 'The Onus of Proof in Proceedings under Part XA of the Workplace Relations Act 1996' (2002) 15 *Australian Journal of Labour Law*, 198–208.

Kahn-Freund, O, 'Servants and Independent Contractors' (1951) 14 *Modern Law Review* 504.

—— 'Status and Contract in Labour Law', (1967) *Modern Law Review*.

—— 'On Uses and Misuses of Comparative Law (1974) *Modern Law Review* 1.

Kalleberg, AL, 'Precarious Work, Insecure Workers: Employment Relations in Transition' (2009) *American Sociological Review* 74.

Klerck, G, 'Rise of the temporary employment industry in Namibia: A regulatory "fix" ' (2009) 27(1) *Journal of Contemporary African Studies*, 85–103.

Kochhar, R, Survey of Mexican Migrants, Part 3, 'The Economic Transition to America' (Washington, DC: Pew Hispanic Center, December 6, 2005).

Kumar, HL, 'Workman Under the Industrial Disputes Act, 1947' (2005) *Factories and Labour Reports*.

Laparra, M, *La construcción del empleo precario Dimensiones, causas y tendencias de la precariedad laboral* (Madrid, Fundación FOESSA, 2007).

Leonardi, S, *Parasubordinazione e Contrattazione Collettiva Una Lettura Trasversale* (Milan, IRES, 2001) available at www.atipici.net/osservatorio/files/Parasubordinazione_e_contrattazione_collettiva_IRES.pdf.

Ley por la que se regula el trabajo autónomo dependiente, exposición de motivos (Madrid, Instituto Complutense de Estudios Internacionales, 2002).

Liebman, S, 'Employment situations and workers' protection: Italy', Paper prepared for Meeting of Experts on Workers in Need of Protection, Geneva, 2000.

Lippel, K, 'Precarious Employment and Occupational Health and Safety Regulation in Quebec' in L Vosko (ed), *Precarious Employment: Understanding Labour Market Insecurity* (Montreal, McGill-Queen's University Press, 2006).

Lund, F and Ardington, C, 'Employment Status, Security and the Management of Risk: A Study of Workers in Kwamsane, KwaZulu-Natal', Working Paper No 45, UKZN Centre for Development Studies (2006).

Lyon-Caen, A, 'Actualité du contrat de travail' (1988) *Droit Social*.

—— *Le droit du travail non-salarié* (Paris, Ed Sirey, 1990).

—— *Evolución del Pensamiento Juslaboralista—Estudios en Homenaje al Prof Héctor-Hugo Barbagelata, '¿Derecho del Trabajo o Derecho del Empleo?'* (Montevideo, FCU, 1997).

——, Pèlisser, J, and Supiot, A, *Droit du travail* (Paris, Dalloz, 1998).

Mangan, J, *Workers Without Traditional Employment: An International Study of Non-Standard Work* (Cheltenham, Edward Elgar Publishing, 2000).

Mangarelli, C, 'Arrendamiento de servicios', in *Cuarenta y dos Estudios sobre la descentralización empresarial y el derecho del trabajo* (Montevideo, FCU, 2000).

Márquez Garmendia, M and Beñarán Burastero, P, 'Trabajadores parasubordinados', in *Cuarenta y dos Estudios sobre la descentralización empresarial y el derecho del trabajo* (Montevideo, FCU, 2000).

Maunzich, N, 'Enmienda Constitucional N° 45 y las nuevas competencias: de la extensión al fortalecimiento de la justicia del trabajo' (2006) 1 *Revista del Departamento de Derecho del Trabajo y de la Seguridad Social, Facultad de Derecho de la Universidad de San Pablo.*

Menghini, L, 'Subordinazione e dintorni: itinerari della giurisprudenza' (1998) 21 *Quaderni di Diritto del Lavoro e delle Relazioni Industriali* 224.

Morvan, P, 'La Chimère du Contrat de Travail Unique, la fluidité et la créativité' (2006) *Droit Social* 959.

Motala, S, *Organising in the informal economy: A Case Study of Street Traders in South Africa* (Geneva, ILO, 2002).

Msweti, S, 'Labour Talk' (2003) 6(46) *Public Eye.*

Müchenberger, U, Wank, R and Buchner, H, 'Ridefinire la nozione di subordinazione? Il dibattito in Germania'(2000) 2 *Gironale di Diritto del Lavoro e Relazioni Industriali.*

Mureinik, E, 'The Contract of Service: An Easy Test for Hard Cases' (1980) 97 South African Law Journal 246.

Nascimento, AM, *Iniciação ao Direito do Trabalho,* 32nd edn (Sao Paulo, LTR, 2006).

Nossar, R, Johnstone and Quinlan, M, 'Regulating Supply Chains to Address the Occupational Health and Safety Problems Associated with Precarious Employment: The Case of Home-Based Workers in Australia' (2004) 17 *Australian Journal of Labour Law,* 1–24.

OECD, 'Partial Renaissance of Self-Employment', OECD Employment Outlook (Paris, OECD, 2000).

O'Reilly, J and Fagan, C, *Part-Time Prospects: An International Comparison of Part-Time Work in Europe, North America, and the Pacific Rim* (New York, Routledge, 1998).

Osti, C, 'Riflessioni sull'abuso di dipendenza economica', (1999) *Mercato concorrenza regole.*

Ouchi, S, 'Labor Law Coverage and the Concept of 'Worker" Paper presented at the 7th Comparative Labor Law Seminar of JILPT in March 2004, available at www.jil.go.jp/english/events_and_information/documents/clls04_ouchi.pdf.

Owens, R, 'Working Precariously: The Safety Net after Work Choices' (2006) 19 *Australian Journal of Labour Law* 161.

Padilla Páez, OV, 'La Precarización del Empleo en las Grandes Ciudades Latinoamericanas', in R Cordera, P Ramírez Kuri and A Ziccardi (eds), *Pobreza, Desigualdad y Exclusión Social en la Ciudad del Siglo XXI* (México, Siglo XXI: UNAM, Instituto de Investigaciones Sociales, 2008).

Pedrazzoli, M, 'Opera (prestazioni coordinate e continuative)', in *Novissimo Digesto Italiano – Appendice,* V (Torino, Utet, 1986).

Perugini, AH, La Relación de dependencia (Buenos Aires, Hammurabi, 2004).

Perulli, A, *Economically dependent/quasi-subordinate (parasubordinate) employment: Legal, social and economic aspects* (Brussels, EC, 2003).

—— and Lyon-Caen, A, *Efficacia e Diritto del Lavoro,* (Padova, Cedam, 2008).

Pinto, V, 'La Categoria Giuridica delle Collaborazioni Coordinate e Continuative e il Lavoro a Progetto', Massimo D'Antona Working Paper 34/2005, 7, available at www.lex.unict.it/eurolabor/ricerca/wp/it/pinto_n34–2005it.pdf.

Plá Rodríguez, A, *Los Principios del Derecho del Trabajo,* 3rd edn, (Buenos Aires, Depalma, 1978).

Polivka and Nardone, T, 'On the definition of "contingent work" ' (1989) 112(12) *Monthly Labor Review* 9.

Qu, L, Taylor, B and Frost, S, 'Labour Relations and Deregulation in Vietnam: Theory and Practice', Working Paper No 53, Southeast Asia Research Centre, City University of Hong Kong, September 2003.

Quadri, R, 'Nullità e tutela del contraente debole, (2002) *Commercio Internazionale.*

Ramírez Gronda, JD, *Tratado de Derecho del Trabajo* (Buenos Aires, La Ley, 1964).

Bibliography

Ratha, D, et al, Migration and Remittances Team, Development Prospects Group, World Bank, 'Outlook for Remittance Flows 2009–2011: Remittances expected to fall by 7–10 per cent in 2009', Migration and Development Brief No 10 (13 July 2009).

Rawling, M, 'The Regulation of Outwork and the Federal Takeover of Labour Law' (2007) 20 *Australian Journal of Labour Law*, 189–206.

Riley, J, 'A fair deal for the entrepreneurial worker? Self-employment and independent contracting post work choices' (2006) 19 *Australian Journal of Labour Law*, 246–262.

Rivas, D, *La subordinación. Criterios distintivos del contrato de trabajo* (Montevideo, FCU, 1995).

—— 'El trabajo autónomo' in *Cuarenta y dos Estudios sobre la descentralización empresarial y el derecho del trabajo* (Montevideo, FCU, 2000).

Rolph, D, 'A Carton of Milk, A Bump to the Head and One Legal Headache: Vicarious Liability in the High Court of Australia' (2006) 19 *Australian Journal of Labour Law* 294.

Romagnoli, U, 'Arriva un bastimento carico di "A" ', in D'Antona (ed.), *Politiche di flessibilità e mutamenti del diritto del lavoro: Italia e Spagna* (Napoli, ESI, 1990).

—— *Evolución del Pensamiento Juslaboralista—Estudios en Homenaje al Prof Héctor-Hugo Barbagelata, 'El derecho del trabajo ¿Qué futuro?'* (Montevideo, FCU, 1997).

Salas, C, 'Between Unemployment and Insecurity in Mexico: NAFTA enters its second decade', Economic Policy Institute Briefing Paper No 173, (28 September 2006).

—— 'Mexico Labor Report, 2001–2006' (9 March 2007) 8, online: Global Policy Network, http://www.gpn.org/data/mexico/mexico-eng.pdf.

Santoro Passarelli, G, *Il lavoro parasubordinato* (Milan, Giuffré, 1979).

—— 'La nuova figura del lavoro a progetto', in *Annuario di Diritto del Lavoro* (Rome, 2005)

Scott, RE, 'NAFTA's Legacy: Rising Trade Deficits Lead to Significant Job Displacement and Declining Job Quality for the United States', Economic Policy Institute Briefing Paper No 173 (28 September 2006) 18, online: www.epinet.org/briefingpapers/173/bp173.pdf.

Servais, JM, *Droit Social de l'Union Européenne* (Brussels, Bruylant, 2008).

Shrivastava, MP, ' "Contract Labour" and "Principal Employer"—Its Implication for Industrial Disputes under Industrial Disputes Act, 1947' (2006) *Factories and Labour Reports* 39.

Simon, H, 'A Formal Theory of the Employment Relation' (1951) 19 *Econometrica*, 295–305.

Siqueira Neto, JF, *Informe Sobre as Situações de Trabalho e de Proteção dos Trabalhadores no Brasil* (Geneva, OIT, 1998), available at wwwiloorg/public/english/dialogue/ifpdial/downloads/wpnr/brazilpdf.

Standing, G, *Global Labour Flexibility: Seeking Distributive Justice* (Basingstoke, Macmillan Press, 1999).

Stewart, A, 'Redefining Employment? Meeting the Challenge of Contract and Agency Labour' (2002) 15 *Australian Journal of Labour Law* 235.

—— 'Work Choices and Independent Contractors: The Revolution that Never Happened' (2008) 18 *Economic and Labour Relations Review* 53.

—— *Fair Work: The New Workplace Law and the Work Choices Legacy*, (Sydney, Federation Press, 2009).

—— 'A Question of Balance: Labor's New Vision for Workplace Regulation' (2009) 22 *Australian Journal of Labour Law* 3.

Supiot, A, 'Introducción a las reflexiones sobre el trabajo' (1996) 115(6) *International Labour Review*.

—— *Au-delà de l'emploi : transformations du travail et devenir du droit du travail en Europe : rapport pour la Commission des communautés européennes avec la collaboration de l'Université Carlos III de Madrid* (Paris, Flammarion, 1999).

—— 'The transformation of work and the future of labour law in Europe: A multidisciplinary perspective' (1999) 138(1) *International Labour Review*, 31–46.

—— 'Wage employment and self-employment', Report to the 6th European Congress for Labour Law, (Warsaw, September 1999).

—— 'Les nouveaux visages de la subordination' (2000) 2 *Droit Social*, 131–145.

—— *Beyond Employment: Changes in Work and the Future of Labour Law in Europe* (Oxford, Oxford University Press, 2001).

——Pellissier, J, and Jeammaud, A, *Droit du Travail* (Paris, Dalloz, 2006).

Suppiej, G, 'Il rapporto di lavoro (costituzione e svolgimento)', in Mazzoni (dir), *Enciclopedia Giuridica del Lavoro* IV (Padua, Cedam, 2002).

Theron, J, 'The erosion of workers' rights and the presumption as to who is an employee' (2002) 6 *Law, Democracy and Development*, 27–56.

—— 'Labour's casualisation cancer spreads' (2005) 29(2) *SA Labour Bulletin* 27–31.

Thompson, C, 'The Changing Nature of Employment' (2003) 24 *Industrial Law Journal (SA)* 1793.

Treu, T, 'Labour law and social change', Public Lecture, Geneva, International Labour Office, November 2002.

—— 'Diritto del lavoro: realtà e possibilità', (2000) *Argomenti di Diritto del Lavoro*.

Tucker, E, ' "Great Expectations" Defeated?: The Trajectory of Collective Bargaining Regimes in Canada and the United States Post-NAFTA' (2004) 26 *Comparative Labor Law and Policy Journal*, 97–150.

Underhill, E, 'Labour Hire and Independent Contracting in Australia: Two Inquiries, How Much Change?' (2006) 19 *Australian Journal of Labour Law*, 306–314.

Vallebona, A, 'Lavoro a progetto: incostituzionalità e circolare di pentimento', (2004) *Argomenti di diritto del lavoro*, 293–297.

Vallée, G, 'Towards Enhancing the Employment Conditions of Vulnerable Workers: A Public Policy Perspective' (2005) Canadian Policy Research Networks, Vulnerable Workers Series No 2, 2.

Valodia, I, Lebani, L, Skinner, C, and Devey, R, 'Low-Waged and Informal Employment in South Africa' (2006) *Transformation*, 60.

Veneziani, B, 'The Evolution of the Contract of Employment', in B Hepple (ed), *The Making of Labour Law in Europe: A Comparative Study of Nine Countries up to 1945* (London, Mansell, 1986).

Verma, V, 'The Mexican and Caribbean Seasonal Agricultural Workers Program: Regulatory and Policy Framework, Farm Industry Level Employment Practices, and the Future of the Program under Unionization' (December 2003), online: The North-South Institute, www.nsi-ins.ca/english/pdf/csawp_verma_final_report.pdf.

Vettori, S, *The Employment Contract and the Changed World of Work* (Ashgate, Aldershot, 2007).

Virassamy, GJ, *Les contrats de dépendance* (Paris, LGDJ, 1986)

Vosko, LF, Zukewich N and Cranford, C, 'Precarious jobs: A new typology of employment' (2003) 4(10) *Perspectives on Labour and Income*, 16–26.

Wank, R, *Arbeitnehmer und Selbständige* (Munich, CH Beck'sche Verlagsbuchhandlung, 1988).

—— 'Tipi contrattuali con prestazioni di servizio nella RFT' (1997) 2 *Lavoro e Diritto*.

—— 'Germany', in 'Labour Law in Motion' (2005) *Bulletin of Comparative Labour Relations*.

Weber, M, 'The Origins of Industrial Capitalism in Europe', in WG Runciman (ed), *Weber Selections in Translations* (Cambridge, Cambridge University Press, 1978).

Webster, E, 'Making a Living, Earning a Living: Work and Employment in Southern Africa' (2005) 26(1) *International Political Science Review* 55.

—— and von Holdt, K, 'Work Restructuring and the Crisis of Social Reproduction: A Southern Perspective' in Webster and von Holdt (eds), *Beyond the Apartheid Workplace: Studies in Transition* (Durban, University of Kwazulu-Natal Press, 2005).

Williamson, O, 'Transaction-Cost Economics: The Governance of Contractual Relations', (1979) 22 *Journal of Law and Economics*, 233–261.

Zieger, R and Gall, GJ, *American Workers, American Unions: The Twentieth Century*, 3rd edn (Baltimore and London, The Johns Hopkins University Press, 2002).

Index

Index

Index

Index

Index

Index

Index

Index

Index

Index

Index

Index

DATE DUE	RETURNED